Instructor's Annotated Edition

HOUGHTON MIFFLIN
COLLEGE READING SERIES

Book One

Second Edition

HOUGHTON MIFFLIN COMPANY   Boston   New York

VP, Publisher: Patricia Coryell
Senior Sponsoring Editor: Lisa Kimball
Senior Development Editor: Judith Fifer
Editorial Associate: Peter Mooney
Senior Project Editor: Cecilia Molinari
Editorial Assistant: Sean McGann
Manufacturing Coordinator: Chuck Dutton
Senior Marketing Manager: Annamarie Rice
Senior Composition Buyer: Sarah L. Ambrose
Art and Design Manager: Gary Crespo
Senior Photo Editor: Jennifer Meyer Dare
Senior Designer: Henry Rachlin

Cover image: © The Image Bank/Alain Daussin

Photo Credits
Page 46: Wendy Smith © 2004 by Houghton Mifflin Company. Reproduced by permission from *The American Heritage Dictionary, Fourth Edition;* © SuperStock, Inc.;
Elizabeth Morales © 2004 by Houghton Mifflin Company. Reproduced by permission
from *The American Heritage Dictionary, Fourth Edition.*

Printed in the U.S.A.

Library of Congress Control Number: 2004117808

Student Edition ISBN: 0-618-54186-1
Instructor's Annotated Edition ISBN: 0-618-54189-6

1 2 3 4 5 6 7 8 9-CRW-09 08 07 06 05

Contents

CHAPTER **10**   Reading Longer Selections   467

Combined Skills Tests   497

Preface

The *Houghton Mifflin College Reading Series, Second Edition,* is a three-level series that uses a progressive, unified approach to improving students' reading comprehension and critical thinking skills—and all at an affordable price! Praised in the first edition by users across the country, the second edition of this innovative series contains additional features and support materials that will enhance students' abilities to become effective readers.

Special Features of the Text

The *Houghton Mifflin College Reading Series, Second Edition,* includes the following features:

▶ **Affordable Price:** Each book in the series contains the same topics and content as do other comparable textbooks, but for a price that is more than a third less than that of similar books.

▶ **Integration of Skills and Strategies:** Along with presenting the major reading skills—identifying the main idea, supporting details, implied main idea, transitions, patterns of organization, and others—the book introduces students to the world of reading strategies that will enable them to practice good habits while reading. Strategies such as SQ3R, annotating, and note taking will help students improve their comprehension of what they read and will enable them to learn different strategies that will help them comprehend and analyze what they read.

▶ **Consistent Chapter Structure:** Each chapter covers skills and strategies in a consistent and clear manner.

▶ **Coverage of Visuals:** Chapter 7 is unique to this text in that it covers visuals students may encounter in their personal and professional reading, such as charts, graphs, tables, and figures.

▶ **Critical Thinking:** In addition to a multitude of skills exercises designed to help students build comprehension, the text features questions at the end of the reading selections that build on important critical thinking skills. Many practice exercises, too, require the application of critical thinking.

▶ **Vocabulary Building:** Every chapter covers a particular vocabulary concept and relates that concept to reading selections from the chapters.

▶ **Focus on Academic Achievement:** Tips and selected readings about studying and succeeding in school are integrated throughout the text.

Chapter Organization

In addition, each chapter in each level of the *Houghton Mifflin College Reading Series, Second Edition,* contains the following elements:

▶ **Goals:** A list of goals at the beginning of each chapter tells students what they will learn when they have completed the chapter.

▶ **Test Yourself:** These pre-tests, which appear in Chapters 2 through 10, assess the student's knowledge of the skill to be introduced. This assessment helps both instructors and students target specific areas for improvement.

▶ **Explanation:** Each chapter is broken up into sections, with each section devoted to explanation and practice of a particular concept. Every attempt has been made to divide material into manageable sections of information that are followed by practice of a specific skill.

▶ **Exercises:** An ample number and variety of exercises is included in every chapter. Most of the exercises contain paragraphs from textbooks, magazines, newspapers, and journals so that students can read various types of selections and learn new information about a variety of different subjects. Exercises are arranged using a step-by-step progression to build concepts and skills gradually.

▶ **Chapter Review:** A cloze exercise tests students' knowledge of the concepts presented in each chapter.

▶ **Longer Reading Selections:** Longer reading selections follow the explanatory material in Chapters 1 through 9 and are included to give students practice in identifying different skills in context. Readings have been chosen for their high interest, diverse topics, and cultural relevance for today's students. In addition, each reading was selected with the level of student in mind as well as students' ethnic, cultural, and educational experiences. New to this edition is the "Practicing the Active Reading Strategy," which asks students to apply active reading techniques to longer selections before, as, and after they read.

▶ **Questions for Discussion and Writing:** These questions ask students to think about their own experiences as well as what they have read in the longer reading selections. The main points, topics, and theses of the longer readings are used as springboards to encourage student reflection on personal experiences and as stimuli for strengthening academic skills such as research, argument, and summary. These questions give students the opportunity to develop their writing skills by responding to a professional reading selection.

▶ **Vocabulary:** Vocabulary is integrated in several different ways throughout each chapter. First, definitions of words or phrases that may be new to beginning students now appear as footnotes. In addition, words that may be unfamiliar are taken from the longer reading selection that appears later in Chapters 1 through 9 and used in a vocabulary exercise that follows the selection. Students are given the opportunity to glean the meanings of certain words from context and expand their overall vocabulary. Lastly, each chapter includes instruction in a specific vocabulary concept, such as context clues, that will help students improve their reading comprehension. The instruction is followed by one or more exercises that draw examples from readings in the text to give students practice with that particular concept.

- ▶ **Reading Strategy:** Every chapter ends with a reading strategy that students can use to help them comprehend and remember what they've read.

- ▶ **Chapter Tests:** Several different tests follow each skills-based chapter and are designed to assess students' progress from the beginning of the chapter, when they completed the "Test Yourself" section (in Chapters 2 through 10). These tests cover all of the individual skills presented in the chapter.

- ▶ **Combined Skills Tests:** A section following the final chapter contains combined skills tests that provide a thorough review of the book's contents. New to this edition, each test includes an opportunity for students to apply various reading strategies to the reading selection.

What's New in the Second Edition

Based on user and reviewer response, several new features have been added.

- ▶ **New and Expanded Information on Purpose and Tone:** Chapter 9 has been renamed to reflect new coverage of purpose and expanded information on tone.

- ▶ **Vocabulary Footnotes:** Definitions of difficult words as well as allusions in many of the examples, exercises, and readings now appear as footnotes so that students don't have to go to outside sources to look them up.

- ▶ **New Grade-Level-Appropriate Examples and Readings:** Examples and readings have been carefully reviewed and replaced when necessary to ensure grade-level appropriateness for each text.

- ▶ **Reading Strategy Now at the End of Each Chapter:** In order to increase the flexibility of the text, the reading strategy now appears at the end of the chapter. This new placement allows instructors to skip this portion of the text if they so choose.

- ▶ **New "Practicing the Active Reading Strategy" exercises:** New exercises that appear before and after the longer, end-of-chapter readings ask students to apply the active reading strategy to that selection.

- ▶ **A More Engaging Chapter 1:** Several of the first edition readings in Chapter 1 have been replaced in order to increase student interest.

- ▶ **Clearer Direction Lines:** Instructions throughout have been rewritten for clarity and consistency.

- ▶ **Expanded Skill Definitions:** Definitions of the skill presented in each chapter now appear after the chapter objectives, and most have been expanded so that students have a better idea of what they are being asked to do in the "Test Yourself" section.

Ancillaries

The *Houghton Mifflin College Reading Series, Second Edition,* is supported by an innovative teaching and learning package.

▶ **Improved! EduSpace for Houghton Mifflin Reading—Level 1.** EduSpace, Houghton Mifflin's online learning tool powered by Blackboard, dynamically expands students' learning opportunities and instructors' teaching options. EduSpace offers cumulative pre- and post-tests as well as interactive tests keyed to almost every chapter in the *Houghton Mifflin College Reading Series*. The EduSpace course for this second edition now contains more questions, including more on vocabulary as well as additional reading selections in the form of combined skills tests. Students get plenty of extra practice, immediate feedback, a score, and grammar or writing targets for further work. Instructors praise EduSpace's flexible course management system, which features an online gradebook linked to the exercises (so that keeping track of student progress is easy); one convenient environment for course objectives, syllabi, and other class information; and the chance to stay connected with students through live online hours, discussion boards, chat rooms, and an announcement center. Visit http://www.eduspace.com/ for more information or to sign up for a demonstration.

▶ **Test Bank.** A printed test bank contains additional, cumulative pre- and post-tests as well as two post-tests for each of the chapters. An answer key to the tests is also provided.

▶ **The Phonics Supplement.** A series of thirty-two exercises leads students from learning how various consonants and vowels sound to ultimately dividing words into syllables and sounding them out. An answer key is provided.

Thanks to the following reviewers who helped shape the second edition:

Barbara Belroy, Cerritos College; Sharon D'Agastino, Hudson County Community College; Daniel E. Davis, Montgomery College; Susan B. Deason, Aiken Technical College; Nancy D. Hunter, Maysville Community College; Terri Jo Jensen, Anoka Ramsey Community College–Cambridge Campus; Evelyn Koperwas, Broward Community College; Linda McGarrah, Northwest Arkansas Community College; Linda Huber Mininger, Harrisburg Area Community College; Aubrey Moncrieffe Jr., Housatonic Community College; Jerolynn A. Roberson, Miami Dade College; Kimberly Shepherd, Washtenaw Community College; Marguerite C. Weber, DA, Harrisburg Area Community College.

CHAPTER 1

Improving Reading and Thinking

GOALS FOR CHAPTER 1

▶ Explain why effective reading is critical to academic, professional, and personal success.

▶ Explain how reading improves thinking skills.

▶ Describe four techniques for improving reading skills.

▶ List the different goals of reading for information.

▶ Explain the four types of mental skills required for reading.

▶ Describe the organization and features of this book.

▶ Explain and apply the steps of active reading.

Do you enjoy reading? If your answer is no, why not? Like many people, you may have several reasons for disliking the printed word. You might think reading is too passive, requiring you to sit still for too much time. You may not like it because it takes too long. You may say that most of the things you read just don't interest you or seem relevant to your life. You may object to reading because it seems too hard—you don't like having to struggle to understand information. These are the most common reasons people give to explain their dislike of reading.

What people don't realize is that most of these reasons arise from a lack of experience and effort. When you first decided you didn't like to read, you probably began to avoid reading as much as possible. This avoidance led to a lack of practice, which set up a vicious cycle: lack of practice led to undeveloped skills. This lack of skills meant more difficult and unrewarding experiences when you did read. As a result, you probably read less and less, and you gave yourself few opportunities to practice your reading skills. Thus, the cycle began again.

You can break this cycle, though, and make your reading experiences more enjoyable. The first step is to realize how much you already know about the reading process.

1

The Importance of Good Reading Skills

As Figure 1.1 shows, a college student spends a lot of his or her daily communication time reading. Obviously, then, good reading skills are an essential component of success in college.

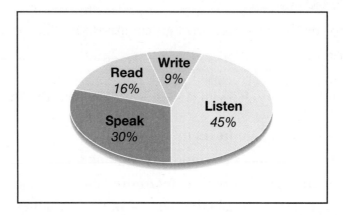

Figure 1.1   What You Do with Your Communication Time

Source: L. Barker et al., "An Investigation of Proportional Time Spent in Various Communication Activities of College Students," *Journal of Communication Research* 8 (1981): 101–109. Reprinted by permission.

Reading and Academic Success

Solid reading skills will be critical to your success in college. Most college courses require a great deal of reading. Your professors will ask you to read textbooks, articles, books, stories, and handouts. You'll be responsible for remembering much of this information and revealing your knowledge of it on tests. You'll have to read the instructor's notes, and you'll have to read your own notes on lecture material to prepare for your tests. In addition, you'll be asked to conduct research, which requires reading all types of sources, including websites on the Internet. Various assignments will ask you to read not only your own writing but also that of your classmates.

Not only will you have to simply read and remember information, you also will be asked to evaluate it, judge it, agree or disagree with it, interpret it, compare it with something else, summarize it, and synthesize it with other things you've read. You can accomplish all of these tasks only if you can first attain a solid grasp of the ideas and information in the source.

Exercise 1.1

Answer the following questions about Figure 1.1 on page 2. Write your answers on the blanks provided.

1. For a college student, what percentage of daily communication time is spent in reading? _16 percent._

2. How do you think your reading time compares with the average figure in the chart? _Answers will vary._

3. The information in the visual relates to a college student. How do you think the four percentages included in the chart change for someone who is not attending college? _Answers will vary._

_____

_____

Exercise 1.2

In the following list, place a check mark beside every reading-related activity you've already done at least once. Then, respond to the questions that follow by writing your answers on the blanks provided. Answers will vary.

_____ Read a textbook

_____ Read a magazine or journal article assigned by a teacher

_____ Read information on a website for a class assignment

_____ Read a novel or another book assigned by a teacher

_____ Researched a topic in the library by reading several sources about it

_____ Read a memo at work

_____ Read a letter from a friend

_____ Read an e-mail message from a friend, teacher, or colleague

_____ Read subtitles[1] while watching a foreign film

_____ Read the newspaper

_____ Read a story to a child

1. **subtitles:** translations of the dialogue

1

_____ Read aloud in class

_____ Read a prepared speech to an audience

1. If you could choose anything to read, what would it be? Why?

   Answers will vary. _____

   _____

   _____

2. What types of reading situations do you find the most difficult?

   Answers will vary. _____

   _____

   _____

3. What do you think you need to do to become a better reader?

   Answers will vary. _____

   _____

   _____

4. What would you like to learn in this textbook that you think would help
   you become a better reader? Answers will vary. _____

   _____

Reading and Professional Success

When you enter the work force, you may be surprised by how much reading
you'll need to do. Many jobs will require you to read e-mail messages, letters,
memorandums, policy and procedure manuals, instructions, reports, logs and
records, summaries of meetings, newsletters, and many other types of
documents.

Often, a lot is at stake concerning your comprehension of these materials.
Your personal safety may depend on your understanding of the information
in manuals or other instructions. Your efficient and effective job performance
may rest on your ability to comprehend written information sent to you by
your supervisors and coworkers. Even your promotions and raises may de-

pend, in part, on your ability to read and understand materials such as reports about trends, new research, or other innovations in your field.

Exercise 1.3

Read the following memo and then write your answers to the questions on the blanks provided.

To: All Employees of Ace Storage Facilities

From: Dan Denton, President

Date: January 2, 20xx

Re: New Bonus for Your Money-Saving Idea

To all employees:

On behalf of the executive team at Ace Storage Facilities, I'd like to thank each and every one of you for your hard work and commitment to this corporation. As you know, we value your input about making our company more efficient and effective. Therefore, we have created a new policy to encourage you to share more of your ideas with your management team.

Effective immediately, you may be able to earn a $500 bonus for an idea that saves our company money. To be eligible for this bonus, you must complete a new form that is now available in all break rooms. The information required on this form must be typed, and all sections of the form must be filled out. In the section about your suggestion, you must describe your idea and your estimate of its cost savings in two hundred words or fewer. Completed forms should be placed in the box beside the time clock. You may submit as many ideas as you like, but each of them should be described on a separate form.

All ideas will be reviewed by the senior management team. If your idea is selected for implementation,[1] you will receive a $500 bonus in your next month's paycheck. So please share with us your thoughts about making our company more cost-effective, and contact Betty in the Human Resources Office if you have any questions about this new policy.

---

1. **implementation:** use

1

1. Are all ideas submitted by employees rewarded with a $500 bonus?
   No, only those that are selected for implementation.

2. Does President Dan Denton want you to call his office if you have questions about his new policy? _No, he wants you to call Betty in the Human
   Resources Office._

3. Can you write the information by hand on the form you fill out?
   No, the information must be typed.

4. How long can the description of your idea be? _Up to 200 words long_

5. What should you do if you have more than one money-saving idea?
   Fill out a separate form for each idea.

6. Where can you get one of the forms you need to fill out? _In one of
   the break rooms_

Reading and Personal Success

There are many occasions in your personal life when you will need to read
well. For example, you may want to learn more about a hobby or subject
area that interests you. If so, you'll need to read books, articles, and webpages to increase your knowledge. You may want to find out how to improve
your personal finances by learning how to save or invest your money. You
may need to assemble something you purchased—such as a child's toy or a
barbecue grill—by following the directions. You or one of your loved ones
may become sick with a particular disease or disorder, causing you to want
more information about treatment options. You may even want to read for
entertainment, picking up a *People* magazine or a Stephen King novel just for
the fun of it.

   You'll also have to read personal correspondence such as letters and
e-mail messages, legal documents such as contracts, and reports from your
children's teachers, among other things. You'll read all of these documents
more capably and confidently when you improve your reading skills.

Exercise 1.4

Read the following selection. Then, write your answers to the questions on the blanks provided.

Man See No Dirt, Hear No Dirt, Clean No Dirt

I like to think that I am a modest person. (I also like to think that I look like Brad Pitt naked, but that is not the issue here.)

There comes a time, however, when a person must toot his own personal horn, and for me, that time is now. A new book has confirmed a theory that I first proposed in 1987, in a column explaining why men are physically unqualified to do housework. The problem, I argued, is that men—because of a tragic genetic flaw—cannot see dirt until there is enough of it to support agriculture. This puts men at a huge disadvantage against women, who can detect a single dirt molecule 20 feet away.

This is why a man and a woman can both be looking at the same bathroom commode,[1] and the man—hindered by Male Genetic Dirt Blindness (MGDB)—will perceive the commode surface as being clean enough for heart surgery or even meat slicing; whereas the woman can't even *see* the commode, only a teeming, commode-shaped swarm of bacteria. A woman can spend two hours cleaning a toothbrush holder and still not be totally satisfied; whereas if you ask a man to clean the entire New York City subway system, he'll go down there with a bottle of Windex and a single paper towel, then emerge 25 minutes later, weary but satisfied with a job well done.

When I wrote about Male Genetic Dirt Blindness, many irate[2] readers complained that I was engaging in sexist[3] stereotyping, as well as making lame excuses for the fact that men are lazy pigs. All of these irate readers belonged to a gender that I will not identify here, other than to say: Guess what, ladies? There is now scientific proof that I was right.

This proof appears in a new book titled *What Could He Be Thinking? How a Man's Mind Really Works*. I have not personally read this book, because, as a journalist, I am too busy writing about it. But according to an article by Reuters, the book states that a man's brain "takes in less sensory[4] detail than a woman's, so he doesn't see or even feel the dust and household mess in the same way."

1. **commode:** toilet
2. **irate:** angry
3. **sexist:** unfairly generalizing about the other gender
4. **sensory:** of the senses

1

And this is only one of the differences between men's and women's brains. Another difference involves a brain part called the "cingulate gyrus," which is the sector where emotions are located. The Reuters article does not describe the cingulate gyrus, but presumably in women it is a structure the size of a mature cantaloupe, containing complex emotional data involving thousands of human relationships; whereas in men it is basically a cashew filled with NFL highlights.

In any event, it turns out that women's brains secrete more of the chemicals "oxytocin" and "serotonin," which, according to biologists, cause humans to feel they have an inadequate supply of shoes. No, seriously, these chemicals cause humans to want to bond with other humans, which is why women like to share their feelings. We men, on the other hand, are reluctant to share our feelings, in large part because we often don't have any. Really. Ask any guy. A lot of the time, when we look like we're thinking, we just have this low-level humming sound in our brains. That's why, in male-female conversations, the male part often consists entirely of him going "hmmmm." This frustrates the woman, who wants to know what he's really thinking. In fact, what he's thinking is, literally, "hmmmm."

So anyway, according to the Reuters article, when a man, instead of sharing feelings with his mate, chooses to lie on the sofa, holding the remote control and monitoring 750 television programs simultaneously by changing the channel every one-half second, his mate should *not* come to the mistaken conclusion that he is an insensitive jerk. In fact, he is responding to scientific biological brain chemicals as detailed in the scientific book *What Could He Be Thinking? How a Man's Mind Really Works*, which I frankly cannot recommend highly enough.

In conclusion, no *way* was that pass interference.*

1. According to Dave Barry, what "flaw" makes men unable to see dirt on the bathroom commode? <u>Male Genetic Dirt Blindness (MGDB)</u>

2. How long would it take a man to clean the entire New York subway system, according to Barry? <u>25 minutes</u>

3. Barry offers scientific proof that he is right about men and dirt. Why, according to the book that Barry mentions, do men not see dirt like women do? <u>Men's brains take in less sensory detail than women's brains do.</u>

---

* "Man See No Dirt, Hear No Dirt, Clean No Dirt" by Dave Barry. Reprinted by permission of TMS Reprints.

1

4. What chemicals do women's brains secrete more of than men's do, causing them to "share their feelings"? <u>oxytocin and serotonin</u>

5. Is this essay meant to entertain readers or inform them about "Male Genetic Dirt Blindness"? How do you know? <u>It's meant to entertain.</u>
<u>It's humorous, and Barry is clearly making up the names of conditions (MGDB),</u>
<u>the names of brain parts, and the "research" he mentions in support of his theory.</u>

Reading and Better Thinking

Better reading skills help you improve your chances for academic, professional, and personal success. They will also help you improve your overall thinking skills. This is because reading requires you to follow and understand the thought processes of the writer. When you can do that effectively, you get opportunities to sharpen a variety of your own mental skills:

1. You evaluate information and decide what's important.

2. You learn to see relationships among things, events, and ideas.

3. You make new connections among things, events, and ideas.

4. You practice following the logic (or seeing the lack of logic) of someone else's thoughts.

5. You add more information to your memory.

These are the very skills that will strengthen your ability to make decisions, think creatively, and think logically in every area of your life.

Exercise 1.5

Read the following letter to the editor from a newspaper and write your answers to the questions on the blanks provided.

I think the best way to prevent most traffic accidents is to ban the use of cell phones while driving. In the past ten years, since cell phones were introduced to the American public and became part of everyone's life, traffic accidents and deaths in cars have increased significantly. In many of these accidents, it is a fact that someone talking on a cell phone has caused the accident.

It is a proven scientific fact that people cannot do two things at once, so why do people think that they can drive and talk on the phone at the same time?

However, I don't think that cell phones are the only cause of accidents or the only thing that should be banned. I think that in addition to banning the use of cell phones in cars, people should not be allowed to eat, chew gum, change the radio station they are listening to, sing along to the song on the radio, put on makeup while they drive, talk to anyone else in the car, or look out any window besides the windshield in front of them while driving. In my opinion, banning these activities will significantly cut down on the number of traffic accidents, injuries, and deaths that occur every day.

In the last three years, my car has been hit fourteen times, all by people either using cell phones, talking to someone else in their car, eating, or singing along to the radio. I have also witnessed a number of accidents and near-accidents involving drivers engaged in the activities mentioned above.

People should keep their eyes on the road at all times. Concentration is the key to being a good, safe driver, so by banning many activities that most of us associate with driving—talking on the phone, eating while driving, and singing—we will have safer roads in America.

1. What new piece of information did you learn by reading this excerpt?
   Answers will vary.
   _____

2. Which sentence gave you your first clue that the author is not logical?
   "It is a proven scientific fact that people cannot do two things at once, so why do
   people think that they can drive and talk on the phone at the same time?"

3. Can you think of another solution to decreasing the number of traffic accidents besides the ones the author suggests? *Answers will vary.*
   _____

How to Improve Reading Skills

Now that you understand *why* it's so important to read well, you're probably wondering *how* you can become a better reader. The obvious answer is practice. The more you read, the more opportunities you'll have for improving your abilities. But simply reading everything in sight will not necessarily improve your skills. In general, you should commit yourself to doing four other things as well.

1. Understand the different purposes for reading

2. Be aware of the mental skills required for reading

3. Develop individual reading skills

4. Learn and use different reading strategies

Understand the Different Purposes for Reading

When you set out to read something, you should know *why* you're reading it. The two basic purposes for reading are to gain information and to be entertained. Obviously, when you read for entertainment, your primary goal is your own pleasure. When you read for information, though, you may have one or more different goals:

1. **Gain a general understanding of the ideas or points.** For example, as you're reading this section of this textbook, you're trying to comprehend the ideas being presented.

2. **Discover the facts or answer questions about the material.** When you read the paragraphs in the exercises of this book, for example, you read them to find answers to the questions you must answer.

3. **Memorize the information.** You often read a textbook chapter so that you'll recall its information when you take a test.

4. **Find information or ideas that prove a point you want to make.** When you conduct research for a paper you need to write, you read to find statements or information that back up your opinions.

5. **Make a decision based on the information.** You read brochures from businesses, for example, to decide whether to buy their particular products or services.

When you read something, you may need to accomplish just one of these goals or perhaps all five at the same time. In any case, getting the most out of everything you read means clearly identifying your purpose before you begin.

Exercise 1.6

Read the following reading situations. Then, place a check mark on the blank next to every MAJOR purpose for reading that applies to that situation. (More than one choice may apply.)

1

1. You read a newspaper article to find out about a fire that burned down a house in your neighborhood.

   _____ Gain a general understanding of the ideas or points

   _✔_ Discover the facts or answer questions

   _____ Memorize the information

   _____ Find information or ideas that prove a point you want to make

   _____ Make a decision based on the information

2. You read the notes you wrote down during your professor's lecture as you prepare for your history exam.

   _✔_ Gain a general understanding of the ideas or points

   _____ Discover the facts or answer questions

   _✔_ Memorize the information

   _____ Find information or ideas that prove a point you want to make

   _____ Make a decision based on the information

3. You read the technical instructions that came with the bicycle you purchased and need to assemble.

   _____ Gain a general understanding of the ideas or points

   _✔_ Discover the facts or answer questions

   _____ Memorize the information

   _____ Find information or ideas that prove a point you want to make

   _____ Make a decision based on the information

4. You read a flyer sent to you by a candidate running for office in your town or city. This flyer states the opinions of the candidate.

   _✔_ Gain a general understanding of the ideas or points

   _____ Discover the facts or answer questions

   _____ Memorize the information

   _____ Find information or ideas that prove a point you want to make

   _✔_ Make a decision based on the information

1

5. You read a report to find out about the number of traffic accidents that oc-curred last year at an intersection in your neighborhood. You plan to argue that your city government needs to install a traffic light at that intersection.

_____ Gain a general understanding of the ideas or points

___✔___ Discover the facts or answer questions

_____ Memorize the information

___✔___ Find information or ideas that prove a point you want to make

_____ Make a decision based on the information

Be Aware of the Mental Skills Required for Reading

"Reading" is actually a collection of different mental skills. They include atti-tude, concentration, memory, and logical thought. These skills are all interre-lated and connected. Some of them depend upon others. When you become aware that these different skills are at work, you can learn to improve them.

Attitude. A positive attitude is the first essential mental component for suc-cessful reading. Your attitude includes your feelings about reading, about *what* you read, and about your own abilities. If these feelings are negative, your reading experiences will be negative. If these feelings are positive, your experiences will be more enjoyable.

A positive attitude not only makes reading more pleasurable; it also cre-ates the right mental environment for gaining new information. As a matter of fact, all of the other mental skills required for reading are useless unless you approach each reading task in the right frame of mind. If you are quick to pronounce a particular text "boring" or "worthless," you are likely to cre-ate a mental block that will prevent you from absorbing the information. Instead, approach each new reading task with intellectual curiosity. Expect to find something of value, something you'll be able to use in your life.

Also, don't let a poor attitude about your own reading abilities get in your way. If you expect to fail, if you tell yourself you just don't get it, then you virtually guarantee your failure. If you believe you can improve, however, then you'll create the necessary mental foundation for improving your skills and becoming a good reader.

Exercise 1.7

Read the following selection and respond to the questions by writing your answers on the blanks provided.

Toward Right Livelihood

Visit Sena Plaza in downtown Santa Fe, and you will see a public garden that is a wonderland of color and texture. The person responsible for this beautiful garden is Barbara Fix, a graduate of Stanford Law School who chose gardening over a high-powered law career. She says, "I've been offered many jobs in my life. I could have been on Wall Street making six figures, but the only job I ever hustled for was this one—six dollars an hour as the gardener at Sena Plaza."

Barbara Fix is an example of someone who appears to have achieved "right livelihood." The original concept of right livelihood apparently came from the teachings of Buddha.[1] In recent years, the concept has been described by Michael Phillips in his book *The Seven Laws of Money* and by Marsha Sinetar in her book *Do What You Love . . . The Money Will Follow.* Right livelihood is work consciously chosen, done with full awareness and care, and leading to enlightenment.[2] When Jason Wilson gave up a challenging business career to become a carpenter, he embraced the concept of right livelihood. He later started his own home construction business. Ronald Sheade, once a vice president at a Fortune 1,000 company,[3] now teaches eighth-grade science in a suburb of Chicago. He doesn't make big money anymore, but he loves teaching and now gets to spend more time with his family.*

1. When you read the title of the selection "Toward Right Livelihood," what did you think the selection would be about? Why? Answers will vary.

   _____

2. Did you assume the passage would be boring or too difficult? If so, why?
   Answers will vary.

   _____

3. As you read this passage, did you discover a fact or idea that interested you? Did you discover some information in this passage you could actu-

---

1. **Buddha:** Siddhartha Gautama, Indian spiritual leader
2. **enlightenment:** full and complete understanding
3. **Fortune 1,000 company:** a company that has achieved success and earned recognition as one of the most successful companies in the United States

---

* Adapted from Barry L. Reece and Rhonda Brandt, *Effective Human Relations in Organizations,* 7th ed. (Boston: Houghton Mifflin Co., 1999), 458–459. Copyright © 1999 by Houghton Mifflin Company. Reprinted with permission.

ally use in your life? If so, what was it? <u>Answers will vary.</u>

_____

4. If you followed the concept of right livelihood, what kind of work would

you do? <u>Answers will vary.</u> _____

_____

Concentration. Once your positive attitude has prepared your mind to absorb new information, you're ready to employ the second mental skill necessary for reading: concentration. Concentration is the ability to focus all of your attention on one thing while ignoring all distractions. You cannot understand or remember information unless you read with concentration.

Many people, however, find concentration difficult to achieve, especially when they read more challenging material. Too often, they allow distractions to pull their thoughts away from the sentences and paragraphs before them. But you can learn to concentrate better. How? By practicing effective techniques for combating the two types of distractions: external and internal.

External distractions are the sights, sounds, and other sensations that tempt you away from your reading. These distractions include ringing phones, people talking or walking nearby, the sound of a stereo, or a friend who stops by to chat. Though they are powerful, they are also the easier of the two types of distractions to eliminate.

To avoid having to deal with external distractions, you merely prevent them from happening by choosing or creating the right reading environment. Try to select a location for reading—such as an individual study area in your library or a quiet room in your house—where distractions will be minimal. Before a reading session, notify your friends and family that you'll be unavailable for conversation and socializing. If you must read in places with more activity, try wearing earplugs and/or sitting with your back to the action so you're not tempted to watch the comings and goings of others.

Internal distractions are often more challenging to overcome. They are the thoughts, worries, plans, daydreams, and other types of mental "noise" inside your own head. They will prevent you from concentrating on what you're reading and from absorbing the information you need to learn.

You can try to ignore these thoughts, but they will usually continue trying to intrude. So how do you temporarily silence them so you can devote your full attention to your reading? Try the following suggestions:

1. Begin every reading task with a positive attitude. A negative attitude produces a lot of grumbling mental noise like complaints and objections to

the task at hand. When you choose to keep a positive attitude, you'll eliminate an entire category of noisy thoughts that interfere with your concentration.

2. Instead of fighting internal distractions, try focusing completely on them for a short period of time. For five or ten minutes, allow yourself to sit and think about your job, your finances, your car problems, your boyfriend or girlfriend, the paper you need to write, or whatever is on your mind. Better yet, write these thoughts down. Do a free-writing exercise (a quick writing of your own thoughts on paper without censoring them or worrying about grammar and spelling) to empty your mind of the thoughts that clutter it. If you can't stop thinking about all of the other things you need to do, devote ten minutes to writing a detailed "To Do" list. Giving all of your attention to distracting thoughts will often clear them from your mind so you can focus on your reading.

3. Keep your purpose in mind as you read. As discussed earlier, having a clear goal when you read will help you concentrate on getting what you need to know from a text.

4. Use visualization to increase your interest and improve your retention of the information. As you read, let the words create pictures and images in your mind. Try to "see" in your mind's eye the scenes, examples, people, and other information presented in the text.

Exercise 1.8

Freewrite for ten minutes about what's going on inside your mind at this moment. Write your thoughts on a separate sheet of paper for this activity. Answers will vary.

Exercise 1.9

Read the following passage and practice the visualization techniques you read about earlier. Write your answers to each question on the blanks provided.

Do you remember a student in primary or secondary school who always insulted, teased, or threatened other students or started fights? These students are described as *bullies*. Bullying is a specific type of aggression in which (1) the behavior is intended to harm or disturb others, (2) the behavior occurs repeatedly over time, and (3) there is an imbalance of power, with a more powerful person or group attacking a less powerful one. The bully may be physically or psychologically more powerful, and the aggression may be verbal, physical, or psychological. If two adolescents of equal strength quarrel or fight, however, it is not considered bullying.*

1. Identify one specific type of aggression listed in the paragraph that describes bullying. _Answers will vary, but students should answer verbal,_ _physical, or psychological._

2. Visualize a specific bully from your past. Describe this person's physical appearance and personality traits. _Answers will vary._

3. Visualize a specific type of bullying from your past and describe it, identifying it as either verbal, physical, or psychological in nature.
   Answers will vary.

Memory. Memory, the ability to store and recall information, is also essential to the reading process. You use your memory constantly as you read. You must remember the meanings of words. You must remember what you know about people, places, and things when you encounter references to them. You must remember all of the ideas and information presented before that point in the text. You must remember the text's overall main point while you read the subpoints or details. You must remember your own experiences that either support or contradict the text's message. You may also need to remember other texts you've read that either agree or disagree with the new information you're reading.

There are many techniques you can use to improve your memory. A few of the most common are described next:

1. **Improve your concentration.** The more intensely you focus on something, the better the chance you'll remember it.

2. **Repeat and review.** Most of the time, the more you expose yourself to new information, the more easily you'll recall it.

3. **Recite.** Saying information aloud helps strengthen your memory of it.

4. **Associate new information with what you already know.** Making connections between your present knowledge and what you need to learn helps you to store new information in your mind more effectively.

* Adapted from Paul S. Kaplan, *Adolescence* (Boston: Houghton Mifflin Co., 2004), 197.

Exercise 1.10

Read the following passage through once; then cover it so you can't see it and test your memory of the information by writing, on the blanks provided, your answers to the questions.

On the evening of March 5, 1770, an angry crowd of poor and working-class Bostonians gathered in front of the guard post outside the Boston customs house. The crowd was protesting a British soldier's abusive treatment a few hours earlier of a Boston apprentice[1] who was trying to collect a debt from a British officer. Suddenly, shots rang out. When the smoke had cleared, four Bostonians lay dead, and seven more were wounded, one mortally. Among those in the crowd was an impoverished[2] twenty-eight-year-old shoemaker named George Robert Twelve Hewes. Hewes had already witnessed, and once experienced, abuses by British troops, but the appalling[3] violence of the "Boston Massacre," as the shooting became known, led Hewes to political activism.[4] Four of the five who died were personal friends, and he himself received a serious blow to the shoulder from a soldier's rifle butt. Over the next several days, Hewes attended meetings and signed petitions denouncing[5] British conduct in the shooting, and he later testified against the soldiers. Thereafter, he participated prominently[6] in such anti-British actions as the Boston Tea Party.*

1. In what year did the Boston Massacre take place? <u>1770</u>

2. What was the crowd protesting? <u>The treatment of a Boston apprentice who</u>
   <u>was trying to collect a debt from a British officer</u>

3. What was George Hewes's profession? <u>shoemaker</u>

4. What kind of injury did Hewes sustain in the massacre? <u>A blow to</u>
   <u>his shoulder</u>

5. What other anti-British action did Hewes take part in? <u>the Boston</u>
   <u>Tea Party</u>

---

1. **apprentice:** one who is learning a trade
2. **impoverished:** poor
3. **appalling:** frightful
4. **activism:** action as a means of achieving a goal
5. **denouncing:** openly condemning or criticizing
6. **prominently:** noticeably or openly

---

* Adapted from Paul Boyer et al., *The Enduring Vision* (Boston: Houghton Mifflin Co., 2004), 123.

1

Logical thought. Another mental skill required for effective reading is logical thinking. Logical thought is composed of many different mental tasks, including those in the following list:

Sequencing and ordering: seeing the order of things and understanding cause/effect relationships

Matching: noticing similarities

Organizing: grouping things into categories

Analysis: understanding how to examine the different parts of something

Reasoning from the general to the particular and from the particular to the general: drawing conclusions and making generalizations

Abstract thought: understanding ideas and concepts

Synthesis: putting things together in new combinations

If you want to improve your ability to think logically, try one or more of the following suggestions:

1. **Practice active reading.** Using outlining, in particular, forces you to work harder to detect relationships in information.

2. **Play with games and puzzles.** Card games, computer games, and board games such as chess, checkers, and backgammon will give you opportunities to sharpen your analytical skills.

3. **Solve problems.** Work math problems. Read mysteries (or watch them on television) and try to figure out who committed the crime before the detective does. Try to think of ways to solve everyday problems, both big and small. For example, come up with a solution for America's overflowing landfills. Or figure out how to alter backpacks so they don't strain your back.

4. **Practice your argument and debating skills.** Discuss controversial issues with people who hold the opposing viewpoint.

5. **Write more.** Writing requires a great deal of logical thought, so write letters to your newspaper editor or congressional representatives about issues that are important to you.

Exercise 1.11

Read this passage from a newspaper. Then, on the blanks provided, write your answers to the questions that follow.

1

Hard to Be a Boy in a Girls' World

A *BusinessWeek* cover piece titled "The New Gender Gap" details the lamentable[1] state of boydom. One of the reasons, some experts say, is female schoolteachers who don't have the foggiest[2] notion of what it is like to be a boy.

The experts do not blame female teachers entirely for what has happened to boys. Some of them simply assert that girls are different, wired by nature to have nimbler fingers that produce beautiful handwriting and are endowed[3] with the innate[4] ability to remain in their seats. A boy, on the other hand, requires frequent recesses lest he go stark raving mad.

Whatever the reason, it's clear that something very bad is happening to boys. They are 30% more likely to drop out of school, something like four to six times as likely to kill themselves and 85% more likely to commit murder than girls. When they get older, they don't go to college or graduate school in the numbers women do and don't bother to vote, either.

If they weren't (real) men, they would demand some sort of preferential[5] treatment. You go, guy.

What's happening? Probably several things. Not only do boys continue to be taught by women who think they are just unruly[6] girls, but girls are now purposely favored. It was girls, remember, who supposedly were overlooked in school and whose self-esteem suffered accordingly. This has become conventional wisdom, even though it hardly conformed to my own school experience and seemed, moreover, to be counterintuitive.[7] Why would female teachers ignore girls? Boys nowadays also have all the wrong role models: rap singers and inarticulate[8] athletes, for instance. Much of the entertainment industry panders[9] to the worst in boys.

My gut also tells me that the incredible overemphasis on sports is bad for boys. In the minds of too many of them, it has gone from being a recreational activity to a supposed career path. Why study to make a modest income when you can play to make really big bucks?

Alas for the home team, none of the possible answers fully satisfies. It seems, instead, that girls are doing better than boys because girls are really better than boys. In a society that no longer needs brawn[10] or values aggression—that

1. **lamentable:** sad
2. **foggiest:** vaguest
3. **endowed:** supplied
4. **innate:** inborn
5. **preferential:** partial to; in this context, better treatment
6. **unruly:** undisciplined, out of control
7. **counterintuitive:** against intuition or instinct
8. **inarticulate:** not well-spoken
9. **panders:** caters
10. **brawn:** strong muscles

1

is, in some respects, more feminine—girls are better endowed by nature to succeed. A socialist[1] (if there are any left) might even suggest that the entire women's liberation movement[2] was capitalism's[3] response to the need for more and better workers—people with better motor skills, the astounding ability to empathize and express feelings and the patience to sit still.

Because this is about boys and men—and supposedly this is a man's world—the tendency is to dismiss this problem. But never mind the cost to society of countless male dropouts. Think instead of individual boys and men—angry, confused, depressed. The statistics on suicide alone tell a sad story. Boys will be boys, all right, but some of them don't make it to be men.

So boys, depressed and beaten down, fall further and further behind—zonked on Ritalin,[4] diagnosed as learning-disabled and prepared by evolution for roles that are no longer valued.

Much has changed since Henry Higgins[5] bellowed, "Why can't a woman be more like a man?" The answer, Mr. Higgins, is now plain: It simply doesn't pay.*

1. The author gives several possible reasons for boys' struggles. What is one of these reasons? <u>Answers will vary. They can include these:</u>

   <u>1) Boys are taught by women who don't understand them.</u>

   <u>2) Girls are now purposely favored. 3) Boys have the wrong role models.</u>

   <u>4) Sports are overemphasized for boys.</u>

2. Think of another possible reason, one that is not mentioned by the author.
   <u>Answers will vary.</u>

   _____

3. Predict two possible effects of having a society that contains too many "depressed and beaten down" men.

   Effect#1: <u>Answers will vary.</u>

   Effect#2: <u>Answers will vary.</u>

1. **socialist:** someone who believes that power and wealth should be distributed equally within a specific community
2. **women's liberation movement:** a 1960s effort by U.S. women to end discrimination and gain equal rights and pay
3. **capitalism:** economic system in which private individuals and companies control production of goods
4. **Ritalin:** drug prescribed for hyperactive children
5. **Henry Higgins:** a character in the play *My Fair Lady*

---

* "Hard to Be a Boy in a Girls' World" by Richard Cohen. Copyright © 2003, The Washington Post Writers Group. Reprinted with permission.

4. Do your own experiences support or refute the author's opinion about boys? Explain your answer. Answers will vary. _____

_____

5. Argue *against* the author's main point about boys. Give facts and/or examples in support of your opinion. Answers will vary. _____

_____

Develop Individual Reading Skills

Another way to improve your reading comprehension is to develop the isolated skills you must use to read well. For example, you can learn techniques for recognizing the main idea of a paragraph or for detecting patterns used to organize information. The rest of this book is designed to help you develop and practice these skills.

Exercise 1.12

Check off in the following list the skills you believe you need to improve. Next to each item that you check, write on the blank provided the number of the chapter in this book that focuses on helping you strengthen that skill. Answers will vary.

_____ Recognizing the overall point (the main idea) of a reading selection (Chapter 2) _____

_____ Understanding how details support the main idea of a reading selection (Chapter 3) _____

_____ Figuring out how a reading selection is organized (Chapter 6) _____

_____ Understanding visuals—maps, charts, graphs—in reading selections (Chapter 7) _____

_____ Reading critically, or figuring out if a reading selection is accurate or trustworthy (Chapter 9) _____

_____ Understanding longer reading selections (Chapter 10) _____

_____ Figuring out implied main ideas, points that are not stated directly in a reading selection (Chapter 4) _____

_____ Recognizing transitions, words that link sentences and paragraphs together (Chapter 5)

_____ "Reading between the lines" (making inferences) by drawing conclusions from the information in a reading selection (Chapter 8)

Learn and Use Different Reading Strategies

Reading strategies are techniques you use when you read. Some of them—such as active reading—are designed to improve your comprehension and retention of information. Others—such as skimming and scanning—provide you with tools you can use to find what you need in certain circumstances.

This book explains a different reading strategy in each chapter. Make sure you understand each of them so that you can begin using them to read better right away.

How This Book Will Help You Improve

Goals of this Book

The Houghton Mifflin College Reading Series is one of three books in a series designed to help you improve your reading skills. This text—the first in the sequence—focuses on the basic skills necessary to effective reading. Each chapter concentrates on one essential skill you can immediately use to strengthen your reading comprehension.

This book, along with the other two in the series, is based on the belief that you can indeed become a better reader. Even if you have struggled in the past, you can learn and practice the skills you need to get more out of anything you read.

Organization and Features

This book is organized into two sections. The first part includes ten chapters, one for each essential reading skill. The second includes a variety of tests designed to give you more practice with the skills covered in the first ten chapters.

Each of the ten chapters includes several helpful features.

Test Yourself. At the beginning of each chapter, except Chapter 1, a section called Test Yourself will help you identify what you already know about the skill covered in that chapter. It will also help you pinpoint specific areas you need to target for improvement.

Exercises. Throughout each chapter, you'll have numerous opportunities to check your understanding with practice activities. As you complete each exercise and receive feedback on your answers, you will progress toward better reading comprehension.

Chapter review. Filling in the blanks in a brief summary of the major points and concepts in the chapter will help you reinforce them in your mind.

Interesting readings. The readings within practices, along with the longer reading selection in each chapter, are drawn from a variety of interesting sources. These readings have been carefully chosen to be enjoyable and/or useful. They have also been selected to clearly demonstrate a particular skill or concept. Furthermore, they'll give you practice reading different kinds of sources, including textbooks, magazine articles, newspaper articles, and essays.

The longer reading selection in each chapter is followed by questions designed to check your comprehension and increase your vocabulary. It also includes discussion questions that will encourage you to sharpen your thinking skills and find ways to apply the information to your own life.

Vocabulary. Each chapter presents a different vocabulary concept. In this section, you will learn techniques for discovering the meanings of unfamiliar words. You will also learn about different types of specialized vocabulary in order to improve your overall reading comprehension. A practice activity draws from the readings in the chapter to give you an opportunity to check your understanding.

Reading strategy. Each chapter concludes with the explanation of a different reading strategy. Strategies are techniques you can use to get more out of what you read. Using these techniques, you can begin to improve your reading comprehension right away.

Tests. Each chapter concludes with a series of tests designed to help you measure your understanding of the concepts and skills presented. They will verify your mastery of the information and also identify areas for further study and review.

Exercise 1.13

Preview this textbook. Write your answers, on the blanks provided, to the following questions about its features and organization.

1

1. How many chapters does this book contain? 10 _____

2. In what chapter is the topic of "Main Ideas" covered? Chapter 2 _____

3. In what chapter will you learn the different patterns of organization that writers use? Chapter 6 _____

4. In what chapter will you find the most "visual" material—that is, charts, graphs, maps, and photos—and find out how to read them? Chapter 7 _____

5. In what chapter will you find information on how to read longer selections? Chapter 10 _____

6. In what chapter will you learn how to use the dictionary? Chapter 1 _____

7. Look at Chapter 8 and define the term *inference*. An inference is a _____
   conclusion you draw that's based upon the stated information. _____

8. How many additional readings appear in the combined skills test section?
   5 _____

9. Look at the table of contents and count the number of reading selections contained in Part One of this text. 11 _____

10. How many different reading strategies are presented in this text? 10 _____

CHAPTER 1 REVIEW

Write the correct answers in the blanks in the following statements.

1. Good reading skills are important to ____academic____, ____personal____, and
   __professional__ success.

2. Reading helps strengthen ____thinking____ skills.

3. The two basic purposes for reading are to gain ____information____ and to be entertained.

4. When you read for information, you may have one or more of the following goals: gain a general ____understanding____ of the ideas or points; discover ____facts____ or answer questions; memorize the information;

1

find information or ideas that prove a ___point___ you want to make; make a ___decision___ based on the information.

5. Reading is actually a collection of mental skills that include ___attitude___, concentration, ___memory___, and ___logical___ thought.

6. A positive ___attitude___ makes reading more pleasurable and more productive.

7. ___Concentration___ is the ability to focus all of your attention on one thing while ignoring distractions.

8. The two types of distractions are ___external___ and ___internal___.

9. ___Memory___ is the ability to store and recall information.

10. Logical thought includes mental tasks such as sequencing and ordering, ___matching___, ___organizing___, analysis, ___reasoning___ from the general to the particular and from the particular to the general, ___abstract___ thought, and synthesis.

11. Reading ___strategies___ are techniques you can use to get more out of what you read.

READING STRATEGY: Active Reading

Many people don't get everything they can out of reading simply because they are *passive* readers. Passive readers are people who try to read by just running their eyes over the words in a passage. They expect their brains to magically absorb the information after just one quick reading. If they don't, they blame the author and pronounce the work "dull" or "too difficult." They don't write anything down. If they come to a word they don't know, they just skip it and keep reading. If they get bored, they let their attention wander. They "read" long sections and then realize they have no memory or understanding of the information or ideas.

To read more effectively, you must become an **active reader.** Active readers know they have to do more than just sit with a book in front of them. They know they have to participate by interacting with the text and by thinking as they read. They read with a pen or pencil in their hand, marking key words or ideas or jotting notes in the margins. They reread the text if necessary. Also, they consciously try to connect the text's information to their own experiences and beliefs.

1

Active reading is essential to understanding and remembering ideas and information, especially those in more difficult reading selections. It includes any or all of the following tasks:

- Identifying and writing down the point and purpose of the reading

- Underlining, highlighting, or circling important words or phrases

- Determining the meanings of unfamiliar words

- Outlining a passage to understand the relationships in the information

- Writing down questions when you're confused

- Completing activities—such as reading comprehension questions—that follow a chapter or passage

- Jotting down notes in the margins

- Thinking about how you can use the information or how the information reinforces or contradicts your ideas or experiences

- Predicting possible test questions on the material

- Rereading and reviewing

- Studying visual aids such as graphs, charts, and diagrams until you understand them

Remember: The purpose of all these activities is to comprehend and retain more of what you read. So for challenging reading, such as textbook chapters or journal articles, active reading is a must. Also, you should perform these tasks for any reading that you're expected to remember for a test.

However, even if you won't have to demonstrate your mastery of a reading selection, you should still get in the habit of reading actively when you read for information. Even if you're just reading for your own pleasure, you'll remember more by using active reading techniques.

To read actively, follow these steps:

1. When you sit down to read a book, get pens, pencils, and/or highlighter markers ready, too.

2. As you read each paragraph, mark points or terms that seem important. You may choose to underline them, highlight them, or enclose them in boxes or circles—this includes any words or key information phrases that are in bold print because the author wishes to

Continued

1

call attention to them. Consider jotting down an outline or notes in the margins as you read. If you're reading a textbook, write in the margins the questions you want to remember to ask your instructor.

3. As you read, continually ask yourself these questions: How can this information help me? How can I use this information? What will my instructor probably want me to remember? How does this reading support or contradict my own ideas or beliefs and experiences?

4. After you have read the entire selection, complete any activities that follow it.

The following passage has been actively read.

It's Better to Be Looked Over Than Overlooked

The first [stage] is the "attention getting" phase. Young men and women do this somewhat differently. As soon as they enter the bar, both males and females typically ① establish a territory—a seat, a place to lean, a position near the jukebox or dance floor. Once settled, they ② begin to attract attention to themselves.

Tactics vary. Men tend to pitch and roll their shoulders, stretch, stand tall, and shift from foot to foot in a swaying motion. They also exaggerate their body movements. Instead of simply using the wrist to stir a drink, men often employ the entire arm, as if stirring mud. The normally smooth motion necessary to light a cigarette becomes a whole-body gesture, ending with an elaborate shaking from the elbow to extinguish the match. And the whole body is employed in hearty laughter—made loud enough to attract a crowd. Thus simple gestures are embellished, overdone.

Then there is the swagger with which young men often move to and fro. Male baboons on the grasslands of East Africa also swagger when they foresee a potential sexual encounter. A male gorilla walks back and forth stiffly as he watches a female out of the corner of his eye. This parading gait is known to primatologists as bird-dogging. Males of many species also preen. Human males pat their hair, adjust their clothes, tug their chins, or perform other self-clasping or grooming movements that diffuse nervous energy and keep the body moving.

Older men often use different props, advertising their availability with expensive jewelry, clothing, and other accoutrements that spell success. But all of these signals can be reduced to one basic, three-part

Main point: Men and women use body language to attract attention and signal availability.

This is true!

Men: simple gestures are exaggerated.

embellished = add more details
Men swagger (bird-dog) and preen, too. Author compares men to gorillas.

gait = way of moving

Older men display their wealth and success.

accoutrements = accessories

1

message: "I am here; I am important; I am harmless." What a difficult mixture of signals to give out simultaneously—importance and approachability. Yet men succeed; women regularly court men.

"It is better to be looked over than overlooked," Mae West once said. And women know it. Young women begin the attention getting phase with many of the same maneuvers that men use—smiling, gazing, shifting, swaying, preening, stretching, moving in their territory to draw attention to themselves. Often they incorporate a battery of feminine moves as well. They twist their curls, tilt their heads, look up coyly, giggle, raise their brows, flick their tongues, lick their upper lips, blush, and hide their faces in order to signal, "I am here."

Some women also have a characteristic walk when courting; they arch their backs, thrust out their bosoms, sway their hips, and strut. No wonder many women wear high-heeled shoes. This bizarre Western custom, invented by Catherine de Medici in the 1500s, unnaturally arches the back, tilts the buttocks, and thrusts the chest out into a female come-hither pose. The clomping noise of their spiky heels helps draw attention too. With this high-heeled gait, puckered lips, batting eyes, dancing brows, upturned palms, pigeoned toes, rocking bodies, swaying skirts, and gleaming teeth, women signal approachability to men.*

> Women use same tactics as men use.
>
> Women also use feminine moves.
> coyly = shyly
>
> Women have a distinctive walk that signals availability.
>
> Men's walk is natural, but women's walk is not?

Now, try applying the active reading strategy yourself. Complete steps 1 through 4 in the previous list to actively read the following passage from a textbook. Then respond to the questions by writing your answers on the blanks provided.

Altering Your Body Image

A growing number of people seem to be unhappy with how they look. Specifically, they are dissatisfied with the appearance of their body. *Psychology Today* uses the term "body image" to describe the perceptions people have of their physical appearance, attractiveness, and beauty. Body image is our mental representation of ourselves; it is what allows us to contemplate[1] ourselves. The image we see in the mirror influences much of our behavior and self-esteem.

Continued

1. **contemplate:** to think about

---

* "It's Better to Be Looked Over Than Overlooked" from *Anatomy of Love: The Natural History of Monogamy, Adultery, and Divorce* by Helen E. Fisher. Copyright © 1992 by Helen E. Fisher. Used by permission of W. W. Norton & Company, Inc.

1

A negative body image can begin to take shape early in life. Teasing during childhood can have a crushing effect on body image. Memories of being teased haunt many people for years. Through adolescence, the pressure to achieve an attractive body image is intense, especially among women. Body weight has a major influence on overall satisfaction with appearance. In many cases, the ever-present media portray desirable women as thin.

Appearance is more important today than it was in the past, according to Mary Pipher, author of *Reviving Ophelia.* She notes that we have moved from communities of primary relationships in which people know each other to cities where secondary relationships are much more common:

In a community of primary relationships, appearance is only one of many dimensions[1] that define people. Everyone knows everyone else in different ways over time. In a city of strangers, appearance is the only dimension available for the rapid assessment of others. Thus it becomes incredibly important in defining value.

Preoccupation[2] with body image follows many people throughout adulthood. Large numbers of people wish to conform to the body-size ideals projected in the media. The motivation to be thinner helps support a $50-billion-a-year diet industry. People have learned to judge themselves, in many cases, by the standards of physical attractiveness that appear in fashion magazines and television commercials.

Some people have found ways to remake their self-image and move away from a preoccupation with body image. One approach is to develop criteria[3] for self-esteem that go beyond appearance. To make appearance less significant in your life, you develop other benchmarks[4] for self-evaluation. These might include succeeding at work, forming new friendships, or achieving a greater feeling of self-worth through volunteer work. Another approach is to engage in exercise that makes you feel good about yourself. Exercise for strength, fitness, and health, not just for weight loss. You can also identify and change habitual[5] and negative thoughts about your body. When you look in the mirror, try to say nice things about your body.*

1. **dimensions:** aspects
2. **preoccupation:** worry; concern with
3. **criteria:** standards

4. **benchmarks:** standards for measuring or judging something
5. **habitual:** happening again and again

* From Barry L. Reece and Rhonda Brandt, *Effective Human Relations in Organizations,* 7th ed. (Boston: Houghton Mifflin Co., 1999), 116–117. Copyright © 1999 by Houghton Mifflin Company. Reprinted by permission.

1

1. Professionals in the field of psychology say that people with low self-esteem rely too much on the views of others for a sense of self-worth. Is this a problem you currently face in your life? Explain. <u>Answers will vary.</u>

_____

2. Mary Pipher says that in large communities appearance is the only dimension available for rapid assessment of others. Do you find yourself placing a heavy emphasis on appearance when assessing the worth of others? <u>Answers will vary.</u>

3. Joan Borysenko, director of the Mind/Body Clinic at Harvard Medical School, says you need to accept yourself as you are. Acceptance, she says, means actually honoring yourself as you are now. Is this good advice? Is it realistic advice? Explain. <u>Answers will vary.</u>

_____

4. If you currently have a negative body image, what other criteria could you use to help enhance your self-esteem? <u>Answers will vary.</u>

_____

Reading Selections

Chapters 2 through 9 in this text contain a longer reading selection at the end, followed by vocabulary, comprehension, and discussion questions. To get you acquainted with the different types of selections you will be reading, this chapter contains one website selection, one literary selection, and one textbook selection. Read the following selections and answer the questions that follow, either independently or with other members of your class.

Practicing the Active Reading Strategy:
Before and As You Read

You can use active reading strategies before, as, and after you read a selection. The following are some suggestions for active reading strategies that you can employ before you read and as you are reading.

1. Skim the selection for any unfamiliar words. Circle or highlight any words you do not know.

1

2. As you read, underline, highlight, or circle important words or phrases.
3. Write down any questions about the selection if you are confused by the information presented.
4. Jot notes in the margin to help you understand the material.

WEBSITE SELECTION

Learning Styles and Maximizing Your Success in School

1 College is different from high school. Entering any new environment brings new challenges and distractions. Also, each step of the learning process usually brings more and harder work. You obviously learned to succeed at your last educational stop. However, you may need to readjust now. This is especially true for adult returning students and students beginning a new field of study. By expanding on your current learning skills, you will better meet the challenges ahead. We hope that the following will provide useful information and tools to make this next educational step a success.

Learning Styles

2 **What are they? How do they match with teaching styles?** There are many types of learning styles. Often, these types match our personality style. Each of us has a different style or combination of styles. The majority of us can use most styles. However, we tend to rely on or prefer certain styles. Hopefully, these are the styles that have brought us success in the past. If this is not the case, it may be helpful to look again at one's approach. We all learn differently, but we can all learn effectively. It is important to understand your own learning style and use it to your best advantage in the classroom.

3   There are also many teaching styles. We do best when our learning styles match with an instructor's teaching style. Below is some information about learning styles, teaching styles, and how to bridge the two.

Eyes or Ears

4 **Do you remember best what is said to you or what you read? Do you prefer television or newspapers as your source of news?** Some people learn best by reading. They need to see something to remember it. Others learn best by listening. Information sticks once they hear it.

5   If you have a visual style, you may have difficulty with an instructor who believes telling people what to learn and know is enough. Instructors who rely heavily on class discussion will also cause you some anxiety. Handouts, reading assignments, and written information on the blackboard are most helpful to you.

6   On the other hand, if you have an auditory style, you may be in trouble with an instructor who writes a lot and assigns reading that is not discussed in class. Class discussions and study groups are a better way for you to learn.

Movement

7 **Does it help you to rewrite your notes or take notes as you read?** Some people's learning is improved by movement. In other words, they learn as they write notes in class. Or when they are reading an assignment, they remember the content best if they take notes as they read. Sometimes the act of highlighting important information while reading works in the same way.

Group or Solitary

8 **Do you find you remember more when you study in a group or alone?** Some people draw their energy from the outside world. They like to interact with other people, activities, or things. This is often called extroversion. Others prefer to gain their energy from their own internal ideas, emotions, or impressions. Some people call this introversion.

9 If you tend to be more extroverted, you communicate freely and like to have other people around. Thus, working in groups and talking material over with others helps you understand and process new ideas better. You may be impatient and distracted working on your own. A class that is less varied and not as action-oriented may be a particular challenge. You like instructors who are active, energetic, and enthusiastic. You also prefer a more friendly and personal approach. In addition, you probably find larger classes exciting.

10 If you are more introverted, you probably work happily alone. You don't mind working on one project for a long time without interruption. You may be quiet in the classroom and dislike classes with a lot of oral presentations and group interaction and work. Sometimes having to communicate with others is hard. You work best if

you read lessons over or write them out before discussion, think before participating, and ask questions before completing tasks or exercises. You like classes that require being thoughtful and introspective. You may dislike a professor with a more personal style of attention and closeness. A quiet and tactful style works best for you. Smaller classes are your preference.

Practical or Innovative

11 **Do you like to follow an established way of doing things? Or would you rather follow your inspirations?** Some people prefer to take information in through their five senses, taking note of what is actually there. They want, remember, and trust facts. They are sometimes called practical types. Others prefer to take information in through a "sixth sense," focusing on what might be. These people like to daydream and think about what might be in the future. One could call them innovative.

12 If you are a practical type, you probably like an established, routine way of doing things. You prefer using skills you already know rather than new ones. Taking note of details, memorizing facts, and reaching a conclusion step-by-step is your ideal. You learn best if you have clear directions to follow. Films, audiovisuals, hands-on exercises, and practical examples are most helpful. You learn best when instructors are factual and thorough, working out details in advance and showing you why things make sense.

13 If you are more innovative, you probably like to solve new problems. You may dislike doing the same thing repeatedly and may be impatient with routine details. You may also find yourself daydreaming during factual lectures. You work best when you can see the

big picture, have independence and freedom, and use new approaches in your work. You like enthusiastic instructors who point out challenges and future benefits and then let you figure out your own way.

Thinking or Feeling

14 **Do you respond more to people's thoughts or feelings?** Some people prefer to organize information in a logical way. They respond more easily to people's thoughts and are more analytical. If you are such a person, emotions play less of a part In your life, decisions, and interactions with others. You work best if you can organize and outline a subject, know your objectives and goals, get to the task, and receive rapid feedback. You are most motivated when you can see logical reasons for studying certain material or working on a particular project. You probably prefer teachers who are task-focused, logical, well-organized, less emotional, and generous with feedback.

15   Other people prefer to organize and structure information in a personal, value-oriented way. If this sounds familiar, you are likely to be very aware of other people and their feelings. You prefer harmony. You probably learn best if you can identify with what you are doing and have an emotional connection to it. You like an environment with little competition and with opportunity to respond more personally. You probably prefer teachers who are friendly and easy to work with. You also like a teaching style that is positive, tells you why what you are doing is valuable, and supports your personal goals.

Open-Ended or Closure-Driven

16 **Do you like to get things settled and finished? Or would you rather leave things open for alterations?** Some people prefer to live a planned and organized life. They go on vacation and plan out all of their activities before they go. Other people like to be more open-ended, living more spontaneously and flexibly.

17   If you need closure, you probably work best when you can plan your work and follow that plan. You like to get things finished and do not like to be interrupted. In an effort to complete a task, however, you may make decisions too quickly. You learn best if you can stick to a routine and follow a specific time frame and precise guidelines. You probably prefer instructors who are structured, timely, precise, and organized. You also like specific performance guidelines.

18   For those who are more open-ended, you probably like change and undertaking many projects at once. You may have trouble making decisions and may postpone unpleasant jobs. You probably learn best if you can be original, physically active, and spontaneous. You like instructors who are more open, creative, spontaneous, and informal. You dislike deadlines and too much direction, wanting to follow your own path.

Solutions

19 **What if your learning style and a teaching style are mismatched?**
It is tempting to respond to this problem by thinking, "If people would only change their approach, my life would be much easier." However, this doesn't get anyone very far, and there are better solutions.

- Try to get as much as you can out of every course.

- Try to "translate" the material into a form you understand.

- Practice approaching the class in another way. Be open to a new way of learning. Adapt to the instructor's style and see what you can learn. You may be surprised. If you are successful, you will add new skills without giving up what you already do well.

- Ask questions. Talk to the instructor. Ask for what you need (i.e., more structure, more freedom, additional readings, more explanation of course goals). A clear, direct, respectful, and responsible communication is best. Also remember that communication is both verbal and nonverbal.*

VOCABULARY

Read the following questions about some of the vocabulary words that appear in the previous selection. Then circle the letter of the correct answer.

1. If your learning style is *auditory*, what does that mean? (paragraph 6)

   (a.) You learn best when you hear something.
   b. You learn best by doing something.
   c. You learn best by holding something in your hand.
   d. You learn best by seeing something repeatedly.

2. If you are *extroverted* (paragraph 9), you are

   a. shy   c. depressed
   b. reserved   (d.) outgoing

3. Conversely, if you are *introverted* (paragraph 10), you are

   a. easily distracted   c. unhappy
   b. easily motivated   (d.) shy

4. A synonym (a word that means the same thing that another word does) for *introspective* (paragraph 10) is

   a. shy   c. delighted
   (b.) thoughtful   d. manipulative

5. "One could call them *innovative*." In paragraph 11, *innovative* means

   (a.) inventive   c. neurotic
   b. old-fashioned   d. mean-spirited

* Developed by Dr. Lauren Slater, Staff Psychologist, Pace University Counseling Center, Westchester campuses, NY, www.pace.edu.

1

Practicing the Active Reading Strategy:
After You Read

Now that you have read the selection, answer the following questions, using the active reading strategies that you have learned in this chapter.

1. Identify and write down the point and purpose of this reading selection.

2. Besides the vocabulary words included in the exercise on page 35, are there any other vocabulary words that are unfamiliar to you? If so, write a list of them. When you have finished writing your list, look up each word in a dictionary and write the definition that best describes the word as it is used in the selection.

3. Predict any possible test questions that may be used on a test about the content of this selection.

4. How could you use the information contained in this selection? Does the information contained in the selection reinforce or contradict your ideas and experiences? Explain.

QUESTIONS FOR DISCUSSION AND WRITING

Answer the following questions based on your reading of the selection. Write your answers on the blanks provided.

1. Did you learn anything new from this article about your learning style? If so, what did you learn? Answers will vary.

_____

2. Will understanding your learning style help you become a better student? Why or why not? Answers will vary.

_____

3. If you had to think about your academic career up to this point, do you think you would have done better in school if you had identified your learning style earlier? Why or why not? Answers will vary.

_____

Practicing the Active Reading Strategy:
Before and As You Read

You can use active reading strategies before, as, and after you read a selection. The following are some suggestions for active reading strategies that you can employ before you read and as you are reading.

1. Skim the selection for any unfamiliar words. Circle or highlight any words you do not know.

2. As you read, underline, highlight, or circle important words or phrases.

3. Write down any questions about the selection if you are confused by the information presented.

4. Jot notes in the margin to help you understand the material.

LITERARY SELECTION

My Life

by Golda Meir

1 I started school in a huge, fortresslike[1] building on Fourth Street near Milwaukee's famous Schlitz beer factory, and I loved it. I can't remember how long it took me to learn English (at home, of course, we spoke Yiddish,[2] and luckily, so did almost everyone else on Walnut Street), but I have no recollection of the language ever being a real problem for me, so I must have picked it up quickly. I made friends quickly, too, Two of those early first- or second-grade friends remained friends all my life, and both live in Israel now. One was Regina Hamburger (today Medzini), who lived on our street and who was to leave America when I did; the other was Sarah Feder, who became one of the leaders of Labor Zionism[3] in the United States. . . .

2 More than fifty years later—when I was seventy-one and a prime minister—I went back to that school for a few hours. It had not changed very much in all those years except that the vast majority of its pupils were now black, not Jewish, as in 1906. They welcomed me as though I were a queen. Standing in rows on the creaky old stage I remembered so well, freshly scrubbed and neat as pins, they serenaded me with Yiddish and Hebrew songs and raised their voices to peal out the Israeli anthem "Hatikvah" which made my eyes fill with tears. Each one of the classrooms had been

---

1. **fortresslike:** like a fort prepared for military action
2. **Yiddish:** language of European Jews
3. **Labor Zionism:** The Labor Zionist Party was committed to the development of a democratic-socialist political economy in Israel.

beautifully decorated with posters about Israel and signs reading SHALOM[1] (one of the children thought it was my family name), and when I entered the school, two little girls wearing headbands with Stars of David on them solemnly presented me with an enormous white rose made of tissue paper and pipe cleaners, which I wore all day and carefully carried back to Israel with me.

3   Another of the gifts I got that day in 1971 from the Fourth Street School was a record of my grades for one of the years I had spent there: 95 in reading, 90 in spelling, 95 in arithmetic, 85 in music, and a mysterious 90 in something called manual arts. Which I cannot remember at all. But when the children asked me to talk to them for a few minutes, it was not about book learning that I chose to speak. I had learned a lot more than fractions or how to spell at Fourth Street, and I decided to tell those eager, attentive children—born as I myself had been, into a minority and living, as I myself had lived, without much extravagance (to put it mildly)—what the gist of that learning had been. "It isn't really important to decide when you are very young just exactly what you want to become when you grow up," I told them. "It is much more important to decide on the way you want to live. If you are going to get involved with causes which are good for others, not only for yourselves, then it seems to me that that is sufficient, and maybe what you will be is only a matter of chance." I had a feeling that they understood me.*

VOCABULARY

Read the following questions about some of the vocabulary words that appear in the previous selection. Then circle the letter of the correct answer.

1. When something is *creaky*, what does that mean? (paragraph 2) "standing in rows on the *creaky* old stage I remembered so well . . ."
   a. new
   b. eerie
   (c.) old; in disrepair
   d. fantastic

2. One sentence includes these words: "they *serenaded* me with Yiddish and Hebrew songs and raised their voices" (paragraph 2). What does the word *serenade* mean?
   a. recited
   (b.) sang
   c. spoke
   d. danced

1. **shalom:** peace; a traditional Jewish greeting or farewell

---

* Excerpt from *My Life* by Golda Meir. Reprinted by permission of Weidenfeld & Nicolson, a division of The Orion Publishing Group, as the Publisher.

1

3. One sentence includes these words: "and raised their voices to *peal* out the Israeli anthem" (paragraph 2). What does the word *peal* mean in this context?

   a. ring   c. pretend
   b. say softly   d. remove

4. One sentence includes these words: "born as I myself had been, into a minority and living, as I myself had lived, without much *extravagance*" (paragraph 3). What does the word *extravagance* mean in this context?

   a. abundance or wealth   c. willfulness
   b. poverty   d. hopefulness

5. What is the *gist* of something? One sentence includes these words: "what the *gist* of that learning had been" (paragraph 3).

   a. despair   c. central idea
   b. hope   d. miscommunication

Practicing the Active Reading Strategy:
After You Read

Now that you have read the selection, answer the following questions using the active reading strategies that you have learned in this chapter.

1. Identify and write down the point and purpose of this reading selection.

2. Besides the vocabulary words included in the exercise on pages 38–39, are there any other vocabulary words that are unfamiliar to you? If so, write a list of them. When you have finished writing your list, look up each word in a dictionary and write the definition that best describes the word as it is used in the selection.

3. Predict any possible test questions that may be used on a test about the content of this selection.

4. How could you use the information contained in this selection? Does the information contained in the selection reinforce or contradict your ideas and experiences? Explain.

QUESTIONS FOR DISCUSSION AND WRITING

Answer the following questions based on your reading of the selection. Write your answers on the blanks provided.

1. Did you enjoy the selection? Why or why not? _Answers will vary._

   _____

2. Based on your reading of the selection, what do you know about Golda Meir's childhood? Her adult life? _Meir had a very humble upbringing_ _but went on to become a respected world leader._

3. Based on your reading of the selection, would you like to learn more about Golda Meir? Why or why not? _Answers will vary._

   _____

Practicing the Active Reading Strategy:
Before and As You Read

You can use active reading strategies before, as, and after you read a selection. The following are some suggestions for active reading strategies that you can employ before you read and as you are reading.

1. Skim the selection for any unfamiliar words. Circle or highlight any words you do not know.
2. As you read, underline, highlight, or circle important words or phrases.
3. Write down any questions about the selection if you are confused by the information presented.
4. Jot notes in the margin to help you understand the material.

TEXTBOOK SELECTION

Developing Wisdom

by Skip Downing

1 As you have discovered, colleges require you to take general education courses. These courses are designed to give you the foundation for academic success. They include subjects like mathematics, composition, speech, history, and science.

The Curriculum of Life

2 The University of Life also requires you to take general education courses. Its courses are a little different, however. These courses are offered by the Department of Adversities. They include subjects like Problems 101,

Obstacles 203, Mistakes 305, Failures 410, and for some, a graduate course called Catastrophes 599. Tests are given often. There are no answers in the back of the book. In fact, there is no textbook in these courses. There are only your experiences from which to learn.

3   People who change their beliefs and behaviors to create the best possible results in their lives believe that each course in the curriculum of life is especially designed to teach them exactly what they need to know at that moment. So they look carefully at their response to adversities: What do I **think**? How do I **feel**? What do I **do**? As always, our responses are guided by our deepest core beliefs about ourselves, about other people, and about the world. Adversities can destroy us, or they can teach us the greatest lessons life has to offer. The choice is ours. The prize is wisdom. Wisdom, I suggest, is the deep and profound understanding that allows us to consistently make wise choices. These choices move us steadily and happily toward the creation of a life worth living.

Avoiding Learned Helplessness

4 Psychologist Martin Seligman, author of *Learned Optimism*, has spent years studying how people respond to adversity. He compares experiencing adversity to being punched in the stomach. The punch will hurt and maybe even knock the person down. Some people get back up. Others stay down for the count. Folks who stay on the floor typically believe that nothing they do will make any difference. They feel helpless, so they quit.

5   These people are not necessarily any less capable than others, but they *believe* they're helpless in the face of adversity. So they are.

Their belief becomes their reality. They have learned to be Victims.

6   Seligman says people quit when they believe the causes of their difficulties are permanent, pervasive, and/or personal. A student who fails an exam may explain her defeat by saying, *I'll never pass these exams* (permanent). *I mess up everything I do* (pervasive). Or, *I'm so stupid* (personal). These, of course, are the harsh self-judgements of her Inner Critic, the internal voice that criticizes us for all that goes wrong.

7   The student who responds to her failure more positively is listening to very different inner voices. According to Seligman, the inner conversation of an optimistic student blames the failure on causes that are temporary, specific, and impersonal. She thinks, *Okay, I failed, but I know I can do better next semester* (temporary—she can improve the situation in the future). *I'm doing fine in my other courses* (specific—the problem is limited to this one area of her life). *I'll be able to do better when I make more time to study* (impersonal—the problem is not a flaw in her, but rather something she can fix by changing her behavior). She believes, *I'll do better next time because I'll learn from my failure and do something different.* This hopeful version of reality allows her to stand up, brush herself off, and get back on course wiser than before.

Lessons from Adversity

8 The research of Seligman and others shows that adversity teaches many people to doubt their ability to go on. By contrast, other people learn to have hope even in the face of life's inevitable challenges. This lesson allows them to focus on solutions rather than problems. It allows them to keep going instead of quitting. People who overcome

adversity learn the great wisdom that each challenge has to teach.

9   A student named Luanne didn't pass English 101 until her seventh try. Luanne could very well have quit after any of her previous six "failures," but somehow she had learned to persevere. Luanne's experience demonstrates that you have not truly failed until you quit. Once you quit, all possibilities for success die. Some people need only one try to succeed; others need many. Wise people know that refusing to give up is a critical ingredient of success. But Luanne didn't succeed just because she wouldn't quit. She succeeded because she was also willing to learn a new way to overcome her obstacles and to change what she had been doing for six previous semesters. And that is a sign of wisdom also.

10   The roll call of the world's successful people is full of "students" of life's adversities. R. H. Macy stumbled seven times before his department store became very profitable. Henry Ford didn't taste success in the automobile industry until he had experienced going broke five times. Winston Churchill failed the sixth grade on his way to becoming prime minister of England. Albert Einstein didn't learn to read until he was seven. Walt Disney went bankrupt before building Disneyland. Abraham Lincoln lost six elections for various political offices before being elected the sixteenth president of the United States.

11   Don't settle in college for being stuffed full of facts and information while starving for wisdom. Courses in the University of Life offer you deeper insights into yourself, other people, and the world. Adversities can show you how to stay on course to a particular goal. They can also teach you how to make the choices that create a rich, personally fulfilling life. And that is the greatest wisdom of all.*

Vocabulary

Read the following questions about some of the vocabulary words that appear in the previous selection. Then circle the letter of the correct answer.

1. Based on your reading of the entire selection, what does *adversity* mean (paragraphs 2 and 3)? "*Adversities* can destroy us, or they can teach us the greatest lessons life has to offer" (paragraph 2).
   - (a.) difficulty
   - b. advantage
   - c. benefit
   - d. mistakes

2. In paragraph 6, what does *pervasive* mean? "Seligman says people quit when they believe the causes of their difficulties are permanent, *pervasive*, and/or personal."
   - a. out of nowhere
   - (b.) present everywhere
   - c. distant
   - d. in the past

*Adapted from Skip Downing, *On Course*, 4th ed. (Boston: Houghton Mifflin Co., 2005), 176–178. Copyright © 2005. Reprinted by permission of Houghton Mifflin Company.

3. What does *inevitable* mean (paragraph 8)? "By contrast, other people learn to have hope even in the face of life's *inevitable* challenges."

    a. unexpected   c. inviting

    (b.) expected   d. awful

4. What does *persevere* mean (paragraph 9)? "Luanne could very well have quit after any of her previous six "failures," but somehow she had learned to *persevere*."

    (a.) continue   c. talk

    b. stop   d. debate

Practicing the Active Reading Strategy:

After You Read

Now that you have read the selection, answer the following questions, using the active reading strategies that you have learned in this chapter.

1. Identify and write down the point and purpose of this reading selection.

2. Besides the vocabulary words included in the exercise on pages 42–43, are there any other vocabulary words that are unfamiliar to you? If so, write a list of them. When you have finished writing your list, look up each word in a dictionary and write the definition that best describes the word as it is used in the selection.

3. Predict any possible test questions that may be used on a test about the content of this selection.

4. How could you use the information contained in this selection? Does the information contained in the selection reinforce or contradict your ideas and experiences? Explain.

QUESTIONS FOR DISCUSSION AND WRITING

Answer the following questions based on your reading of the selection. Write your answers on the blanks provided.

1. Did you enjoy this selection? Why or why not? <u>Answers will vary.</u>

    _____

1

2. According to the author, what do "people who change their beliefs and behaviors to create the best possible results in their lives" believe?

   They believe that each course in the curriculum of life is especially designed to

   teach them exactly what they need to know at that moment.

3. What did you learn from this selection that you did not previously know? *Answers will vary.*

▶ Vocabulary: Using the Dictionary

To increase your vocabulary and to ensure your comprehension of what you read, you'll need to keep a dictionary close by. The best dictionaries for college-level reading are those that include the word *college* or *collegiate* in their title and are not older than five years. For example, *The American Heritage College Dictionary* would be a good reference to have at home. You should also get in the habit of carrying a paperback dictionary with you to class.

Most dictionaries contain the following information:

- The spelling and pronunciation of the word, including its syllables and capital letters

- The word's part of speech (noun, verb, adjective, etc.)

- Words made from the main word, including plurals and verb forms

- The different meanings of the word, including special uses

- Synonyms (words that mean the same thing) for the word

- The history of the word

- Labels that identify the word's subject area or level of usage (for example, *slang* or *informal*)

The entry for a word may also contain a sentence that demonstrates the correct usage of the word. In addition, an entry may include antonyms, or words with the opposite meaning.

To use the dictionary effectively, you must understand how to locate a word and how to read the entry for that word once you find it.

Guide Words

All dictionaries list words in alphabetical order, which helps you find a word quickly. Another feature that helps you locate a particular word is the two **guide words** at the top of the page. The first guide word identifies the first word listed on that page. The second guide word tells you the last word on the page. Refer to Figure 1.2 to see an example of a dictionary page with guide words. If you want to find the word *codeine*, for example, you'd know to look for it on the page labeled with the guide words *cocktail table* and *coeno-* because the first three letters of *codeine, cod,* come between *coc* and *coe*.

But what do you do if you're not sure how to spell a word you need to find? In that case, you'll have to try different possibilities based on the sound of the word. For example, let's say you were looking for the word *quay*, which means a wharf or dock. This is a tough one because the word sounds like *kay* and its letter *u* is silent. The beginning sound could be a *k*, a *c*, or a *q*. The long *a* sound could be spelled *a, ay, ey, uay,* or *eigh*. So you would try different combinations of these sounds until you found the right spelling. You could also try typing your best guess into a word processing program. Many of them include spell checkers that suggest other alternatives when you misspell a word.

Understanding a Dictionary Entry

Every dictionary includes a guide at the front of the book that explains how to read the entries. This guide explains the abbreviations, symbols, and organization of meanings, so you may need to consult it to know how to decipher the information. Various dictionaries differ in these details. However, they all usually contain certain types of standard information, as follows.

The main entry. Each word in a dictionary appears in bold print with dots dividing its syllables. This word is correctly spelled, of course, and any alternative spellings for the word follow.

Pronunciation key. Usually in parentheses following the main entry, the word's pronunciation is represented with symbols, letters, and other marks. The guide at the front of the dictionary will provide a list of the corresponding sounds for each letter or symbol. For example, the symbol ∂ is pronounced like "uh." The accent mark shows you what syllable to stress when you say the word. For example, the pronunciation key for the word *codominant* on the sample dictionary page in Figure 1.2 tells you to emphasize the second syllable when you say the word.

Main Entries

Meaning

Pronunciation Key

Part of Speech

History of Word

Guide Words

277

cocktail table

coeno–

regimen. **3.** An appetizer, such as mixed fruit served with juice or seafood served with a sharp sauce: *shrimp cocktail.* ❖ *adj.* **1.** Of or relating to cocktails: *a cocktail party.* **2.** Suitable for wear on semiformal occasions. [?]

cocktail table *n.* See **coffee table.**

cock•y (kŏk′ē) *adj.* **-i•er, -i•est** Overly self-assertive or self-confident. —**cock′i•ly** *adv.* —**cock′i•ness** *n.*

Co•co (kō′kō) A river rising in N Nicaragua and flowing c. 483 km (300 mi) to the Caribbean Sea.

co•coa (kō′kō) *n.* **1a.** A powder made from cacao seeds after they have been fermented, roasted, shelled, ground, and freed of most of their fat. **b.** A beverage made by mixing this powder with sugar in hot water or milk. **2.** A moderate brown to reddish brown. [Alteration (influenced by *coco*, coconut palm; see COCONUT) of CACAO.] —**co′coa** *adj.*

cocoa bean *n.* See **cacao** 2.

cocoa butter *n.* A yellowish-white fatty solid obtained from cacao seeds and used in cosmetics, chocolate, and soap.

co•co•nut also **co•coa•nut** (kō′kə-nŭt′, -nət) *n.* **1.** The fruit of the coconut palm, consisting of a fibrous husk surrounding a large seed. **2.** The large, brown, hard-shelled seed of the coconut, containing white flesh surrounding a partially fluid-filled central cavity. **3.** The edible white flesh of the coconut. **4.** A coconut palm. [Port. *côco*, grinning skull, goblin, coconut (prob. < LLat. *coccum*, shell; see COCOON) + NUT.]

coconut milk *n.* **1.** A milky fluid extracted from the flesh of the coconut, used in foods or as a beverage. **2.** The watery fluid in the central cavity of the coconut, used chiefly as a beverage.

coconut oil *n.* An oil or semisolid fat obtained from the flesh of the coconut, used in foods, cosmetics, and soaps.

coconut palm *n.* A feather-leaved palm *(Cocos nucifera)* extensively cultivated in tropical regions for food, beverages, oil, thatching, fiber, utensils, and ornament.

co•coon (kə-ko͞on′) *n.* **1a.** A protective case of silk or similar fibrous material spun by the larvae of moths and other insects that serves as a covering for their pupal stage. **b.** A similar natural protective covering or structure, such as the egg case of a spider. **2.** A protective plastic coating that is placed over stored military or naval equipment. **3.** Something suggestive of a cocoon in appearance or purpose. ❖ *v.* **-cooned, -coon•ing, -coons** —*tr.* To envelop in or as if in a cocoon. —*intr.* To retreat as if into a cocoon. [Fr. *cocon* < Provençal *coucoun*, dim. of *coco*, shell < LLat. *coccum* < Lat., berry, oak gall < Gk. *kokkos*, seed, berry.]

coco plum or **co•co•plum** (kō′kō-plŭm′) *n.* An evergreen shrub or small tree *(Chrysobalanus icaco)* native to the American and African tropics and having plumlike fruit. [Alteration of Sp. *icaco* < Arawak *ikaku.*]

Co•cos Islands (kō′kōs) also **Kee•ling Islands** (kē′lĭng) An Australian-administered island group in the E Indian Ocean SW of Sumatra.

co•cotte (kô-kôt′) *n.* A woman prostitute. [Fr., chicken, prostitute < fem. dim. of *coq*, cock < OFr. See COCK[1].]

co•co•yam (kō′kō-yăm′) *n.* See **taro** 2. [COCO(A) + YAM.]

Coc•teau (kŏk-tō′, kôk-), **Jean** 1889–1963. French writer and filmmaker whose works include the novel *Les Enfants Terrible* (1929) and the film *Beauty and the Beast* (1945).

Co•cy•tus (kō-kī′təs, -sī′-) *n.* *Greek Mythology* One of the five rivers of Hades.

cod[1] (kŏd) *n., pl.* **cod** or **cods** Any of various marine fishes of the family Gadidae, esp. *Gadus morhua*, a food fish of northern Atlantic waters. [ME.]

cod[2] (kŏd) *n.* **1.** A husk or pod. **2.** *Archaic* The scrotum. **3.** *Obsolete* A bag. [ME < OE *codd.*]

Cod, Cape A hook-shaped peninsula of SE MA extending E and N into the Atlantic Ocean.

COD *abbr.* **1.** cash on delivery **2.** collect on delivery

co•da (kō′də) *n.* **1.** *Music* The concluding passage of a movement or composition. **2.** A conclusion or closing part of a statement. [Ital. < Lat. *cauda*, tail.]

cod•dle (kŏd′l) *tr.v.* **-dled, -dling, -dles 1.** To cook in water just below the boiling point. **2.** To treat indulgently; baby. [Poss. alteration of CAUDLE.] —**cod′dler** *n.*

code (kōd) *n.* **1.** A systematically arranged and comprehensive collection of laws. **2.** A systematic collection of regulations and rules of procedure or conduct: *a traffic code.* **3a.** A system of signals used to represent letters or numbers in transmitting messages. **b.** A system of symbols, letters, or words given certain arbitrary meanings, used for messages requiring secrecy or brevity. **4.** A system of symbols and rules used to represent instructions to a computer; a computer program. **5.** The genetic code. **6.** *Slang* A patient whose heart has stopped beating, as in cardiac arrest. ❖ *v.* **cod•ed, cod•ing, codes** —*tr.* **1.** To systematize and arrange (laws and regulations) into a code. **2.** To convert (a message, for example) into code. —*intr.* **1.** To specify the genetic code for an amino acid or a polypeptide. **2.** To write or revise a computer program. **3.** *Medicine* To go into cardiac arrest. [ME < OFr. < Lat. *cōdex*, book. See CODEX.]

code blue *n.* A medical emergency that involves signaling personnel to aid a person in cardiac arrest.

co•dec•li•na•tion (kō′dĕk-lə-nā′shən) *n.* *Astronomy* The complement of the declination.

co•de•fen•dant (kō′dĭ-fĕn′dənt) *n.* *Law* A joint defendant.

co•deine (kō′dēn′, -dē-ĭn) *n.* An alkaloid narcotic, $C_{18}H_{21}NO_3$, derived from opium or morphine and used as a cough suppressant, analgesic, and hypnotic. [Fr. *codéine* : Gk. *kōdeia*, poppy head (< *kōos*, cavity) + *-ine*, alkaloid; see –INE[2].]

code name *n.* A name assigned to conceal the identity or existence of something or someone.

co•de•ter•mi•na•tion (kō′dĭ-tûr′mə-nā′shən) *n.* Cooperation, esp. between labor and management, in policymaking.

code word *n.* **1.** A secret word or phrase used as a code name or password. **2.** A euphemism.

co•dex (kō′dĕks′) *n., pl.* **co•di•ces** (kō′dĭ-sēz′, kŏd′ĭ-) A manuscript volume, esp. of a classic work or of the Scriptures. [Lat. *cōdex, cōdic-*, tree trunk, wooden tablet, book, var. of *caudex*, trunk.]

cod•fish (kŏd′fĭsh′) *n., pl.* **codfish** or **-fish•es** See **cod**[1].

codg•er (kŏj′ər) *n.* *Informal* A somewhat eccentric man, esp. an old one. [Perh. alteration of obsolete *cadger*, peddler. See CADGE.]

cod•i•cil (kŏd′ə-sĭl) *n.* A supplement or appendix, esp. to a will. [ME < OFr. *codicille* < Lat. *cōdicillus*, dim. of *cōdex, cōdic-*, codex. See CODEX.] —**cod′i•cil′la•ry** (kŏd′ə-sĭl′ə-rē) *adj.*

cod•i•fy (kŏd′ĭ-fī′, kō′də-) *tr.v.* **-fied, -fy•ing, -fies 1.** To reduce to a code: *codify laws.* **2.** To arrange or systematize. —**cod′i•fi•ca′tion** (-fĭ-kā′shən) *n.* —**cod′i•fi′er** *n.*

cod•ling[1] (kŏd′lĭng) also **cod•lin** (-lĭn) *n.* **1.** A greenish elongated English apple used for cooking. **2.** A small unripe apple. [Alteration of ME *querdlyng*, poss. < AN **querdelion*, lionheart : OFr. *cuer*, heart; see COURAGE + *de*, of (< Lat. *dē*; see DE–) + OFr. *lion*, lion; see LION.]

cod•ling[2] (kŏd′lĭng) *n., pl.* **codling** or **-lings** A young cod.

codling moth also **codlin moth** *n.* A grayish moth *(Carpocapsa pomonella)* whose larvae are destructive to various fruits.

cod-liv•er oil (kŏd′lĭv′ər) *n.* An oil obtained from the liver of cod and related fishes, used as a source of vitamins A and D.

co•dom•i•nance (kō-dŏm′ə-nəns) *n.* A condition in which both alleles are codominant.

co•dom•i•nant (kō-dŏm′ə-nənt) *adj.* **1.** *Genetics* Of or being two alleles of a gene pair in a heterozygote that are both fully expressed. **2a.** *Ecology* Being one of two or more of the most characteristic species in a biotic community. **b.** Influencing the presence and type of other species in the community. ❖ *n.* *Ecology* A codominant species in a biotic community.

co•don (kō′dŏn′) *n.* A sequence of three adjacent nucleotides constituting the genetic code that determines the insertion of a specific amino acid in a polypeptide chain during protein synthesis. [COD(E) + –ON[1].]

cod•piece (kŏd′pēs′) *n.* A pouch at the crotch of the tight-fitting breeches worn by men in the 15th and 16th centuries. [ME *codpece* : *cod*, bag, scrotum (< OE *codd*, bag) + *pece*, piece; see PIECE.]

cods•wal•lop (kŏdz′wŏl′əp) *n.* *Chiefly British Slang* Nonsense; rubbish. [?]

Co•dy (kō′dē), **William Frederick** Known as "Buffalo Bill." 1846–1917. Amer. frontier scout who after 1883 toured the US and Europe with his Wild West Show.

co•ed or **co-ed** (kō′ĕd′) *Informal* *n.* A woman who attends a coeducational college or university. ❖ *adj.* **1.** Coeducational. **2.** Open to both sexes. [Short for *coeducational.*]

co•ed•it (kō-ĕd′ĭt) *tr.v.* **-ed•it•ed, -ed•it•ing, -ed•its** To edit (a print publication or a film) jointly with another or others. —**co•ed′i•tor** *n.*

co•ed•u•ca•tion (kō-ĕj′ə-kā′shən) *n.* The system of education in which both sexes attend the same institution or classes. —**co•ed′u•ca′tion•al** *adj.* —**co•ed′u•ca′tion•al•ly** *adv.*

co•ef•fi•cient (kō′ə-fĭsh′ənt) *n.* **1.** A number or symbol multiplied with a variable or an unknown quantity in an algebraic term, as 4 in the term $4x$ or x in the term $x(a + b)$. **2.** A numerical measure of a physical or chemical property that is constant for a system under specified conditions.

–coel or **–coele** or **–cele** *suff.* Chamber; cavity: *blastocoel.* [NLat. *-coela* < Gk. *koilos*, hollow.]

coe•la•canth (sē′lə-kănth′) *n.* Any of various mostly extinct fishes of the order Coelacanthiformes. [NLat. *Coelacanthus*, former genus name : Gk. *koilos*, hollow; see –COEL + Gk. *akantha*, spine.] —**coe′la•can′thine′** (-kăn′thīn′, -thĭn), **coe′la•can′thous** (-thəs) *adj.*

coe•len•ter•ate (sĭ-lĕn′tə-rāt′, -tər-ĭt) *n.* See **cnidarian.** [< NLat. *Coelenterāta*, phylum name : *coelenter(on)*, coelenteron; see COELENTERON + Lat. *-āta*, neut. pl. of *-ātus*, -ate; see –ATE[1].] —**coe•len′ter•ate′, coe•len•ter′ic** (-tĕr′ĭk) *adj.*

coe•len•ter•on (sĭ-lĕn′tə-rŏn′, -tər-ən) *n., pl.* **-te•ra** (-tər-ə) The saclike cavity within the body of a coelenterate. [NLat. : Gk. *koilos*, hollow; see –COEL + ENTERON.]

coe•li•ac (sē′lē-ăk′) *adj.* Variant of **celiac.**

coe•lom also **ce•lom** or **coe•lome** (sē′ləm) *n.* The cavity within the body of all animals higher than the cnidarians and certain primitive worms, formed by the splitting of the embryonic mesoderm into two layers. [Ger. *Koelom* < Gk. *koilōma*, cavity < *koilos*, hollow.] —**coe•lom′ic** (sĭ-lŏm′ĭk, -lō′mĭk) *adj.*

coe•lo•mate (sē′lə-māt′) *adj.* Possessing a coelom: *a coelomate animal.* —**coe′lo•mate** *n.*

coeno– or **ceno–** *pref.* Common: *coenocyte.* [NLat. < Gk. *koino-*

coconut palm
Cocos nucifera

Buffalo Bill Cody

coelacanth
Latimeria chalumnae

ă	pat	oi	boy
ā	pay	ou	out
âr	care	o͝o	took
ä	father	o͞o	boot
ĕ	pet	ŭ	cut
ē	be	ûr	urge
ĭ	pit	th	thin
ī	pie	*th*	this
îr	pier	hw	which
ŏ	pot	zh	vision
ō	toe	ə	about, item
ô	paw		

Stress marks:
′ (primary);
′ (secondary), as in
lexicon (lĕk′sĭ-kŏn′)

Figure 1.2 Dictionary Page

From *The American Heritage College Dictionary*, 4th ed. (Boston: Houghton Mifflin Co., 2002), 277. Reprinted by permission of Houghton Mifflin Company.

1

The part of speech. The next part of the entry is an abbreviation that identifies the word's part of speech. *N.* means noun, *v.* means verb, *adj.* stands for adjective, and so on. Refer to the list of abbreviations in the guide at the front of the dictionary to find out what other abbreviations mean.

The meanings of the word. The different meanings of a word are divided first according to their part of speech. All of the meanings related to a particular part of speech are grouped together. For example, the word *contact* can function as both a noun and a verb. All of its noun meanings appear first, followed by all of its verb meanings. Dictionaries order each set of meanings in different ways, usually from most common to least common or from oldest to newest. Different senses, or shades of meaning, are numbered. Following the list of meanings, the dictionary may provide synonyms and/or antonyms for the word.

The history of the word. Some dictionaries provide information about the origin of a word. This history usually includes the word's language of origin, along with its various evolutions.

Vocabulary Exercise 1

Write these words in alphabetical order on the blanks provided.

oleander	okra
omelet	oleander
once	olive
olive	omega
omen	omelet
omnivore	omen
omega	omnivore
okra	once

Vocabulary Exercise 2

Beneath each set of guide words, circle each word that would appear on the same page labeled with those guide words.

1

1. **playbook / pledge**

    (please)   play   (plaything)

    (plead)   pledger   plenary

2. **scamper / scarcely**

    (scar)   (scant)   (scarce)

    scarcity   scamp   scarecrow

3. **cellophane / census**

    cello   cent   (cement)

    (cellular)   (censure)   cell

4. **infantryman / infinitive**

    (infect)   infinity   induction

    (infield)   (infer)   infant

5. **photobiology / photophobia**

    (photocopy)   photophobic   (photon)

    photoactive   (photograph)   (photolysis)

Vocabulary Exercise 3

Write your answers to the following questions on the blanks provided.

1. What is the plural of *shelf*? <u>Shelves</u>

2. How many different parts of speech can the word *right* be? <u>Four (noun,</u>
<u>adjective, adverb, verb)</u>

3. What is a synonym for the word *ridicule*? <u>Mock, taunt, deride, gibe</u>

4. What language does the word *tattoo* come from? <u>Polynesian</u>

5. How many different pronunciations does your dictionary provide for the
word *harass*? <u>Two</u>

6. Does the verb *slough* rhyme with *tough* or *plow* or *flew*? <u>Tough</u>

7. How many syllables does the word *schizophrenia* contain? <u>5</u>

Vocabulary Exercise 4

On the blank following each sentence, write the correct meaning for the italicized word.

1. The company president presented her with a *plaque* to recognize her twenty years of service.

   Definition: <u>A plate, slab, or disk ornamented or engraved for mounting</u>

2. A buildup of *plaque* within the arteries can cause a heart attack.

   Definition: <u>A deposit of fatty material on the inner lining of an arterial wall</u>

3. He won first prize for his science *project,* a study of bumblebees in a zero-gravity environment.

   Definition: <u>An extensive task undertaken by a student or group of students</u>

4. A ventriloquist *projects* his voice so the dummy appears to talk.

   Definition: <u>To direct one's voice so it can be heard at a distance</u>

5. During her vacations at the beach, she was *content.*

   Definition: <u>Satisfied</u>

6. The *content* of late night television shows is not appropriate for young children.

   Definition: <u>Subject matter</u>

CHAPTER 1 TESTS

Name _____ Date _____

TEST 1

1. A dislike for reading often arises from undeveloped reading skills.
   - (a.) true   b. false

2. Good reading skills are critical to success in college.
   - (a.) true   b. false

3. Reading is actually a collection of different mental skills.
   - (a.) true   b. false

4. A negative attitude about reading will not affect reading comprehension.
   - a. true   (b.) false

5. You cannot understand or retain information unless you read with concentration.
   - (a.) true   b. false

6. Thinking about your plans for the weekend while you're trying to read is an example of an external distraction.
   - a. true   (b.) false

7. When you visualize, you pay extra attention to the visuals (such as graphs, charts, and photos) in a text.
   - a. true   (b.) false

8. To improve memory, a reader can associate new information with what he or she already knows.
   - (a.) true   b. false

9. Analysis is one type of logical thought.
   - (a.) true   b. false

10. Reading strategies are techniques you use when you read.
    - (a.) true   b. false

For additional tests, see the Test Bank.

1

TEST 2

Review the following passage from a textbook and respond to the questions that follow by circling the letter of the correct answer.

1   In a period of extreme stress, an outbreak of witchcraft accusations occurred in Salem Village (now Danvers), Massachusetts. Like their contemporaries[1] elsewhere, seventeenth-century New Englanders believed in the existence of witches, whose evil powers came from the Devil. If people could not find other explanations for their troubles, they tended to suspect they were bewitched. Before 1689, 103 New Englanders, most of them middle-aged women, had been charged with practicing witchcraft. Their accusers were usually neighbors who blamed their misfortunes on the suspected witch. Only a few of the accused were convicted, and fewer still were executed. Most such incidents were isolated; nothing else in New England's history came close to matching the Salem Village disaster.

2   The crisis began in early 1692 when a group of girls and young women accused some older female neighbors of having bewitched them. Before the hysteria was over ten months later, nineteen people (including several men, most of them related to convicted female witches) were hanged; one was pressed to death with heavy stones, and more than 100 persons were jailed. Historians have proposed various explanations for this puzzling episode, but to be understood it must be seen in the context of political and legal disorder, Indian war, and religious and economic crisis. Puritan[2] New Englanders must have felt as though their entire world was collapsing. At the very least they could have had no sense of security about their future.

3   Nowhere was that more true than in Salem Village, a farming town torn between old and new styles of life because of its position on the edge of the bustling port of Salem. And no residents of the village had more reason to feel insecure than those who made the first accusations. Many of them had been orphaned in the recent Indian attacks on Maine; they were living in Salem Village as domestic servants. Their involvement with witchcraft began as an experiment with fortune-telling as a means of foreseeing their futures, in particular the identities of their eventual husbands. As the most powerless people in a town apparently powerless to direct its fate, they offered their fellow New Englanders an interesting explanation for their seemingly endless chain of troubles: their home was under direct attack from the Devil and his legion

1. **contemporaries:** people living at the same time

2. **Puritan:** related to the beliefs of the Puritans, who insisted on strict religious discipline and simplification of church ceremonies

1

of witches. Therefore, it is not so much the number of witchcraft prosecutions that seems surprising but rather their sudden end in the fall of 1692.

4   There were three reasons for the rapid end to the crisis. First, the accusers grew too bold. When they began to charge some of the colony's most distinguished and respected residents with associating with the Devil, the people in charge began to doubt their honesty. Second, the colony's ministers, led by Increase Mather,[1] formally expressed strong reservations about the worth of the evidence used against most of the accused. Third, a new royal charter[2] ended the worst period of political uncertainty, eliminating a major source of stress. King William's War[3] continued, but, although the Puritans were not entirely pleased with the new charter, at least order had formally been restored.*

1. Seventeenth-century people blamed witches for

    a. the existence of the Devil.   (c.) their misfortunes.
    b. women's premature aging.   d. King William's War.

2. The people accused of witchcraft in Salem Village were witches.

    a. true   (b.) false

3. Which of the following is NOT true about those who accused others of practicing witchcraft?

    a. Many experimented with fortune-telling.
    b. Many were orphans.
    (c.) Many were the town's most powerful people.
    d. They offered an explanation for New Englanders' troubles.

4. Which of the following is a possible reason for the witchcraft hysteria in Salem Village?

    (a.) New Englanders felt like their world was collapsing.
    b. The powerful New Englanders wanted to rid their village of troublemakers.
    c. Those accused of being witches were plotting to take over the town's government.
    d. The accusers were tired of working as farmers.

1. **Increase Mather (1639–1723):** American clergyman
2. **charter:** contract

3. **King William's War:** 1689–1697 battle between England and France for North American territory

* Adapted from Mary Beth Norton et al., *A People and a Nation,* vol. 1, 5th ed. (Boston: Houghton Mifflin Co., 1998), 86–87.

5. Which of the following is NOT a reason for the end of the Salem crisis?

    a. The accusers began targeting some of the village's most respected residents.

    b. A new royal charter ended the stress of political uncertainty.

    c. Ministers began to doubt the evidence offered by the accusers.

    ⓓ Most of the male townspeople had to go fight in King William's War.

Read the memo below and answer the questions that follow.

TO:	All Employees
FROM:	Dan Rogers
DATE:	March 15, 20xx
SUBJECT:	Proper Lifting Techniques

In the past three months, our company has seen a 60 percent increase in on-the-job back injuries. These accidents cost thousands of dollars in worker's compensation claims each year. Even worse, though, a back injury can cause long-term disability. Someone who hurts his or her back may never be able to return to work or handle simple, everyday tasks like combing hair or picking up a baby. So please review the proper procedures for picking up heavy objects, both at work and at home. These techniques will significantly reduce your risk of experiencing back strain.

- Plan ahead what you want to do and don't be in a hurry. Position yourself close to the object you want to lift. Separate your feet shoulder-width apart to give yourself a solid base of support. Bend at the knees. Tighten your stomach muscles as you stand up. Don't try to lift by yourself an object that is too heavy or is an awkward shape. Get help.

- To lift a very light object from the floor, such as a piece of paper, lean over the object, slightly bend one knee and extend the other leg behind you. Hold on to a nearby chair or table for support as you reach down to the object.

- Whether you're lifting a heavy laundry basket or a heavy box on the job, remember to get close to the object, bend at the knees, and lift with your leg muscles. Do not bend at your waist. When lifting luggage, stand alongside the luggage, bend at your knees, grasp the handle, and straighten up.

- While you are holding the object, keep your knees slightly bent to maintain your balance. If you have to move the object to one side, avoid twisting your body. Point your toes in the direction you want to move and pivot[1] in that direction. Keep the object close to you when moving.

- If you must place an object on a shelf, move as close as possible to the shelf. Spread your feet in a wide stance, positioning one foot in front of the other, to give you a solid base of support. Do not lean forward and do not fully extend your arms while holding the object in your hands.

- If the shelf is chest high, move close to the shelf and place your feet apart and one foot forward. Lift the object chest high, keep your elbows at your side, and position your hands so you can push the object up and onto the shelf. Remember to tighten your stomach muscles before lifting.

- When sitting, keep your back in a normal, slightly arched position. Make sure your chair supports your lower back. Keep your head and shoulders erect. Make sure your working surface is at the proper height so you don't have to lean forward.

- Once an hour, if possible, stand and stretch. Place your hands on your lower back and gently arch backward.

Following these procedures will help protect you from a costly and painful injury. Please call my office at extension 613 if you have any questions about this information.*

6. Which of the following is NOT a reason (according to this memo) to protect yourself from back injury?
   a. It costs your company money.
   b. It can prevent you from being able to work again.
   c. It can prevent you from being able to do simple, everyday activities.
   d. It can result in an addiction to painkilling drugs.

7. To lift a light object from the floor, you should lean over the object, bend one knee, and
   a. stretch one arm high into the air.
   b. stretch your other leg out behind you.
   c. lower the other knee to the floor.
   d. bend at the waist.

1. **pivot:** turn

* Adapted from "Preventing Back Pain at Work and at Home," American Academy of Orthopaedic Surgeons website, http://orthoinfo.aaos.org. Reprinted by permission.

1

8. When lifting a heavy object, you should never
   a. bend your knees.
   b. lift with your leg muscles.
   c. bend at the waist.
   d. get close to the object.

9. If you sit all day, what should you try to do once every hour?
   a. lift something heavy
   b. stand and stretch
   c. tighten your stomach muscles
   d. pivot from side to side

Read the selection below and answer the questions that follow by circling the letter of the correct answer.

A Night Out on the Antarctic Ice: Who Can Stick It Out?

1   God, I wish I were fat.

2   At least, that's what I was thinking a few weeks ago when I lay shivering on the ice in Antarctica, the coldest place on Earth.

3   In Antarctica, blubber is *de rigueur*.[1] The penguins have it. The seals have it. The whales have it.

4   Alas, I didn't have it, and I was clearly out of my element.

5   Of course, this didn't stop me from joining several dozen ambitious globetrotters in camping overnight on the most remote of continents, something only a handful of people have done.

6   The outing was part of a ten-night expedition to the White Continent. For most of the trip we spent the day exploring the stunning but frigid landscape and retreated each night to the warmth of the ice-hardened *Akademik Ioffe*, our chartered Russian research vessel. But on one night we would test our mettle[2] against this harshest of climates.

7   How did we fare? Ask just about anyone who was there that cold and windy night, and he'll tell you he was snug as a bug in the 10-below-zero-rated sleeping bags given to us and placed in trenches in the snow.

8   They're all lying. As a journalist, I am sworn to the truth, and I must report that sleeping on the ice, without tents, in Antarctica, was an absolutely, positively miserable experience.

9   We were freezing.

10 I stuck it out until morning. I can't say I was happy, although the scenery was out of this world: soaring mountains, glaciers, a pristine[3] bay full of icebergs. And I suspect I was far from alone in such sentiments. When I awoke

---

1. *de rigueur*: the norm or standard
2. **mettle**: courage
3. **pristine**: pure, uncorrupted by civilization

just before breakfast, more than half the campers already had fled to the ship—some just hours after arriving for the night. I was told later that one was so cold she could not stop shivering.

11   Not that anyone would admit it come dinnertime. By then, our adventure had grown to epic[1] proportions. Like Ernest Shackleton[2] himself, we had braved the worst The Ice could throw at us, and we not only survived; we thrived.

12   We were true Antarctic heroes.*

10. Gene Sloan, the author of this selection, states that he wishes he were fat. Why?
    a. Fat would have kept him warm in the sub-zero climate.
    b. He wouldn't have been as hungry during the trip.
    c. Everyone else on the trip was fat.
    d. Because he has always been too thin.

11. How many nights did the author spend on the "White Continent"?
    a. five   c. eight
    b. six   d. ten

12. Where did Sloan and the other members of his trip spend most of their nights?
    a. in a snow bank
    b. in Russia
    c. on a chartered research vessel
    d. in a hotel

13. How does the author describe the one night that he and his fellow travelers spent in sleeping bags in the snow?
    a. as a positively miserable experience
    b. as a great experience that he wants to have again
    c. as something that made him stronger
    d. as something that he would love to have his children experience

1. **epic:** unusually large or impressive

2. **Ernest Shackleton:** British explorer who went on expeditions to the Antarctic

* "A Night Out on the Antarctic Ice: Who Can Stick It Out?" by Gene Sloan, from *USA Today*, December 26, 2003. Copyright © 2003 *USA Today*. Reprinted with permission.

14. How many people lasted until morning in the snow?

    a. two   c. more than half

    (b.) fewer than half   d. none

15. How does Sloan describe himself and the people with whom he traveled?

    (a.) Antarctic heroes   c. snug as bugs in a rug

    b. crazy   d. nature lovers

TEST 3

For each of the following reading situations, choose the MAJOR purposes for reading that apply. Circle the letter of as many as apply.

1. You visit a website on the Internet that provides information about a company in which you are considering investing.

    a. Gain a general understanding of the ideas or points.

    (b.) Discover the facts or answer questions.

    c. Memorize the information.

    d. Find information or ideas that prove a point you want to make.

    (e.) Make a decision based on the information.

2. You read a letter that explains why your auto insurance rates have gone up and how to compare the rates of various insurance companies.

    (a.) Gain a general understanding of the ideas or points.

    (b.) Discover the facts or answer questions.

    c. Memorize the information.

    d. Find information or ideas that prove a point you want to make.

    (e.) Make a decision based on the information.

3. You read the guidelines for selecting employees issued by a company for which you would like to work.

    (a.) Gain a general understanding of the ideas or points.

    (b.) Discover the facts or answer questions.

    c. Memorize the information.

    d. Find information or ideas that prove a point you want to make.

    e. Make a decision based on the information.

1

4. You read your state's driver's license handbook in preparation for taking your driving test.

   a. Gain a general understanding of the ideas or points.

   (b.) Discover the facts or answer questions.

   (c.) Memorize the information.

   d. Find information or ideas that prove a point you want to make.

   e. Make a decision based on the information.

5. You read a magazine article to see if it contains statistics that prove a statement you want to make in your research paper.

   a. Gain a general understanding of the ideas or points.

   b. Discover the facts or answer questions.

   c. Memorize the information.

   (d.) Find information or ideas that prove a point you want to make.

   e. Make a decision based on the information.

Main Ideas

2

GOALS FOR CHAPTER 2

▸ Define the terms *general* and *specific*.

▸ Order groups of sentences from most general to most specific.

▸ Identify the topic of a paragraph.

▸ Determine the main idea of a paragraph.

▸ Recognize the topic sentence of a paragraph.

▸ Recognize topic sentences in different locations in a paragraph.

▸ Describe the characteristics of an effective reading environment.

To read successfully, you must learn to determine the main idea of a paragraph or longer selection. The **main idea** is the overall point the author is trying to make. The rest of the paragraph or longer selection consists of information or examples that help the reader understand the main point.

What process do you go through to help you figure out the main idea of a selection? Take this test to find out how much you already know about identifying and understanding main ideas.

TEST YOURSELF

Read the following paragraph and respond to the questions by writing your answers on the blanks provided.

Clogging is the latest fitness/dance craze. *American Fitness* magazine has reported that the traditional Appalachian[1] dance is great exercise. With its rapid-fire footwork, it burns about 400 calories an hour and has been found

1. **Appalachia:** a rural region in the eastern United States

2

to improve blood pressure, endurance, strength, lung capacity, muscle tone, flexibility, and coordination. It's also considered a stress reliever.*

1. What is the main idea of this paragraph? How do you know?

   <u>Clogging is a popular new fitness/dance craze. You know this because the first</u>

   <u>sentence states this point, and the rest of the paragraph explains it.</u>

2. To figure out the main idea, what part of the paragraph did you look at first?

   <u>Answers will vary.</u>

What is the main idea of each of the following passages? Write your answers on the blanks provided.

3. Without a deadline, you might stretch the pursuit of a goal over your whole life, never reaching it. Therefore, effective goals have specific deadlines. A short-term goal usually has a deadline within a few months. A long-term goal generally has a deadline of a year or more, maybe even five or ten years away. These deadlines help to motivate you so that you will put forth the energy to accomplish the goal.

   Main Idea: <u>Effective goals have specific deadlines.</u>

4. Effective goals are also realistic. It would be unrealistic to say you'll complete a marathon next week if your idea of a monster workout has been jogging around the block a few times a week. A more realistic goal would be to set the goal of running two or three miles within a certain amount of time. You're less likely to give up on goals that you know are achievable for you.

   Main Idea: <u>Effective goals are realistic.</u>

5. Effective goals focus your energy on what you *do* want rather than on what you *don't* want. So effective goals are positive goals. For example, "I will stop being late to classes" is a negative goal, but "I will arrive on time to every class" is a positive goal. I recall a race car driver who explained how he miraculously kept his spinning car from smashing into the retaining wall: "I kept my eye on the track, not the wall." You, too, will stay on course if you focus your thoughts and actions on where you *do* want to go rather than on where you *don't* want to go.

   Main Idea: <u>Effective goals are positive.</u>

6. Effective goals state outcomes in specific, measurable terms. It's not enough to say, "My goal is to do better this semester" or "My goal is to work harder at my job." How will you know if you've achieved these goals? What concrete evidence will you have? More effective goals are "I will achieve a 3.5

* From Pat Curry, "Hot Feet Need TLC," *USA Weekend,* February 20–22, 2004, 22.

or better grade average this semester" and "On my job, I will volunteer for all offerings of overtime." Being specific keeps you from fooling yourself into believing you've achieved a goal when, in fact, you haven't.*

Main Idea: <u>*Effective goals state outcomes in specific, measurable terms.*</u>

General and Specific

Before you practice finding main ideas, it's helpful to learn how to tell the difference between the terms **general** and **specific.** You must apply these concepts to figure out the relationships of sentences within a paragraph. Understanding these relationships is the first step in improving your comprehension of the author's meaning.

The word *general* means "broad" and "not limited." When we say a word or idea is general, we mean that it includes or refers to many different things in a large category. For example, *weather* is a general word that includes many different types of conditions, including wind, rain, snow, and hail. *Coins* is another general word that refers to a large group of items, including pennies, dimes, nickels, and quarters.

The word *specific* means "definite" or "particular." Specific things or ideas are limited or narrowed in scope, and they refer to one certain something within a larger group. In the previous paragraph, for instance, *wind, rain, snow,* and *hail* are all certain types of weather, so we say they are more specific. *Pepsi, Coca-Cola,* and *RC* are all specific colas. *Math, English,* and *science* are three specific subjects we study in school.

The terms *general* and *specific* are relative. In other words, they depend upon or are connected to the other things with which they are being compared. For example, you would say that *school subject* is a general term and that *math* is one specific subject. However, *math* becomes the more general term when you think of specific kinds of math, such as *algebra, trigonometry,* and *calculus.* Words and concepts, therefore, can change from being general or specific, depending on their relationships to other words and concepts. Look at this list:

weather

storm

hurricane

category 4 hurricanes

Hurricane Floyd

* Adapted from Skip Downing, *On Course,* 4th ed. (Boston: Houghton Mifflin Co., 2005), 59–60.

The words in this list are arranged from most general to most specific. In other words, each item on the list is more specific than the one above it. The last item, Hurricane Floyd, names one specific storm, so it is the most specific of all.

Exercise 2.1

Put these lists of words in order from most general to most specific. Write your answers on the blanks provided.

1. Taurus   car   Ford   machine
   machine   car   Ford   Taurus
   _____

2. strawberry   fruit   food   plant
   plant   food   fruit   strawberry
   _____

3. subject   science   biology   microbiology
   subject   science   biology   microbiology
   _____

4. hip-hop singer   performer   Lil' Kim   singer
   performer   singer   hip-hop singer   Lil' Kim
   _____

5. Le Bron James   sports   basketball   Cleveland Cavaliers
                       players   players   team members
   sports players basketball players Cleveland Cavaliers team members Le Bron James
   _____

To read well, you will need to be able to recognize the most general idea within a passage. Let's practice that skill by looking at groups of related items in different ways. Can you select the most general word in the list?

mixer   appliances   toaster   blender

Three of the words in the group are specific, and one of the words is the most general. If you chose *appliances* as most general, you are correct. The other three items are specific kinds of appliances.

Now examine this list and decide how the items are related. Come up with a word that includes all three items in the list.

mouse   rat   hamster

Did you say *rodent*? The three creatures are all specific types of rodents.

Finally, see if you can think of three specific examples of this phrase:

supernatural occurrences

Some possible answers include *ghosts, monsters,* and *UFOs.*

Exercise 2.2

The following groups of words include one general word and three specific words. Circle the most general word in each group.

1. (dance)   ballet   tap   modern
2. hockey   basketball   (sports)   baseball
3. running   jogging   aerobics   (exercise)
4. Roy Rogers   McDonald's   (fast-food restaurants) Wendy's
5. oak   walnut   maple   (trees)

Exercise 2.3

On the blank following each group, write a general term that includes all of the items in the list.

1. looking up words   checking spelling   reading definitions

   General Idea: _using a dictionary_

2. hamburgers   turkey   ice cream

   General Idea: _food_

3. nurse   doctor   X-ray technician

   General idea: _medical professionals_

4. pine   redwood   weeping willow

   General Idea: _trees_

5. attending class   using a textbook   taking notes

   General Idea: _going to school_

Exercise 2.4

Write on the blanks provided at least three specific ideas included in the general idea. Answers will vary.

1. General Idea: Doing laundry

   Specific Ideas: _sorting clothes, pouring in detergent, folding clean clothes_

2

2. General Idea: States in the United States

    Specific Ideas: <u>New York, Florida, Texas (or any of the other 47 states)</u>

3. General Idea: Maintaining your car

    Specific Ideas: <u>changing the oil, getting gas, putting air in the tires</u>

4. General Idea: U.S. presidents

    Specific Ideas: <u>George W. Bush, Bill Clinton, Jimmy Carter (or any of the other</u>

    <u>presidents)</u>

5. General Idea: Using e-mail

    Specific Ideas: <u>writing a message, sending a message, receiving messages</u>

General and Specific Sentences

Now that you've reviewed how words can be general and specific, you'll be able to see how the sentences that express ideas are also general and specific in relation to each other. Paragraphs are composed of both general and specific sentences. A *general sentence* is one that states the broadest idea in the paragraph. This idea can often be explained or interpreted in a variety of different ways. The *specific sentences* in a paragraph are those that offer explanation or details that help us understand and accept the idea in the general sentence. Specific sentences are essential in helping readers correctly determine the meaning of the general statement.

We saw earlier how the terms *general* and *specific* are relative when applied to words. Sentences within a paragraph, too, are relatively general and specific. For example, read the following three statements:

Dessert is my favorite part of a meal.

I especially love to eat pie.

The after-dinner treat I like most to eat is a slice of warm cherry pie.

The first sentence states the most general idea; then the second sentence clarifies a specific type of dessert—pie—that the writer enjoys. The third sentence is even more specific because it identifies the particular kind of pie the writer likes most. So in this group of sentences, each statement is more specific than the one above it.

Exercise 2.5

Put these sentences in order from most general to most specific. Number them by writing 1, 2, or 3 on the blanks to indicate the most general (1) to the most specific (3).

1. __2__ Paris is her favorite destination.

   __1__ Marcy has always loved to travel.

   __3__ She loves to visit Paris landmarks such as the Eiffel Tower and the Louvre.[1]

2. __3__ Fresh, homegrown vegetables are a delicious addition to family meals.

   __2__ You can grow your own food in your back yard.

   __1__ Gardening is a rewarding hobby.

3. __1__ Many people suffer from foot pain.

   __3__ Firemen, nurses, and people in service jobs experience more foot pain than people in other professions.

   __2__ People whose jobs require that they stand for long periods of time have the most foot problems.

4. __3__ Courage, teamwork, and excellence are three of her father's values that she celebrates in her book.

   __1__ Sharon Robinson, daughter of baseball great Jackie Robinson, wanted to honor her father and his values.

   __2__ Sharon Robinson published a collection of essays and stories about nine values embraced by her father.

5. __1__ If you're looking for news and information, you can get it on the World Wide Web.

   __3__ *U.S. News and World Report* posts its articles on its website.

   __2__ Twenty-three of the fifty largest U.S. magazines are available online.*

---

1. Louvre: famous Paris art museum

---

* Adapted from Joe Saltzman, "Too Much Information, Too Little Time," *USA Today,* September 1997, 67.

2

Paragraphs are combinations of sentences that all work together to develop a main idea. So sorting out the general and specific relationships among related sentences is the first step toward understanding what you read. Look at the three sentences below and try to identify the one that is the most general.

Surveys show that adults typically watch four hours of TV per day.

Americans watch too much television.

The average American school child watches about twenty-eight hours of TV per week.

Did you choose the second sentence as most general? The other two sentences offer specific facts—the number of hours of TV adults and children watch—that help explain the idea of "too much television."

Now read these three specific sentences:

High school dropouts are 50 percent more likely than high school graduates to go on welfare.

Fewer than 50 percent of high school dropouts find jobs when they leave school.

When they do find jobs, high school dropouts earn 60 percent less income than high school graduates.

How could you state the general idea these three sentences explain or support? All three are examples of the negative effects of dropping out of high school, so the sentence "Dropping out of high school has several negative consequences" would be an accurate statement of the general idea they develop.

Finally, read this general sentence:

In many ways, college is tougher than high school.

What three specific sentences could you write to explain this sentence? Some possibilities include:

The course work is more difficult.

The instructors are more demanding.

The learning pace is much faster.

Exercise 2.6

The following groups of sentences include one general sentence and three specific sentences. Label each sentence on the blank provided with either a G for *general* or an S for *specific*.

1. __G__ I enjoy eating fruit.

   __S__ I put strawberries in my cereal.

   __S__ I eat blueberry topping on my ice cream.

   __S__ I enjoy peach pancakes.

2. __S__ In Florida, there has been much damage to homes and businesses as a result of hurricanes.

   __G__ Hurricanes can be very dangerous.

   __S__ Hurricane Floyd wiped out much of the beach area where I live.

   __S__ Many people died during Hurricane Andrew.

3. __S__ She has a television show that millions of people watch.

   __S__ Her magazine, *O,* is a great success.

   __G__ Oprah Winfrey is a very successful businesswoman and entertainer.

   __S__ She made a movie called *Beloved,* in which she starred.

4. __S__ Many town pools have rules requiring the use of "water wings" on children under age five.

   __G__ There are safety standards at many public swimming areas to prevent drownings.

   __S__ The lake in my town requires that a lifeguard be on duty until dark.

   __S__ The local YMCA requires that swimmers wait thirty minutes after eating before getting back in the pool to avoid getting cramps.

5. __G__ For most college graduates working in an office from 9 to 5 is hard to get used to.

   __S__ Many college graduates find it difficult to conform to others' schedules.

   __S__ A lot of new graduates are used to sleeping very late and staying up past midnight.

   __S__ Many recent graduates do not like having to report to a boss after being on their own for four years.

6. __S__ Most student drivers, have a difficult time merging onto highways and into traffic.

   __S__ For a new driver, changing lanes during rush hour is very hard to do.

2

___G___   Learning to drive can be very difficult.

___S___   Parking was the hardest part for me when I was a new driver.

7. ___S___   My grandmother's apple pie won awards at county fairs.

___G___   My grandmother was a great cook.

___S___   Grandma Rose studied cooking at a very famous cooking school.

___S___   A soup manufacturer tried to buy her recipe for chicken soup.

8. ___S___   Running tones your muscles.

___S___   Running two times a week increases the number of calories burned by 10 percent.

___G___   Running is the best form of exercise.

___S___   When I run, I feel great.

9. ___S___   Janet meets a lot of new people when she walks her dog.

___G___   Janet enjoys walking her dog.

___S___   When Janet walks her dog, she gets to spend time outdoors.

___S___   Janet gets a lot of exercise when she walks her dog.

10. ___G___   My house needs to be painted.

___S___   The paint is chipping off the side of my house by the driveway.

___S___   Mold is growing underneath the shingles from dirt and rain.

___S___   I don't like the color of my house.

Exercise 2.7

Read the three specific sentences given. Then, in the list that follows them, circle the letter of the general sentence best supported by those three specific sentences.

1. Women and minorities make up the majority of people applying to colleges.

   Prior to 1980, the majority of college applications came from white men.

   Fewer men are applying to colleges because they are going directly into the work force.

General Sentences:

(a.) There is a change in the types of people who are applying to college.
b. More women go to college than before.
c. Prior to 1980, fewer women and minorities applied to college.

2. Every American uses 80 to 100 gallons of water a day.

U.S. citizens spend more than $5 million a year on bottled water.

Many Americans frequently visit spas for relaxing and revitalizing water treatments.*

General Sentences:

(a.) Water can heal mental and physical ailments.
b. Americans use too much water.
c. Water is an important part of American life.

3. Flextime[1] saves businesses money because they don't need as much office space.

Flextime allows workers to more effectively balance their career schedules and personal lives.

Flextime helps businesses recruit the best workers and keep them from leaving.†

General Sentences:

a. Flextime can work only with clear-cut guidelines for employees.
(b.) Flextime, or flexible hours, offers several advantages.
c. Flextime and telecommuting are becoming more widespread in American companies.

4. Composting[2] involves making use of kitchen, lawn, and garden waste that would otherwise go to a landfill.

Putting grass clippings in your compost heap cuts down on the use of plastic bags used for gardening.

As the chemicals in the materials react and start to decompose, the compost heats up and yields rich, dark earth, perfect for fertilizing a garden.‡

1. **flextime:** working hours other than a 9 AM to 5 PM, 40–hour week

2. **composting:** adding discarded vegetable matter to a pile of organic waste

* Adapted from Marisa Fox, "Water Cures," *O Magazine,* June 2001, 171.
† Adapted from "Flextime Programs Gain Popularity," *USA Today Newsview,* April 1998, 5.
‡ Adapted from "Ask Martha," *New York Times,* June 2, 2001, 3e.

General Sentences:

a. Composting is one of the best things you can do for your garden and for the environment.

b. Composting is best done in the summer when it is hot.

c. Composting is easy.

5. *Riverdance,* a Broadway show that features Irish dance and music, is a big hit.

The Chieftains, an Irish group that has been playing together for many years, is suddenly selling more CDs than ever before.

Irish dancing is increasing in popularity with children enrolling in Irish step-dance classes.

General Sentences:

a. Irish culture is popular in other countries.

b. Irish culture, especially dance and music, is very popular now.

c. Many people take Irish dancing lessons.

Exercise 2.8

Read the general sentence given and then circle the letters of the three sentences from the list that best explain or support that statement.

1. General Sentence: Stephen Huneck is fast becoming a folk artist of cult status in America, mostly because of his smile-provoking art involving dogs.

Specific Sentences:

a. Stephen Huneck has many dogs.

b. One of his dogs is Sally, a black Labrador.

c. He has created woodcut prints involving dogs.

d. One of his sculptures shows dogs eating ice cream cones.

e. Huneck's dining room table is held up by four carved dogs.

f. Some of his sculptures show dogs with their heads sticking out of car windows.*

2. General Sentence: A growing number of researchers say it is a good idea to let families have easier access to patients during emergency treatment in hospitals.

---

* Adapted from Craig Wilson, "Art and Religion, Gone to the Dogs," *USA Today,* June 5, 2001, Section D, Life.

Specific Sentences:

(a.) Family members can comfort patients in a way no health-care provider can.

(b.) When the patient is less scared and is surrounded by family members, procedures go more smoothly.

c. Health decisions are left to the physician in charge.

d. Few hospitals have formal rules on this issue.

(e.) This way of treating emergency room patients is most effective when the patient is a child and a parent can stay with him or her during treatment.

f. One physician thinks that this should be done on a case-by-case basis.*

3. General Sentence: Television host Regis Philbin is a very busy man.

(a.) His talk show, *Live with Regis and Kelly*, is on five days a week from 9 AM to 10 AM.

b. Regis Philbin is a graduate of Notre Dame University and discusses his loyalty to the school and its sports teams on his television show.

(c.) Regis frequently guest stars on sitcoms.

d. Regis is married to Joy Philbin and is the father of two adult daughters.

(e.) Besides his hosting duties on *Live,* Regis is often seen on David Letterman's show as a guest.

f. Regis has a house in Connecticut and an apartment in New York City.

4. General Sentence: Stephen King, sometimes called the "master of horror," is considered the most popular fiction writer ever and is loved by his fans.

(a.) He has sold more than a billion books since his first one was published.

b. He published a book after being hit by a car and suffering terrible injuries.

c. He is a frequent guest on popular talk shows because he is very funny.

d. His first manuscript was rejected.

(e.) Fans line up in front of bookstores in anticipation of one of his book's publication and buy all copies available on the first day.

(f.) He gets bags full of fan mail every day.

5. General Sentence: It is important that children, especially those who can't swim, be supervised by their parents or guardians around pools and bodies of water.

(a.) Many children drown every summer because they have not been supervised properly.

(b.) Even if children can swim, it is important that a parent be close by in case the children experience cramping in their legs or feet.

(c.) Lifeguards should not be expected to supervise everyone's children, especially at a crowded swimming facility.

d. Some children learn to swim at a very young age.

* Adapted from Pat Wingert, "Family Notes," *Newsweek*, June 11, 2001, 60.

e. The ocean is fun to swim in.

f. Lakes are safer than oceans because there are no waves.

Determining the Topic

Now that you've reviewed the distinction between general and specific, let's look at the most general aspect of a paragraph: its topic. To understand what you read, you must be able to identify the topic, or subject, of a reading selection. The **topic** is the person, place, thing, event, or idea that the passage is about, and it is usually expressed in just a word or brief phrase. For example, read this paragraph:

The Slinky has been a popular toy for more than fifty years. The Slinky is available on every continent except Antarctica. Ninety percent of Americans know what this coiled wire toy is. Since 1946, 250 million Slinky toys have been sold. Today, both boys and girls still enjoy this inexpensive plaything.

The topic of this paragraph is the Slinky. Every sentence in the paragraph refers to or mentions the Slinky.

To find the topic of a selection, look for the person, place, thing, event, or idea that is repeated again and again.

Exercise 2.9

Read each paragraph and write the correct topic on the blank provided.

1. How you spend the hours before bedtime plays a big role in how well you'll sleep, Dr. Maas points out in his recent book, *Power Sleep* (Harper Perennial). Although a big meal is forbidden for three hours before you settle in, having a light snack, high in carbohydrates and low in protein, will help you drift off—crackers, a cookie or two, or camomile[1] tea. Milk, of course, has always been a popular recommendation because it speeds the amino acid tryptophan to the brain, where it is converted to sleep-inducing serotonin. Other tried-and-true before-bed aids: yoga, visualization, and deep breathing.*

   Topic: Things to do before bedtime to induce sleep

2. For the very young, the very old, and people with lung disease, air pollution is not only annoying but also dangerous. Smog causes inflammation

1. camomile: an herb

* Adapted from "Follow the Milky Way," *Victoria,* January 2001, 81.

or swelling of the airway, which makes breathing more difficult. Exposure to high smog levels can trigger asthma attacks and worsen emphysema.[1] Long-term exposure can cause scarring of the lungs.*

Topic: _air pollution (or smog)_

3. Success in school and in life is largely a matter of cultivating effective habits. The new habit that you choose does not have to make headlines. It can be one simple, small change in behavior. All of the researchers on studying and success in school agree that forming good habits regarding your school work is essential to your success.†

Topic: _Good habits_

4. A writing center should have a table with chairs around it, containers of writing tools, and newsprint or unlined paper in various sizes and colors. Children like to experiment with colored felt-tipped pens, crayons, pencils, and chalk for individual chalkboards. Resource materials to encourage children to write include greeting cards, note pads, books and magazines, envelopes, special words related to a unit or holiday, magnetic letters, and the alphabet in uppercase and lowercase letters. Writing centers may also contain notice or message boards for the children and teacher to use for exchanging information.‡

Topic: _Writing centers_

5. It is said that women gossip more than men do. However, men gossip, too, though they tend to call it "networking." What really differs is the content of their gossip. Men are much more interested in who is up and who is down, an interest that arises from their enjoyment of competitive game playing. Women tend to gossip more about social inclusion[2] and morality. They are more interested in who has merit.§

Topic: _Gossip_

1. **emphysema:** a lung disease that makes breathing difficult

2. **inclusion:** the act of being included or the state of being included

* Adapted from Anita Manning, "There's No Breathing Easy With Air Pollution," *USA Today,* April 16, 2004, 8A.

† Adapted from Dave Ellis, *Becoming a Master Student* (Boston: Houghton Mifflin Co., 2000), 120. Copyright © 2000 by Houghton Mifflin Company. Reprinted with permission.

‡ From Paul Burns et al., *Teaching Reading in Today's Elementary Schools,* 7th ed. (Boston: Houghton Mifflin Co., 1999), 69.

§ Adapted from Nigel Nicholson, PhD, "The New Word on Gossip," *Psychology Today,* May/June 2001, 44.

2

When you are deciding on the topic of a paragraph or passage, make sure your choice is not too *broad* or too *narrow*. A topic that is too broad suggests much more than the paragraph actually offers. A topic that is too narrow does not include everything the paragraph covers. For example, look at the following paragraph:

> Many popular inventions were created by accident. In 1886, a pharmacist trying to create a nerve and brain tonic[1] made a syrup that became Coca-Cola. In 1853, a chef accidentally created potato chips for a restaurant guest who complained that his French fries were too thick. In the 1920s, Yale University students who liked to toss and catch pie plates made by the Frisbie Pie Company accidentally came up with the popular toy known as the Frisbee.

Which of these is the correct topic of the paragraph?

_____ inventions

_____ the invention of Coca-Cola

✔ accidental inventions

If you checked accidental inventions, you're correct. The first topic, inventions, is too broad because it includes all kinds of inventions, even those that were created intentionally. The second topic, the invention of Coca-Cola, is too narrow because the paragraph discusses potato chips and Frisbees, too. Accidental inventions is the right topic because the paragraph gives examples of three different products that were all discovered by accident.

Now read another example:

> Miss America Heather Whitestone overcame many obstacles on her path to the crown. When she was eighteen months old, the H influenza virus almost killed her. Although she survived, the illness left her almost totally deaf. During her childhood she spent countless hours in speech therapy. It took her six years to learn to say her last name. She pushed herself to attend a regular high school instead of one for deaf students. She endured her parents' heartbreaking divorce. When she began entering pageants, she won only first runner-up in two Miss Alabama pageants. But she refused to give up, and in 1995, she became the first person with a disability to win the Miss America pageant.

Which of the topics below is the correct one?

_____ Miss America pageant

1. **tonic:** a drink with healthful qualities

_____✔_____ Heather Whitestone

_____ Heather Whitestone's speech therapy

The first choice, Miss America pageant, is too broad. This paragraph focuses on just one specific winner of that pageant. The last choice, Heather Whitestone's speech therapy, is too narrow because this paragraph also discusses other obstacles she overcame. Therefore, Heather Whitestone is the correct topic. This paragraph describes her difficulties and ultimate triumph over them.

Exercise 2.10

Following each paragraph are three topics. On each blank, label the topic *B* if it is too broad, *N* if it is too narrow, and *T* if it is the correct topic of the paragraph.

1. Working in the fishing industry is one of the most dangerous jobs in America. Fishermen average 71 fatalities per 100,000 workers, which is more than twenty times the fatality rate of the average U.S. worker. Fishermen must put in very long hours during short fishing seasons. They work with heavy gear and dangerous machinery. And they tend to go out even in rough, stormy seas because they have to catch a lot of fish to make any money, and they have only a short amount of time to do it. Not surprisingly, drowning is the most common cause of death.*

    The fishing industry: __T__

    Long hours of fishermen: __N__

    Dangerous jobs: __B__

2. Reciting is saying each fact or idea in your notes out loud, in your own words, and from memory. Recitation is an extremely powerful aid to memory. Recitation makes you think, and thinking leaves a trace in your memory. Experiments show that students who recite retain 80 percent of the material; students who reread but do not recite retain only 20 percent when tested two weeks later. Without retention, there is no learning.†

    Memory aids: __B__

    Reciting: __T__

    Memory experiments: __N__

---

* Adapted from Les Christie, "America's Most Dangerous Jobs," *CNN/Money*, October 13, 2003, http://money.cnn.com/2003/10/13/pf/dangerousjobs.

† From Walter Pauk and John Fiore, *Succeed in College!* (Boston: Houghton Mifflin Co., 2000), 47. Copyright © 2000 by Houghton Mifflin Company. Reprinted with permission.

2

3. Most people engage in *linear thinking*; that is, they begin a task, finish it, and then go on to something else. Teenagers using the Internet today, however, are *multitasking;* that is, as they are online, they are also doing other things. They may be watching television or visiting two sites at the same time. Eighty-six percent of teenage girls listen to the radio while they are using the computer. Adolescents may be e-mailing a friend and looking something up at the same time.*

Multitasking adolescents: __T__

Teenagers: __B__

Teenagers who listen to the radio while using a computer: __N__

4. Goals are specific changes you'd like to make in yourself or in your environment. To help achieve your goals, state them as results you can measure. Think in detail about how things would be different if your goal were attained. List the specific changes in what you'd see, feel, touch, taste, hear, be, do, or have. Some goals that will aid you with your schoolwork include setting aside a specific time to study every day, taking good notes in class, and reviewing those notes from time to time to make sure you are retaining information.†

Goals: __T__

Changing yourself: __B__

Taking notes in class: __N__

5. Until now, people who wanted hybrid gas-electric cars that conserved fuel could choose only among two Honda models and a Toyota. But by 2005, consumers will be offered a variety in all sizes and shapes. Hybrid versions of three sport-utility vehicles, the Ford Escape, Toyota Highlander, and Lexus RX400, are just months away from showrooms. Hybrid versions of the Honda Accord and Dodge Ram pickup aren't far behind.‡

Cars: __B__

Hybrid sport-utility vehicles: __N__

New hybrid cars: __T__

---

* Adapted from Paul S. Kaplan, *Adolescence* (Boston: Houghton Mifflin Co., 2004), 266.
† Adapted from Dave Ellis, *Becoming a Master Student* (Boston: Houghton Mifflin Co., 2000), 59.
‡ Adapted from "Hybrid Car Market Revs Up," *USA Today,* May 3, 2004, 12A.

Determining the Main Idea

Once you've found the topic of a paragraph, you can determine its **main idea,** the general point the writer expressed about the topic. The main idea is what the writer wants to prove or explain. It's the point he or she wants you to know or to believe when you finish reading the paragraph. Therefore, being able to identify main ideas is a fundamental skill for successful reading.

To find the main idea, ask yourself what the writer is saying *about* the topic. For example, read this paragraph:

> The Eagles' *Greatest Hits* album is the most successful album in history. It has sold 26 million copies, more than any other album. It was the first album ever to gain platinum status for sales of one million copies. *Greatest Hits* was the number one album on the Billboard Charts for five weeks, and it spent a total of 133 weeks on the charts altogether.

The topic of this paragraph is the Eagles' *Greatest Hits* album. It's the thing that is mentioned in every sentence of the paragraph. But what is the author's point about this topic? In the first sentence, she states that this album was more successful than any other. Then, all of the other sentences in the paragraph offer details to explain that idea.

As you read the next paragraph, try to identify the topic and main idea.

> Single mothers face many challenges. Their greatest difficulties are usually financial. They are the primary family breadwinners, so their greatest struggles, especially for those who are younger and less educated, often involve making ends meet. To make matters worse, single moms often do not receive regular child support from their children's fathers. They also must curtail[1] their work hours due to childcare limitations, so many can't earn full-time wages.

Did you say that the topic is *single mothers' financial challenges*? That is correct. Every sentence of this paragraph mentions single mothers, single moms, or includes a pronoun (*they* or *their*) that refers to single moms. Also, each sentence refers to difficulties related to money. Now, what does the author want you to know or believe about that topic? The second sentence says that financial difficulties are their greatest hardship. Then, the remainder of the paragraph explains why the reader should accept that idea as true.

1. **curtail:** shorten

2

Exercise 2.11

Read each paragraph and then circle the letter of the correct topic.

1. In any subject, learning is enhanced when we ask questions. And there are no dumb questions. To master math and science, ask whatever questions will aid your understanding. Don't worry about what other students do or don't ask. What you need to ask may not be the same as for the other people in your class.*

   Topic:
   a. learning math and science
   b. asking questions to aid understanding
   c. students in higher education

2. Most college lecturers speak about 120 words per minute. In a fifty-minute lecture, you hear up to 6,000 words expressing ideas, facts, and details. To make sure that students understand the ideas, facts, and details they are presenting, lecturers use signal words and phrases. Signal words help lecturers convey[1] important information. Some signal words and phrases include *to illustrate, before/after, furthermore, as a result,* and *more importantly.* Being able to recognize signal words and phrases will improve your reading, writing, speaking, and listening, as well as your note taking.†

   Topic:
   a. fifty-minute lectures
   b. signal words and phrases
   c. college lecturers

3. Developing the ability to concentrate is an important study skill. Keep your mind on what you're doing and try hard to ignore distractions. Remove the telephone and the television set, and try to eliminate any other interruptions. Find a quiet place where you'll be isolated from things that might disturb you. Sometimes low-level noise like instrumental music or a steady flow of traffic helps stimulate concentration. And don't try to study if you are hungry. That's a sure way to break your concentration.‡

1. convey: communicate

---

* Adapted from Dave Ellis, *Becoming a Master Student* (Boston: Houghton Mifflin Co., 2000), 181.

† Adapted from Walter Pauk and John Fiore, *Succeed in College!* (Boston: Houghton Mifflin Co., 2000), 38.

‡ Adapted from Sharon Sherman and Alan Sherman, *Essential Concepts of Chemistry* (Boston: Houghton Mifflin Co., 1999), xxxi.

2

Topic:

a. developing the ability to concentrate
b. low-level noise
c. eliminating interruptions

4. As I looked back and evaluated my own college training, I saw that the training and experience I had had in public speaking had been of more practical value to me in business—and in life—than everything else I had studied in college all put together. Why? Because it had wiped out my timidity[1] and lack of self-confidence confidence and given me the courage and assurance to deal with people. It had also made clear that leadership usually gravitates[2] to the man who can get up and say what he thinks.*

Topic:

a. college
b. public speaking
c. courage

5. The recent tragedy involving thirteen-year-old Brittanie Cecil, who was hit and killed by a flying puck at a hockey game, could have been prevented. American hockey stadiums, like those in Europe, need to install protective netting. Even fans who are alertly watching the game cannot dodge a puck traveling 100 miles per hour, so nets would protect spectators from getting injured or killed. Some fans of the game argue that nets are difficult to see through or distracting. But in Europe, where nets are common, they are barely visible. So protective netting should be mandatory[3] in order to prevent any more deaths or injuries.

Topic:

a. hockey
b. protective nets for hockey stadiums
c. hockey fans

1. **timidity:** shyness
2. **gravitates:** moves toward; is attracted to
3. **mandatory:** required

* Excerpted from Dale Carnegie, *How To Stop Worrying and Start Living* (New York: Pocket Books, 1984), xvi.

Exercise 2.12

Now, read each paragraph again and write a check mark in the blank beside the correct main idea in the list.

1. In any subject, learning is enhanced when we ask questions. And there are no dumb questions. To master math and science, ask whatever questions will aid your understanding. Students come to higher education with widely varying backgrounds in these subjects. What you need to ask may not be the same as for the other people in your class.*

Main Idea:

_✔_ Asking questions helps students learn.

_____ Students' questions are very different.

_____ Math and science are tough subjects to master.

2. Most college lecturers speak about 120 words per minute. In a fifty-minute lecture, you hear up to 6,000 words expressing ideas, facts, and details. To make sure that students understand the ideas, facts, and details they are presenting, lecturers use signal words and phrases. Signal words help lecturers convey important information. Some signal words and phrases include *to illustrate, before/after, furthermore, as a result,* and *more importantly.* Being able to recognize signal words and phrases will improve your reading, writing, speaking, and listening, as well as your note taking.†

Main Idea:

_____ Most college lectures last for fifty minutes.

_✔_ Signal words and phrases help students better understand lectures.

_____ Most college lecturers speak too quickly.

3. Developing the ability to concentrate is an important study skill. Keep your mind on what you're doing and try hard to ignore distractions. Remove the telephone and the television set, and try to eliminate any other interruptions. Find a quiet place where you'll be isolated from things that might disturb you. Sometimes low-level noise like instrumental music

* Adapted from Dave Ellis, *Becoming a Master Student* (Boston: Houghton Mifflin Co., 2000), 181.
† Adapted from Walter Pauk and John Fiore, *Succeed in College!* (Boston: Houghton Mifflin Co., 2000), 38.

or a steady flow of traffic helps stimulate concentration. And don't try to study if you are hungry. That's a sure way to break your concentration.*

Main Idea:

___✔___ The ability to concentrate can be developed.

_____ Interruptions are sure ways to break your concentration.

_____ Hunger inhibits effective studying.

4. As I looked back and evaluated my own college training, I saw that the training and experience I had had in public speaking had been of more practical value to me in business—and in life—than everything else I had studied in college all put together. Why? Because it had wiped out my timidity and lack of self-confidence and given me the courage and assurance to deal with people. It had also made clear that leadership usually gravitates to the man who can get up and say what he thinks.†

Main Idea:

_____ College training is invaluable.

___✔___ Public speaking is a practical and valuable skill.

_____ Saying what you think is the key to effective leadership.

5. The recent tragedy involving thirteen-year-old Brittanie Cecil, who was hit and killed by a flying puck at a hockey game, could have been prevented. American hockey stadiums, like those in Europe, need to install protective netting. Even fans who are alertly watching the game cannot dodge a puck traveling 100 miles per hour, so nets would protect spectators from getting injured or killed. Some fans of the game argue that nets are difficult to see through or distracting. But in Europe, where nets are common, they are barely visible. So protective netting should be mandatory in order to prevent any more deaths or injuries.

Main idea:

_____ Hockey is a very dangerous game.

___✔___ Hockey stadiums need to install nets to protect fans.

_____ Hockey fans are very safety-conscious.

---

* Adapted from Sharon Sherman and Alan Sherman, *Essential Concepts of Chemistry* (Boston: Houghton Mifflin Co., 1999), xxi.

† Excerpted from Dale Carnegie, *How to Stop Worrying and Start Living* (New York: Pocket Books, 1984), xvi.

2

The Topic Sentence

The **topic sentence** is the single statement that presents the main point or idea of the paragraph. Topic sentences have two parts: they state the topic, and they state what the author has to say about that topic. Writers do not have to include such a sentence. Chapter 4 of this book will discuss in more detail paragraphs that lack a topic sentence. However, writers often include a topic sentence to help readers quickly and easily see the main idea.

To find the topic sentence, look for the most general statement in the paragraph and then make sure the other sentences all offer information or details. See if you can locate the topic sentence in the following paragraph:

> Within hours of its collapse, the debate began over what—if anything —should be built to replace the World Trade Center in New York City. Some suggested rebuilding exact replicas[1] of the original towers—a signal to terrorists that the city's spirit is intact.[2] Others suggested creating a park as a memorial to the attack's victims. The World Trade Center's current manager, Larry Silverstein, has suggested erecting something new: a cluster of four 50-story buildings.*

If you chose the first sentence, you're right. That statement expresses the paragraph's main idea, and the rest of the paragraph explains that idea.

Exercise 2.13

For each of the following paragraphs, write the correct topic on the blank provided. Write on the second blank provided the number of the sentence that expresses the main idea.

1. (1) Cheating in high school is very common. (2) Three out of every four high school students admit to breaking the rules by cheating on a test at least once. (3) Seventy-five percent of students have also confessed to handing in work that was completed by someone else. (4) A quarter of all students say they've been dishonest by working with others when they were instructed to work by themselves.

   Topic: _Cheating_____

   Topic Sentence: __1__

1. **replicas:** in this context, buildings that look exactly like the original World Trade Center towers; copies

2. **intact:** remaining together or uninjured

* Adapted from Michael Dolan, "Standing Tall," *Popular Science*, December 2001, 78.

2. (1) Teenagers are master rationalizers.¹ (2) Some say that sports and other activities interfered with homework. (3) They also claim that they cheated because the assignment seemed meaningless or boring. (4) Many cited the pressure to get good grades. (5) Indeed, to many of these kids, high school seems like simply a tedious hurdle. (6) Once in college, though, many students appear to start taking school more seriously, at least when classes seem relevant to their goals. (7) They say, "I've never cheated in my major, but when it comes to general education requirements—those courses don't matter."

Topic: <u>Teenagers' reasons for cheating</u>

Topic Sentence: <u> 1 </u>

3. (1) Students also cite famous cheaters as examples of what it takes to succeed. (2) As one student wrote: "This world is full of cheaters because cheaters are the ones who most often get to the top. (3) News flash: Cheaters do prosper!" (4) In past surveys, names like Michael Milken² and Donald Trump³ came up. (5) This year, a student put it this way: "If Clinton⁴ can do it and get away with it, why can't we?"*

Topic: <u>Famous cheaters</u>

Topic Sentence: <u> 1 </u>

Locations of Topic Sentences

Main ideas are often stated in the first sentence of the paragraph. However, they can appear in other places in a paragraph, too. Writers sometimes place the topic sentence in the middle of a paragraph or even at the end.

1. **rationalizers:** people who come up with self-satisfying but incorrect reasons for their behavior

2. **Michael Milken:** wealthy American executive who went to prison for fraud and other crimes

3. **Donald Trump:** wealthy American business executive who has come close to bankruptcy

4. **Clinton:** Bill Clinton, 42nd president of the U.S., who was caught lying about having an extramarital relationship

---

* All excerpts in Exercise 2.13 adapted from Emily Sohn, "The Young and the Virtueless," *U.S. News and World Report*, www.usnews.com/usnews/issue/010521/education/cheating.b.htm.

2

Topic Sentence as First Sentence

It's very common for writers to announce the main idea in the first sentence of the paragraph. Then, the remainder of the paragraph explains why the reader should accept that point. In the following paragraph, for example, the topic sentence, which is in boldface type, is at the beginning.

> **Newspapers have definite advantages over other sources of information.** The wonderful thing about the newspaper is that all the work is done for you. There is nothing to turn on, nothing to search for, nothing between you and the information. Somebody else has already categorized, organized, edited, and condensed[1] the information for you in a form easily handled and assimilated.[2] Another great thing about the newspaper is it brings the family together. Different sections of the paper can be parceled[3] out to members of the family. There is something wonderful about the habit of a family reading and digesting the daily newspaper. Ideas are shared, opinions voiced, and lives and deaths verified.*

Topic Sentence as Second or Third Sentence

Sometimes, though, a writer needs to present a sentence or two of introductory information before stating the main point. This means that the topic sentence might occur in the second or third sentence of the paragraph. Take a look at this example:

> As many as 80 percent of websites on the Internet include inaccurate information. If you're doing research, how do you make sure the information you find is true? **You can examine certain parts of a website to evaluate its reliability.** Websites with addresses that include *.org, .gov,* or *.edu* are usually accurate. Websites that give the sources of their information, too, tend to be more trustworthy. Also, look for identification of the site's creators as well as contact information for those people.

The main idea is "You can examine certain parts of a website to evaluate its reliability" because most of the paragraph is about what those parts are. However, the writer included some background information and a question at the beginning of the paragraph. Both of these sentences led up to the topic sentence in the third statement.

---

1. **condensed:** shortened   3. **parceled:** divided
2. **assimilated:** absorbed

---

* Adapted from Joe Saltzman, "Too Much Information, Too Little Time," *USA Today,* September 1997, 67.

Topic Sentence in the Middle

A topic sentence can also appear somewhere in the middle of the paragraph. For example, read the following paragraph:

> An old saying in business claims that 80 percent of a company's profits come from 20 percent of its customers. That's why Centura Bank ranks its 650,000 customers on a scale of one to five. Those with the best ratings get better customer service. **This company and others are beginning to concentrate more on their best customers.** Continental Airlines, for instance, plans to give its agents access to each customer's history so they can give the best service to their top clients. First Union Bank codes its credit card customers. When a person calls for service, the bank's representatives know when they're talking to one of their best patrons.*

This paragraph begins with an introductory statement in the first sentence. Then, the second sentence offers the first of three examples given to explain the main idea in the fourth sentence. After the main idea is stated, the paragraph offers two more examples.

Topic Sentence as Last Sentence

A writer might choose to save the topic sentence for the end of the paragraph, offering it as the last sentence. This next paragraph is an example of one that builds up to the main point:

> People who attend religious services more than once a week live seven years longer than people who never attend religious services. Spiritual people also recover more quickly from surgery. Regular church-goers are less likely to have heart disease or high blood pressure. They have lower rates of depression and anxiety, too. **Obviously, being faithful has positive health benefits.**†

In this paragraph, the writer offers all of her explanations first. Then, she summarizes the point in a topic sentence at the paragraph's end.

Topic Sentence as First and Last Sentence

Finally, the topic sentence might occur twice: once at the beginning of the paragraph and then again, in different words, at the end. Writers often restate the topic sentence to emphasize or reinforce the main idea for the reader.

---

* Adapted from Diane Brady, "Why Service Stinks," *Reader's Digest,* May 2001, 161–168.

† Adapted from Elena Serocki, "Heaven Can Wait," *Reader's Digest,* May 2001, 112.

Here is an example:

> **Jigsaw puzzles, which were created in the 1760s, are still a popular pastime.** Thirty million jigsaw puzzles were sold in 2000. Eighty percent of American homes contain a jigsaw puzzle for adults. Eighty-three percent of American homes contain at least one child's jigsaw puzzle. There's even a National Jigsaw Puzzle Championship every year. This contest offers puzzle enthusiasts[1] $10,000 in prizes. **It's clear that many people still enjoy this centuries-old hobby.***

This paragraph identifies the main point in the first sentence, offers explanation, and then makes the same point again in the final sentence.

Steps for Locating the Topic Sentence

To find the topic sentence regardless of where it is located, look for the most general statement in the paragraph. Then, verify that the rest of the sentences in the paragraph offer information, details, or explanation for that general idea. Here's a specific step-by-step procedure you can follow when you're trying to determine the main idea and topic sentence in a paragraph:

Step 1: Read over the entire paragraph to get an idea of the subject matter included.

Step 2: Read the first sentence to see if it gives a general picture of the entire paragraph. If it doesn't, it may provide some general background or contrasting information. Or the first sentence may pose a question that the next few sentences go on to answer.

Step 3: If the first sentence does not state the main idea, read the last sentence to see if it gives a general picture of the entire paragraph. Turn the last sentence into a question, and then see if the other sentences in the paragraph answer that question. If they do, that last sentence may be the topic sentence.

Step 4: If either the first or the last sentence gives that general overview of the paragraph, the main idea, you have found your topic sentence.

Step 5: If neither the first nor the last sentence is identified as the topic sentence, then you must evaluate each sentence in the middle of the paragraph to see if one of the sentences states the general idea or the main idea information. Test each possibility by turning it into a ques-

1. **enthusiasts:** fans

* Adapted from John Tierney, "Playing with the Puzzle People," *Reader's Digest*, May 2001, 118–123.

tion and then determining if the other sentences in the paragraph answer that question.

Step 6: Once the topic sentence is located, then you must look for the general phrase located in the topic sentence that states the overall main idea.

Exercise 2.14

Below each paragraph, write on the blank provided the number of the sentence (or sentences) that state(s) the main idea.

1. (1) The atmosphere in Escalante's room was much like that in the locker room at a football game. (2) Class began with warm-up exercises. (3) All the students slapped their hands against their desks and stomped their feet on the floor in rhythm while chanting an opening ritual. (4) When attention dropped, Escalante would begin the "wave," a cheer in which row after row of students, in succession,[1] stood, raising their hands, then sat quickly, creating a ripple across the room like a pennant[2] billowing in victory. (5) The intensity of drills and quizzes was relieved with jokes, demonstrations, and an occasional round of volleyball. (6) Just as the classroom clock never registered the correct time, the routine usually varied, keeping the team alert and focused *

   Topic Sentence: ____1____

2. (1) Many young children and adults believe supplements[3] will make them faster and stronger. (2) In reality, people who take steroids[4] are jeopardizing their health. (3) Steroid use puts people at greater risk for heart attacks and strokes, increases aggressiveness, and stunts[5] growth for both genders. (4) It also can lead to a number of sexual side effects in males, including breast development, premature balding, testicular atrophy,[6] and decreased sperm count. (5) Many of these side effects are irreversible.†

   Topic Sentence: ____2____

1. **succession:** one after another
2. **pennant:** flag
3. **supplements:** products people eat or drink to become larger or stronger
4. **steroids:** supplements that some people take to improve their physical performance

5. **stunts:** decreases or stops
6. **atrophy:** wasting away or deterioration

---

* From Ann Byers, *Jaime Escalante: Sensational Teacher* (Springfield, NJ: Enslow Publishers, 1996).

† Adapted from Joe Biden, "Baseball Drug Testing Needs to Get Beyond First Base," *USA Today*, March 8, 2004, 13A.

2

3. (1) Cell phones are pulling drivers' attention from the road. (2) Navigation systems and e-mail are already available in vehicles. (3) Audio systems are becoming more complicated to operate. (4) Automakers are installing all kinds of potential distractions in cars. (5) There are customized information services that shower drivers with news items and shopping tips. (6) There are TVs in the backseats, too.*

Topic Sentence: ___4___

4. (1) In the old days, kids headed off to camp with a few postcards. (2) Now a laptop might do better. (3) In today's world of camping, kids don't leave technology behind when they go off to summer camp. (4) According to Peg Smith, executive director of the American Camping Association, about 70 percent of summer camps are online and many allow e-mail. (5) Some also post daily shows of activities on websites; a few even have live Webcams.

Topic Sentence: ___3___

5. (1) Although he is one of the highest paid ball players in history, he always takes the time to sign autographs for kids at the ball field. (2) He has his own charity organization, to which he devotes a lot of time. (3) He talks about his great family in interviews, and how much he loves his mother, father, and younger sister. (4) And he's a great fielder and hitter. (5) That's what makes Derek Jeter one of the most popular professional athletes in America today.

Topic Sentence: ___5___

Exercise 2.15

Following each paragraph, write on the blank provided the number of the sentence that is the topic sentence.

1. (1) Stress is hard to define because it means different things to different people. (2) However, stress is usually a negative reaction, either mental or physical, to some demand (a force, a pressure, or a strain) placed upon an individual. (3) This negative reaction can take the form of worry, anxiety, and irritability. (4) It can disrupt concentration and interfere with good decision-making. (5) The negative reaction can take the form of physical problems such as increased blood pressure, headaches, muscle tension, and insomnia.[1]

Topic sentence: ___2___

1. **insomnia:** sleeplessness

---

* Adapted from Dann McCosh, "Driven to Distraction," *Popular Science,* December 2001, 86.

2. (1) Many people cope with stress in unhealthy ways. (2) Some use alcohol or drugs to escape or calm themselves down. (3) Some take up smoking to soothe their nerves. (4) Some people refuse to deal with problems through avoidance or procrastination.[1] (5) Others overeat. (6) Still others allow themselves to burn out, give up, and succumb[2] to depression. (7) And some people allow themselves to become angry and withdrawn.

Topic sentence: __1__

3. (1) Other people deal with stress by engaging in aerobic exercise, which can reduce anxiety by up to 50 percent. (2) They make sure they get proper nutrition, eating the right foods to improve their ability to respond to stress. (3) They get an adequate amount of sleep every night. (4) They reduce their intake of caffeine and give up smoking. (5) These methods are the healthy physical ways to cope with stress.

Topic sentence: __5__

4. (1) Another good way to counteract stress is to meditate. (2) Taking just ten to twenty minutes a day for quiet reflection often brings relief from stress. (3) You can also use visualization, using your imagination to picture in your mind how to manage a stressful situation more successfully. (4) These and other mental strategies are good stress management techniques. (5) For example, you can decide to be more realistic about how many obligations[3] you can take on at one time, and you can give up the idea that you can reach perfection in everything you do.

Topic sentence: __4__

CHAPTER 2 REVIEW

Write the correct answers on the blanks in the following statements.

1. Paragraphs are composed of ___general___ and ___specific___ statements.

2. The most general sentence in the paragraph expresses its ___main idea___, the idea or point the writer wants you to know or to believe.

3. The sentence that states the writer's main idea is called the ___topic sentence___.

4. The topic sentence has two parts: the ___topic___, or subject, of the paragraph and what the writer wants to say about that topic.

5. The topic sentence can occur anywhere in the ___paragraph___.

1. **procrastination:** putting things off   3. **obligations:** duties or responsibilities
2. **succumb:** give in

Reading Selection

> ## Practicing the Active Reading Strategy:
> ### Before and As You Read
>
> You can use active reading strategies before, as, and after you read a selection. The following are some suggestions for active reading strategies that you can employ before you read and as you are reading.
>
> 1. Skim the selection for any unfamiliar words. Circle or highlight any words you do not know.
> 2. As you read, underline, highlight, or circle important words or phrases.
> 3. Write down any questions about the selection if you are confused by the information presented.
> 4. Jot notes in the margin to help you understand the material.

Is Gossip Beneficial or Harmful?

by Dr. Offra Gerstein

1 Gossip, the practice of sharing information about other people's lives, is familiar to all of us. We enjoy this form of idle talk and are often unaware of its harm.

2 The origins of gossip date to early man. Primitive societies used negative information to damage the reputation of their rivals and defeat them. In Old English, gossip evolved from "god-sibb." This word referred to a close female friend present at the birth of a child. This woman would assume the role of a godparent. She listened to the new mother and served as her confidant. Later, the term evolved to describe friends' intimate sharing of personal information. It further expanded to the current use of talk about a person not present.

3 If your mother tells you that gossiping is bad, she is right. If researchers inform you that gossip is unavoidable and beneficial, they too are right. The distinction is between "good" and "bad" gossip. As psychologist James Lynch puts it: "Human dialogue can be a great healer or a great destroyer."

4 According to researchers, gossip has some benefits. Exchanging information can create a healthy connection. It can build rules for acceptable and unacceptable behavior. It can improve society.

5 Similarly, gossip is useful in the business world. Gossip researcher Professor Frank McAndrew says, "If people are talking about good things others do, we want to emulate that good behavior. It is a nice way of socially controlling people." When a company faces bad times, gossip about the future of the employees can reduce fear and uncertainty. It can also create a feeling of fellowship.

6 However, bad gossip, the negative talk about other people's lives, can be destructive. Disappointingly enough, the researchers spend little time on this form of malice.

People engage in negative gossip for several reasons. They may do it to bond with another person. They may do it to pass the time or to deny problems. They may gossip to build themselves up through comparisons with others, or they may want to hurt others.

7   Bonding with another individual brings pleasure, even when it is done at the expense of someone else. People who criticize someone else feel superior to the criticized person. "We think that what she did is outrageous. We would never do anything like this to anyone." This false feeling of superiority temporarily raises the level of self-esteem of the "gossipers." For those who compare themselves with others to create better self-esteem, the practice of knocking others becomes an unfortunate habit.

8   Another use of gossip for emotional connection is the revealing of confidential information. If someone told us a secret, we share it with another person to gain the listener's friendship while *betraying* the holder of the secret. Some people ask the listener to promise not to further relate the secret. And thus begins the chain of evil betrayal.

9   Gossip also serves as a nondemanding way of engaging in idle talk. It is an activity to pass the time with someone. It requires no strain on the brain. We can just pass judgments on what the neighbors are doing as a form of entertainment.

10   For some people, gossip is a way to avoid dealing with their own problems by concentrating on how poorly others solve theirs. It is a way to avoid criticism or even appreciation from others. When we focus on what others should do better, we are free from becoming accountable for ourselves.

11   Some people use gossip to harm others. This is terrible behavior. It is never justified.

12   Ancient Indian mythology considers gossip a form of mental illness. Religions hate and forbid it. Psychoanalysts report that gossip is harmful to the individual. It creates many emotional problems, such as suspicion, fear, mistrust, and depression. Gossip is poison to one's soul and destroys friendships and relationships.

13   Feeling "better than" or "less than" other people is a tragic way to understand one's worth. Self-esteem must come from within the individual. It must be based on one's character and on actions that lead to self-respect.

14   To deal with gossip better:

- Create healthy ways of connecting with others that do not require negative talk about someone else.

- When you are told something about another person, ask for proof of the information. If you trust what is said without challenging its truth, you become a partner in spreading gossip.

- If you hear negative talk, refuse to listen and politely attempt to stop the speaker.

- Ask the "gossiper" to tell you positive things about the individual he is criticizing.

- When you are entrusted with a secret, feel honored and never repeat it to anyone. Repeating confidences is like stealing one's dignity.

- Feel free to share positive gossip with others. But make sure your facts are correct.

- It may be enjoyable to bond with someone temporarily through gossip. However, the damage to all parties is enormous. Resist the temptation and gain a wholesome sense of self-respect.*

* "Is Gossip Beneficial or Harmful?" by Offra Gerstein as appeared in the *Santa Cruz Sentinel*, January 18, 2004. Reprinted by permission of Offra Gerstein.

2

Vocabulary

Read the following questions about some of the vocabulary words that appear in the previous selection. Then circle the letter of the correct answer to each question.

1. "We enjoy this form of *idle* talk and are often unaware of its harm." (paragraph 1) What does *idle* mean?

   a. important

   (b.) unimportant

   c. distracting

   d. sad

2. A *confidant* (paragraph 2) is

   (a.) someone to whom one tells private information.

   b. someone to fear.

   c. someone to avoid.

   d. someone to admire.

3. If you *emulate* behavior (paragraph 5) you

   (a.) imitate it.

   b. criticize it.

   c. do not notice it.

   d. destroy it.

4. What is *malice* (paragraph 6)?

   a. conversation

   b. thirst for danger

   c. bad attitude

   (d.) desire to harm others

5. Information that is *confidential* (paragraph 8) is

   a. important.

   b. complicated.

   (c.) secret.

   d. dangerous.

Topic, Topic Sentence, and Main Ideas

Respond to each of the following questions by circling the letter of the correct answer.

1. The topic of paragraph 2 is

   a. primitive man.

   (b.) the origins of gossip.

   c. Old English.

   d. friends' sharing of information.

2. What is the topic of paragraph 6?

   (a.) bad gossip

   b. gossip researchers

c. negative talk

d. hurting others

3. What is the main idea of paragraph 7?

   (a.) Some people gossip to bond with others or to feel better about themselves.

   b. People love having a false sense of superiority.

   c. People who gossip have high self-esteem.

   d. Gossip is always bad.

4. What is the topic sentence of paragraph 8?

   (a.) the first sentence

   b. the second sentence

   c. the third sentence

   d. the fourth sentence

5. What is the main idea of paragraph 9?

   a. Gossip is fun.

   b. Gossip is destructive.

   c. Gossip makes us feel connected.

   (d.) Gossip is a way to pass the time.

Practicing the Active Reading Strategy:
After You Read

Now that you have read the selection, answer the following questions, using the active reading strategies that you learned in Chapter 1.

1. Identify and write down the point and purpose of this reading selection.

2. Besides the vocabulary words included in the exercise on page 94, are there any other vocabulary words that are unfamiliar to you? If so, write a list of them. When you have finished writing your list, look up each word in a dictionary and write the definition that best describes the word as it is used in the selection.

3. Predict any possible test questions that may be used on a test about the content of this selection.

4. How could you use the information contained in this selection? Does the information contained in the selection reinforce or contradict your ideas and experiences? Explain.

QUESTIONS FOR DISCUSSION AND WRITING

Answer the following questions based on your reading of the selection. Write your answers on the blanks provided.

1. Do you agree or disagree with the statement "Bonding with another individual brings pleasure, even when it is done at the expense of someone else"? Why? Answers will vary.

2. Do you agree that some gossip can be positive? Why or why not?
Answers will vary.

3. List any new information you learned from this selection. Did you find the selection interesting? Why or why not?
Answers will vary.

▶ Vocabulary: Synonyms

Synonyms are words that have the same, or similar, meanings. Synonyms serve four purposes in texts. First of all, they add variety to a reading selection. Instead of writing the same word over and over again, authors will use different words with the same meanings to keep sentences lively and interesting. For example, in the paragraph about the Slinky, the author refers to the Slinky as both a *toy* and a *plaything*.

Secondly, authors use synonyms to express their thoughts as precisely as possible. For example, the paragraph about protective netting for hockey stadiums refers to "the recent *tragedy*." The author could have used the word *situation* or *incident* or *misfortune*, but she used the more specific and emotional word *tragedy*, which clearly communicates how she feels about Brittanie Cecil's death.

A third use of synonyms is to connect ideas and sentences together and to reinforce ideas. Do you remember the paragraph about the reliability of websites? Notice how the italicized words are synonyms that keep the paragraph focused on the main idea:

As many as 80 percent of websites on the Internet include inaccurate information. If you're doing research, how do you make sure the information you find is **true?** You can examine certain parts of a website to evaluate its **reliability.** Websites with addresses that include *.org, .gov,* or *.edu* are usually **accurate.** Websites that give the sources of their information, too, tend to be more **trustworthy.** Also, look for identification of the site's creators as well as contact information for those people.

Finally, texts include synonyms to help readers figure out what other words mean. For example, in the sentence below, the author provides a synonym to help the reader understand what the word *inflammation* means:

Smog causes inflammation or swelling of the airway, which makes breathing more difficult.

Swelling is another way to say *inflammation,* so it's a synonym used to define a word.

Vocabulary Exercise

The following paragraphs come from examples in this chapter. On the blanks following each paragraph, write two synonyms used in the paragraph for the italicized, boldface word or phrase.

1. ***People who attend religious services*** more than once a week live seven years longer than people who never attend religious services. Spiritual people also recover more quickly from surgery. Regular church-goers are less likely to have heart disease or high blood pressure. They have lower rates of depression and anxiety, too.

   Two synonyms for italicized phrase: <u>spiritual people, regular church-goers</u>

2. Single mothers face many ***challenges.*** Their greatest difficulties are usually financial. They are the primary family breadwinners, so their greatest struggles, especially for those who are younger and less educated, often involve making ends meet. To make matters worse, single moms often do not receive regular child support from their children's fathers. They also must curtail their work hours due to childcare limitations, so many can't earn full-time wages.

   Two synonyms for italicized word: <u>difficulties, struggles</u>

3. ***Cheating*** in high school is very common. Three out of every four high school students admit to breaking the rules by cheating on a test at least once. Seventy-five percent of students have also confessed to handing in work that was completed by someone else. A quarter of all students say they've been dishonest by working with others when they were instructed to work by themselves.

   Two synonyms for italicized word: <u>breaking the rules, being dishonest</u>

4. Developing the ability to concentrate is another important study skill. Keep your mind on what you're doing and try hard to ignore distractions.

Remove the telephone and the television set, and try to eliminate any other interruptions. Find a quiet place where you'll be isolated from *things that might disturb you.* Sometimes low-level noise like instrumental music or a steady flow of traffic helps stimulate concentration. And don't try to study if you are hungry. That's a sure way to break your concentration.

Two synonyms for the italicized phrase: *distractions, interruptions*

5. An old saying in business claims that 80 percent of a company's profits come from 20 percent of its **customers.** That's why Centura Bank ranks its 650,000 customers on a scale of one to five. Those with the best ratings get better customer service. This company and others are beginning to concentrate more on their best customers. Continental Airlines, for instance, plans to give its agents access to each customer's history so they can give the best service to their top clients. First Union Bank codes its credit card customers. When a person calls for service, the bank's representatives know when they're talking to their best patrons.

Two synonyms for the italicized word: *clients, patrons*

READING STRATEGY: Creating an Effective Reading Environment

If you're like most students, you probably read both at home and outside your home: perhaps somewhere on your college campus and maybe even at work during your breaks. Your reading environment can greatly affect your comprehension, so give some thought to how you can create or select the right reading environments. The right environment allows you to stay alert and to focus all of your concentration on the text, especially when it's a challenging one.

When you're at home, you can usually create effective conditions for reading. You might want to designate a particular place—a desk or table, for example—where you always read. Make sure the place you choose is well lit, and sit in a chair that requires you to sit upright. Reading in a chair that's too soft and comfortable tends to make you sleepy! Keep your active reading tools (pens, highlighter markers, notebook or paper) and a dictionary close at hand.

Before you sit down for a reading session, try to minimize all potential external distractions. Turn off your phone, the television, and

2

the radio. Notify your family members or roommates that you'll be unavailable for a while. If necessary, put a "Do not disturb" sign on your door! The more interruptions you must deal with while you read, the harder it will be to keep your attention on the task at hand.

Overcoming internal distractions, which are the thoughts, worries, plans, daydreams, and other types of mental "noise" inside your own head, is often even more challenging for readers. However, it's important to develop strategies for dealing with them, too. If you don't, they will inhibit you from concentrating on what you are reading. Internal distractions will also prevent you from absorbing the information you need to learn. You can try to ignore these thoughts, but they will usually continue trying to intrude. So how do you temporarily silence them so you can devote your full attention to your reading? Instead of fighting them, try focusing completely on these thoughts for a short period of time. For five or ten minutes, allow yourself to sit and think about your job, your finances, your car problems, your boyfriend or girlfriend, the paper you need to write, or whatever else is on your mind. Better yet, write these thoughts down. To empty your mind onto a piece of paper, try a freewriting exercise, which involves quickly writing your thoughts on paper without censoring them or worrying about grammar and spelling. If you can't stop thinking about all of the other things you need to do, devote ten minutes to writing a detailed "To Do" list. Giving all of your attention to distracting thoughts will often clear your mind so you can focus on your reading.

If you're reading somewhere other than at home (on your college campus, for instance), it will be more difficult to achieve ideal reading conditions. However, you can still search for places that have the right characteristics. First of all, find a location—such as the library—that is well lit and quiet. Try to sit at an individual study carrel[1] so you can block out external distractions. If no carrels are available, choose a table that's out of the flow of traffic, and sit with your back to others so you're not tempted to watch their comings and goings. If you must read in a more distracting place like your college cafeteria or a bench on the grounds, you might want to get in the habit of carrying a pair of earplugs in your book bag so you can reduce external noise. Finally, don't forget to keep your active reading tools and dictionary with you so you'll have them on hand no matter where you end up reading.

Continued

1. **study carrel:** cubicle or boxed-in area
   in which to study

2

Read and answer the following questions:

1. Where were you when you read this information about creating an effective reading environment? Describe your surroundings.

   Answers will vary.

2. Is this the place where you do most of your reading? If not, where do you usually read?

   Answers will vary.

3. What external distractions pulled your attention from the book as you read?

   Answers will vary.

4. Could you have done anything to prevent these external distractions from happening?

   Answers will vary.

5. Did you battle any internal distractions as you read? Briefly describe the thoughts that intruded upon your concentration.

   Answers will vary.

6. Based on the information in this section, where could you create the most ideal environment for reading? What objects and/or procedures will you need to create that environment?

   Answers will vary.

CHAPTER 2 TESTS

Name _____ Date _____

TEST 1

A. Circle the letter of the option that puts each list of words or phrases in order from most general to most specific.

1. (1) maintaining healthy teeth
   (2) brushing teeth
      a. 1-2-4-3
      b. 4-3-1-2

   (3) daily health care
   (4) healthy habits
      c. 3-4-2-1
      d. 4-1-3-2

2. (1) facial expression
   (2) expressing emotion
      a. 4-1-3-2
      b. 3 4 2-1

   (3) showing joy
   (4) smiling
      c. 1-2-4-3
      d. 2-3-1-4

3. (1) hobby
   (2) gardening
      a. 4-1-2-3
      b. 3-1-4-2

   (3) growing vegetables
   (4) leisure activity
      c. 4-3-1-2
      d. 1-3-4-2

4. (1) former *Friends* cast member
   (2) Jennifer Aniston
      a. 1-3-2-4
      b. 4-3-1-2

   (3) entertainment personality
   (4) TV star
      c. 3-4-1-2
      d. 2-4-3-1

5. (1) BIC
   (2) writing instrument
      a. 4-2-3-1
      b. 1-3-2-4

   (3) pen
   (4) means of communication
      c. 3-2-4-1
      d. 4-1-2-3

For tests on identifying the topic sentence, see the Test Bank.

2

B. Each of the following groups of words includes one general word and three specific words. Circle the letter of the most general word in each group.

6. writing   drawing   creating   sculpting

    a. writing   (c.) creating

    b. drawing   d. sculpting

7. trumpet   instrument   flute   harp

    a. trumpet   c. flute

    (b.) instrument   d. harp

8. university   Harvard   Yale   Princeton

    (a.) university   c. Yale

    b. Harvard   d. Princeton

9. lamp   flashlight   lantern   lighting device

    a. lamp   c. lantern

    b. flashlight   (d.) lighting device

10. anger   emotion   happiness   sorrow

    a. anger   c. happiness

    (b.) emotion   d. sorrow

C. For each group of words, circle the letter of the general category that includes all the specific items listed.

11. newspaper   magazine   brochure   book

    a. reference materials   c. electronic media

    (b.) printed materials   d. free information

12. juice   soda   water   milk

    a. healthy foods   c. nutritious drinks

    b. energy sources   (d.) things to drink

13. forest green   sky blue   blood red   flaming yellow

    (a.) colors   c. rock groups

    b. places   d. landscapes

14. Christmas   Easter   Chanukah   Kwanzaa

    a. school breaks   (c.) holidays

    b. societies   d. religions

15. Russian   French   Dutch   Portuguese

    a. countries   c. plants

    b. automobiles   (d.) languages

2

D. For each general idea, circle the letter of the more specific idea that it includes.

16. General Idea: room in a house

    Specific Idea:

    a. dishwasher   c. hanger

    (b.) kitchen   d. back yard

17. General Idea: means of transportation

    Specific Idea:

    a. store   (c.) train

    b. fishing   d. reading

18. General Idea: earning money

    Specific Idea:

    a. wearing a hat   c. sleeping soundly

    b. paying an admission price   (d.) working at a job

19. General Idea: taking a photograph

    Specific Idea:

    (a.) aim the camera   c. have fun with friends

    b. walk to a beautiful spot   d. cook a meal

20. General Idea: reference sources

    Specific Idea:

    a. hardware store   c. shopping mall

    (b.) encyclopedia   d. novel

TEST 2

A. For each group of sentences, circle the letter of the option that places them in order from most general to most specific.

1. 1. Andrea regularly goes to the dentist to avoid problems with her teeth.

   2. Good dental health is an essential part of good overall health.

   3. During Andrea's last dental appointment, her dentist filled a cavity.

   4. Watching over your health is vital for achieving a happy life.

     a. 2-1-4-3   c. 3-4-2-1

     (b.) 4-2-1-3   d. 1-4-3-2

2. 1. The right windshield wiper doesn't work correctly anymore.

   2. My car has developed plenty of ailments in its old age.

   3. When you switch on the windshield wipers, the right one goes back and forth too fast.

   4. Old cars often have plenty of things that go wrong.

     a. 2-4-3-1   c. 1-2-4-3

     b. 4-1-3-2   (d.) 4-2-1-3

3. 1. In the mornings, I drink too much coffee.

   2. I have some bad habits I'd like to break.

   3. I'd like to make some improvements in my life.

   4. The caffeine leaves me feeling stressed and irritated.

     (a.) 3-2-1-4   c. 1-2-4-3

     b. 4-1-2-3   d. 3-4-2-1

4. 1. A PG-13 rating means the film contains a limited number of curse words and other exclamations.

   2. A panel of the Motion Picture Association of America assigns a movie's rating by using a formula that counts the frequency of particular words and body parts.

   3. *Behind Enemy Lines* contained, for instance, only seven mentions of the word *hell*.

2

4. For example, the movie *Behind Enemy Lines,* which contains about fifty curse words, got a PG-13 rating.

   a. 2-3-4-1   c. 2-1-4-3
   b. 1-2-3-4   d. 2-4-3-1

5. 1. In particular, Irwin routinely interacts with and handles a number of vicious predators.[1]

   2. Steve Irwin, host of TV's *The Crocodile Hunter,* works with dangerous animals.

   3. He is best known for his encounters with reptiles.

   4. On many occasions, for example, he has single-handedly caught huge, bad-tempered alligators.

   a. 2-1-3-4   c. 2-3-4-1
   b. 1-2-3-4   d. 4-3-2-1

B. Each of the following groups of sentences includes one general sentence and three specific sentences. For each group, circle the letter of the *general* sentence.

6. 1. There were many who wanted to sell magazine subscriptions.

   2. A small group wanted to sell cakes and other baked goods.

   3. For our school band's fundraiser, we decided to have a sale.

   4. Most people wanted to sell grapefruit fresh from the orchard.

   a. 1   c. 3
   b. 2   d. 4

7. 1. Mary Peterson is known for her wide selection of boots.

   2. I think more people wear sneakers than any other type of shoes.

   3. Frank Evans usually dresses casually, but he always wears black dress shoes with tassels.

   4. There's no dress code at our office, so people wear all kinds of shoes.

   a. 1   c. 3
   b. 2   d. 4

1. **predators:** meat-eating animals

2

8. 1. *Hard skills* are the special knowledge one needs to perform a particular job.

   2. All nurses need good nursing skills such as knowing how and where to insert an intravenous[1] feeding tube.

   3. A lawyer must possess legal skills such as knowing what the current inheritance laws are.

   4. An accountant must be familiar with how to complete a tax return.*

     (a.) 1   c. 3

     b. 2   d. 4

9. 1. Juan liked the excitement, the culture, and the crowds of the city.

   2. Juan and Marie wanted to settle down and buy a house.

   3. Marie favored the comforts and convenience of the suburbs.

   4. Both of them found that the simple, quiet beauty of the countryside was the best choice of all.

     a. 1   c. 3

     (b.) 2   d. 4

10. 1. The kids clean up and vacuum their rooms and change their beds.

    2. Frederick vacuums the rest of the house and cleans the bathrooms.

    3. Winona dusts the entire house and polishes the furniture.

    4. One day a week, the entire family does their cleaning chores.

      a. 1   c. 3

      b. 2   (d.) 4

C. For each item, read the three specific sentences given. Then circle the letter of the general sentence best supported by those three specific sentences.

11. The most appealing and most expensive option was tile.

   A cheaper and quite practical choice was linoleum.

   It was also possible to leave the carpeting that was already there.

---

1. intravenous: inserted into a vein

---

* Adapted from Skip Downing, *On Course,* 4th ed. (Boston: Houghton Mifflin Co., 2005), 15.

General Sentences:

a. While renovating their new house, Sally and Bob had many arguments over how much space they needed.

b. Sally wanted to add two new rooms to the house as an extension to the kitchen.

(c.) Sally and Bob were having a hard time deciding on what to use for their new kitchen floor.

d. Bob was against the addition of two new rooms because he liked having a large back yard.

12. Seventy percent of Americans have watched a movie starring Elvis Presley, and 44 percent have danced to an Elvis song.

When it comes to purchasing Elvis-related products, 31 percent of Americans have bought Elvis records, CDs, and videos.

One in ten Americans (10 percent) has visited Graceland, Elvis's home, and 34 percent (72 million people) have seen an Elvis impersonator.[1]*

General sentences:

a. Elvis Presley was the most popular entertainer who ever lived.

b. Elvis Presley is more popular now than when he was alive.

(c.) Elvis Presley has touched the lives of millions of Americans.

d. Elvis Presley was a talented singer and actor.

13. Margie is allergic to eggs.

Terrence is allergic to lactose.

Susan is allergic to cat dander.

General Sentences:

a. Margie should never have eggs for breakfast.

(b.) My friends suffer from different types of allergies.

c. Cat dander is a common allergy.

d. Allergies can be annoying.

1. **impersonator:** someone who imitates someone else

* Adapted from Joy Marie Sever, "Elvis Presley Has Touched the Lives of The Vast Majority of Americans," *Harris Interactive,* August 12, 2002, www.harrisinteractive.com/harris_poll/index.asp?PID=317.

14. The company that made my computer told me that it was a software problem and that I should call the software company.

    I called the company that made my software, but a representative said it was a hardware problem.

    When I called my Internet service provider, a service person said there was probably a problem with my telephone connection.

    General Sentences:

    a. The company that made my computer has excellent technical support.

    b. My computer has generally been working well, so this problem doesn't bother me.

    c. I think my Internet service provider had the correct solution.

    (d) Each person I called for help gave me a different opinion about the problem's source.

15. Gayle canceled her cell phone service and paid all she owed, but the phone company keeps sending her more bills.

    When Gayle calls the phone company, the customer service people are always polite and always say they have solved the problem.

    Every time a customer service person says that Gayle owes the company nothing, Gayle receives another bill the following week.

    General Sentences:

    (a.) The phone company has well-meaning customer service people but a terrible billing system.

    b. Gayle should never have canceled her cell phone service.

    c. The phone company has a policy of continuing to bill its customers in hopes that these customers will eventually reinstate their service.

    d. The phone company's customer service people choose not to help those who cancel their phone service.

D. For each item, read the general sentence and then circle the letter of the three specific sentences that explain or support that statement.

16. General Sentence: Gas-electric "hybrid" cars like the Toyota Prius and Honda Insight are better than other automobiles.

    Specific Sentences:

    1. Their exhaust is less polluting than that of other cars.

    2. The Honda Insight is not the ideal trip or family car.

3. These cars combine an internal-combustion engine with an electric motor.

4. It is as much fun to drive these cars as it is to drive conventional cars.

5. They deliver exceptional gas mileage.

6. They are less expensive than other vehicles to operate and maintain.

7. Both the Prius and Insight come in a wide variety of colors.*

    a. 1, 4, 7   c. 3, 4, 7

    b. 2, 3, 6   (d.) 1, 5, 6

17. General Sentence: Martial arts training offers many benefits.

Specific Sentences:

1. Learning a martial art will improve your physical fitness.

2. Some martial arts use swords, spears, staffs, and other weapons.

3. The martial arts teach useful self-defense techniques that will allow you to protect yourself during a street confrontation or attack.

4. Martial arts training fosters mental, emotional, and spiritual development.

5. Martial arts traditions are thousands of years old.

6. Some martial arts are called "hard" because they use direct force while others are termed "soft" because they use the redirection of force.

7. Karate, Kung Fu, Aikido, and Tae Kwon Do are all different types of martial arts.

    (a.) 1, 3, 4   c. 4, 6, 7

    b. 2, 4, 6   d. 2, 3, 7

18. General Sentence: Before you begin to paint a room, you have to make sure the room is prepared for painting.

Specific Sentences:

1. Have a good meal and get plenty of rest before you begin painting.

2. Take off the covers from all heating–air conditioning ducts to protect them from splattering paint.

3. Turn off the electricity to the room.

* Adapted from Ralph Kinney Bennett, "Lean, Green Driving Machines," *Reader's Digest*, December 2001, 86.

4. If you're new at painting, start with a small, out-of-the-way room.

5. Make sure the colors you select for the room will work well with the rest of your home.

6. Remove all nails, screws, and picture hangers from surfaces to be painted.

7. Wear gloves and old clothes you won't mind getting full of paint.

   a. 3, 5, 7   c. 2, 4, 5

   b. 1, 2, 6   (d.) 2, 3, 6

19. General Sentence: Doing the wrong thing is becoming more common nationally.

Specific Sentences:

1. The 2002 Ethics of American Youth survey found that three out of four high school students admitted to having cheated on at least one test during the previous year.

2. Thirty-eight percent of students taking the survey acknowledged stealing something from a store.

3. Teachers see no increase in classroom cheating incidents.

4. Thirty-seven percent of students taking the Ethics of American Youth survey said that they would lie in order to get a good job.

5. Many adults do not think it is acceptable to cheat on one's income taxes.

6. Millions of young people do volunteer work for charities.

7. Cheating is not a crime.*

   (a.) 1, 2, 4   c. 2, 4, 6

   b. 1, 3, 4   d. 3, 4, 5

TEST 3

A. Read each paragraph and then circle the letter of the correct topic.

1. A website might be thought of as a special type of publication. In some cases, the entire contents of an individual website are contributed by the Web author. In other instances, a website consists of some material

* Adapted from Katy Kelly, "Parents in a Haze?" *U.S. News and World Report,* May 26, 2003, 44.

2

developed by the Web author and connections to other resources found on computers throughout the Internet. A Web user does not have to keep track of who authored what in the website. The user simply follows links embedded[1] within the content of webpages from one topic of interest to another.*

Topic:

a. publications

(b.) websites

c. the World Wide Web

d. links in websites

2. Here are some reasons for attending college that you may or may not have considered. In the courses you will take, you will be exposed to new ideas, beliefs, and ways of looking at the world. At times, you will be excited by what you are learning; at other times, you will be frustrated by opinions and values that challenge your own. A college education can help you develop a flexible and open mind, sharpen your ability to think, and enrich your life. Best of all, you may discover in yourself talents, skills, and interests that you did not know you possessed.†

Topic:

a. college courses

b. educational challenges

(c.) reasons for attending college

d. talents, skill, and interests

3. If you're like me, you probably have one or two really close friends and a lot of great acquaintances. But that's good because that's what you need. According to Dr. John Litwac of the University of Massachusetts Medical Center, people in modern society require a variety of friends to meet their needs. And the variety of friends we need varies over time. What Dr. Litwac says in a book, *Adult Friendships,* is that the friendships we enjoy when we are young differ a lot from those we experience as we grow older. As we develop, so does the complexity and intimacy of our relationships.‡

(a.) friendships

b. experience

c. modern society

d. complexity

1. embedded: enclosed; part of

---

* Adapted from Mark Grabe and Cindy Grabe, *Integrating Technology for Meaningful Learning* (Boston: Houghton Mifflin Co., 1998), 204.

† Adapted from Carol C. Kanar, *The Confident Student,* 5th ed. (Boston: Houghton Mifflin Co., 2004), 91.

‡ From Michael Osborn and Suzanne Osborn, *Public Speaking* (Boston: Houghton Mifflin Co., 2000), 356.

2

4. A routine trip to the family doctor may be a lot different in the near future. Patients will be able to go online and schedule their own appointments. They will be able to opt for[1] group visits with nurse educators and other patients during which they can swap tips for managing illnesses such as diabetes or asthma. Their doctors will tap into a national database of evidence-based medical guidelines which will be regularly updated with medical findings relevant to family practice. In the same visit, patients will meet with nutritionists, psychologists, or health coaches. Or patients with routine questions may skip the office visit altogether by e-mailing their doctor or nurse.*

a. doctors   c. nurses

(b.) innovations in health care   d. managing illnesses

5. I can accept that many people take fashion seriously, but I have never been a fashion buff. To me, dressing in style is pointless. I can, however, accept that many people love to dress in style, but there is one particular fashion "statement" that totally baffles[2] me. I mean, specifically, wearing a fashionable watch. To me, it is beyond comprehension that multitudes pay hundreds or thousands of dollars for their watches. My watch cost me $13.00. It keeps accurate time, and it has a stopwatch, an alarm, and when I want it, a very good light for telling the time in the dark. My watch may not be "stylish," but I suppose you could say it's part of how I "dress in style."

a. fashion statements   c. fashionable watches

(b.) dressing in style   d. watches

B. For each item, decide whether the topic listed for the paragraph is too broad, too narrow, or the correct topic for the paragraph. Circle the letter of the correct answer.

6. Why do people dance? The urge springs from the same desire to express that motivates the other arts, but the medium[3] is the most accessible[4]— the human body. Dancing is in a sense "body language." We have all felt the need to express fear, sorrow, anger, love, and joy with gesture and

---

1. **opt for:** choose
2. **baffles:** confuses
3. **medium:** means of communication or expression
4. **accessible:** easily obtained or used

---

* Adapted from Liz Szabo, "Doctors Heal the System, "*USA Today,* March 31, 2004, 8D.

with movement. One can express an emotion in movement before it can be put into words and also gesture feelings beyond the limits of words.*

Topic: How people express themselves

a. too broad   c. the correct topic

b. too narrow

2

7. Education significantly increases an individual's earning power. According to a recent study by the Employment Policy Foundation, someone without a high school diploma can anticipate average lifetime earnings of $872,396. But a person with a high school diploma can expect lifetime earnings of $1,204,343. A person who has completed some college can expect $1,363,031, and a person with a bachelor's degree can expect to earn $2,043,889. An individual who completes a master's degree will earn an average of $2,402,929. A professional degree raises the total to $2,910,720.†

Topic: Lifetime earnings of people with college degrees

a. too broad   c. the correct topic

b. too narrow

8. Otto von Bismarck (1815–1898), the most important figure in German history between Luther[1] and Hitler,[2] has been the object of enormous interest and debate. A great hero to some, a great villain to others, Bismarck was above all a master of politics. Bismarck had a strong personality and an unbounded desire for power. Yet in his drive to secure power for himself and for Prussia, Bismarck was extraordinarily flexible and pragmatic.[3] He kept his options open, pursuing one policy and then another as he moved with skill and cunning toward his goal.‡

Topic: Otto von Bismarck

a. too broad   c. the correct topic

b. too narrow

1. **Luther:** a fifteenth and sixteenth-century German theologian
2. **Hitler:** a despicable twentieth-century German dictator
3. **pragmatic:** practical

* From Mary Ann Frese Witt et al., *The Humanities,* Vol. II (Boston: Houghton Mifflin Co., 1997), 181.
† Adapted from Skip Downing, *On Course,* 4th ed. (Boston: Houghton Mifflin Co., 2005), 101.
‡ Adapted from John P. McKay et al., *A History of World Societies,* Vol. II (Boston: Houghton Mifflin Co., 1996), 834.

9. Today's obese American child is prone to diseases potentially more dangerous than scurvy[1] and rickets,[2] which were routinely diagnosed in malnourished children a century ago. Conditions once seen exclusively in adults, such as type-2 diabetes and hypertension, now show up in adolescents and preteens. A study in 2003 by the American Academy of Pediatrics' Center for Child Health Research found that at least 4 percent of adolescents and almost 30 percent of overweight adolescents have developed "metabolic syndrome"—a condition that makes them susceptible to[3] premature heart disease. Other research links obesity in children to higher rates of depression and suicide.*

Topic: Children

(a.) too broad   c. correct topic

b. too narrow

10. Noise can increase the secretion of adrenaline[4] in humans, perhaps because our distant ancestors associated loud sounds, like a lion's roar or a baby's scream, with danger. The greater the sound, the greater the adrenaline rush. Dr. Les Blomberg theorizes that racetracks try to be as loud as possible because the noise excites the fans. "That's why exercise classes crank up the decibels,[5] and rock bands, and action movies," he observes. "In effect, noise becomes a drug they're pumping out and into you."†

Topic: Noise

a. too broad   (c.) correct topic

b. too narrow

C. Read each paragraph and circle the letter of the main idea.

11. That ache in your spine could be an infection. Researchers at the Royal Orthopaedic Hospital in Birmingham, England, found that a surprising number of patients with sciatica—pain extending from the back into the

1. **scurvy:** disease caused by lack of vitamin C

2. **rickets:** disease caused by lack of vitamin D

3. **susceptible to:** likely to be affected by

4. **adrenaline:** hormone produced in response to stress

5. **decibels:** units for measuring sound

---

* Adapted from Suzanne Leigh, "Too Much Food, Not Too Little, Plagues U.S. Children," *USA Today,* March 10, 2004, 13A.

† Adapted from Richard Wolkomir and Joyce Wolkomir, "Noise Busters," *Smithsonian,* March 2001, 99.

2

legs—had infectious microorganisms in the area of the sciatic nerve. In one group, 43 of 140 people had the bacteria; among 36 patients with severe sciatica, 19 carried the bug. The researchers theorize[1] that some cases of lower-back pain are actually chronic low-grade infections and that these occur when microscopic tears in spinal disks allow the organisms entry.*

Main Idea:

a. There is a research lab at the Royal Orthopaedic Hospital in Birmingham, England.

b. Sciatica is pain extending from the back into the legs.

(c.) Lower back pain is sometimes the result of an infection.

d. Out of 36 patients with severe sciatica, 19 carried infectious microorganisms.

12. Genetic engineering[2] can do remarkable things to flowering of plants. Not everyone agrees it's desirable to fool Mother Nature this way, but there's no denying the potential significance of the results. Getting a plant to flower even slightly earlier or later than normal can extend the geographical range of a particularly favored variety. Fast flowering also means faster breeding.†

Main Idea:

a. Not everyone agrees that genetic engineering should be used on plants.

(b.) Genetic engineering can remarkably affect the flowering of plants.

c. Flowering even slightly earlier can mean faster plant breeding.

d. You can extend the geographical range of a particularly favored variety.

13. Emergency medical services in many cities have begun advising 911 callers to give a person who has collapsed chest compressions but *not* mouth-to-mouth resuscitation.[3] In emergencies, lives are generally saved

1. **theorize:** speculate; propose to be true

2. **genetic engineering:** altering the basic material in living organisms

3. **resuscitation:** bringing back to consciousness

---

* Adapted from John O'Neill, as quoted in the *New York Times*, "Bacterial Back Pain," *Reader's Digest,* January 2002, 48.

† Adapted from Rosie Mestel, "Rhythm and Blooms," *Natural History,* June, 2000, 74.

2

or lost in the first six minutes, so trying to explain mouth-to-mouth procedures to callers was wasting precious time and doing more harm than good. In addition, new research suggests that mouth-to-mouth resuscitation is not effective in the first few minutes after a collapse. Therefore, emergency medical dispatchers are explaining to untrained callers only how to perform chest compressions to mimic[1] a steady heartbeat until paramedics can arrive.*

Main Idea:

(a.) Many emergency medical services dispatchers are no longer explaining to callers how to give a victim mouth-to-mouth resuscitation.

b. Emergency medical services are advising people not to try to save someone who has collapsed.

c. Mouth-to-mouth resuscitation is very difficult to perform properly.

d. Research has shown that mouth-to-mouth resuscitation does more harm than good.

14. Many fast-food burgers are loaded with calories. The Hardee's Two-thirds Pound Double Bacon Cheeseburger has 1,301 calories. That number is between 46 and 81 percent of the recommended number of calories an adult should consume in an entire day. Jack in the Box's Bacon Ultimate Cheeseburger contains, 1,120 calories, or 40 to 70 percent of an adult's recommended maximum calories. And Burger King's Double Whopper with Cheese has 1,060 calories, or 38 to 66 percent of the calories one should eat in a day.†

Main Idea:

a. Many fast-food restaurants specialize in burgers.

b. Hardee's Two-thirds Pound Double Bacon Cheeseburger is the biggest hamburger sold at any fast-food restaurant.

c. Americans eat too many calories in a day.

(d.) Several fast-food burgers have a lot of calories in them.

15. President Franklin Delano Roosevelt recognized the importance of radio for informing the nation and embarked[2] on a series of radio talks to

---

1. **mimic:** copy or imitate   2. **embarked:** began

---

* Adapted from Robert Davis, "Simpler Method for CPR Adopted," *USA Today,* February 24, 2004, 1A.

† Adapted from Jeff Elder, "Which Burgers Have the Most Calories?" *Charlotte Observer,* March 31, 2004, 2A.

promote his administration's policies. The popular broadcasts became known as "fireside chats." Roosevelt delivered thirty-one fireside chats over the radio during his thirteen years as president. Historians agree that the chats reassured Americans during the Great Depression,[1] and mobilized[2] them to fight Japan and Germany during World War II.*

Main Idea:

a. Radio is an important method of informing the nation.

b. President Roosevelt's "fireside chats" were a popular and effective use of radio.

c. Americans needed reassurance during the Great Depression.

d. During Franklin Roosevelt's thirteen years as president, he delivered thirty-one "fireside chats."

D. Read each paragraph and then circle the letter of the main idea.

16. In calculating report card grades, teachers do not evaluate students based on a single test or sample of performance. Combining several trustworthy scores from several different tests will increase the reliability substantially. Teachers base grades on points accumulated[3] from a variety of sources. Therefore, the final grade is likely to be reliable even though a single test may not be.†

Main Idea:

a. Teachers combine a variety of trustworthy scores in calculating reliable report card grades.

b. Teachers often use a single major test as a reliable guide for calculating report card grades.

c. There are many different methods teachers use to calculate report card grades.

d. When scores are accumulated from a variety of sources, teachers often discard the highest and lowest scores.

1. **Great Depression:** period of poverty and job losses lasting from 1929 to World War

2. **mobilized:** assembled

3. **accumulated:** gathered

* Adapted from Joseph Turow, *Media Today* (Boston: Houghton Mifflin Co., 1999), 178.

† From Sharon J. Sherman, *Science and Science Teaching* (Boston: Houghton Mifflin Co., 2000), 183.

2

17. A composer's working methods are unique to his personality. Some composers are fluent[1] and fast: Rossini, it is said, preferred rewriting a page to
picking up a leaf of manuscript fallen to the floor, and Mozart appears to
have been able to keep the totality of a work in his mind's ear at every turning point. Beethoven worked with great difficulty; Mahler revised compulsively,[2] forever tinkering with bass drum strokes and cymbal crashes.*

Main Idea:

a. Beethoven worked with great difficulty.

b. Some composers work quickly, seemingly without effort.

(c.) Every composer has unique working methods.

d. Mozart could keep track of several musical parts simultaneously.

18. Earth's origins lie in the creation of the universe. Just how this came
about remains unclear, but many scientists accept some version of the
"big bang" theory, which goes like this. At first all energy and matter
(then only subatomic[3] particles) were closely concentrated. About 15,000
million years ago, a vast explosion scattered everything through space.
Star studies prove the universe is still expanding, and background radiation hints at its initial heat.†

Main Idea:

a. The universe is still expanding.

b. Some scientists do not accept the "big bang" theory.

c. Energy and matter were at first subatomic materials that were closely
concentrated.

(d.) Many scientists accept the "big bang" theory of the universe's origins.

19. The War of 1812 saw the birth of an American icon:[4] "Uncle Sam." He appears to have arisen in 1813 in Troy, New York, but little more than that is

1. **fluent:** expressing oneself easily
2. **compulsively:** obsessively
3. **subatomic:** relating to the parts of an atom, the smallest unit of an element
4. **icon:** image or symbol

* Adapted from D. Kern Holoman, *Masterworks: A Musical Discovery* (New York: Prentice-Hall, 1998), 7.
† From David Lambert and the Diagram Group, *The Field Guide to Geology* (New York: Facts on File, 1988), 16.

2

known. The inspiration for Uncle Sam is sometimes traced to one Samuel Wilson, an army inspector in Troy, but it seems more probable[1] that the name was merely derived from the initials *U. S.* The top-hatted, striped-trousered figure we associate with the name was popularized in the 1860s in the cartoons of Thomas Nast and later reinforced by the famous I WANT YOU recruiting posters of the artist James Montgomery Flagg.*

Main Idea:

(a.) "Uncle Sam" possibly originated in 1813 and was later popularized by Thomas Nast and James Montgomery Flagg.

b. Americans first saw "Uncle Sam" in the top-hatted, striped-trousered cartoon figure created by Thomas Nast in the 1860s.

c. Samuel Wilson, an army inspector in Troy, was definitely the inspiration for the original "Uncle Sam."

d. It is possible that the American icon "Uncle Sam" was merely derived from the initials *U. S.*

20. By 1066, the English social system was elaborate and stable. There were many strata.[2] At the bottom were serfs or slaves; next cottagers or cottars; then villeins, who farmed as much perhaps as fifty acres; then thanes, who drew rents in kind from the villeins; then earls, each ruling one of the six great earldoms that covered the country; and above all, the king.†

Main Idea:

a. There were six ruling English earldoms in 1066.

b. In 1066, villeins were people who farmed perhaps as many as fifty acres.

(c.) The English social system in 1066 was stable and had many strata.

d. At the top of the entire English social system in 1066 was the king.

1. probable: likely   **2. strata:** levels

---

* Adapted from Bill Bryson, *Made in America* (New York: Avon Books, 1994), 65.
† Adapted from David Howarth, *1066* (New York: Penguin, 1977), 14.

CHAPTER 3
Supporting Details, Mapping, and Outlining

GOALS FOR CHAPTER 3

▶ Define the terms *major details* and *minor details.*

▶ Recognize major and minor details in paragraphs.

▶ Define the term *transitions.*

▶ Locate transitions that often identify major details and minor details.

▶ Recognize transitions in paragraphs.

▶ Use mapping to show major and minor details in a paragraph.

▶ Use outlining to show major and minor details in a paragraph.

▶ Describe the principles of effective time management.

In the previous chapter, you practiced finding the main idea of a paragraph. The main idea is the general point the writer wants you to know or to believe when you've finished reading the paragraph. Often, though, readers cannot understand or accept this point as true unless they get more information. The **supporting details** in a paragraph provide this information.

Before continuing, take this test to find out what you already know about supporting details.

TEST YOURSELF

Identify the main idea and write it on the blank following each paragraph. Then, choose one sentence that offers a *major* detail to support that main idea. Write the number of that sentence in the blank below your main idea statement.

3

1. (1) The United States is home to many highly regarded universities with an African-American tradition. (2) From a shanty[1] and church in rural Alabama, African-American visionary Booker T. Washington built the future Tuskegee Institute, which has been around for 120 years. (3) Another example, Howard University, in Washington, D.C., is the largest of these schools. (4) It has a fine reputation as an educational institution. (5) Nashville is the home to Fisk, which was founded in 1866. (6) Fisk is noted for having W. E. B. DuBois[2] among its graduates. (7) And finally, the state of Georgia has Morehouse University, whose graduates include Martin Luther King Jr.,[3] and Spike Lee.[4]*

Main Idea: _The United States is home to many highly regarded universities with an African-American tradition._

Major Supporting Detail: _Sentence 2, 3, 5 or 7 (Answers will vary.)_

2. (1) There are certain things you should do to keep children safe around cars in warm weather. (2) First, teach children not to play in, on, or around cars. (3) Second, never leave a child or pet unattended in a motor vehicle, even with the window slightly open. (4) Car temperatures can rise to 122 degrees within 20 minutes and 150 degrees within 40 minutes on a hot day. (5) Always lock car doors and trunks—even at home—and keep keys out of children's reach. (6) And finally, watch children closely around cars, particularly when loading or unloading. (7) Check to ensure that all children leave the vehicle when you reach your destination. (8) Don't overlook sleeping infants. (9) Following all of these suggestions will ensure safety when it comes to children and automobiles in hot weather.†

Main Idea: _There are certain things you should do to keep children safe around cars in warm weather._

Major Supporting Detail: _Sentence 2, 3, 5 or 6 (Answers will vary.)_

1. **shanty:** old, dilapidated dwelling or home
2. **W.E.B. DuBois:** American civil rights leader
3. **Martin Luther King Jr.:** American civil rights leader
4. **Spike Lee:** American film director

* Adapted from "Don't Know Much About Historically Black Colleges," *USA Weekend,* July 6–8, 2001, 14.

† Adapted from Cathy Elcik, "Summer Safety: Kids and Cars Don't Mix," *Westchester Family,* July 2001, 24.

3. (1) The benefits of walking go well beyond the purely physical. (2) More than any other activity, walking is a sure way to jump-start the brain, set thoughts in motion, and calm our troubles. (3) Prompted by our modest exertions,[1] just a few minutes into a walk the body begins to produce endorphins, chemical compounds that reduce pain and stress and enhance memory and judgment as they course through the brain. (4) Walking also produces increased levels of serotonin, an important brain neurotransmitter that increases feelings of well-being. (5) For this reason, doctors recommend walking as a treatment for mild depression and anxiety.*

Main Idea: _The benefits of walking go well beyond the purely physical._

Major Supporting Detail: _Sentence 2, 3, or 4 (Answers will vary.)_

4. (1) Jack Lemmon was one of the finest, funniest, and most popular movie actors of the second half of the last century. (2) He was a middle-class Everyman forever tugging at his collar. (3) His shoulders hunched in anticipation of trouble on the way, and his smile was more nervous than an expression of pleasure. (4) Lemmon represented the white-collar American male, always having problems, but lovable. (5) People loved him because his characters were never larger than life; they were people most Americans could identify with.†

Main Idea: _Jack Lemmon was one of the finest, funniest, and most popular movie actors of the second half of the last century._

Major Supporting Detail: _Sentence 2, 4, or 5 (Answers will vary.)_

5. (1) If you live with a chronic[2] snorer, take a hard look at his habits. (2) Some simple changes could stop a snoring problem for good. (3) For example, being overweight is the most common cause of snoring, so if you can get your bedmate to take off a few pounds, the snoring may become less frequent. (4) Also, don't allow your bedmate to drink alcohol before going to bed, as that can increase the frequency of snoring during the night. (5) Sleeping on the back is another cause of snoring. (6) And finally, encourage your bedmate to quit if he smokes cigarettes; smoking is known as a leading cause of snoring in addition to being an unhealthy habit.‡

1. **exertions:** efforts

2. **chronic:** happening over and over again

* Adapted from Gregory McNamee, "Wandering Soles," *Modern Maturity,* September/October 2001, 76.
† Adapted from David Ansen, "Nobody's Perfect, but Some Get Close," *Newsweek,* July 9, 2001, 61.
‡ Adapted from Ellie McGrath, "How to Sleep with a Snorer," *Good Housekeeping,* May 2000, 64–68.

Main Idea: _Some simple changes can stop a snoring problem for good._

Major Supporting Detail: _Sentence 3, 4, 5, or 6 (Answers will vary.)_

Supporting details are the specific facts, statistics, examples, steps, anecdotes, reasons, descriptions, definitions, and so on that explain or prove the general main idea stated in the topic sentence. They support, or provide a solid foundation for, this main idea.

Supporting details should answer all of the questions raised by the topic sentence. For example, read the following statement:

> Female surgeons are treated differently from male surgeons by their colleagues, nurses, and patients.

This topic sentence immediately raises the questions *how* and *why* in the reader's mind. To answer the questions, the paragraph must go on to offer the reasons and other explanations that prove this point.

As you read this next paragraph, notice how the supporting details clarify the main idea, which is in boldface, and explain why it's true.

> **If you want to become rich, you must follow four important rules.** The first rule is to establish a reasonable income base. To reach and maintain that stable, middle-income base, you should earn a college degree, marry someone with an equal or higher education and stay married, and work as long as you are able to. The second rule for becoming rich is to avoid frivolous temptations. For example, don't drive expensive luxury cars; instead, buy medium-priced cars. Following rule #2 will allow you to save more money, which is rule #3. Average people who become rich often do so because they save more of their money, even if they must make sacrifices to do so. Finally, the fourth rule to becoming rich is take advantage of compound interest. If you invested $2,000 every year from age 22 to age 65 and that money earned 10 percent interest per year, you'd have over a million dollars when you retired.*

The topic sentence of this paragraph raises the question *What are these rules for becoming rich?* Then, the paragraph goes on to answer that question by explaining the four things you must do to increase your wealth. The reader would not be able to understand the topic sentence without reading the

---

* Adapted from Richard B. McKenzie and Dwight R. Lee, "Becoming Wealthy: It's Up to You," *USA Today,* September 1998, 16–19.

details in the rest of the paragraph. It's important to learn to recognize supporting details, for they determine your understanding and interpretation of what you read.

Major and Minor Details

There are two kinds of supporting details: major details and minor details. The **major details** are the main points that explain or support the idea in the topic sentence. They offer *essential* reasons or other information that the reader must have in order to understand the main idea.

Minor details offer more explanation of the major details. Minor details are not usually critical to the reader's comprehension of the main idea, though they do offer more specific information that helps clarify even more the points in the paragraph.

To see the difference between major and minor details, read the following paragraph:

> **Many Americans believe in the supernatural.** For one thing, they believe in supernatural beings. A recent Gallup poll revealed that 69 percent of people believe in angels, half of them believe they have their own guardian angels, and 48 percent believe that there are aliens in outer space. Americans also believe in the existence of supernatural powers. For example, over 10 million people have called the Psychic Friends network to get advice about their present and future.*

The topic sentence of this paragraph, which is in boldface, raises the question *What kinds of supernatural things do they believe in?* The second and fourth sentences of the paragraph answer that question. They tell the reader that Americans believe in supernatural beings and supernatural powers. The other sentences in the paragraph offer minor details. In this case, the minor details offer examples of the kinds of beings and powers people believe are real. Therefore, they offer nonessential information that helps explain the main idea even more.

Remember the explanation of general and specific sentences back in Chapter 2? You learned that the topic sentence is the most general statement in a paragraph while the other sentences offer more specific information. Well, these other sentences (the supporting details) are also related to each other in general and specific ways. It might be helpful to visualize these relationships in a diagram form as shown at the top of the next page.

* Adapted from Jill Neimark, "Do the Spirits Move You?" *Psychology Today,* September 19, 1996, 48.

```
                    ┌─────────────────────────────┐
                    │  Many Americans believe     │
                    │  in the supernatural.       │
                    │                             │
        ┌───────────┴─────────────┬───────────────┴──────────────┐
        │ For one thing, they     │ Americans also believe in    │
        │ believe in              │ the existence of             │
        │ supernatural beings.    │ supernatural powers.         │
        ├─────────────────────────┼──────────────────────────────┤
        │ A recent Gallup poll    │ For example, over 10 million │
        │ revealed that           │ people have called the       │
        │ 69 percent of people    │ Psychic Friends network to   │
        │ believe in angels,      │ get advice about their       │
        │ half of them believe    │ present and future.          │
        │ they have their own     │                              │
        │ guardian angels, and    │                              │
        │ 48 percent believe that │                              │
        │ there are aliens in     │                              │
        │ outer space.            │                              │
        └─────────────────────────┴──────────────────────────────┘
```

This diagram offers a useful visual image of the general and specific relationships among sentences in paragraphs. The major details—represented in the blocks beneath the topic sentence—provide the solid foundation of support for the main idea. You could not remove any of these blocks without significantly weakening the base on which the main idea rests. The minor details in the next row of blocks make the structure even sturdier. Though the main idea would still be supported by the major details even if the minor details were removed, the minor details make the whole base even stronger.

To better understand what you read, you may want to try to visualize the sentences in a diagram like the one above. Sorting out these relationships is critical not only to comprehending a paragraph but also to deciding whether or not you can agree with the author's ideas.

Exercise 3.1

Read the following paragraphs and then label the list of sentences that follow as MI for main idea, MAJOR for major detail, or MINOR for minor detail.

1. (1) Walkie-talkies are becoming a fashionable way for families to stay in touch during outings at places like malls and amusement parks. (2) One reason for walkie-talkies' popularity is their low cost. (3) Cell phones charge monthly fees, but walkie-talkies cost an average of just $35 each, with no extra fees beyond the cost of batteries. (4) Another reason more parents and children are using walkie-talkies is their ease of use. (5) You don't have to dial a number; you just push a button to talk and release it to listen.*

* Adapted from Leonard Wiener, "Hello? Can You Hear Me? Walkie-Talkies Are the Rage," *U.S. News and World Report Online*, July 2, 2001, www.usnews.com/usnews/issue/010702/tech/walkie.htm.

<u>MI</u>   Sentence 1

<u>MAJOR</u> Sentence 2

<u>MINOR</u> Sentence 3

2. (1) Doctors now have several new treatments that alter the soft palate (the roof of the mouth) and help quiet nighttime snoring. (2) In one procedure, a form of microwave energy is used under local anesthesia to scar and shrink the soft tissue in the back of the throat so that it vibrates less. (3) Another new treatment involves injecting a substance into the palate to chemically scar the tissue. (4) If you don't want the back of your throat burned, then a third option is having three small polyester inserts placed in the soft palate to make it stiffer and less prone to vibrate.*

<u>MI</u>   Sentence 1

<u>MAJOR</u> Sentence 3

<u>MAJOR</u> Sentence 4

3. (1) Learning to ride a motorcycle can be a very difficult thing to do. (2) First, balancing yourself on two wheels can be frightening, especially since if you fall, a thousand-pound machine can land on top of you! (3) It is also hard to manage the coordination between the gear shift and the gas pedal, although Harley Davidson makes a motorcycle that is easier to handle than most. (4) It can be a little intimidating, too, to ride a motorcycle on a major highway with cars going past you at 60 miles an hour. (5) It is fun, however, to feel the wind whipping through your hair as you ride.

<u>MI</u>   Sentence 1

<u>MAJOR</u> Sentence 2

<u>MAJOR</u> Sentence 3

4. (1) You can become a good writer if you put your mind to it. (2) The best thing to do if you want to learn to write well is to write every day. (3) Writing every day increases confidence in your skills, so you should set aside time in your schedule every day to write for fun, for school, or just for practice. (4) You should also make sure that you have a good, quiet place to write as that can increase your concentration.

* Adapted from Daniel K. Hoh, "Sound (Free) Sleep," ABCNEWS.com, April 8, 2004, www.abcnews.go.com/sections/Living/GoodMorningAmerica/snoring_treatments_040408.htm.

<u>MI</u>   Sentence 1

<u>MAJOR</u> Sentence 2

<u>MINOR</u> Sentence 3

5. (1) Working with a personal trainer is a good way to begin an exercise program. (2) Personal trainers will make sure that you are in good enough health to start exercising and will tailor a program to fit your fitness level, your body type, and your schedule. (3) Furthermore, you will see results faster if you work with a trainer. (4) A trainer will encourage you to stick with your program and make it harder for you to quit.

<u>MI</u>   Sentence 1

<u>MAJOR</u> Sentence 3

<u>MINOR</u> Sentence 4

Exercise 3.2

Read each paragraph and write an abbreviated form of each sentence in the boxes that follow to indicate their general and specific relationships.

1. Since she discovered tennis at the age of 10, Zina Garrison has encountered extraordinary, inspiring people at tennis camps and in early matches. Althea Gibson, the first great African-American tennis player, taught her about the physical and mental requirements for becoming a professional. Arthur Ashe[1] taught her about a slice backhand and dedication to the sport. Once she had made the choice to be dedicated,

Since she discovered...		
Althea Gibson, the first great African-American...	Arthur Ashe taught her about...	Once she had made that choice, Motown's...
		"No matter what," he said...

1. **Arthur Ashe:** another great African-American tennis player

3

Motown's Berry Gordy taught her about grace under pressure. "No matter what," he said, "win like a champion, lose like a champion."*

2. There are at least five important elements in the American view of the political system. The first is liberty. Americans believe they should be free to do pretty much as they please, with some exceptions, as long as they don't hurt other people. The second element is equality. Americans believe everybody should have an equal vote and an equal chance to participate and succeed. Democracy is the third element. Americans think government officials should be accountable to the people. Fourth is civic duty. Americans generally feel people ought to take community affairs seriously and help out when they can. Finally, Americans believe in individual responsibility. A characteristically American view is that, barring some disability, individuals are responsible for their own actions and well-being.†

There are at least five...				
The first is liberty...	The second element is equality...	Democracy is the third element...	Fourth is civic duty...	Finally, Americans believe in individual responsibility...
Americans believe...	Americans believe everybody...	Americans think government...	Americans generally feel...	A characteristically American view...

3. If you find that procrastination, or putting things off, hurts your progress, here are some ways to break the habit. First, look at the benefits of doing the work at hand. Will you feel a sense of accomplishment when the job is done, and will you feel less stressed and more relieved? Next, break the job into smaller parts. Break the work into fifteen-minute segments, take a break after each segment, and work slowly to build up your capacity to work. Another strategy is to reward yourself when you are done. Finally, if you simply can't break the procrastination habit, just sit down and force yourself to complete the task.‡

---

* Adapted from Elizabeth Kaye, "After Youth, Then What?" *O Magazine*, June 2001, 160.

† Adapted from James Q. Wilson and John J. DiIulio Jr., *American Government: The Essentials*, 9th ed. (Boston: Houghton Mifflin Co., 2004), 78–79.

‡ Adapted from Sharon Sherman and Alan Sherman, "Getting Yourself to Study," *Essential Concepts of Chemistry* (Boston: Houghton Mifflin Co., 1999), xxxi–xxxii.

If you find that procrastination...			
First, look at the benefits...	Next, break the job into...	Another strategy is to reward...	Finally, if you simply...
Will you feel a sense of...	Break the work into...		

4. Several publications and materials are the means by which the people at your college express their interest in you, your needs, and your success as a student. Your *college newspaper* contains information of interest to the college community along with articles that report on local and world events from a student's point of view. Your college may also provide a *student bulletin* or other weekly publication that keeps you informed of campus activities and events and contains additional items of general interest. A *student handbook* condenses[1] and summarizes information contained in the catalog concerning the college's policies and regulations,[2] but it is usually written in a style that is more appealing to students. Throughout your campus you will find various *informational flyers* about services and events that are printed by people or departments sponsoring the events. These flyers will contain only the essentials about the service or event: the time, the place, and whether it costs anything. *

Several publications and materials are the means...			
Your college newspaper...	Your college may also provide a student bulletin...	A student handbook condenses...	Throughout your campus you will find various informational flyers...
			These flyers will contain...

1. **condenses:** shortens   2. **regulations:** rules

---

* Adapted from Carol Kanar, *The Confident Student,* 5th ed. (Boston: Houghton Mifflin Co., 2004), 23.

5. Americans tend to believe several long-standing myths about families past and present. The first myth concerns the roles of family members. Many people think that the 1950s, an era of breadwinning dads and stay-at-home moms, was the last decade in a long era of stable families, but 1950s families actually reversed a 100-year trend of rising divorce rates. A second myth concerns the best family structure. People assume that a return to roles common within a 1950s family would decrease the number of broken homes, but today, sole breadwinning males are often less competent fathers, and stay-at-home women often feel isolated and depressed. Another myth relates to the number and severity of family problems. Though people believe that modern families face worse problems, the truth is that families in all eras of history have dealt with difficulties like drug and alcohol addiction and abuse.*

3

	Americans tend to believe...	
The first myth concerns the roles...	A second myth concerns the best family...	Another myth relates to the number...
Many people think that the 1950s, an era...	People assume that a return to roles common...	Though people believe that modern...

Exercise 3.3

Read the paragraph below and respond to the questions that follow by circling the letters of the correct answers.

(1) Are you interested in the idea of vacationing at a farm? (2) Before booking your trip, there are a few important things to consider, according to guidebook author Jay Golan, who stayed on farms while researching *Frommer's Philadelphia & the Amish Country,* his book about farm vacations. (3) First, he says, some people could be put off by rural America's old-fashioned ways. (4) For the most part, men do the farm work, and women do the household chores. (5) If you don't want your children to experience that lifestyle, you may not want to visit. (6) Second, there are often smells that can bother city slickers who aren't used to them. (7) On farms that have cattle and chickens,

* Adapted from "Unrealistic Family Myths," *USA Today Newsview,* December 1997, 1–2.

3

there can be overpowering smells in the air that people who live in and around the city find hard to take. (8) Third, you may get dirty. (9) City people sometimes show up in designer clothing, which is not the thing to wear on the farm. (10) You have to expect that you will pick up dirt or manure on your shoes or boots if you are going to be on a farm. (11) Indeed, at one farm, the owner's one rule is that people visiting the chicken house must scrub their shoes before returning to the farmhouse. Chicken droppings, it turns out, are surprisingly sticky!*

1. The main idea is expressed in sentence
   a. 1. c. 3.
   b. 2. d. 4.

2. The supporting details of this paragraph relate to
   a. farms.
   b. things about a farm you may not like.
   c. cows and cattle.
   d. smells on the farm.

3. Which of the following sentences is NOT a *major* detail in this paragraph?
   a. "Third, you may get dirty."
   b. "Second, there are often smells that can bother city slickers who aren't used to them."
   c. "City people sometimes show up in designer clothing, which is not the thing to wear on the farm."
   d. "First, he says, some people could be put off by rural America's old-fashioned ways."

4. Which of the following would be considered a *minor* detail in this paragraph?
   a. "First, he says, some people could be put off by rural America's old-fashioned ways."
   b. "You have to expect that you will pick up dirt or manure on your shoes or boots if you are going to be on a farm."
   c. "Second, there are often smells that can bother city slickers who aren't used to them."
   d. "Before booking your trip, there are a few important things to consider, according to guidebook author Jay Golan, who stayed on farms while researching *Frommer's Philadelphia & the Amish Country,* his book about farm vacations."

* Adapted from Gene Sloan, "Farmers Are Bullish on City Tourists," *USA Today,* June 29, 2001, 4d. Copyright © 2001, *USA Today.* Reprinted with permission.

5. People who are not used to farm life often show up with designer clothing because
   (a.) they are not prepared for the realities of farm life.
   b. they like to wear designer clothes all of the time.
   c. they think farmers wear designer clothes too.
   d. they are too materialistic.

Transitions

3

To help readers recognize the general and specific relationships among sentences in a paragraph, paragraphs usually include transitions. **Transitions** are words that assist readers in distinguishing between major and minor details because they make connections and distinctions between the different details. In particular, sentences that offer major details are likely to begin with words such as:

first, second, third	finally
In addition	one
and	another
also	furthermore
next	

These words signal that the sentence will offer another new point in support of the topic sentence. For an example of transitions that indicate major details, read the following paragraph. These transitions are in bold print:

> Several states are considering extending daylight-saving time so that it would start earlier in the spring and end later in the fall. **One reason** for doing so is to save energy costs. With longer daylight time, need for electricity would be reduced, and both governments and individuals would pay less. **Another reason** for lengthening daylight-saving time is increased safety. More daylight into the evening would reduce the number of rush-hour traffic accidents and make Halloween trick-or-treating safer for children.*

The transitions in the previous list are not the only ones that identify major details. Others will be discussed later in Chapter 5. However, because

---

* Adapted from "More Daylight Makes Sense," *USA Today Online,* June 18, 2001,
  www.usatoday.com/usatonline/20010618/3408445s.htm.

they commonly introduce important supporting details, readers should be aware of their function within the paragraph.

A paragraph might also include transitions to indicate minor details. Sentences that offer minor details are sometimes introduced with words such as:

for example	to illustrate
one example	specifically
for instance	in one case

These words can indicate that the sentence is about to offer more specific information to develop the last idea further. In the next paragraph, the transitions that signal minor details are in boldface print while those that identify major details are in italics.

> Certain traits separate the good bosses from the bad bosses. *The first characteristic* is the boss's response to his or her employees. **For example**, a bad boss orders employees around while a good boss treats employees with respect by recognizing their skills and experience. *The next characteristic* is the boss's response to his employees' ideas. A bad boss, **for instance**, is close-minded and disregards others' input, but a good boss encourages workers to contribute their ideas and then listens to and seriously considers those ideas. *Finally*, a good boss and a bad boss differ in the way they handle their own egos. A bad boss cares only about his own power and prestige[1] while a good boss focuses instead on providing the best, most efficient product or service.*

It is important to note here that the transitions in the list above can also be used to introduce *major* details in a paragraph. Chapter 5 will offer more specific information about how paragraphs use transitions in different ways.

Exercise 3.4

Read each paragraph and then underline the topic sentence, circle the transitions that signal major details, and underline transitions that signal minor details.

1. There are some basic principles of outlining you should keep in mind when preparing an outline. First, each point in your outline should contain only one idea or piece of information. Second, your outline should accurately

---

1. **prestige:** respect; high standing among others

---

* Adapted from Paul B. Hertneky, "You and Your Boss," *Restaurant Hospitality*, August 1, 1996, 78.

reflect relationships among ideas and supporting material. (Third), you should use a consistent system of symbols and indentations.[1] (Fourth), write out transitions and relevant portions of introductions and conclusions.*

2. According to management experts, a business must do two things to be successful. (First) it must put the customer first—by listening, understanding, and providing customer service. (Second) a company—both its managers and its employees—must act with speed and flexibility. In one case, Dell Computers, the company scores A+ on both counts. Specifically, in just fourteen years, Dell has made its mark in the computer industry because of its ability to see an opportunity that larger competitors like Compaq and IBM ignored.†

3. One of the brain's primary jobs is to manufacture images so we can use them to make predictions about the world and then base our behavior on those predictions. (For one thing), when a cook adds chopped onions, mushrooms, and garlic to a spaghetti sauce, he has a picture of how the sauce will taste and measures each ingredient according to that picture. (And) when an artist creates a painting or sculpture, he has a mental picture of the finished piece. (Another example) would be that of the novelist who has a mental image of the characters she wants to bring to life.‡

4. Denis Leary is a comedian who is also devoted to a couple of charities. (One) charity is called the Kerry Chesire Fund, which helps handicapped people in Ireland. (Another) is the Cam Neely[2] Foundation, which provides a home away from home for cancer patients. (Finally) the Leary Firefighters

1. indentations: blank spaces	**2. Cam Neely:** Neely was a professional hockey player for the Boston Bruins

* Adapted from James Andrews and Patricia Andrews, *Public Speaking* (Boston: Houghton Mifflin Co., 1999), 184–186. Copyright © 1999 by Houghton Mifflin Company. Reprinted with permission.

† Adapted from William Pride et al., *Business,* 6th ed. (Boston: Houghton Mifflin Co., 1999), 24.

‡ Adapted from Dave Ellis, "Notice Your Pictures and Let Them Go," *Becoming a Master Student* (Boston: Houghton Mifflin Co., 2000), 132.

Foundation raises money to help firefighters get new and improved equipment that could help save their lives during a fire.*

5. A 2001 survey of high school students conducted by the National Institute on Drug Abuse pointed out two disturbing trends. First, adolescents now tend to become involved with drugs at an earlier age. Specifically, substance use has increased substantially for those in sixth through ninth grades. Second, the percentage of adolescents who appreciate the dangers of drugs has declined greatly. Fewer students indicate that they understand the consequences of drug use.†

Mapping and Outlining

Earlier in this chapter, you saw how you can visualize the relationships among sentences in a paragraph by inserting each one into a block. The main idea went into the block at the top, the major supporting details went into the row of blocks just beneath the main idea, and the minor details, if any, were in the third row.

	MAIN IDEA	
MAJOR DETAIL	MAJOR DETAIL	MAJOR DETAIL
Minor Detail	Minor Detail	Minor Detail

This diagram is a form of **mapping**, a technique that involves using lines, boxes, circles, or other shapes to show how sentences in a paragraph are related.

In mapping, you lay out a visual to help you see the main idea, major supporting details, and minor supporting details. Here are some other, different ways to visualize these relationships:

* Adapted from Frank DeCaro, "Denis Leary Gets Serious," *Rosie*, July, 2001, 88.
† Adapted from Paul S. Kaplan, *Adolescence* (Boston: Houghton Mifflin Co., 2004), 496.

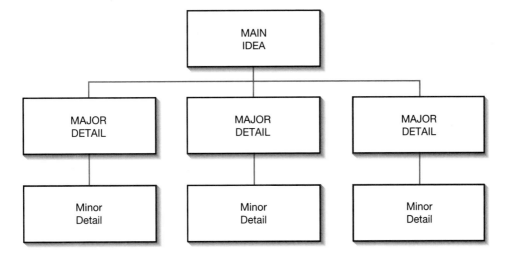

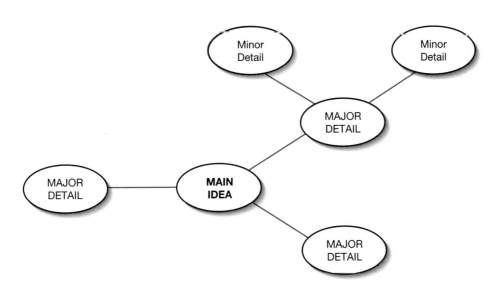

For example, using the diagram above, you might map the paragraph about good and bad bosses on page 134 like this.

3

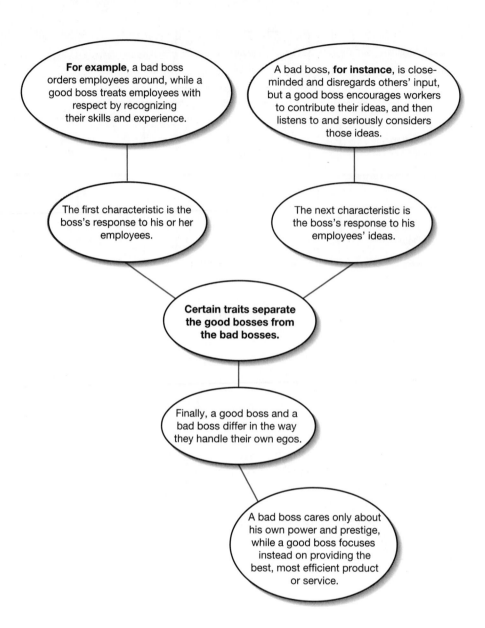

Exercise 3.5

Read each paragraph and then fill in the map that follows with an abbreviated form of each sentence.

1. There are two models for explaining dropping out of high school. The *frustration–self-esteem model* argues that continuous failure leads to low self-esteem and problem behaviors such as absenteeism,[1] which finally end in dropping out. The *participation-identification model* argues that lack of participation in school activities leads to poor school performance and alienation[2] from school, which lead to dropping out.*

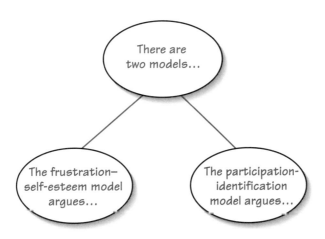

2. Companies are finding that business e-mail messages clog computer networks and increasingly take up employees' time, so several companies are encouraging workers to curb e-mail. Intel has recently started classes on how to manage e-mail. And IBM is increasingly using instant messaging instead of e-mail because messaging is less taxing on networks. Another company called Computer Associates asks its employees to place large files on internal networks where they can be viewed by many, and, like Intel, offers e-mail training.†

1. **absenteeism:** repeated failure to attend

2. **alienation:** isolation

---

* Adapted from Paul S. Kaplan, *Adolescence* (Boston: Houghton Mifflin Co., 2004), 248.

† Adapted from Jon Swartz, "E-mail Overload Taxes Workers and Companies," *USA Today*, June 26, 2001, 1A.

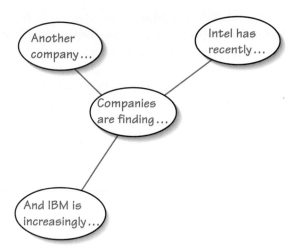

3. Some companies are using wireless devices in a variety of ways and reaping big benefits. One Illinois cleaning company called Service-Master, which scrubs Greyhound buses, uses its hand-held wireless network to keep track of customer satisfaction. After each bus is cleaned, a Greyhound supervisor rates the job using an electronic form on one of the company's other computers. Another company is Office Depot, which has cut the time it spends filing and searching for delivery paperwork by 50 percent thanks to a wireless system that links trunks on 22,000 delivery routes. And police officers in Coos Bay, Oregon, no longer have to make two one-hour detours back to headquarters each shift, thanks to a wireless computer in patrol cars that allows them to submit entries to the police log through a wireless network.*

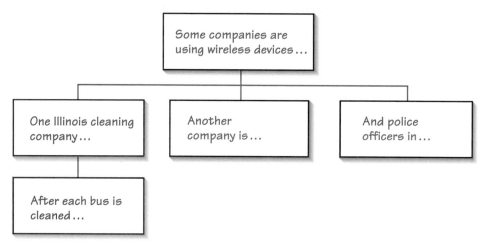

* Adapted from Michelle Kessler, "Gadgets Give Workers on the Run a Leg Up," *USA Today*, June 26, 2001, 5F.

4. According to the Weber Grill-Watch survey, nearly all Americans fall into one of four categories of barbecue grilling personalities. The first category is the Gallant[1] Grillers. These people, who make up 33 percent of barbecue grill owners, are adventurous and love to treat their guests to grilled food experiments. The next group is the Careful Cooks. These grillers—32 percent of grill owners—love to entertain, too, but they are more cautious and follow recipes closely. Busy Barbecuers are the third group. These people, who make up 19 percent of grill owners, like to

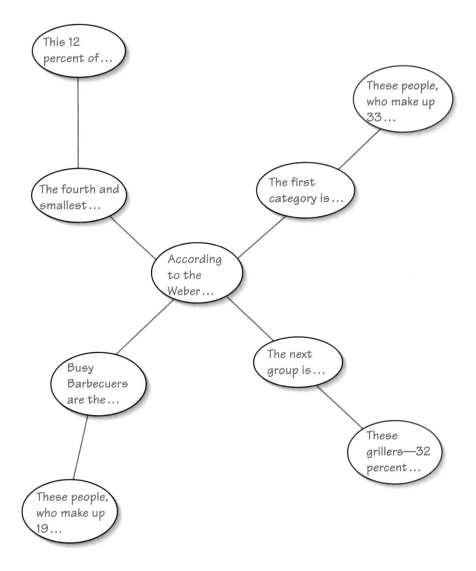

1. **gallant:** boldly stylish

cook only those foods that don't take much time, and they rarely try new things. The fourth and smallest category is the Need-It-Nows. This 12 percent of grill owners views barbecueing only as a way to produce food, not as a way to entertain or spend time with the family.*

5. There are some dos and don'ts that you should keep in mind when you are exercising with a dog. First, don't run with toy breeds or short-nosed dogs such as bulldogs because they don't have a human's endurance. Second, don't run a dog on hot pavement. If the surface is too hot to put your hand on, it's too hot for the dog. Third, if the dog is scared of traffic or panics next to your bicycle, neither of you will enjoy the workout. Think of alternatives—running in a park or on side streets rather than on a busy street, for instance. Fourth, if the dog is overweight, is suspected of having heartworms, or has any other health problems, check with a veterinarian before beginning an exercise program. Finally, always keep the dog's abilities and limits in mind. Set your pace to match what the dog can do and cut the workout short if the dog looks tired or stressed.†

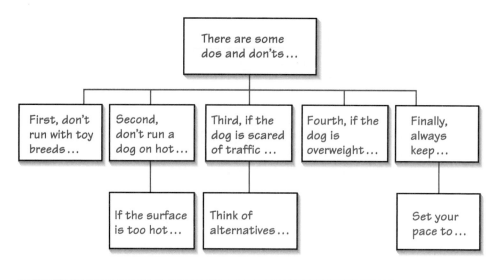

Another good way to identify the main idea and supporting details is to create an outline. An **outline** is a list of these details labeled with a system of

* Adapted from "What's Your Barbecue Profile?" *USA Today*, May 1998, 10.

† Excerpt from "Do's and Don'ts When Exercising a Dog" by Aline McKenzie from *The Journal News*, June 25, 2001, 1E. Reprinted by permission of the Chicago Tribune.

numbers and letters that show their relationships to one another. Outlines often use the Roman numeral system, which effectively identifies the main idea and different topics or details. Outlines can be in sentence form or in topic form. The latter is useful for creating a brief summary that allows you, at a glance, to see the general and specific relationships.

I. Main Idea
   A. Major detail
      1. Minor detail
      2. Minor detail
   B. Major detail
      1. Minor detail
      2. Minor detail

For example, you could outline the paragraph about daylight-saving time on page 133, as follows:

I. Reasons for extending daylight-saving time
   A. Save energy costs
      1. Reduce electricity needs
      2. Governments and individuals would pay less
   B. Increased safety
      1. Fewer rush-hour traffic accidents
      2. Halloween safer for children

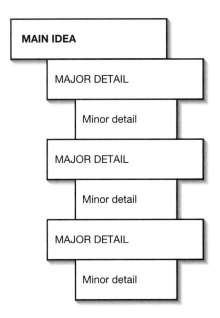

To create an outline, line up the major details along one margin and label them with capital letters. Beneath each major detail, indent minor details with numbers: 1, 2, 3, etc.

If you do not like the formality of a Roman numeral outline, you can also outline a paragraph in a more visual way by using a series of indented boxes in place of the numbers and letters.

This diagram, like the Roman numeral outline, arranges major details along one margin line and indents minor details beneath each one. You could create an outline of this type for the paragraph about becoming wealthy on page 124, as follows:

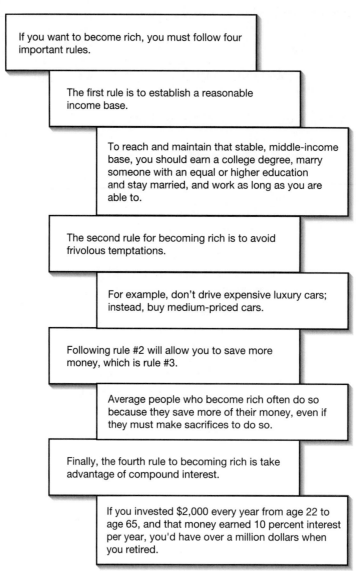

If you want to become rich, you must follow four important rules.

The first rule is to establish a reasonable income base.

To reach and maintain that stable, middle-income base, you should earn a college degree, marry someone with an equal or higher education and stay married, and work as long as you are able to.

The second rule for becoming rich is to avoid frivolous temptations.

For example, don't drive expensive luxury cars; instead, buy medium-priced cars.

Following rule #2 will allow you to save more money, which is rule #3.

Average people who become rich often do so because they save more of their money, even if they must make sacrifices to do so.

Finally, the fourth rule to becoming rich is take advantage of compound interest.

If you invested $2,000 every year from age 22 to age 65, and that money earned 10 percent interest per year, you'd have over a million dollars when you retired.

Exercise 3.6

Complete the outline that follows each paragraph by filling in the blanks provided.

1. Celebrities, and in particular movie stars, find it very hard to have long-term relationships for a number of reasons. For one thing, celebrity couples rarely work on movies together. This means that they are often in two different locations at the same time for extended periods of time. It is also hard to have a relationship under the constant eye of tabloid[1] newspapers, television reporters, and photographers. Oftentimes, the media mistake photos taken from movies or friends seen together as romantic encounters and report on a star's unfaithfulness to his or her significant other. And finally, it is hard to stay faithful when you are surrounded by great-looking people all day long, as is the case with most movie stars. Many stars have confessed to having romantic relationships with costars from a movie project because of the long hours, the time away from home, and just being attracted to a costar.

I. _Reasons for celebrities' difficulties in having long-term relationships_

   A. _Rarely work on movies together_

   B. _Under constant eye of media_

   C. _Surrounded by great-looking people all day_

2. More than one out of four teens nationwide does some type of volunteer work, and they are not only helping others but also benefiting themselves. Research confirms that teens who learn early to be social, caring, and responsible perform better in school. As a matter of fact, volunteering improves their chances of graduating at the top of their class, armed with critical leadership skills. It also makes teens feel good about themselves. For example, studies show that teens who volunteer just two hours per week have higher self-esteem and more resiliency,[2] and they are 50 percent less likely to smoke, drink, or do drugs.*

I. _Benefits of teens' volunteer work_

   A. _Better performance in school_

      1. _Improves chances of graduating at top of class_

      2. _Develops critical leadership skills_

1. **tabloid:** sensational

2. **resiliency:** ability to recover quickly from misfortune

* Adapted from Ann Pleshette Murphy, "Give It Up," *ABC News*, June 18, 2003, http://www.abcnews.go.com/sections/GMA/AmericanFamily/GMA030618Teen volunteers.html

B. <u>Makes teens feel good about themselves</u>

    1. <u>Higher self-esteem</u>

    2. <u>More resiliency</u>

    3. <u>Less likely to smoke, drink, do drugs</u>

3. Right after having a baby, a woman might experience one of three kinds of postpartum[1] depression. One kind of depression is called the postpartum blues. This type affects about 85 percent of new mothers and causes mood swings for up to two weeks. The second, more severe type is called postpartum depression. This condition affects about 10 percent of mothers, especially those who don't enjoy motherhood, and can produce eating or sleeping disorders for months at a time. The third and worst kind of depression is called postpartum psychosis. Fortunately, this type occurs in only one out of 1,000 mothers because it causes a woman to experience delusions[2] and believe the baby would be better off dead.*

I. <u>Three kinds of postpartum depression</u>

    A. <u>Postpartum blues</u>

        1. <u>Affect 85 percent of new mothers</u>

        2. <u>Cause mood swings for two weeks</u>

    B. <u>Postpartum depression</u>

        1. <u>Affects about 10 percent of mothers</u>

        2. <u>Can produce eating or sleeping disorders</u>

    C. <u>Postpartum psychosis</u>

        1. <u>Occurs in only one out of 1,000 mothers</u>

        2. <u>Causes a woman to experience delusions</u>

4. The U.S. justice system should not treat violent juvenile[3] offenders as adults. First of all, these children do not yet possess the intellectual or moral capacity to understand the consequences of their actions. Also, they are not totally responsible for their crimes. They should not have

1. postpartum: after giving birth   **3. juvenile:** young
2. delusions: false beliefs

* Adapted from "Most Mothers Affected by 'Blues,'" *USA Today Online*, June 22, 2001, www.usatoday.com/usatonline/20010622/3424834s.htm.

access to deadly weapons such as guns. The adults who allowed them to get their hands on weapons are at least as accountable as the kids themselves. Finally, the juvenile system still gives these kids a chance to turn their lives around. Adult facilities have all but abandoned any attempt to rehabilitate[1] inmates. Juvenile facilities, on the other hand, still offer opportunities for kids to evolve into productive members of society.*

I. Reasons for not treating violent juvenile offenders as adults

   A. Children can't understand consequences of their actions

   B. Children aren't totally responsible for their crimes

      1. Should not have access to deadly weapons

      2. Adults are just as accountable

   C. Children can turn their lives around in juvenile system

      1. Adult facilities don't rehabilitate

      2. Juvenile facilities still give kids a chance

5. European-American parents tend to employ one of three distinct socialization patterns, as described by Diana Baumrind. *Authoritarian parents* tend to be strict, punitive,[2] and unsympathetic. They value obedience from children and try to shape their children's behavior to meet a set standard and to curb the children's wills. They do not encourage independence. They are detached and seldom praise their youngsters. In contrast, *permissive parents* give their children complete freedom and lax[3] discipline. The third group, *authoritative parents,* fall between these two extremes. They reason with their children, encouraging give and take. They allow children increasing responsibility as they get older and better at making decisions. They are firm but understanding. They set limits but also encourage independence. Their demands are reasonable, rational, and consistent.†

1. **rehabilitate:** to restore to a good life or condition

2. **punitive:** punishing

3. **lax:** loose; not strict

---

* Adapted from Jessica Reaves, "Should the Law Treat Kids and Adults Differently?" *Time.com,* May 21, 2001, www.time.com/time/nation/printout/0,8816,110232,00.html.

† Adapted from Douglas A. Bernstein et al., *Psychology* (Boston: Houghton Mifflin Co., 1997), 410.

I. Three socialization patterns of parents

    A. Authoritarian parents

        1. Strict, punitive, unsympathetic

        2. Value obedience, shape behavior, curb children's wills

        3. Don't encourage independence

        4. Detached and seldom praise

    B. Permissive parents

        1. Complete freedom

        2. Lax discipline

    C. Authoritative parents

        1. Reason with children

        2. Allow children increasing responsibility

        3. Firm but understanding

        4. Set limits but encourage independence

        5. Demands are reasonable, rational, consistent

CHAPTER 3 REVIEW

Write the correct answers in the blanks in the following statements.

1. __Supporting details__ are the specific facts, statistics, examples, steps, anecdotes, reasons, descriptions, definitions, and so on that explain or prove the general __main idea__ stated in the topic sentence.

2. There are two kinds of supporting details: __major__ details and __minor__ details. The __major__ details are the main points that explain or support the idea in the topic sentence. __Minor__ details offer more explanation of the major details.

3. __Transitions__ are words that assist readers in distinguishing between major and minor details because they make connections and distinctions among the different details.

4. __Mapping__ is a technique that involves using lines, boxes, circles, or other shapes to show how sentences in a paragraph are related.

5. An __outline__ is a list of supporting details labeled with a system of numbers and letters that show the relationships of the details to one another.

Reading Selection

3

Practicing the Active Reading Strategy:
Before and As You Read

You can use active reading strategies before, as, and after you read a selection. The following are some suggestions for active reading strategies that you can employ before you read and as you are reading.

1. Skim the selection for any unfamiliar words. Circle or highlight any words you do not know.

2. As you read, underline, highlight, or circle important words or phrases.

3. Write down any questions about the selection if you are confused by the information presented.

4. Jot notes in the margin to help you understand the material.

College Lectures: Is Anybody Listening?
by Robert Holkeboer and Thomas Hoeksema

1 Today, American colleges and universities (originally modeled on German ones) are under strong attack from many quarters. Teachers, it is charged, are not doing a good job of teaching, and students are not doing a good job of learning. American businesses and industries suffer from unenterprising, uncreative executives educated not to think for themselves but to mouth outdated truisms the rest of the world has long discarded. College graduates lack both basic skills and general culture. Studies are conducted and reports are issued on the status of higher education, but any changes that result either are largely cosmetic or make a bad situation worse.

2 One aspect of American education too seldom challenged is the lecture system. Professors continue to lecture and students to take notes much as they did in the thirteenth century, when books were so scarce and expensive that few students could own them. The time is long overdue for us to abandon the lecture system and turn to methods that really work.

3 To understand the inadequacy of the present system, it is enough to follow a single imaginary first-year student—let's call her Mary—through a term of lectures on, say, introductory psychology (although any other subject would do as well). She arrives on the first day and looks around the huge lecture hall, taken a little aback to see how large the class is. Once the hundred or more students enrolled in the course discover that the professor never takes attendance (how can he?—calling the roll would take far too much time), the class shrinks to a less imposing size.

4 Some days Mary sits in the front row, from where she can watch the professor read from a stack of yellowed notes that

seem nearly as old as he is. She is bored by the lectures, and so are most of the other students, to judge by the way they are nodding off or doodling in their notebooks. Gradually she realizes the professor is as bored as his audience. At the end of each lecture he asks, "Are there any questions?" in a tone of voice that makes it plain he would much rather there weren't. He needn't worry; the students are as relieved as he is that the class is over.

5   Mary knows very well she should read an assignment before every lecture. However, as the professor gives no quizzes and asks no questions, she soon realizes she needn't prepare. At the end of the term she catches up by skimming her notes and memorizing a list of facts and dates. After the final exam, she promptly forgets much of what she has memorized. Some of her fellow students, disappointed at the impersonality of it all, drop out of college altogether. Others, like Mary, stick it out, grow resigned to the system, and await better days when, as juniors and seniors, they will attend smaller classes and at last get the kind of personal attention real learning requires.

6   I admit this picture is overdrawn. Most universities supplement lecture courses with discussion groups, usually led by graduate students, and some classes, such as first-year English, are always relatively small. Nevertheless, far too many courses rely principally or entirely on lectures, an arrangement much loved by faculty and administrators but scarcely designed to benefit the students.

7   One problem with lectures is that listening intelligently is hard work. Reading the same material in a textbook is a more efficient way to learn because students can proceed as slowly as they need to until the subject matter becomes clear to them. Even simply paying attention is very difficult; people can listen at a rate of four hundred to six hundred words a minute while the most impassioned professor talks at scarcely a third that speed. This time lag between speech and comprehension leads to daydreaming. Many students believe years of watching television have sabotaged their attention span, but their real problem is that listening attentively is much harder than they think.

8   Worse still, attending lectures is passive learning, at least for inexperienced listeners. Active learning, in which students write essays or perform experiments and then have their work evaluated by an instructor, is far more beneficial for those who have not yet fully learned how to learn. While it's true that techniques of active listening, such as trying to anticipate the speaker's next point or taking notes selectively, can enhance the value of a lecture, few students possess such skills at the beginning of their college careers. More commonly, students try to write everything down and even bring tape recorders to class in a clumsy effort to capture every word.

9   Students need to question their professors and to have their ideas taken seriously. Only then will they develop the analytical skills required to think intelligently and creatively. Most students learn best by engaging in frequent and even heated debate, not by scribbling down a professor's often unsatisfactory summary of complicated issues. They need small discussion classes that demand the common labors of teacher and students rather than classes in which one person, however learned, propounds his or her own ideas.

10   The lecture system ultimately harms professors as well. It reduces feedback to a minimum so that the lecturer can neither judge how well students understand the material nor benefit from their questions or comments. Questions that require the speaker to clarify obscure points and comments that challenge sloppily constructed arguments are indispensable to scholarship. Without them, the liveliest mind can atrophy. Undergraduates may not be able to make telling contributions very often, but lecturing insulates a professor from even the beginner's naïve question that could have triggered a fruitful line of thought.

11   If lectures make so little sense, why have they been allowed to continue? Administrators love them, of course. They can cram far more students into a lecture hall than into a discussion class, and for many administrators that is almost the end of the story. But the truth is that faculty members, and even students, conspire with them to keep the lecture system alive and well. Lectures are easier on everyone than debates. Professors can pretend to teach by lecturing just as students can pretend to learn by attending lectures, with no one the wiser, including the participants. Moreover, if lectures afford some students an opportunity to sit back and let the professor run the show, they offer some professors an irresistible forum for showing off. In a classroom where everyone contributes, students are less able to hide and professors less tempted to engage in intellectual exhibitionism.

12   Smaller classes in which students are required to involve themselves in discussion put an end to students' passivity. Students become actively involved when forced to question their own ideas as well as their instructor's. Their listening skills improve dramatically in the excitement of intellectual give and take with their instructors and fellow students. Such interchanges help professors do their job better because they allow them to discover who knows what—before final exams, not after. When exams are given in this type of course, they can require analysis and synthesis from the students, not empty memorization. Classes like this require energy, imagination, and commitment from professors, all of which can be exhausting. But they compel students to share responsibility for their own intellectual growth.

13   Lectures will never entirely disappear from the university scene both because they seem to be economically necessary and because they spring from a long tradition in a setting that rightly values tradition for its own sake. But the lectures too frequently come at the wrong end of the students' educational careers—during the first two years, when they most need close, even individual instruction. If lecture classes were restricted to junior and senior undergraduates and to graduate students, who are less in need of scholarly nurturing and more able to prepare work on their own, they would be far less destructive of students' interests and enthusiasms than the present system. After all, students must learn to listen before they can listen to learn.*

* Adapted from Robert Holkeboer and Thomas Hoeksema, "College Lectures: Is Anyone Listening?" *The College Success Reader* (Boston: Houghton Mifflin Co., 1998), 62–65. Copyright © 1998 by Houghton Mifflin Company. Reprinted with permission.

VOCABULARY

Read the following questions about some of the vocabulary words that appear in the previous selection. Circle the letter of the correct answer.

1. In paragraph 1, what does *unenterprising* mean?
   - a. not living
   - (b.) not showing initiative
   - c. not breathing
   - d. not drinking

2. In paragraph 5, what does *impersonality* mean?
   - (a.) detachment
   - b. warmth
   - c. energy
   - d. feeling

3. In paragraph 7, what does *impassioned* mean?
   - a. insensitive
   - b. remote
   - (c.) emotional
   - d. demented

4. In paragraph 7, what does *sabotaged* mean?
   - a. refunded
   - b. replaced
   - c. energized
   - (d.) damaged

5. In paragraph 10, what does *obscure* mean?
   - a. transparent
   - b. lucid
   - (c.) unclear
   - d. damaged

6. In paragraph 10, what does *indispensable* mean?
   - (a.) essential
   - b. not needed
   - c. independent
   - d. insufficient

7. In paragraph 10, what does *atrophy* mean?
   - a. wasted
   - (b.) wither
   - c. award
   - d. plaque

8. In paragraph 10, what does *insulates* mean?
   - (a.) protects
   - b. defends
   - c. warrants
   - d. models

9. In paragraph 11, what does *conspire* mean?
   - (a.) plot
   - b. determine
   - c. ward off
   - d. protect

10. In paragraph 11, what does *exhibitionism* mean?
    - a. showing
    - (b.) display
    - c. mirror
    - d. nakedness

TOPIC, TOPIC SENTENCE, MAIN IDEAS, AND SUPPORTING DETAILS

Respond to each of the following questions by circling the letter of the correct answer.

1. What is the topic of paragraph 2?

   a. American education   c. methods that really work
   (b.) the lecture system   d. books that are scarce

2. Which of the following is the topic sentence of paragraph 7?

   (a.) "One problem with lectures is that listening intelligently is hard work."
   b. "Reading the same material in a textbook is a more efficient way to learn because students can proceed as slowly as they need to until the subject matter becomes clear to them."
   c. "Even simply paying attention is very difficult; people can listen at a rate of four hundred to six hundred words a minute, while the most impassioned professor talks at scarcely a third that speed."
   d. "This time lag between speech and comprehension leads to daydreaming."

3. What is the main idea of paragraph 10?

   a. The lecture system reduces feedback.
   b. Undergraduates ask naïve questions.
   c. Lecturing insulates a professor from questions.
   (d.) Lectures harm professors as well as students.

4. Which of the following is a *major* supporting detail in paragraph 11?

   a. "If lectures make so little sense, why have they been allowed to continue?"
   (b.) "Administrators love them, of course."
   c. "They can cram far more students into a lecture hall than into a discussion class, and for many administrators that is almost the end of the story."
   d. "In a classroom where everyone contributes, students are less able to hide and professors less tempted to engage in intellectual exhibitionism."

5. Which of the following is a *minor* supporting detail in paragraph 10?

   a. "The lecture system ultimately harms professors as well."
   b. "It reduces feedback to a minimum so that the lecturer can neither judge how well students understand the material nor benefit from their questions or comments."
   c. "Questions that require the speaker to clarify obscure points and comments that challenge sloppily constructed arguments are indispensable to scholarship."
   (d.) "Without them, the liveliest mind can atrophy."

Practicing the Active Reading Strategy:
After You Read

Now that you have read the selection, answer the following questions, using the active reading strategies that you learned in Chapter 1.

1. Identify and write down the point and purpose of this reading selection.

2. Besides the vocabulary words included in the exercise on page 152, are there any other vocabulary words that are unfamiliar to you? If so, write a list of them. When you have finished writing your list, look up each word in a dictionary and write the definition that best describes the word as it is used in the selection.

3. Predict any possible test questions that may be used on a test about the content of this selection.

4. How could you use the information contained in this selection? Does the information contained in the selection reinforce or contradict your ideas and experiences? Explain.

QUESTIONS FOR DISCUSSION AND WRITING

Answer each of the following questions based on your reading of the selection. Write your answers on the blanks provided.

1. In what type of environment do you learn best? Have you ever been in a college lecture hall like the one described? If so, does your experience match Mary's, or was it different? How? Answers will vary.

2. What is one aspect of your learning experience or learning environment that you wish you could change? Why? Answers will vary.

3. In your opinion, is there a student population for which the types of lectures described in the selection work effectively? Answers will vary.

◗ Vocabulary: Context and Meaning

When you encounter an unfamiliar word as you read and go to the dictionary to look it up, you'll often find several different meanings and variations for that word. How do you know which definition is the right one? You have to look at the context—the words, phrases, and sentences surrounding that word—to determine which meaning applies.

To figure out the right definition, you may first need to determine the word's part of speech in the sentence. Many words can function as different parts of speech (for example, the word *left* can be a noun, a verb, an adjective, or an adverb), so you'll have to figure out how the word is being used before you can decide which definition applies. For example, the word *interest* is both a noun and a verb. The noun form means both "a state of curiosity" and "a charge for a loan." Which of the noun form meanings is being used in the following sentence?

> Finally, the fourth rule to becoming rich is to take advantage of compound **interest**.

You know the word refers to a charge for a loan because of the other words around it. The whole passage that contains this sentence is about becoming wealthy, so you know the word *interest* refers to money.

Vocabulary Exercise

The following sentences all come from paragraphs throughout this chapter. Look up the boldfaced, italicized words in a dictionary and write on the blank provided the definition that best describes how each word is being used.

1. Many people think that the 1950s, an era of breadwinning dads and stay-at-home moms, was the last decade in a long era of *stable* families, but 1950s families actually reversed a 100-year trend of rising divorce rates.

   steadfast, permanent, enduring

2. There are two *models* for explaining dropping out of high school.

   descriptions of theories

3. People loved him [actor Jack Lemmon] because his *characters* were never larger than life; they were people most Americans could identify with.

   people portrayed in an artistic piece

3

4. One kind of *depression* is called the postpartum blues. <u>condition of feeling</u>

 <u>sad or despondent</u>

5. Always lock car doors and *trunks*—even at home—and keep keys out of

 children's reach. <u>covered compartments for storage in the rear of an automobile</u>

6. Another company is Office Depot, which has cut the time it spends filing and searching for delivery paperwork by 50 percent thanks to a wireless

 system that links *trunks* on 22,000 delivery routes. <u>lines of a communication</u>

 <u>system</u>

7. Companies are finding that business e-mail messages *clog* computer net-works and increasingly take up employees' time, so several companies are

 encouraging workers to curb e-mail. <u>block up</u>

8. Companies are finding that business e-mail messages clog computer net-works and increasingly take up employees' time, so several companies are

 encouraging workers to *curb* e-mail. <u>check or restrain</u>

9. Prompted by our *modest* exertions, just a few minutes into a walk the body begins to produce endorphins, chemical compounds that reduce pain and stress and enhance memory and judgment as they course

 through the brain. <u>moderate or limited</u>

10. Prompted by our modest exertions, just a few minutes into a walk the body begins to produce endorphins, chemical compounds that reduce pain and stress and enhance memory and judgment as they *course* through

 the brain. <u>move swiftly</u>

READING STRATEGY: Reading and Time Management

How often should you read? How long should you try to read in one sit-ting? How many times should you read a chapter? Is it better to read the whole chapter at once or just a section at a time?

    There are no right or wrong answers to these questions. The most ef-fective length, amount, and frequency of reading time will differ from student to student and from class to class. You will have to experiment to discover what works best for you, and you will probably need to make adjustments for each different course you take.

However, be aware of the following general principles of effective time management:

- Schedule time to read. Don't just try to fit reading in whenever you can; actually make an appointment to read by blocking out regular times on your calendar.

- The best time to read is the time of day or night when you are most mentally alert. If you're a night owl, read at night. If you're a morning person, try to fit in your reading time at the beginning of your day.

- Take frequent breaks during reading sessions. Regularly stand up and stretch, walk around, and rest your eyes for a few minutes.

- Keep up with the reading assignments in a course by following the schedule provided by your instructor. Following the schedule will give you the basic understanding of the material you'll need in order to get the most out of class lectures, discussions, and activities.

- Try to schedule time for multiple readings of the same chapter. Repeated exposure to information helps increase your retention of the material. If you hurriedly read large chunks of information all at once just before a test, you probably won't remember much of it. If you digest information slowly and regularly over a longer period of time, you'll remember more.

Write your answers to the following questions on the blanks provided.

1. Describe the typical length, amount, and frequency of reading time that seems to work best for you. Answers will vary.

2. Describe a time when you took a class that required you to alter significantly the length, amount, and/or frequency of your reading.
Answers will vary.

3. What time of day are you most mentally alert? Is that the time of day when you usually read? Answers will vary.

4. Which of the guidelines listed above do you already practice?

   Answers will vary.

   _____

5. Which of the guidelines above do you think you should implement in order to get more out of your reading?   Answers will vary.

   _____

Name _____ Date _____

TEST 1

A. Read the following paragraphs and identify each of the sentences listed as a main idea, major supporting detail, or minor supporting detail. Circle the letter of the correct answer.

(1) Athletes can become heroes. (2) Jackie Robinson suffered years of blatant[1] discrimination that would have caused lesser men to lash out at their tormentors and postpone the racial integration of Major League Baseball. (3) Hall of Fame outfielder Roberto Clemente lost his life in a plane crash bringing food and supplies to earthquake victims in Nicaragua. (4) After serving in World War II, baseball legend Ted Williams returned to active duty in the Korean conflict, where he flew thirty-nine combat missions. (5) The three men are heroic figures because of the courage and exemplary[2] behavior they exhibited as human beings, not as athletes.*

1. Sentence 1 is a

   a. main idea.
   b. major supporting detail.
   c. minor supporting detail.

2. Sentence 3 is a

   a. main idea.
   b. major supporting detail.
   c. minor supporting detail.

3. Sentence 4 is a

   a. main idea.
   b. major supporting detail.
   c. minor supporting detail.

1. **blatant:** obvious

2. **exemplary:** worthy of imitation or copying

---

* Adapted from George J. Bryjak, "Don't Call Jocks Sports 'Heroes,'" *USA Today*, February 18, 2002, 13A.

For more tests on word mapping and outlines, see the Test Bank.

3

(1) Forming a stereotype, a belief that associates a whole group of people with certain traits, requires performing two related processes. (2) The first process is categorization, or sorting people into groups. (3) A specific gender, race, age, occupation, political party, or another common attribute[1] may be the basis for each group. (4) The second process involves perceiving the groups to which we belong as being different from the groups to which we don't belong and then assuming that everyone in the other groups is alike. (5) For example, people who don't live in New York City talk about the typical New Yorker, liberals lump together all conservatives, and teenagers think that all old people are the same.*

4. Sentence 1 is a
   a. main idea.
   b. major supporting detail.
   c. minor supporting detail.

5. Sentence 2 is a
   a. main idea.
   b. major supporting detail.
   c. minor supporting detail.

6. Sentence 5 is a
   a. main idea.
   b. major supporting detail.
   c. minor supporting detail.

(1) Delivering painful information requires a complex set of skills—whether you're a doctor speaking to a patient, a manager firing an employee, or a teacher telling a parent, "Your son is failing." (2) To start with, experts say, find a private, quiet place to begin the conversation, as opposed to conducting it in a crowded hallway or over the phone. (3) Then, open with what's called a verbal warning shot. (4) Medical students learn to say, "I'm afraid I have some difficult news that we need to talk about today," so the patient has time to steel herself for what's coming. (5) Also, avoid saying, "I don't know" (a better reply is "I'll find out"), and withhold details the listener isn't ready to hear. (6) For example, a doctor should spare a cancer patient specifics about her inevitable chemotherapy and radiation treatments.†

1. **attribute:** trait or characteristic

---

* Adapted from Sharon S. Brehm et al., *Social Psychology*, 5th ed. (Boston: Houghton Mifflin Co., 2002), 133–135.

† Adapted from Amy O'Connor, "How to Tell Hard Truths," *O*, January 2002, 144.

7. Sentence 2 is a

    a. main idea.

    (b.) major supporting detail.

    c. minor supporting detail.

8. Sentence 4 is a

    a. main idea.

    b. major supporting detail.

    (c.) minor supporting detail.

9. Sentence 6 is a

    a. main idea.

    b. major supporting detail.

    (c.) minor supporting detail.

(1) Men no longer dominate the workplace because women are entering in greater numbers than ever before and are achieving management positions. (2) One result of these changes has been a realization that men and women tend to speak in distinctly different "genderlects," just as people from various cultures speak different dialects.[1] (3) Men are more likely to talk about money, sports, and business; women prefer talking about people, feelings, and relationships. (4) Even when discussing the same topic, men and women may be on different wavelengths because their gender-specific focus is different. (5) For example, if a man and woman are discussing an upcoming layoff in their organization, the man might approach it from a cost-cutting point of view, and the woman may focus on the feelings of the people involved. Neither view is wrong, but the resulting conversation can frustrate both parties.*

10. Sentence 2 is a

    (a.) main idea.

    b. major supporting detail.

    c. minor supporting detail.

11. Sentence 3 is a

    a. main idea.

    (b.) major supporting detail.

    c. minor supporting detail.

1. **dialects:** language particular to specific groups

---

* Adapted from Barry Reece and Rhonda Brandt, *Effective Human Relations in Organizations*, 7th ed. (Boston: Houghton Mifflin Co., 1999), 39.

12. Sentence 5 is a

    a. main idea.
    b. major supporting detail.
    (c.) minor supporting detail.

(1) When it comes to relating to others, there are four kinds of people. (2) One type includes the *dependent* people. (3) These people believe that they can't achieve their goals by themselves; they need other people to do most of the work for them. (4) The second type of people includes *codependent* individuals, who believe that they'll pursue their own goals as soon as they've helped others reach their goals. (5) Then there are the *independent* people. (6) They believe that by working hard, they can get what they want all by themselves. (7) Finally, the *interdependent* people believe that they can get some of what they want by working alone but realize that they'll accomplish more and have more fun if they give and receive help.*

13. Sentence 1 is a

    (a.) main idea.
    b. major supporting detail.
    c. minor supporting detail.

14. Sentence 3 is a

    a. main idea.
    b. major supporting detail.
    (c.) minor supporting detail.

15. Sentence 5 is a

    a. main idea.
    (b.) major supporting detail.
    c. minor supporting detail.

B. Read the following paragraphs and respond to each of the questions by circling the letter of the correct answer.

(1) You can use the following three techniques to stay focused as you read. (2) First, visualize the material by forming mental pictures of the concepts as they are presented. (3) For instance, if you read that a voucher[1] system can help control cash disbursements, picture a voucher handing out dollar bills. (4) Second, read it out loud—especially complicated material. (5) Some of us remember better and understand more quickly when we hear an idea instead

1. **voucher:** related to written
    authorization

---

* Adapted from Skip Downing, *On Course*, 4th ed. (Boston: Houghton Mifflin Co., 2005), 111.

of seeing it in print. (6) Third, get a "feel" for your subject. (7) For example, if you're reading about a paramecium[1] in your biology text, imagine what it would feel like to run your finger around the long, cigar-shaped body of the organism and feel the hairy little cilia as they wiggle in your hand.*

16. The topic of this selection is
    a. reading.
    b. visualization.
    c. techniques for staying focused while reading.
    d. reading out loud.

17. The main idea is stated in
    a. sentence 1.   c. sentence 3.
    b. sentence 2.   d. sentence 4.

18. How many major supporting details develop the main idea?
    a. 1   c. 4
    b. 3   d. 6

(1) Nothing gets in the way of Hollywood's movie machinery—even the death of the film's star. (2) *Queen of the Damned,* singer/actress Aaliyah's last movie, was released after she died in a plane crash. (3) Oliver Reed died of a heart attack while shooting 2000's Oscar-winning *Gladiator,* but director Ridley Scott used computer-generated imagery to patch him into some scenes. (4) Phil Hartman was shot and killed by his wife, Brynn, in 1998, six weeks before his action-adventure *Small Soldiers* was to open. (5) No scenes were cut or altered. (6) John Candy died in his sleep of a heart attack in March 1994 while shooting the comedy *Wagons East!* in Mexico. (7) But thanks to a body double[2] and digital wizardry, Candy appeared in several scenes that he had never originally filmed, including one at a bar. (8) Brandon Lee's final film, *The Crow,* opened one year after he died from an accidental gunshot wound in 1993—on Friday the 13th. (9) According to producer Ed Pressman, "Everyone knew how wonderful he was, and it made more sense to continue than to destroy what he'd created." (10) A stand-in salvaged[3] Bruce Lee's unfinished 1973 flick, *Game of Death.* (11) The movie was completed six years after Lee's demise with the surviving actors and a body double.†

1. **paramecium:** a single-celled organism

2. **body double:** person who looks just like a particular actor

3. **salvaged:** saved or rescued

---

* Adapted from Dave Ellis, *Becoming a Master Student,* 9th ed. (Boston: Houghton Mifflin Co., 2000), 112.

† Adapted from Donna Freydkin, "Even in Death, Shows Must Go On," *USA Today,* February 18, 2002, 11B.

19. The topic of this selection is
    a. Aaliyah.
    b. actors and actresses.
    (c.) films that were released after their stars' deaths.
    d. weird things that happen in the film industry.

20. The main idea is stated in
    (a.) sentence 1.   c. sentence 9.
    b. sentence 2.   d. sentence 11.

21. How many major supporting details develop the main idea?
    a. 1   (c.) 6
    b. 3   d. 8

(1) American President Theodore Roosevelt and British Prime Minister Winston Churchill had much in common. (2) Both were from aristocratic[1] families. (3) Churchill was the grandson of the Duke of Marlborough, and Roosevelt's grandfather, Cornelius Van Schaack Roosevelt, owned acres of Manhattan real estate. (4) Both men revered[2] their fathers, even as they tried to avoid what they regarded as their respective single flaws. (5) Specifically, Theodore Roosevelt Sr. hired a substitute to serve in his place in the Civil War, and Lord Randolph Churchill made a political blunder[3] that ended his career. (6) Both men wrote several books. (7) Both took part in cavalry[4] charges in 1898; Roosevelt's was on San Juan Hill in Cuba, and Churchill's at Omdurman in the Sudan. (8) Both men worked to expand and modernize their nations' navies. (9) And both saw history as a story of the expansion of the influence of English-speaking peoples.*

22. The topic of this selection is
    a. Theodore Roosevelt.
    b. Winston Churchill.
    (c.) similarities between Roosevelt and Churchill.
    d. Roosevelt's and Churchill's fathers.

23. The main idea is stated in
    (a.) sentence 1.   c. sentence 8.
    b. sentence 2.   d. sentence 9.

1. **aristocratic:** related to the ruling class or nobility
2. **revered:** respected and adored
3. **blunder:** mistake
4. **cavalry:** troops on horseback

---

* Adapted from Michael Barone, "A Big Stick," *U.S. News and World Report,* February 25, 2002, 52.

24. How many major supporting details develop the main idea?

    a. 1   (c.) 6
    b. 3   d. 8

25. Which of the following sentences is a *minor* supporting detail?

    a. sentence 1   (c.) sentence 5
    b. sentence 4   d. sentence 6

TEST 2

Read each paragraph and respond to the questions that follow by circling the letter of the correct answer.

(1) You can learn techniques to help you remember to do certain things. (2) One technique is to link something you need to remember to another event that you know will take place. (3) For example, if you want to remember that your accounting assignment is due tomorrow, switch your watch (or a ring) from one arm to the other. (4) Then, every time you look at your watch, it becomes a reminder that you were supposed to remember something. (5) Tie a triple knot in your shoelace to remind you to set the alarm for your early morning study group meeting. (6) A second technique is to use imaginary cues. (7) For instance, to remember to write a check for the phone bill, picture your phone hanging onto the front door and picture reaching for the door knob and grabbing the phone instead. (8) When you get home and reach to open the front door, the image is apt[1] to return to you. (9) A third way to remember something is just to tell yourself you will remember it. (10) Specifically, relax and say to yourself, "At any time I choose, I will be able to recall . . . ." (11) The intention to remember can be more powerful than any other memory technique.*

1. The topic sentence of this paragraph is

    (a.) sentence 1.   c. sentence 3.
    b. sentence 2.   d. sentence 4.

2. Which of the following sentences does NOT begin a transition that signals a major supporting detail?

    a. sentence 2   (c.) sentence 7
    b. sentence 6   d. sentence 9

1. apt: likely

---

* Adapted from Dave Ellis, *Becoming a Master Student*, 9th ed. (Boston: Houghton Mifflin Co., 2000), 87.

3. Which of the following sentences begins with a transition that signals a minor supporting detail?

a. sentence 1   c. sentence 9
b. sentence 2   d. sentence 10

(1) Gretchen Grimm, who finally kicked her decades-old habit of stealing when she was 83 years old, illustrates two important truths about shoplifting. (2) The first is the powerful ego boost it can provide, especially to insecure young people. (3) To illustrate, Gretchen began shoplifting when she was just six years old, she believes, to win her mother's attention and affection. (4) The other lesson is that a crime that can be perpetrated[1] by first graders and old ladies is pretty hard to stop. (5) Gretchen, for instance, had only one serious arrest and hid her habit from her family for almost her whole life.*

4. The topic sentence of this paragraph is

a. sentence 1.   c. sentence 3.
b. sentence 2.   d. sentence 4.

5. Which two sentences begin with transitions that signal major supporting details?

a. sentences 1 and 2   c. sentences 2 and 4
b. sentences 2 and 3   d. sentences 3 and 5

6. Which of the following sentences begins with a transition that signals a minor supporting detail?

a. sentence 1   c. sentence 3
b. sentence 2   d. sentence 4

(1) The Internet provides car buyers with a wealth of information. (2) For one thing, they can look at photos and find data about comparative safety, reliability, and owner satisfaction. (3) Also, they can read independent reviews, locate dealers in their geographic area, select options, and compare prices. (4) At the Auto Channel's website, for example, consumers can find data on used-car prices, and the Used-Vehicle Classified Ads website lets shoppers design a search based on geographic area, make, model, price range, year, and desired features. (5) In addition, customers can click on another site that provides a toll-free number to VINguard, which reports on a vehicle's history and tells if a car has ever been in a collision.†

1. **perpetrated:** committed

---

* Adapted from Jerry Adler, "The 'Thrill' of Theft," *Newsweek*, February 25, 2002, 53.

† Adapted from William Pride et al., *Business,* 6th ed. (Boston: Houghton Mifflin Co., 1999), 307. Copyright © 1999 by Houghton Mifflin Company. Reprinted with permission.

7. The topic sentence of this paragraph is
   - (a.) sentence 1.
   - b. sentence 2.
   - c. sentence 3.
   - d. sentence 4.

8. Which of the following sentences does NOT begin with a transition that signals a major supporting detail?
   - (a.) sentence 1
   - b. sentence 2
   - c. sentence 3
   - d. sentence 5

9. Which of the following sentences includes a transition that signals a minor supporting detail?
   - a. sentence 2
   - b. sentence 3
   - (c.) sentence 4
   - d. sentence 5

(1) Most methods of coping with stress can be classified as either problem-focused or emotion-focused. (2) Problem-focused methods involve efforts to alter or eliminate a source of stress. (3) For example, you might deal with the problem of noise from a nearby airport by forming a community action group to push for tougher noise-reduction laws. (4) Emotion-focused techniques attempt to regulate[1] the negative emotional consequences of stress. (5) For instance, you might calm your anger when airport noise occurs by mentally focusing on the group's efforts to improve the situation.*

10. The topic sentence of this paragraph is
    - (a.) sentence 1.
    - b. sentence 2.
    - c. sentence 3.
    - d. sentence 4.

11. The two sentences that provide major supporting details are
    - a. sentences 1 and 2.
    - b. sentences 2 and 3.
    - (c.) sentences 2 and 4.
    - d. sentences 4 and 5.

12. Which of the following sentences begin with a transition that signals a minor supporting detail?
    - a. sentences 2 and 3
    - b. sentences 3 and 4
    - c. sentences 4 and 5
    - (d.) sentences 3 and 5

(1) Janice Boucher, author of *How to Love the Job You Hate*, says it's possible to recapture your love for a job gone bad. (2) One approach is to redesign your job so that it offers more challenge, more variety, or less stress. (3) For

1. **regulate:** control

---

* Adapted from Douglas Bernstein and Peggy Nash, *Essentials of Psychology*, 2nd ed. (Boston: Houghton Mifflin Co., 2002), 359.

instance, you could delegate[1] to someone else some task that you do not like to do, or you could develop a special project that gives your job greater meaning. (4) Also, you can do things that make you feel good about yourself and your job again. (5) As an illustration, a supermarket cashier might begin to pay genuine attention to customers in order to improve service, and a newspaper reporter pressured to emphasize sensationalism[2] could establish higher standards for truth in reporting.*

13. The topic sentence of this paragraph is

   (a) sentence 1.   c. sentence 3.

   b. sentence 2.   d. sentence 4.

14. Which of the following sentences begins with a transition that signals a major supporting detail?

   a. sentence 1   (c) sentence 4

   b. sentence 3   d. sentence 5

15. Which of the following sentences begins with a transition that signals a minor supporting detail?

   a. sentence 1   c. sentence 4

   b. sentence 2   (d) sentence 5

3

1. **delegate:** assign a task

2. **sensationalism:** subject matter characterized by exaggeration or shocking details

---

* Adapted from Barry Reece and Rhonda Brandt, *Effective Human Relations in Organizations*, 7th ed. (Boston: Houghton Mifflin Co., 1999), 190.

Implied Main Ideas

GOALS FOR CHAPTER 4

▶ Define the term *implied main idea.*

▶ Form generalizations based on specific details.

▶ State the implied main idea of a paragraph.

▶ Apply the steps of the SQ3R strategy to reading selections.

When you read Chapter 2 of this book, you learned that many paragraphs include a topic sentence that clearly states the main idea. Other paragraphs, however, do not contain a topic sentence. Does that mean they don't have a main point? No, it means that readers must do a little more work to figure out what that point—which is called an **implied main idea**—is. To see how much you already know about drawing conclusions about a main idea, take the following test.

TEST YOURSELF

The following paragraphs do not include a stated main idea. Read each paragraph and see if you can determine its main point. Circle the letter of the sentence that best states the main idea.

1. Why do we watch reality-based shows such as *Big Brother, Fear Factor,* and *Survivor*? Most people, when responding to a survey, answered that guessing who will be eliminated or who will win is the reason they watch. Others stated that seeing real people facing challenging situations was their motivation for watching the shows while others get a thrill out of imagining themselves in similar situations. Other respondents to the survey cited watching fights among contestants, making fun of contestants, watching physically attractive contestants, and having emotional attachments to contestants as their main reasons for watching reality-based shows. Only 11.4 percent, however, answered that they watched only because there was nothing better on TV.*

* Adapted from "We're Reality-TV Voyeurs," *USA Today,* July 18, 2001, 1D.

a. Reality-based TV shows are popular today.

b. Reality-based TV shows present challenging situations.

(c.) Reality-based TV shows interest people for a number of different reasons.

d. Several surveys have been designed to ask people why reality-based TV shows are popular.

2. For centuries in China, soy has been served as both a food and a drink. In the 1930s, auto magnate[1] Henry Ford used soybeans to make paint enamel. Today, soy can be found in salad dressings, cereals, breads, burgers, energy bars, and frozen desserts. Soy can even be found in moisturizers.*

a. Soy beans are delicious.

(b.) Soy can be used in a variety of ways.

c. Soy may be the key to finding a non-oil based fuel for cars.

d. If you use soy as a moisturizer, you'll see visible results in days.

3. I have clung to a potato cart as it climbed the steep, rugged mountains to Kurdish[2] refugee camps. I have flown in a dark, cold, windowless cargo plane to cover a story in the Mideast desert. I have watched the most graphic and gory bone surgery, standing just inches from the carved limbs. On the other hand, my face flushes hot and my heart races before facing a person with whom I have had a major disagreement. I worry that someone won't like or admire me. I burn with anxiety when I think I'm being talked about behind my back. Nothing unnerves me more than the prospect of being humiliated. Even writing these words, I wonder what friends and family will think when they read them. My sister Leslie, who at least appears fearless, has asked me often over the years: "Why in the world do you care what any of these people think?" I've never had a good answer.†

a. The author has done many dangerous things in her life.

(b.) The author is not afraid to do dangerous things but is afraid of emotional things.

c. The author is concerned about what her friends and family will think of her writing.

d. The author's sister Leslie counsels her on a variety of things.

---

1. **magnate:** powerful, influential person

2. **Kurdish:** related to the Kurds, people inhabiting Kurdistan in southwest Asia

---

* Adapted from Lisa Singer, "The Truth About Soy," *Real Simple*, April 2004, 165.

† "Pulse" by Tracy Chutorian Semler. Copyright © 2001 by Tracy Chutorian Semler. Reprinted by permission of International Creative Management, Inc.

4. Who is a master student? A master student is a person who has attained[1] a level of skill that goes beyond technique. A master student is curious about everything, and the unknown does not frighten him or her. He or she can take a large body of information and sift[2] through it to discover relationships. Mastery of skills is important to the master student, and work is generally effortless; struggle evaporates. Mastery can lead to flashy results, but often the result of mastery is a sense of profound satisfaction, well-being, and timelessness.*

   a. The master student has many different personalities.
   b. The master student understands the importance of developing certain critical skills.
   c. There are many flashy results that can be attained by a master.
   d. The master student feels like he or she needs to be an expert at everything.

5. What do I have planned for the summer? Well, by August, my body fat will match that of a *Survivor*[3] contestant. My abdominal muscles will be flat, my biceps round, my inner thighs carved, and my rear end will be jiggle-free. Oh, and I'll be smarter and far more accomplished, once I finish Plato's *Republic,*[4] watch those French videos, hone[5] my pastry skills, organize my closets, and embrace the power of yoga. It's going to happen. Trust me.†

   a. The author is going to change her body type by August.
   b. The author is going to organize her closet by August.
   c. The author has some very ambitious summer plans.
   d. The author has many different skills.

4

Understanding Implied Main Ideas

Every paragraph contains a main idea. Sometimes, that main idea is stated outright in a topic sentence. Sometimes, though, the main idea is implied. An **implied main idea** is one that is suggested but not said. To determine the

1. **attained:** achieved
2. **sift:** sort
3. *Survivor*: a popular reality television show
4. **Plato's *Republic*:** a philosophical work
5. **hone:** sharpen or improve

* Adapted from Dave Ellis, "The Master Student," *Becoming a Master Student* (Boston: Houghton Mifflin Co., 2000), 26–27.
† Adapted from Linda Wells, "Better, Stronger, Faster," *Allure*, July 2001, 30.

implied main idea, you examine the details presented and draw from them a conclusion about the overall point.

If you think about it, you figure out implied main ideas quite often in your daily life. For example, look at the following conversation:

Mother: How was your day, honey?

Son: Well, I overslept. As I was rushing to get to class, I slipped and fell in a mud puddle. I left an assignment at home that was due today, so I'll lose points for turning it in late. At lunch, my girlfriend told me she wants to break up with me.

The son answered his mother's question with a series of specific details. What conclusion can you draw from them? Every incident he reported caused him pain, trouble, or aggravation, so it's safe to conclude that he had a pretty bad day.

Here's another example: You're in the park. You see a dog. You notice that the dog is not wearing a collar. The dog looks dirty and wet. The dog also appears underfed because you can see its ribs through its skin. The dog appears to be alone, not with a person. What conclusion do you make? Most people would say that the animal is probably a stray.

You yourself notice details, add them together, and draw conclusions all the time. In Chapter 3 of this book, you practiced recognizing supporting details, the information that proves or explains a main idea. A paragraph with an implied main idea contains *only* supporting details. These details are the clues that you put together to figure out the author's point.

To improve your ability to draw these conclusions while you read, it's helpful to remember what you learned about the terms *general* and *specific* back in Chapter 2.

Figuring out an implied main idea requires you to form a generalization based on a series of specific items or ideas. Look at the following group of words:

coat

pants

dress

shirt

What generalization can you make about this list of items? They're all things you wear, so the general term that describes them is *clothing*.

Now, examine another list:

paper

desk

pencil

toothpick

This group is a little trickier. When you read the first three items, you may have thought they were *things in an office* or *things you use at school*. But the last item isn't in either of those categories. When you add up all the details and look for the similarities, you realize that these are all *products made from wood.*

Exercise 4.1

Write on the blank above each group of words a general category that includes all of the items listed.

1. General Idea: <u>Things that fly</u>

   airplane
   helicopter
   bird
   kite

2. General Idea: <u>Yard equipment</u>

   leaf blower
   weed eater
   lawn mower
   hedge clipper

3. General Idea: <u>Things that are round</u>

   steering wheel
   tire
   hula hoop
   donut

4. General Idea: <u>Types of music</u>

   rap
   hip-hop
   disco
   alternative rock

5. General Idea: _Kinds of dessert_

ice cream
cake
pie
cookies

6. General Idea: _Bodies of water_

river
ocean
stream
pond

7. General Idea: _Things that are underground_

subway
basement
root cellar
gas station tanks

8. General Idea: _Dairy products; things made with milk_

cheese
yogurt
cream
butter

9. General Idea: _Things that are rectangular_

dictionary
magazine
notebook paper
football field

10. General Idea: _Ways of communicating; types of communication_

e-mail
phone
letter
face-to-face

As you remember from Chapter 2, a group of specific sentences can also support a general idea. For example, read the following sentences:

Maggie works seven days a week.

Maggie works over ten hours a day.

Maggie hasn't taken a vacation in three years.

What general statement would include all three of those specific sentences? The answer is *Maggie works too much.*

Exercise 4.2

On the blank above each group of sentences, write a general sentence that includes all of the specific details given.

1. General Sentence: <u>Being a police officer can be dangerous.</u>

   Police officers sometimes drive patrol cars in high-speed chases.
   Police officers can be wounded in fights or shot by criminals.
   Police officers have to go into dark buildings or alleys to investigate crimes.

2. General Sentence: <u>Jim likes to read; Jim reads a lot.</u>

   Jim has several newspapers delivered to his home every day.
   Jim belongs to several book clubs and attends book club meetings regularly.
   Jim reads six or seven books a month.

3. General Sentence: <u>Seattle is a rainy city.</u>

   The sun doesn't shine very much in Seattle.
   Seattle has about 200 rainy days a year.
   Some streets often flood in Seattle.

4. General Sentence: <u>Rich spends a lot of time in his garden; Rich enjoys his garden.</u>

   Rich weeds his garden every day.
   Rich has planted four tomato plants in his garden.
   Rich spends a lot of money on flowers for his garden.

5. General Sentence: <u>Jin uses (or enjoys using) the World Wide Web a lot.</u>

   Jin sends e-mail to many of her friends and family members on a weekly basis.
   Jin does most of her shopping on the Internet.
   Jin surfs the Web for information on movies, books, and other things that interest her.

You may not have realized it, but you often form general ideas based on specific details when you read cartoons and comic strips. For instance, look at the following comic strip.

Beetle Bailey © Reprinted with special permission of King Features Syndicate.

This comic strip never states a main idea. However, you can add up all of the details to conclude that these men are complainers who are not happy, no matter what they're doing.

Exercise 4.3

On the blank beneath each of the following cartoons, write the idea the artist hoped to imply.

Cathy © 2001 Cathy Guisewite. Reprinted with permission of
Universal Press Syndicate. All rights reserved.

1. Main Idea:

    Wedding customs have changed to reflect modern times.

Grand Avenue reprinted by permission of United Feature Syndicate, Inc.

2. Main Idea:

    People use cell phones mostly for personal or social reasons.

Family Circus © Bill Keane, Inc. Reprinted by special permission of King Features Syndicate.

3. Main Idea:

    Parents are excited when their child learns to talk, but they are embarrassed

    when the child says things she shouldn't.

Cathy © 2002 Cathy Guisewite. Reprinted with permission of Universal
Press Syndicate. All rights reserved.

4. Main Idea:

Although people try to work out, working out is difficult and causes them to give

up on losing weight.

Determining Implied Main Ideas

To figure out the implied main idea in a paragraph, you can often use a me-
thodical, step-by-step approach. Basically, this procedure involves looking for
clues in the supporting details, adding them together, and drawing a logical
conclusion based on the evidence. These next sections will explain and give
you practice with each of the four steps in this process:

Step 1: Find the subject of each sentence.

Step 2: Determine the *type* of supporting detail in the paragraph.

Step 3: Determine a general topic based on the specific details.

Step 4: State an implied main idea that includes both the topic and what
the author is saying about that topic.

As you become a more proficient reader, you will be able to complete all
of these steps in your head most of the time.

Step 1: Find the Subject of Each Sentence

The first step in discovering an implied main idea is to closely examine the
supporting details. The major and minor details in a paragraph will provide

you with the clues you need to draw a conclusion about the author's point. For example, read the following paragraph:

(1) "Calvin and Hobbes," a comic strip about a little boy and his tiger, often tackles classical, philosophical, and ethical subjects. (2) The "Doonesbury" comic strip takes on political subjects, and even the "Peanuts" comic strip included social commentary on the Vietnam War. (3) "The Far Side" cartoons often focus on scientific ethics. (4) The "Dilbert" comic strip points out the illogic and insensitivity within American corporations. (5) The "For Better or Worse" comic strip often examines morality and family issues.*

Here are the subjects in each of the sentences:

Sentence 1: "Calvin and Hobbes"

Sentence 2: "Doonesbury" and "Peanuts"

Sentence 3: "The Far Side"

Sentence 4: "Dilbert"

Sentence 5: "For Better or Worse"

Exercise 4.4

On the blanks below each paragraph, write the subject of each sentence.

1. (1) Louisiana was named after France's King Louis XIV. (2) South Carolina comes from *Carolus*, the Latin word for Charles I, King of England. (3) Maryland was named after Queen Mary, wife of England's King Charles I. (4) Georgia was named in honor of England's King George II. (5) Both Virginia and West Virginia were named for Elizabeth I, the "virgin" queen.

   Sentence 1 subject: Louisiana

   Sentence 2 subject: South Carolina

   Sentence 3 subject: Maryland

   Sentence 4 subject: Georgia

   Sentence 5 subjects: Virginia and West Virginia

* Adapted from *USA Today Newsview*, August 1997, 5.

2. (1) Teachers, according to 79 percent of public high school students, are too easy on students when it comes to enforcing rules and assigning homework. (2) In addition, half of teens in public schools say their teachers and schools do not challenge them. (3) Too many disruptive students in classrooms, according to 70 percent of teenagers, are interfering with learning. (4) Schools' standards for graduation, say 70 percent of students, are too low. (5) According to three-fourths of students, diplomas are given to students even if they don't learn the required material.*

Sentence 1 subject: <u>teachers</u>

Sentence 2 subject: <u>teachers and schools</u>

Sentence 3 subject: <u>disruptive students</u>

Sentence 4 subject: <u>schools' standards</u>

Sentence 5 subject: <u>diplomas</u>

3. (1) *Ladies' Home Journal* is a magazine that focuses on women's issues and is generally considered appropriate for women in their thirties, forties, and fifties. (2) *Glamour* is a magazine that devotes many pages to issues facing women in their twenties and early thirties. (3) *Mode* is a new magazine devoted entirely to issues affecting "plus-size" women. (4) *Allure* magazine has the most information on beauty products and is for women who are interested in the latest information on makeup and hairstyles. (5) For the most information on home life, however, the best magazine to buy is *Better Homes and Gardens*.

Sentence 1 subject: <u>Ladies' Home Journal</u>

Sentence 2 subject: <u>Glamour</u>

Sentence 3 subject: <u>Mode</u>

Sentence 4 subject: <u>Allure</u>

Sentence 5 subject: <u>Better Homes and Gardens</u>

4. (1) Thomas Jefferson, who wrote the Declaration of Independence, was lean, elegant, remote, and a bit sneaky. (2) John Adams, who contributed

* Adapted from "Teenagers Want More from Public Schools," *USA Today Newsview*, August 1997, 4.

to the Declaration as well, was stout,[1] cheap, and perhaps too honest about himself and everyone else. (3) Considered somewhat eccentric, or odd, Benjamin Franklin was a noted inventor and diplomat who was somewhat chubby and messy, but neither of those things interfered with his ability to help write the most important document in American history. (4) George Washington was a genius at lifting morale[2] and knowing when to retreat to fight another day, so keeping the Founding Fathers agreeable and on task was his major contribution.

Sentence 1 subject: _Thomas Jefferson_

Sentence 2 subject: _John Adams_

Sentence 3 subject: _Benjamin Franklin_

Sentence 4 subject: _George Washington_

5. (1) Philadelphia is known for its "Philly cheese steak." (2) Coney Island in Brooklyn, New York, is known for its hot dogs. (3) Miami is famous for its Cuban food, particularly chicken and rice, or "arroz con pollo." (4) Chicago has made a name for itself by serving great deep-dish pizza. (5) And you can't go to Boston without getting the best clam chowder in the entire United States.

Sentence 1 subject: _Philadelphia_

Sentence 2 subject: _Coney Island_

Sentence 3 subject: _Miami_

Sentence 4 subject: _Chicago_

Sentence 5 subject: _Boston_

Step 2: Determine the *Type* of Supporting Detail in the Paragraph

Once you've determined what each sentence is about, you should be able to conclude what type of supporting details the sentences are. Common types of supporting details include the following.

1. **stout:** plump   2. **morale:** spirits of a person or group

reasons	causes
examples	effects
events	types
steps	parts
points of comparison	descriptive details or features

For an illustration, read the next paragraph:

(1) Quick naps during the day help counteract the negative effects of the sleep deprivation[1] that plagues[2] over 50 percent of Americans. (2) Thus, naps give the body needed rest and actually reduce the risk of getting diseases like obesity, diabetes, and heart attacks. (3) Naps also help us overcome the natural dip in energy that occurs midway through the workday. (4) Therefore, naps keep employees creative, productive, and alert. (5) Thus, naps make people less prone to making mistakes and causing accidents.*

To determine the type of details in this paragraph, first find the subject of each sentence:

Sentence 1: Naps' effect on sleep deprivation

Sentence 2: Naps' effects on the body and diseases

Sentence 3: Naps' effect on the midday dip in energy

Sentence 4: Naps' effects on employees

Sentence 5: Naps' effects on mistakes and accidents

What type of details are these? If you answered *causes* and *effects*, you're right. Understanding the kind of details included in the paragraph will help you form a more accurate statement of the main idea when you get to Step 4.

Be aware that there may be more than one type of supporting detail in a paragraph. A paragraph may, for example, combine examples and reasons or causes and types. Authors can use different types of details together to develop their ideas.

1. **deprivation:** loss or lack of something
2. **plagues:** afflicts; affects

---

* Adapted from Betty Booker, "Catching Some Zzzzzz's at Work," *The News Herald* (Morganton, NC), April 6, 2003, 1C.

Exercise 4.5

In the list below each paragraph, write a check mark on the blank next to the correct type of supporting details in that paragraph.

1. When severe thunderstorms threaten your area, the first thing you should do is listen to your local radio or TV station. Then, get inside a home, large building, or car. Do not stand under a tall tree in an open area, on a hilltop, in an open field, or on a beach. Also, get away from all metal objects such as tractors or other metal farm equipment, motorcycles, bicycles, golf carts, and scooters, and do not hold metal objects such as golf clubs. When you get indoors, do not use the telephone except for emergencies. Do not use bathtubs, water faucets, or sinks because metal pipes can conduct electricity.*

   ____ reasons   ____ points of comparison

   ____ causes and effects   ____ events

   ✔ steps   ____ examples

2. The Physicians' Health Study in the 1980s, a long-term monitoring of 22,000 doctors, found that aspirin taken in small doses every other day may reduce the risk of a first heart attack by 44 percent. Other studies have shown that aspirin can lower the risk of a second heart attack by 30 percent and death during a heart attack by 23 percent. Aspirin also seems to reduce the risk of most strokes and their recurrence[1] by about 25 percent. Research has revealed that regular aspirin use may protect against the risk of colon cancer by as much as 40 to 50 percent; esophageal, or throat, cancer by about 80 to 90 percent; and ovarian cancer by some 25 percent.†

   ____ reasons   ____ points of comparison

   ____ causes and effects   ____ events

   ____ steps   ✔ examples

1. recurrence: happening again

* Adapted from "Emergency Weather Information," *The Westchester County Planning for Emergencies Booklet,* 9.

† Adapted from Jake Page, "Take Two Aspirin and Call Me in the Morning," *Smithsonian,* August 2001, 101.

3. The need to feel important drives people to place enormous value on such symbols as titles, corner offices, and first-class travel. It causes us to feel excessively pleased when someone important recognizes us, and to feel hurt when our doctor or pastor passes us on the street without saying hello, or when a neighbor calls us by our sister's or brother's name. The need to know that we are making a difference motivates doctors and medical researchers to spend hours looking through microscopes in the hope of finding cures for diseases. It drives inventors and entrepreneurs[1] to stay up nights trying to find a better way of providing people with something they need. It causes artists, novelists, and composers to try to add to the store of beauty in the world by finding just the right color, the right word, the right note. And it leads ordinary people to buy six copies of the local paper because it has their name or picture in it.*

_____ reasons   _____ points of comparison

_____ causes and effects   _____ events

_____ steps   ✔ examples

Note: Causes and effects could also be considered correct.

4. Are all fast-food restaurants alike? That depends on what you are looking for. Wendy's has a full salad bar with fresh salads, some soups, and accompanying things like croutons and beans. Its salad dressing selection is great, too. McDonald's doesn't offer a salad bar but does offer salads in easy-to-use cups that can be shaken to distribute dressing evenly throughout the salad. Burger King also offers salads, but they are in rectangular trays, which can be difficult to handle while eating. All of the restaurants mentioned, however, have hamburgers, chicken sandwiches, and fried sandwich selections that are comparable in price and quality.

_____ reasons   ✔ points of comparison

_____ causes and effects   _____ events

_____ steps   _____ examples

5. In the early 1800s, every city and town in America kept its own time, so it might be 11:55 AM in New York City, 11:47 AM in Washington, and 11:35 AM in Pittsburgh. As a result, mid-nineteenth century railroad travelers who

1. **entrepreneurs:** people who start their own businesses

---

* Excerpted from Harold S. Kushner, *Living a Life That Matters* (New York: Knopf, 2001), 6.

moved from city to city began to find all of the different times confusing and inconvenient. In 1872, therefore, the Time-Table Convention searched for a solution, and Charles F. Dowd proposed the creation of time zones, imaginary divisions of the Earth's surface. In 1883, after Congress did not act to solve the problem, the railroads decided to establish four time zones: Eastern, Central, Mountain, and Pacific. On November 18, 1883, they set one standard time, and cities around the country changed their clocks to conform to it.*

_____ reasons	_____ points of comparison
✔ causes and effects	_____ events
_____ steps	_____ examples

Step 3: Determine a General Topic Based on the Specific Details

Once you've discovered the supporting details' subjects and type, you can make a generalization about them. You must make this generalization before you can complete the final step. In using logic to determine an overall category for the details, you are figuring out the overall topic of the paragraph. You'll need to be able to include this topic in your statement of the main idea.

Let's look at the paragraphs in the explanations of steps 1 and 2 as illustrations. In the paragraph about comic strips on page 179, the subjects of each sentence were all examples of comic strips or cartoons. This is the general category that includes those specific details. Now look back at the paragraph about naps on page 182. In that paragraph, the sentences were all causes or effects. What generalization can you make about those details? You might say they're all *effects of naps*. That is the paragraph's overall topic.

Exercise 4.6

Read each of the following paragraphs and write the correct answers on the blank after each one. The types of supporting details are reasons, examples, events, steps, points of comparison, causes, effects, types, parts, and descriptive details or features.

1. (1) Saving most of your income may allow you to retire early, like John Greaney, who retired at the age of 38 after saving aggressively in his

* Adapted from John Steele Gordon, "Standard Time," *American Heritage*, July/August 2001, 22–23.

twenties and early thirties. (2) Experts say that living in the smallest, least expensive home that will meet your needs will give you more money to spend during your retirement. (3) Other things to do so that you can live well while retired include living more cheaply, tapping into your retirement account sooner, or arranging to work a few hours so that you still have some kind of income to help you live.*

Sentence 1 subject: <u>Saving income</u>

Sentence 2 subject: <u>Living in small, less expensive home</u>

Sentence 3 subject: <u>Other things to do so that you can live well</u>

Type of supporting details: <u>Steps</u>

General topic of paragraph: <u>Things to do so that you can retire early</u>

2. (1) At only age sixteen, Mae Jemison entered Stanford University, one of the top colleges in the nation, and earned a bachelor's degree in chemical engineering. (2) After earning this degree, she went to medical school at Cornell University in New York and earned a medical degree in 1981. (3) Then she joined the Peace Corps, working as a medical officer for more than two years in Africa. (4) Next, she entered NASA's astronaut program, and when she rocketed into space aboard the space shuttle *Endeavor* in 1992, she became America's first African-American female astronaut. (5) She worked for NASA for six years and then resigned to found her own company, the Jemison Group, which tries to bring advanced technologies to the developing world. (6) She is also a college professor and has been a professional dancer.†

Sentence 1 subject: <u>Mae Jemison</u>

Sentence 2 subject: <u>Mae Jemison</u>

Sentence 3 subject: <u>Mae Jemison</u>

Sentence 4 subject: <u>Mae Jemison</u>

Sentence 5 subject: <u>Mae Jemison</u>

* Adapted from Linda Stern, "Retire When You Want To," *Reader's Digest*, RD.com, July 17, 2001.

† Adapted from Jim Dawson, "Mae Jemison: Woman of Many Facets," *Star Tribune* (Minneapolis, MN), March 13, 2000.

Type of supporting details: _Events or descriptive details_

General topic of paragraph: _Mae Jemison's achievements_

3. (1) Before you take any family photos, experts advise, look for a good point-and-shoot camera with a flash and a good lens. (2) Next, read the manual that comes with the camera so you can find out, for example, that your camera could, with the flip of a switch, add the date to a print. (3) Third, buy a lot of film; professional photographers might use twenty rolls of film to get one good shot. (4) And last, make sure everyone is in a good mood because good moods lead to good pictures.*

Sentence 1 subject: _Buy the right camera_

Sentence 2 subject: _Read the camera manual_

Sentence 3 subject: _Buy a lot of film_

Sentence 4 subject: _Take photos when subjects are in a good mood_

Type of supporting details: _Steps_

General topic of paragraph: _Things to do to take good photos_

4. (1) What could possibly be on a video made for cats? (2) To start, colorful bird sequences filled with stereo chirps and trills are very attractive to cats. (3) Gerbils scurrying across reddish desert rocks and a chipmunk darting into a grate rate more highly with other furry viewers, who watch intently from their perches until excitement finally propels them to paw the screen or to look behind the television set to find the critters they've been watching. (4) Also popular is the televised aquarium, which makes some kitties jump to the top of the television to try to dip their paws into the image on the screen.†

Sentence 2 subject: _Bird sequences_

Sentence 3 subject: _Gerbils and chipmunk_

Sentence 4 subject: _Televised aquarium_

* Adapted from S. Johanna Robledo, "Group Mug," *Real Simple*, August 2001, 45.
† Adapted from "The Cats' Meow," advertisement, National Syndications, Inc.

Type of supporting details: _Examples or descriptive features_

General topic of paragraph: _Creatures that are attractive to cats_

5. (1) On his own, an orangutan[1] named Fu Manchu figured out how to use a wire lock-pick to escape from his cage at the Omaha Zoo, hiding the tool in his mouth each time he was recaptured. (2) Another orangutan at a Seattle zoo came up with a ploy,[2] too, by pretending to drop or lose a piece of fruit and then asking for a replacement while actually hiding it. (3) A killer whale named Corky let a keeper stand on his head—a trick he had never been taught—to help the man reach a baby whale in danger of dying in a stretcher hanging over the tank. (4) An ape named Chantek who learned to earn coins for doing chores and to trade them for treats came up with the idea to try to expand his money supply by counterfeiting extra coins from tinfoil.*

Sentence 1 subject: _Fu Manchu_

Sentence 2 subject: _Another orangutan_

Sentence 3 subject: _A killer whale named Corky_

Sentence 4 subject: _An ape named Chantek_

Type of supporting details: _Examples_

General topic of paragraph: _Animals_

As you complete this step, remember what you learned in Chapter 2 about topics that are too broad or too narrow. Make sure the topic you choose is neither.

Exercise 4.7

After each paragraph, label each topic by writing *N* on the blank if it's too narrow, *B* if it's too broad, and *T* if it's the correct topic.

1. The mothers of today's "Generation X," the group of Americans born between 1961 and 1981, did 89 percent of the cooking in their homes, but

1. orangutan: a type of ape   **2. ploy:** a sneaky trick

---

* Adapted from Eugene Linden, "What Animals Really Think," *Reader's Digest*, February 2000, 116–123.

their grown children now tend to divide evening meal preparation equally between the husband and the wife. The parents of Generation Xers usually insisted that their families sit down to eat meals together almost every day, but parents and children today eat only about five meals per week as a family. The length of meals has changed, too: in the homes of most older generation people, mealtimes usually lasted at least thirty minutes, but now only half of Generation Xers stay at the table that long.*

_B_ a. Mealtimes

_T_ b. Mealtimes in older generation and Generation X homes

_N_ c. The length of mealtimes in older generation and Generation X homes

2. Although air conditioning is the invention that keeps us cool and comfortable in the middle of the summer, it also has left many of us psychologically unprepared to deal with the outdoors. People now think that they are incapable of handling the discomfort of high temperatures and humidity. Air conditioning has also been blamed for encouraging urban sprawl and draining the South's energy resources. In 1997, for example, Florida alone spent $1.8 billion just on air conditioning. Furthermore, Southern traditionalists accuse air conditioning of speeding up their lifestyles, encouraging an influx[1] of Northerners, and contributing to a decline in neighborly conduct.†

_B_ a. Air conditioning

_N_ b. Air conditioning's effect on psychology

_T_ c. Air conditioning's negative effects

3. The ancient Greeks would tuck rosemary twigs in their hair while studying to help them remember what they were learning. They also wore rosemary garlands to ward off the "evil eye," a look or stare believed to harm others. The popular belief at one time was that only evil people could not grow rosemary. During the Middle Ages, a common practice was to place rosemary under the pillow at night to prevent nightmares. At one time,

1. **influx:** flowing in

---

* Adapted from "Who's Cooking in Gen X Households?" *USA Today*, July 1998, 9–10.

† Adapted from Sean Mussenden, "100 Years of Cool Air Change South," *Orlando Sentinel*, June 21, 2002, www.orlandosentinel.com.

rosemary was used in almost all wedding ceremonies. Sprigs of rosemary were dipped in scented waters and then woven into a bridal wreath for the bride to wear around her head.*

___N___ a. Wedding customs involving rosemary

___B___ b. Superstitions

___T___ c. Historical uses of rosemary

4. Stroll down a country lane. Meander[1] along an ancient footpath. Picnic next to a bubbling stream or a village courtyard. Walking tours will also give you a closer look at a country and its people. You'll get to know your fellow travelers, too. Last but not least, you'll get lots of exercise because walking vacations usually involve several miles of hiking per day.†

___B___ a. Vacations

___T___ b. Things to see and do on walking tours

___N___ c. Meeting people on walking tours

5. *Friends* television show star Matthew Perry was treated for addiction to prescription drugs in 1997 and again in 2001 for addiction to pain killers and alcohol. In 1998, actor Charlie Sheen entered the Promises clinic in Malibu, California, for his substance abuse. *Baywatch* actress Yasmine Bleeth voluntarily entered Promises in 2000 with a cocaine addiction. In 2001, actor Ben Affleck checked into the same clinic to get treatment for alcohol abuse. That same year, actor Robert Downey Jr. entered rehab for addiction to drugs. Jack Osbourne, one of the stars of the reality-TV show *The Osbournes*, checked into rehab in 2003 after becoming addicted to alcohol and prescription drugs.‡

___T___ a. Actors who sought treatment for addictions

___B___ b. Actors and actresses

___N___ c. Actor Matthew Perry

---

1. meander: walk slowly

---

* Adapted from Tim Haas and Jan Haas, "Using Rosemary," *News Herald* (Morganton, NC), March 28, 2004, 5C.

† Adapted from Judy Hammond, "In Step with the World," *Daily News*, July 15, 2001, Travel Section, 12.

‡ Adapted from "Stars Who Faced Their Demons," *USA Today*, March 17, 2004, 3D.

Step 4: State an Implied Main Idea

If you have successfully completed steps 1 through 3, you have systematically gone through each thinking stage necessary to state the paragraph's main idea. It is in this last step that you put together all of the clues you have examined to come up with a statement of the main idea in your own words. This requires you not only to recognize the subjects in the supporting details but also to draw a general conclusion based on *what is being said about each of these subjects*. Then once more, you decide on a general category of ideas or things that include all of those statements.

Remember what you learned about main ideas and topic sentences in Chapter 2. The main idea has two parts: the topic and the point the author wants to make about that topic. The implied main idea is no different. It, too, should include both of those parts. Your statement will begin with the general topic you discovered in step 3 of this process. Then, it will go on to express the conclusion you drew from adding together the specific supporting details.

For example, look again at the paragraph about comic strips on page 179. What is being said about each different comic strip? Each sentence points out a certain type of subject matter that the cartoonists include in their creations:

philosophy and ethics

political and social commentary

scientific ethics

illogic and insensitivity within American corporations

morality and family issues

What generalization can you make about the items in this list? Obviously, they're all serious, important, and weighty issues.

To form a statement of the main idea, begin with the topic you determined in step 3: comic strips and cartoons. Often, you will indicate the type of details the paragraph contains, which is why you completed step 3. Then, add the generalization mentioned above to state the main idea:

Several examples of cartoons and comic strips are often about some serious, important, and weighty issues.

This is the overall point suggested by the paragraph's specific supporting details.

Now, let's follow the same procedure with the paragraph about the effects of taking naps. This list briefly summarizes those effects.

4

Effect #1: Naps counteract sleep deprivation

↓

give body rest

↓

reduce risk of disease

Effect #2: Naps help us overcome natural dip in energy

↓

keep employees creative, productive, and alert

↓

so employees less prone to mistakes and accidents

What generalization can you make based on these effects? You could say that they're all positive results or benefits.

Next, put the generalizations you make about the topic and about the ideas together to form a statement of the main idea. Here is one possibility:

Taking naps offers a number of benefits.

As a final illustration, let's go through all four steps for another paragraph:

(1) In 1959, the Mercury astronauts were household names, but today, few Americans can name even one of the 148 Space Shuttle astronauts currently on NASA's roster. (2) In the early days of America's space program, people were interested in astronauts because they were swaggering, bragging, boastful pilots, but now that two-thirds of them are doctors, scientists, and engineers, they're no longer "glamorous." (3) In the 1960s, astronauts were worshipped by the American public as heroes, but today, most Americans are indifferent[1] to them. (4) People used to stop their lives to pay close attention when astronauts went into space, but now, the Space Shuttle goes up and comes back with little fanfare.*

Step 1:   Sentence 1: Americans' past and present knowledge of astronauts' names

Sentence 2: Americans' past and present interest in astronauts

Sentence 3: Americans' past and present perceptions of astronauts

Sentence 4: Americans' past and present attentiveness to astronauts' missions

1. **indifferent:** not interested

* Adapted from Traci Watson, "Quick: Name an Astronaut," *USA Today*, July 12, 2001, 1A.

Step 2:   Types of details: Points of comparison

Step 3:   Paragraph's topic: Changes in Americans' attitudes about astronauts

Step 4:   Sentence 1: Knew names → don't know names

Sentence 2: Interested → not interested

Sentence 3: Hero worship → indifference

Sentence 4: Attentive → not attentive

Generalization: Americans used to care about astronauts, but now they don't.

Implied main idea: Between the early days of the space program and now, Americans' attitudes toward astronauts have changed from caring to indifference.

As you can see, determining implied main ideas is not only a necessary reading skill; it also helps you sharpen your thinking skills. You must analyze and apply logic as you complete each step of this process to draw a final conclusion. This kind of practice will lead to better thinking in general.

Exercise 4.8

Write the correct answer on each of the blanks that follow the paragraphs below. Answers may vary.

1. (1) In the recent past, U.S. President Bill Clinton lied about his extramarital romantic encounters with a White House intern. (2) Executives at Sony's Columbia Pictures admitted to creating a fake movie critic to write praiseworthy quotations about their films. (3) Pulitzer Prize-winning historian Joseph Ellis was exposed as a liar who invented his whole tour of duty in Vietnam. (4) Journalist David Brock knowingly printed false information about Anita Hill, an attorney who accused Supreme Court Justice nominee Clarence Thomas of sexual harassment.*

Sentence 1 subject: Bill Clinton

Sentence 2 subject: Executives at Sony's Columbia Pictures

* Adapted from Karen S. Peterson, "Would I Lie to You?" *USA Today*, July 5, 2001, 8D.

Sentence 3 subject: <u>Joseph Ellis</u>

Sentence 4 subject: <u>David Brock</u>

Type(s) of supporting details: <u>Examples</u>

General topic of paragraph: <u>High-profile people</u>

Generalization: <u>All of them were caught in lies.</u>

Implied main idea: <u>Many high-profile people have recently been caught lying.</u>

2. (1) Ever wanted to just up and leave your spouse for an extended—but temporary—period of time? (2) Janis Kirstein is a high school art teacher in Louisville who says she is taking a time-out at the Vermont Studio Center in Johnson, Vermont, to spend a month nurturing[1] her creativity and learning more about art. (3) Sally Howald took a leave from her job as a creative director for an ad agency to teach advertising strategies in Holland and to get away from her life as "soccer mom and full-time working mom" and reconnect with the person she was before she married. (4) Joan Mister, however, waited until her children were grown and then drove 30,000 miles alone in six months, having her sixty-fifth birthday on the road. (5) Her trip, she says, was about self-exploration.*

Sentence 2 subject: <u>Janis Kirstein</u>

Sentence 3 subject: <u>Sally Howald</u>

Sentence 4 subject: <u>Joan Mister</u>

Type(s) of supporting details: <u>Examples</u>

General topic of paragraph: <u>Married women who temporarily leave their spouses</u>

Generalization: <u>All three women focused on nurturing their talents or rediscovering themselves.</u>

1. **nurturing:** developing or helping to grow

---

* Adapted from Karen S. Peterson, "Relationship Respite," *USA Today*, July 19, 2001, 1D.

Implied main idea: <u>Some married women temporarily leave their</u>

<u>spouses to nurture their talents or to rediscover themselves.</u>

3. (1) Lakers guard Kobe Bryant, perhaps the best basketball player in the world, faced sexual-assault charges in Colorado. (2) Ravens running back Jamal Lewis, who may be the best football player in the world, was charged with intent to distribute cocaine nearly four years ago. (3) Giants outfielder Barry Bonds, perhaps the best baseball player in the world, has appeared before a grand jury in California investigating steroid distribution, and his personal trainer, Greg Anderson, pleaded not guilty to charges of supplying steroids to professional athletes. (4) And of course, Mike Tyson, formerly the best heavyweight boxer in the world, pleaded guilty in a Brooklyn court to disorderly conduct after a 5:30 AM fistfight with two men in a hotel lobby last June.*

Sentence 1 subject: <u>Kobe Bryant</u>

Sentence 2 subject: <u>Jamal Lewis</u>

Sentence 3 subject: <u>Barry Bonds and Greg Anderson</u>

Sentence 4 subject: <u>Mike Tyson</u>

Type (s) of supporting details: <u>Examples</u>

General topic of paragraph: <u>Athletes</u>

Generalization: <u>The athletes mentioned have been charged with breaking the law.</u>

Implied Main Idea: <u>Many famous athletes have had run-ins with the law.</u>

4. (1) Girls now outnumber boys in student government, honor societies, school newspapers, and debating clubs. (2) A recent study found girls ahead of boys in almost every measure of well-being; for example, girls feel closer to their families, have higher aspirations,[1] and even boast better assertiveness skills. (3) Boys earn 70 percent of the Ds and Fs that teachers dole out. (4) They make up two-thirds of students labeled "learning disabled." (5) They account for 80 percent of high school dropouts.

1. **aspirations:** goals

* Adapted from Steve Rushin, "This Is CourtsCenter," *Sports Illustrated*, March 8, 2004, 15.

(6) And they are less likely to go to college than ever before; by 2007, universities are projected to enroll 9.2 million women to 6.9 million men.*

Sentence 1 subject: _Girls' and boys' school activities_

Sentence 2 subject: _Girls' and boys' well-being_

Sentence 3 subject: _Girls' and boys' grades_

Sentence 4 subject: _Girls' and boys' learning disabilities_

Sentence 5 subject: _Girls' and boys' drop-out rate_

Sentence 6 subject: _Girls' and boys' college enrollment_

Type(s) of supporting details: _Points of comparison_

General topic of paragraph: _Girls' and boys' different characteristics, abilities, and achievements_

Generalization: _Girls outperform boys in many areas._

Implied main idea: _Girls are healthier and more accomplished than boys in a number of different areas._

5. (1) Do cops go easy on celebrities? (2) Consider the case of a high-profile politician who was linked to the disappearance of his girlfriend. (3) Despite evidence linking him to the woman, the police didn't interview him, search his apartment, or give him a lie-detector test early on in the case. (4) Or look at the circumstances surrounding a New York City publicist, who some say backed her car into a group of people waiting to get into a famous nightclub. (5) By the time the police got around to asking her some questions, her lawyer had arrived and instructed her not to say anything, arranging for her to be released on bail and back at home before dawn. (6) Then there's the case of a famous child actor who claims his wife was shot while he went into a restaurant. (7) Police declined to name him a suspect despite the fact that he had a gun in his car, and it was clear that the couple was unhappily married.†

* Adapted from Anna Mulrine, "Are Boys the Weaker Sex?" *U.S. News and World Report*, July 2, 2001.

† Adapted from Rich Hampson, "Do the Cops Go Easy on Celebrities? Maybe Not," *USA Today*, July 19, 2001, 1A. Copyright © 2001, *USA Today*. Reprinted with permission.

Sentence 2 subject: _High-profile politician_

Sentence 4 subject: _New York City publicist_

Sentence 6 subject: _Famous child actor_

Type(s) of supporting details: _Examples_

General topic of paragraph: _Celebrities or prominent people who may have committed crimes_

Generalization: _All of them initially avoided accusations or punishment._

Implied main idea: _Celebrities or prominent people who may have committed crimes seem to get off too easily._

4

Exercise 4.9

Read each paragraph and then circle the letter next to the sentence that correctly states the paragraph's main idea.

1. Problems are the cutting edge that distinguishes between success and failure. Problems call forth our courage and our wisdom; indeed, they create our courage and our wisdom. It is only because of problems that we grow mentally and spiritually. When we desire to encourage the growth of the human spirit, we challenge and encourage the human capacity to deal with problems, just as in school we deliberately set problems for our children to solve. It is through the pain of confronting and resolving problems that we learn. As Benjamin Franklin said, "Those things that hurt, instruct."*

   a. Problems have both positive and negative effects.
   b. Problems produce beneficial outcomes for human beings.
   c. Too many people avoid confronting their problems.
   d. Benjamin Franklin had a lot of problems.

2. The state of North Carolina says that 92 percent of its high school students graduate. According to a recent report by the nonprofit Education Trust, though, the actual rate is about 63 percent. The state of California says 87 percent of its students graduate. However, a more

* Adapted from M. Scott Peck, *The Road Less Traveled* (New York, Simon and Schuster, 1978), 16.

accurate estimate is 67 percent. Maryland reports that 85 percent of its students earn their high school diplomas, but the actual rate is more like 74 percent.*

    a. Dropping out of school brings a number of negative consequences.
    b. Several states do not keep accurate records.
    (c.) States tend to exaggerate their graduation rates.
    d. Across the nation, graduation rates are steadily rising.

3. Hotels hardly ever clean bedspreads in guest rooms. They never clean the ice buckets or the coffee pots; they merely rinse them and wipe them out. Hotels intentionally install heavily patterned carpets to mask dirt and stains. Hotel maids are likely to have given drinking glasses a quick rinse in the sink, wiped them dry, and returned them to the bathroom for the next guests. If a hotel maid is running late, she may not clean the bathtub at all. And hotel bathroom shower curtains, which are breeding grounds for bacteria and mold, are hardly ever cleaned.†

    (a.) Hotel rooms are not always cleaned very thoroughly.
    b. Hotels routinely hire maids who don't know how to clean.
    c. Hotel bathrooms are much dirtier than they look.
    d. Hotel maids are overworked and underpaid.

4. When Sir Edmund Hillary and Tenzing Norgay planted the first flag atop Mount Everest on May 29, 1953, they surveyed an utterly pristine[1] place. Nearly fifty years later, dozens of teams line up to take their crack at the sacred Nepalese[2] monolith.[3] Scores of guides jockey to get high-paying clients to the top. Trash on the roof of the world has become so bad that climbers mount expeditions specifically to clean up after past expeditions. At Everest Base Camp, a Nepalese entrepreneur[4] is planning to open a cyber café—perhaps the world's highest at an altitude of 17,000 feet (5,180 meters). And in 2003, not one but two teams of snowboarders rode down Everest from top to bottom.‡

1. **pristine:** pure and unspoiled by civilization
2. **Nepalese:** related to Nepal, a country in central Asia
3. **monolith:** a large block of stone
4. **entrepreneur:** a person who starts and operates a new business

---

* Adapted from "Major Cause of Joblessness Lies Within U.S. Schools," *USA Today*, March 31, 2004, 22A.

† Adapted from Peter Greenberg, "What You Should Check Out Before You Check In," *Today Show*, March 15, 2004, http://www.msnbc.msn.com/id/4527495/.

‡ Adapted from Alex Salkever, "Everest: Now Just Another Tourist Trap?" *National Geographic News*, April 8, 2003.

a. Sir Edmund Hillary and Tenzing Norgay were cleaner hikers than today's mountain climbers.

b. A cyber café will be created on Mount Everest.

c. Mount Everest is very dirty.

(d.) In fifty years, Mount Everest went from being deserted and untouched to being busy and crowded.

5. Why is Harry Potter such a popular and likeable character? Well, for one thing, he is an orphan who was raised by mean, nasty relatives who didn't want him and still manages to succeed in life. He goes from being an abused little boy to being a star athlete at Hogwarts School of Witchcraft and Wizardry almost overnight. He is very self-sufficient, which is a character trait that many people strive to incorporate into their own personalities. He is also a master magician and makes friends and fights mythic battles against the forces of Darkness, all of which appeal to a wide variety of readers. And not once does he blame his miserable aunt and uncle for his troubles. Harry's never a victim, even though he does have the most powerful evil wizard of all time harboring a grudge against him, which makes Harry Potter readers root for the character.*

a. Harry Potter was an orphan, which makes a lot of readers identify with him.

(b.) Harry Potter has had to overcome a lot of adversity[1] and has a lot of positive character traits, so readers identify with him and enjoy reading about him.

c. Harry Potter does not blame anyone for his troubles.

d. The Harry Potter series is very popular.

CHAPTER 4 REVIEW

Write the correct answer in each of the blanks in the following statements.

1. An ____implied____ main idea is one that is suggested but not stated.

2. An implied main idea paragraph contains specific supporting details but no _topic sentence_.

3. To determine the implied main idea of a paragraph, you can follow four steps.

1. **adversity:** hardship, misfortune

---

* Adapted from Janette Barber, "On Being . . . a Harry Potter Fan," *Rosie*, August 2001, 42–43.

    a. Find the _____subject_____ of each sentence.

    b. Determine the _____type_____ of supporting details in the paragraph.

    c. Determine a general _____topic_____ based on the specific details.

    d. Draw a _____conclusion_____ from the supporting details and state an implied main idea in your own words.

4. An implied main idea, like one that's stated in a topic sentence, includes both the _____topic_____ and what is being said about that topic.

Reading Selection

4

Practicing the Active Reading Strategy:
Before and As You Read

You can use active reading strategies before, as, and after you read a selection. The following are some suggestions for active reading strategies that you can employ before you read and as you are reading.

1. Skim the selection for any unfamiliar words. Circle or highlight any words you do not know.

2. As you read, underline, highlight, or circle important words or phrases.

3. Write down any questions about the selection if you are confused by the information presented.

4. Jot notes in the margin to help you understand the material.

Greatness Knows No Color
by Angela G. King

1 I still remember it vividly. Dozens of small hands shot up into the air throughout packed classrooms and children screamed out the names Martin Luther King Jr., George Washington Carver, and Harriet Tubman, to name a few.

2 The usual short list of well-known blacks was eagerly recited by third-, fourth-, and fifth-graders in response to my query, "Who can name a famous black person in American history?" as I went from school to school in Troy, Michigan.

3 It was 1982, I was 17 years old and, as a debutante for America's oldest black sorority, Alpha Kappa Alpha, I had decided to talk to elementary school kids in my hometown about significant black historical figures.

4   Troy was back then as it is now—a predominately white suburb of Detroit. I happened to be a black girl who lived there, and I figured that all children, not just black children down in the city, needed to know about some of the overlooked Americans who played a pivotal role in pushing this nation forward. Unfortunately, I learned then what still holds true today—that even as we commemorate Black History Month every February, many blacks who made a tremendous contribution in shaping this country languish in obscurity.

5   That's a shame. Knowing about the inventor of the traffic light (Garrett Morgan) or how Elijah McCoy revolutionized the locomotive industry by inventing a self-lubricating oil cap for steam engines or about the partner of Howard Hughes who helped develop the first commercial communications satellite (Frank Mann) isn't just *black* history. It's *American* history.

6   Take the blacks I chose to tell those Troy school children about as my community-service project. Who has heard of Asa Spaulding, founder of the nation's oldest and largest black life insurance firm? Or Percy Lavon Julian, a chemist who synthesized physostigmine, the drug used to treat glaucoma? Or Mary McCleod Bethune, the educa-

tor and promoter of civil and women's rights who founded Bethune-Cookman College, one of this nation's oldest black colleges?

7   I'd never heard of them until I did research for my project back then as a high school senior, and very few of the young students I talked to back then—or, I dare say, their teachers—had heard of them either.

8   I'm sorry to say that it has not been until this year, at age 35, while doing research for a freelance writing project, that I've learned about Dr. Daniel Hale Williams, the first physician to successfully perform open-heart surgery; Jan Ernst Matzeliger, who automated shoe manufacturing with a machine he invented to replace the costly manual method of forming shoes; Julian Francis Abele, one of the nation's first professional black architects, who designed the Philadelphia Museum of Art; and Mary Church Terrell, who founded the National Association of Colored Women to help poor black women fight for women's rights.

9   As the old saying goes, "You can't know where you're going unless you know where you've been." Americans can't move forward together as a nation until we recognize the entire spectrum of people who have helped to shape our nation. That's a lesson not just for February, but all year round.*

VOCABULARY

Read the following questions about some of the vocabulary words that appear in the previous selection. Then circle the letter of the correct answer for each question.

1. In paragraph 1, the author uses the word *vividly* to describe how she recalls a memory she had about her experience in an elementary school classroom. In this context, what does *vividly* mean?

   a. cloudy   c. shaky
   b. clearly   d. faintly

* "Greatness Knows No Color" by Angela King from *Daily News*, February 25, 2000. Copyright © 2000 New York Daily News, L. P. Reprinted with permission.

2. What does the word *query* mean as used in paragraph 2?

   a. eerie

   b. reply

   c. explanation

   (d.) question

3. The author describes herself as having been a *debutante* (paragraph 3). What do you think the word *debutante* means?

   a. a poor woman

   (b.) a young woman who makes a formal debut into society

   c. a college student

   d. an elementary school teacher

4. In paragraph 4, the author writes, "I figured that all children, not just black children down in the city, needed to know about some of the overlooked Americans who played a *pivotal* role in pushing this nation forward." What does the word *pivotal* mean as used here?

   (a.) significant

   b. not worthy

   c. insignificant

   d. happy

5. What does the word *commemorate* mean as used in paragraph 4?

   a. to begin

   (b.) to acknowledge and honor

   c. to design

   d. to declare

6. What do you think the phrase to *languish in obscurity* means? In paragraph 4, the author writes that "many blacks who made a tremendous contribution in shaping this country *languish in obscurity*."

   a. are famous

   b. remain fearful

   (c.) are unknown

   d. stay inside

7. In paragraph 6, the author asks if you know Percy Lavon Julian, a chemist who *synthesized* physostigmine, the drug used to treat glaucoma. What do you think the word *synthesized* means?

   a. shook up

   b. threw out

   (c.) combined or produced

   d. deleted

8. What does the word *spectrum* mean in paragraph 9? "Americans can't move forward together as a nation until we recognize the entire *spectrum* of people . . . ."

   (a.) range

   b. cluster

   c. batch

   d. concentration

Implied Main Ideas, Topics, and Supporting Details

Respond to each of the following questions by circling the letter of the correct answer.

1. What is the implied main idea of paragraphs 1 through 3?
   a. Children in Troy, Michigan, are very smart.
   b. The author was a debutante and a member of a black sorority.
   c. Children know a few names of famous African Americans.
   d. The author is from Troy, Michigan, and was a good student.

2. What is the implied main idea of paragraph 6?
   a. There are many significant figures in black history, and students should know about them.
   b. Mary McCleod Bethune founded a famous college long before women were doing things like that.
   c. Asa Spaulding faced racism in founding the oldest and largest black life insurance firm.
   d. Bethune-Cookman College is one of the nation's oldest black colleges.

3. Reread paragraph 8. What is the implied main idea?
   a. The author's research project was very difficult.
   b. These historical figures are not given proper credit for their achievements.
   c. The author wishes she had known about these important black figures in history earlier in her life.
   d. Mary Church Terrell founded the NACW.

4. The topic of paragraph 5 is
   a. traffic lights.   c. communications satellites.
   b. African-American inventors.   d. shameful behaviors.

5. The type of supporting details in paragraph 8 is
   a. examples.   c. points of comparison.
   b. reasons.   d. steps.

Practicing the Active Reading Strategy:
After You Read

Now that you have read the selection, answer the following questions, using the active reading strategies that you learned in Chapter 1.

1. Identify and write down the point and purpose of this reading selection.

2. Besides the vocabulary words included in the exercise on pages 201–202, are there any other vocabulary words that are unfamiliar to you? If so, write a list of them. When you have finished writing your list, look up each word in a dictionary and write the definition that best describes the word as it is used in the selection.

3. Predict any possible test questions that may be used on a test about the content of this selection.

4. How could you use the information contained in this selection? Does the information contained in the selection reinforce or contradict your ideas and experiences? Explain.

QUESTIONS FOR DISCUSSION AND WRITING

Respond to each of the following questions based on your reading of the selection by writing your answer on the blank.

1. The author writes in paragraph 5 that "knowing about [important black figures in history] . . . isn't just *black* history. It's *American* history." Do you agree or disagree? Why? <u>Answers will vary.</u>

   _____

2. Agree or disagree with the statement "You can't know where you're going unless you know where you've been." Explain your answer. Why do you think the author chose to end her essay with that statement?
   <u>Answers will vary.</u>

   _____

3. What do you think the author is saying about Black History Month as an event? Do you agree or disagree with her? Why? <u>Answers will vary.</u>

   _____

▶ Vocabulary: The Definition/Restatement Context Clue

When you encounter an unfamiliar word as you read, you may be able to figure out its meaning by using context clues. The context of a word is its relationship to the other words, phrases, and sentences that surround it. Sometimes, these nearby elements offer clues you can use to get a sense of what a particular word means.

One type of context clue is **definition** or **restatement**. In this type of clue, either the word's meaning is directly stated, or synonyms are used to restate it. The following sentence, which comes from one of the paragraphs in this chapter, uses restatement:

> Considered somewhat *eccentric*, or odd, Benjamin Franklin was a noted inventor and diplomat who was somewhat chubby and messy, but neither of those things interfered with his ability to help write the most important document in American history.

The word *odd* is a synonym for *eccentric*; therefore, it tells you what *eccentric* means.

Vocabulary Exercise

The following sentences all come from paragraphs in Chapters 2, 3, and 4. In each one, underline the definition or restatement context clue that helps you understand the meaning of the boldfaced, italicized word.

1. You can also use *visualization*, using your imagination to picture in your mind how to manage a stressful situation more successfully.

2. Research has revealed that regular aspirin use may protect against the risk of colon cancer by as much as 40 to 50 percent; *esophageal* (throat) cancer by about 80 to 90 percent; and ovarian cancer by some 25 percent.

3. The mothers of today's *"Generation X,"* the group of Americans born between 1961 and 1981, did 89 percent of the cooking in their homes, but their grown children now tend to divide evening meal preparation equally between the husband and the wife.

4. Doctors now have several new treatments that alter the soft *palate* (the roof of the mouth) and help quiet nighttime snoring.

5. In 1872, therefore, the Time-Table Convention searched for a solution, and Charles F. Dowd proposed the creation of *time zones*, imaginary divisions of the Earth's surface.

6. Prompted by our modest exertions, just a few minutes into a walk the body begins to produce *endorphins*, chemical compounds that reduce pain and stress enhance memory and judgment as they course through the brain.

7. If you find that *procrastination*, or putting things off, hurts your progress, here are some ways to break the habit.

8. They also wore rosemary garlands to ward off the *"evil eye,"* <u>a look or stare believed to harm others.</u>

9. Teenagers using the Internet today, however, are **multitasking**; that is, as they are online, they are also <u>doing other things.</u>

10. In the early days of America's space program, people were interested in as-tronauts because they were ***swaggering,*** <u>bragging, boastful</u> pilots, but now that two-thirds of them are doctors, scientists, and engineers, they're no longer "glamorous."

READING STRATEGY: SQ3R

In Chapter 1, you learned how to use active reading techniques to in-crease your comprehension of the material you read. One specific type of active reading strategy is called the **SQ3R method.** This abbreviation stands for

S urvey

Q uestion

R ead

R ecite

R eview

This series of five steps gives you a clear, easy-to-remember system for reading actively.

Step one is to **survey** the text. "To survey" means look over the text to preview it. Surveying gives you an overall idea of a reading selection's major topics, organizations, parts, and features. When you complete this step, you'll be able to form a mental framework that will allow you to better understand how specific paragraphs, sections, or chapters fit in. At this stage, your purpose is not to read the whole text but to get an overview of what to expect.

If you are preparing to read a longer text, such as a book, read over the title and glance through the table of contents to understand the major topics covered and how they are organized. Flip to one of the chapters and make yourself aware of its important features. A textbook, like this one, for example, may include a list of goals at the beginning of the chapter and a review summary at the end. It will probably also include headings that divide and identify sections of information. It is likely to emphasize key words or concepts with distinctive typeface such as bold print.

Prior to reading a shorter selection—such as one particular chapter, or an article, or an essay—survey it by reading any introductory material, the headings throughout, and the first sentence of each paragraph or each section. Read any review summaries or questions at the end of the chapter to get an idea of the major concepts covered in the selection. Also, glance over any illustrations and their captions.

The second step is to **formulate questions.** Turn the title and the headings into questions; then, when you read, you can actively look for the answers to those questions. For example, if the heading is "The Medieval Castle," you could turn it into "What was the Medieval Castle like?" If the heading is "The War of 1812," you could create the question "What caused the War of 1812?" or "What happened during the War of 1812?"

The next three steps are the three Rs of the SQ3R process. Step three is **read.** In this step, you read entire sentences and paragraphs in a section. However, you read only one section at a time; for example, in a textbook, you'd read from one heading to the next and then stop. As you read, look for the answers to the questions you formed in step two. Mark the text as you go. Highlight or underline those answers and other important information. You may want to write the answers or other details in the margins.

Step four is to **recite.** Reciting means saying something aloud. After you read a section of material, stop and speak the answers to the questions you created in step two. If you can't answer a question, reread the information until you can. Move on to the next section only when you can say the answers for the section you just read.

The last step of the SQ3R method is **review.** Review means "look at again." After you've read the entire selection, go back through it and see if you can still answer all of the questions you formed in step two. You don't have to reread unless you can't answer a particular question.

Practice the SQ3R active reading method with the following passage from a physical science textbook.

Tornadoes

The tornado is the most violent of storms. Although it may have less *total* energy than some other storms, the concentration of its energy in a relatively small region gives the tornado its violent

Continued

4

distinction. Characterized by a whirling, funnel-shaped cloud that hangs from a dark cloud mass, the tornado is commonly referred to as a *twister*.

Tornadoes occur around the world, but are most prevalent[1] in the United States and Australia. In the United States, most tornadoes occur in the Deep South and in the broad, relatively flat basin between the Rockies and the Appalachians. But no state is immune. The peak months of tornado activity are April, May, and June, with southern states usually hit hardest in winter and spring, and northern states in spring and summer. However, tornadoes have occurred in every month at all times of day and night. A typical time of occurrence is between 3:00 and 7:00 PM on an unseasonably warm, sultry[2] spring afternoon.

Most tornadoes travel from southwest to northeast, but the direction of travel can be erratic and may change suddenly. They usually travel at an average speed of 48 km/h (30 mi/h). The wind speed of a major tornado may vary from 160 to 480 km/h (100–300 mi/h). The wind speed of the devastating 1999 Oklahoma tornado was measured by Doppler radar to be 502 km/h (312 mi/h), the highest ever recorded.

Because of many variables, the complete mechanism of tornado formation is not known. One essential component, however, is rising air, which occurs in thunderstorm formation and in the collision of cold and warm air masses.

As the ascending air cools, clouds are formed that are swept to the outer portions of the cyclonic motion and outline its funnel form. Because clouds form at certain heights, the outlined funnel may appear well above the ground. Under the right conditions, a full-fledged tornado develops. The winds increase and the air pressure near the center of the vortex[3] is reduced as the air swirls upward. When the funnel is well developed, it may "touch down" or be seen extending up from the ground as a result of dust and debris picked up by the swirling winds.*

1. **prevalent:** common, widespread
2. **sultry:** hot and humid
3. **vortex:** whirling mass of air

* Adapted from James T. Shipman et al., *An Introduction to Physical Science*, 9th ed. (Boston: Houghton Mifflin Co., 2000), 540. Copyright © 2000 by Houghton Mifflin Company. Reprinted with permission.

Name _____ Date _____

TEST 1

A. Select the correct general category that includes all the specific items listed. Then circle the letter of the correct answer.

1. sport-utility vehicle   convertible

   van   sedan

   a. bicycles   c. toys
   (b.) automobiles   d. publications

2. cardinals   orioles

   robins   blue jays

   a. foods   c. clocks
   b. clothes   (d.) birds

3. bedroom   kitchen

   den   bathroom

   (a.) rooms   c. instruments
   b. sports   d. tasks

4. dog   parakeet

   cat   guinea pig

   (a.) pets   c. trees
   b. foods   d. places

5. oil   electricity

   gas   coal

   a. reference materials   c. countries
   b. home repairs   (d.) energy sources

For additional tests, see the Test Bank.

4

B. For each group of sentences, select the general sentence that includes all the specific details given. Then circle the letter of the correct answer.

6. You can teach a dog to sit on command.

   You can teach a dog to lie down.

   You can teach a dog to come when called.

   a. Dogs know how to come when called.
   b. Dogs are friendly.
   c. Dogs know when to lie down.
   d. Dogs can be trained.

7. Eric always undercooks our eggs.

   Eric makes spaghetti that's too soft.

   Eric usually burns the meat loaf.

   a. Eric doesn't care for eggs.
   b. Eric doesn't like to cook.
   c. Eric is not a good cook.
   d. Eric doesn't cook much.

8. My watch runs too slowly.

   My watch's alarm does not come on at the right time.

   Sometimes my watch stops altogether.

   a. My watch needs to be repaired.
   b. All watches have their own characteristics.
   c. My watch is interesting.
   d. New watches are expensive.

9. Lydia always talks very loudly into her cell phone.

   Lydia uses her cell phone in restaurants, theaters, and even during religious services.

   Lydia interrupts any conversation she's having in order to answer her cell phone.

   a. Lydia never misses messages that come by cell phone.
   b. Lydia needs to learn her cell phone manners.
   c. Lydia thinks her cell phone is one of her most useful appliances.
   d. Lydia is a believer in new phone technology.

10. Some people read the newspaper's sports section before everything else.

    Others are not interested in sports at all.

And there are still others who follow their local team only when it is playing a championship game.

   (a.) People have widely varying tastes when it comes to sports.
   b. Most people like to know how their local sports teams are doing.
   c. People who care deeply about sports usually dress tastefully.
   d. People who don't care about sports are dull.

TEST 2

A. Read each of the following paragraphs and then respond to each of the questions by circling the letter of the correct answer.

(1) Domino's Pizza offers mayonnaise and potato pizza in Tokyo and pickled ginger pizza in India. (2) Heinz varies its ketchup recipe to satisfy the needs of specific markets; in Belgium and Holland, for example, the ketchup is not as sweet. (3) When Haagen-Dazs served up one of its most popular American flavors, Chocolate Chip Cookie Dough, to British customers, they left it sitting in supermarket freezers. (4) What the premium ice-cream maker learned is that chocolate chip cookies aren't popular in Great Britain, and children don't have a history of snatching raw dough from the bowl. (5) After holding a contest to come up with a flavor the British would like, the company launched "Cool Britannia,[1]" vanilla ice cream with strawberries and chocolate-covered Scottish shortbread.*

  1. The subject of sentence 1 is
   (a.) Domino's Pizza.
   b. Tokyo.
   c. mayonnaise.
   d. India.

  2. The subject of sentence 2 is
   a. Belgium and Holland.
   b. recipes.
   (c.) Heinz.
   d. markets.

  3. The subject of sentence 4 is
   (a.) Haagen Dazs.
   b. ice-cream flavors.

1. Britannia: another word for Great Britain

---

* Adapted from William M. Pride et al., *Business,* 6th ed. (Boston: Houghton Mifflin Co., 1999), 338.

    c. contests.
    d. Britain.

4. The major supporting details are

    a. reasons.
    b. points of comparison.
    c. events.
    (d.) examples.

5. The general topic of this paragraph is

    a. pizza.
    (b.) food manufacturers.
    c. ice-cream preferences.
    d. delicious food.

4

(1) Before you choose a contractor to remodel your home, experts advise, look for someone who either lives in your town or has done work there before. (2) Next, meet with the contractor to see if his or her vision for your home matches yours. (3) For example, does the contractor agree with what you've planned to do? (4) If not, you might want to shop around for someone else. (5) Third, get a list of references from the contractor and find out if the people for whom he or she has done work like what was done and feel it was of good quality. (6) And last, make sure the contractor is available on the date on which you would like to start the work.

6. The subject of sentence 1 is

    (a.) contractors.
    b. homes.
    c. experts.
    d. towns.

7. The subject of sentence 2 is

    a. your vision.
    (b.) contractor's vision.
    c. homes.
    d. meetings.

8. The subject of sentence 5 is

    a. contractors.
    (b.) list of references.

    c. people in town.

    d. quality.

9. The type of supporting details is

    a. examples.

    b. events.

    (c.) steps.

    d. points of comparison.

10. The general topic of this paragraph is

    a. your home.

    (b) things to check when choosing a contractor.

    c. steps in remodeling.

    d. home improvement.

(1) Cats spend most of their day sleeping but have been known to prance[1] around at night, to the dismay[2] of their owners. (2) Dogs are awake most of the day but usually sleep all night, just like their human friends. (3) Cats have few needs in the hygiene department; they wash themselves and usually don't need to be bathed by their owners. (4) Dogs should be bathed and groomed on a regular basis in order to keep their coats healthy and free from matting. (5) Cats can be left a bowl of food that they can graze at throughout the day. (6) A dog's bowl should only be filled in the morning and at night. (7) Dogs have been known to eat more than necessary, only to get sick later. (8) Cats can also be left alone for long periods of time. (9) Dogs should have regular companionship and get exercise on a regular basis.

11. The subject of sentence 1 is

    (a) cats.

    b. sleep.

    c. dogs.

    d. cat owners.

12. The subject of sentence 2 is

    a. cats.

    (b) dogs.

    c. sleep.

    d. dog owners.

1. **prance:** walk in a spirited manner   2. **dismay:** upset or alarm

13. The subject of sentence 6 is

    a. dogs.
    b. a dog's bowl.
    c. a sick dog.
    d. feeding schedules.

14. The type of supporting details is

    a. reasons.
    b. steps.
    c. points of comparison.
    d. examples.

15. The general topic of this paragraph is

    a. differences between cats and dogs.
    b. why pet owners buy pets.
    c. feeding cats and dogs.
    d. exercising dogs regularly.

B. After each paragraph and topic statement, circle the letter next to *N* if the topic is too narrow, *B* if it's too broad, and *T* if it's the correct answer.

16. Have you ever noticed how few people drive at the speed limit? Most drivers stretch it at least 10 miles per hour beyond the limit, and many go even faster. In fact, when someone does keep to the speed limit, it makes the motorists behind the driver frustrated and anxious to get past so they can go at their normal fast speed. When police officers give speeding tickets, it's usually when someone is going way beyond the speed limit. But can you imagine how many tickets the police would give out if they stopped everyone who went faster than the speed limit?

    Topic: People who drive at the speed limit.

    a. N
    b. B
    c. T

17. Self-help guru Tony Robbins has sold more than $300 million of his products through infomercials.[1] Football great Fran Tarkenton anchored Robbins' first spots in 1995. Leeza Gibbons anchored another. Ali MacGraw and Lisa Hartman opened the way for actors to appear in infomercials when they turned up in a 1989 makeover spot for Victoria Jackson Cosmetics. Based on

1. **infomercials:** long commercials that have the format of regular TV programs

the success of Jackson's infomercials, actress Victoria Principal began hawking her own skin-care and beauty products. Former Miss America Vanessa Williams has appeared in a spot for Proactive Acne Treatment.*

Topic: Celebrities promoting products on infomercials

 a. N
 b. B
 (c.) T

18. Do speed bumps really make the streets in residential neighborhoods safer? A study published in the April 2004 *Journal of Public Health* looked at children under fifteen years of age who were taken to an Oakland, California, emergency room over a five-year period. The review found that children who live on streets with speed bumps were up to 60 percent less likely to be hit and injured by a vehicle than were children who lived in neighborhoods without speed bumps. Furthermore, although Oakland was the California city with the highest rate of pedestrian[1] deaths in 1995, it decreased child pedestrian deaths by 15 percent after it installed 1,600 speed bumps on residential streets between 1995 and 2000.†

Topic: Ways to make streets safer

 a. N
 (b.) B
 c. T

19. One theory about the derivation[2] of the name *chicken pox* says that it comes from the early years of diagnosis, when the pox blisters were described as looking like chickpeas. Another theory is that the blisters were said to look like chicken bites. A third states that children were once popularly called "chickens." Since the disease mainly struck that age group, the affliction[3] was named for them.‡

Topic: Theories about the origin of the name *chicken pox*

 a. N
 b. B
 (c.) T

1. **pedestrian:** one who travels on foot   3. **affliction:** pain or suffering
2. **derivation:** origin or source

---

* Adapted from Donna Petrozzello, "The Infomercial at 20," *New York Daily News*, February 26, 2004, 89.

† Adapted from Jennifer C. Kerr, "Speed Bumps Help Protect Kids, Study Says," *Charlotte Observer*, March 31, 2004, 10A.

‡ Adapted from "FYI," *Popular Science*, September 2001, 78.

CHAPTER **5**

Transitions

GOALS FOR CHAPTER 5

▶ Define the term *transition.*

▶ Recognize common transitions used to indicate a series of items.

▶ Recognize common transitions used to indicate time order.

▶ Recognize common transitions used to indicate cause/effect.

▶ Recognize common transitions used to indicate comparison/contrast.

▶ Recognize common transitions used to indicate definition and examples.

▶ Recognize transitions in paragraphs organized according to more than one pattern.

▶ Practice the steps involved in summarizing a reading selection.

5

In Chapters 3 and 4, you learned how to recognize supporting details within paragraphs. To help you understand how those details are related to one another, paragraphs include transitions that help you follow the author's train of thought. To discover what you already know about transitions, take the following test.

TEST YOURSELF

Circle the transition words and phrases in the following paragraphs.

1. Starting a vegetable garden can be a rewarding experience, but you have to spend a lot of time tending your plants in order to be able to have a crop at the end of summer. At first, your plants will be small and will not yield any vegetables or fruit. But don't get discouraged! Before long, you will begin to see small sprouts growing, which means that the work you have done is paying off. Eventually, after spending time weeding and trimming your garden, you are sure to have many things to eat from your garden, and you will understand the joys of gardening.

217

2. (Five minutes after) I arrive home, I have to cook dinner for my family. My children are old enough to boil a pot of water, (yet) dinner has become my nightly duty. (Consequently,) we end up getting take-out on many nights because I am just too tired to cook. (As a result,) I feel like our diet is not as healthy as it should be.

3. (When) Janis Klein became a school nurse fifteen years ago, one-sixth of the children in her elementary school had head lice.[1] (As a result,) they couldn't go to school. (So) Klein, who has worked in hospitals and summer camps, quickly became an expert in recognizing head lice. (In time,) she started her own business to help families through the area recognize, treat, and deal with head lice.*

4. You and your dog can do more together than go on long walks, chase balls, and share a bowl of popcorn while watching Saturday-morning cartoons. Take Heidi, (for instance.) Heidi is an English springer spaniel who volunteers with her owner as a therapy dog at a residential treatment school for children who suffer from emotional disorders. (Another example) is Sophie the bull terrier, who works with her owner at a Connecticut-area nursing home whose residents all seem to comment, "She reminds me of a dog I used to have when I was young." (Also,) there are dogs that help the blind or hearing-impaired live a productive life by being good and responsible companions.†

5. There are several types of headache that signal more serious disorders. (First) is "the worst headache of your life" (arterial bleeding). (In addition,) there are the headache with weakness or loss of vision (stroke), headache accompanied by blackout (seizures), and headache associated with fever (meningitis).[2] (However,) not all headaches require medical attention. Some result from missed meals or muscle tension. (Therefore,) they are easily remedied with a cold pack applied directly to the scalp over the angry nerve endings. Aspirin, (too,) works by interfering with enzymes[3] that inflame the nerves.‡

---

1. **head lice:** small insects that can be parasites on animals and humans

2. **meningitis:** disease characterized by fever, vomiting, headache, and stiff neck

3. **enzymes:** proteins in living organisms

---

* Adapted from M. K. Fottrell, "No Nits Here," *Westchester Parent*, August 2001, 16.

† Adapted from "Healing Partners," *AKC Family Dog, New Puppy Edition,* Fall/Winter 2003, 6.

‡ Adapted from Marc Siegel, "What Is a Headache?" *New York Daily News*, February 23, 2004, 44.

Transitions are words and phrases whose function is to show the relationships between thoughts and ideas. The word *transition* comes from the Latin word *trans*, which means "across." Transitions bridge the gaps across sentences and paragraphs and reveal how they are related.

Transitions make sentences clearer, so they help readers understand the ideas in a passage more easily. Without them, the readers have to figure out relationships on their own. For example, read these two sentences:

> She was afraid of guns. She bought a gun and learned to use it to protect herself.

When you read these two sentences, which are not connected, the second one seems to contradict the first one. If someone fears guns, why would she buy one? In the absence of a transition, the reader has to pause and mentally fill in that gap on his or her own. Now look at how the addition of a transition more clearly reveals the contrast between the two thoughts:

> She was afraid of guns. **But** she bought a gun and learned to use it to protect herself.

Characteristics of Transitions

You should be aware of three characteristics of transitions:

1. Some of them are synonyms. In other words, they mean the same thing. For instance, the transitions *also, in addition,* and *too* all have the same meaning. Therefore, they are usually interchangeable with one another.

2. Some transitions can be used to show more than one kind of relationship between details. For example, you may see the word *next* in both series of items and in a paragraph that explains the steps in a process.

   > The *next* component of love is commitment. (series of items)
   > *Next*, prepare an agenda for the meeting. (steps in a process)

3. Different transitions can create subtle but significant changes in the meanings of sentences. For example, reread an earlier example that includes a contrast transition:

   > She was afraid of guns. *But* she bought a gun and learned to use it to protect herself.

   The transition *but* suggests that she bought a gun *in spite of* her fear. Notice, however, how a different transition changes the relationship between the two sentences.

> She was afraid of guns. *So* she bought a gun and learned to use it to protect herself.

Substituting the transition *so*, which is a cause/effect word, suggests that she bought the gun *to overcome* her fear. Altering that one transition significantly alters the meaning of those two sentences.

As you read, then, you'll need to pay attention to transitions so you can accurately follow the train of thought within a reading selection. The remainder of this chapter explains and illustrates the different types of transition words that accompany various patterns of organization. (For more information about patterns of organization, see Chapter 6.)

Transition Words That Indicate a Series

Certain transition words show readers that the sentence will add another item to a series. A series may consist of examples, reasons, or some other kind of point. Here are some common series transitions:

Series Transitions		
also	furthermore	finally
in addition	first, second, third	lastly
too	first of all	most importantly
another	and	moreover
one	for one thing	next

The following pairs of sentences illustrate the use of series transitions:

When you travel in a recreational vehicle, kids feel at home no matter where you go. *And* parents love the freedom, the conveniences, and the relatively low cost.

Hummingbirds are among the smallest warm-blooded animals on earth. *Also*, they are among the meanest.

A sincere apology can have a tremendous amount of healing power. *In addition*, it can set the stage for better communication in the future.

Now, read a paragraph that includes series transition words (boldfaced and italicized). Notice how each transition indicates the addition of another item in the series.

> Your credit score is determined by five factors. ***The first factor*** is your payment record. Thirty-five percent of your score depends on whether you pay your bills on time. ***The second factor*** is the amount you owe. Your total amount of debt accounts for 30 percent of your score. ***The third determinant***[1] of your score is your credit history. The length of time you've been borrowing and paying back money influences 15 percent of your score. Your credit application history is ***the fourth factor***. Ten percent of your score is based on how much new debt you try to acquire. ***The fifth and final factor*** is your credit mix. This last ten percent of your score is based on what kinds of debts you have incurred.[2]*

This paragraph presents a series of five factors that determine an individual's credit score. The series transitions *first, second, third*, and so on indicate each new factor.

Exercise 5.1

Fill in the blanks in the following sentences and paragraphs with appropriate series transitions. Choose words or phrases from the box on page 220. Try to vary your choices. Answers may vary.

1. Pet ownership requires a lot of your time and effort. ___In addition___, having a pet costs money.

2. There are a few things you'll need to bake a cake. ___First___, you will need the right ingredients. ___Second___, you will need the proper baking dish. And ___third___, you will need an oven.

3. A low-fat diet has many benefits. ___First of all___, it can help you stay at a weight that is appropriate for your height and age. ___Most importantly___, it can reduce your risk of heart disease.

4. ___One___ example of an Alfred Hitchcock movie is *Vertigo*, starring Jimmy Stewart and Kim Novak. ___Another___ example is *The Birds*, which made Tippi Hedren a big star.

1. determinant: influencing factor   **2. incurred:** acquired

* Adapted from Paul J. Lim, "They Know Your Credit Score," *Reader's Digest*, July 2001, 164–166.

5. Buddha gave some good advice about what to say and what not to say to others. The founder of Buddhism[1] recommended that a person ask three vital questions before saying anything to another person. _____First_____, ask yourself if the statement is *true*. _____Next_____, ask if the statement is *necessary*. _____Lastly_____, ask if the statement is *kind*. If a statement falls short on any of these counts, Buddha advised that we say nothing.*

6. My mother always gave me a lot of tips before I went out on a date. _____For one thing_____, I was never to order spaghetti. She thought that eating spaghetti on a date was too messy and had the potential for disaster. _____Furthermore_____, I was never to wear patent-leather[2] shoes. She was so old-fashioned that she thought that patent-leather shoes could reflect what you were wearing under your dress or skirt! _____Also_____, I was always supposed to let my date open the door for me. _____Finally_____, her last tip was to never let a boy kiss me on the first date. My mother was certainly behind the times!

7. Many people say that there is nothing worth watching on television. Television critics disagree and give several examples of worthwhile programs. _____One example_____ of a good program is *Seinfeld*. Even though it doesn't air in prime time on a weekly basis anymore, it is still shown daily on television stations across the United States and remains extremely popular because of the excellent script writing that defined the show. _____Another example_____ of a worthwhile program is *The West Wing*. Although some people do not like the liberal[3] focus of the show, most agree that it has good plots, characters, and story lines. _____A third example_____ of a great program is *60 Minutes*. Called the "granddad of news programming," it has been on the air for more than twenty years and remains a program of high quality with ground-breaking news.

1. **Buddhism:** religion that focuses on eliminating desire to end suffering and on meditating to obtain spiritual enlightenment

2. **patent-leather:** black leather finished to a hard, glossy surface

3. **liberal:** related to a political viewpoint that is open-minded and favors reform

* Adapted from Barry L. Reece and Rhonda Brandt, *Effective Human Relations in Organizations*, 7th ed. (Boston: Houghton Mifflin Co., 1999), 213.

Transition Words That Indicate Time Order

Some transition words signal that the sentence is providing another event, step, or stage within a chronological order of details. Here is a list of common time order transitions:

Time Order Transitions			
first, second, third	next	as	finally
before	soon	when	over time
now	in the beginning	until	in the end
then	once	later	during, in, on,
after	today	eventually	*or* by (*followed*
while	previously	last	*by a date*)
	often	meanwhile	

The following pairs of sentences illustrate the use of time order transitions:

On July 29, 1981, Diana Spencer married England's Prince Charles and became the Princess of Wales. *In 1992*, Charles and Diana officially separated.

High-fiber foods take longer to eat and increase your satisfaction. *Then*, when they get to the intestines, fiber-rich foods act as an appetite suppressant.[1]

During the Great Depression, Wal-Mart founder Sam Walton sold magazine subscriptions door-to-door. *After* serving in World War II and *then* managing a Ben Franklin variety store *from 1945 to 1950*, Walton and his wife Helen opened their own Walton's Five and Dime in Bentonville, Arkansas.*

Now, read a paragraph that uses time order transition words (boldfaced and italicized). Notice how each transition indicates another event in the timeline.

1. **suppressant:** something that puts a stop to something else

---

* Adapted from Paul Boyer et al., *The Enduring Vision,* 5th ed. (Boston: Houghton Mifflin Co., 2004), 935.

The famous Leaning Tower of Pisa has been tilting for over eight hundred years, and recent improvements should allow it to continue tilting for another three hundred more. ***On August 9, 1173***, construction began on this well-known Italian bell tower. ***Almost immediately***, it began leaning because it was being erected on the soft silt of a buried riverbed. ***Between 1178 and 1360***, work stopped and started two more times as workers tried to continue the project and figure out how to compensate for the tilt. ***Over the next six centuries***, the tower's lean continued to increase, although tourists were still allowed to visit. ***Then, in 1990***, Italy's prime minister feared the tower would collapse and closed it to the public. ***From 1999 to 2001***, engineers excavated soil from beneath the tower. ***Now***, the tower still leans out about fifteen feet beyond its base, but it should remain stable for several more centuries.*

This paragraph tells the story of the Leaning Tower of Pisa, arranging the details using time order. Each new detail is introduced with a time order transition to help the reader easily follow the progression of events.

Exercise 5.2

Fill in the blanks in the following sentences and paragraphs with appropriate time order transitions. Choose words or phrases from the box on page 223. Try to vary your choices. Answers may vary.

1. Twenty years ago, patients got most medical information from their doctors.
   ____Now____, they can access some 70,000 health-care-related Internet sites.

2. Tiger Woods has won just about every golf tournament that is played.
   ____Eventually____, he has to lose, don't you think?

3. Yesterday, I had my eyes checked at the eye doctor's office. ____Today____, I get the results of my eye exam.

4. ____During____ colonial times, many children died due to disease and poor medical care.

5. You just won big money in the lottery. Now what do you do? ____First____, protect your ticket. Seal it in an envelope and stash it in a safe deposit box

---

* Adapted from Richard Covington, "The Leaning Tower Straightens Up," *Smithsonian*, June 2001, 41–47.

until you can claim your prize. ___Second___, contact lottery headquarters within the time limit. You probably have from 180 days to one year to show up with your winning ticket. ___Third___, you'll have to decide how you want to receive your money. You can either get one lump-sum[1] payment, or you can arrange to be paid a portion every year for, say, twenty years. ___Fourth___, hire a financial advisor and an accountant to help you manage and invest your money. ___Finally___, you'll need to decide whether or not you want to keep your job. Many people think they'd quit right away, but to make the money last through wise investments, you may need to keep on working.*

6. Franklin Roosevelt[2] was not eager to enter World War II, according to many historians. ___On___ December 7, 1941, however, his position changed. ___When___ the Japanese invaded the military base at Pearl Habor, FDR found that he had no choice but to enter the war. ___After___ much thought, he addressed the American people and gave them his decision.

7. ___Previously___, the volunteer program known as "Friends for Life" was a small organization run by four people. ___Now___, it is a successful program that pairs senior citizens with dog friends and has a staff of more than one hundred people nationwide. ___Over time___, the head of "Friends for Life," John Baker, wants to expand the program overseas. ___By___ 2010, he hopes to have programs operating in France, Belgium, and Germany.

Transition Words That Indicate Cause/Effect

Certain transition words indicate that an occurrence about to be presented in a sentence is either a reason for or a result of an occurrence presented in a

1. **lump-sum:** paid all at once

2. **Franklin Roosevelt:** 32nd president of the U.S.

* Adapted from Jack R. Fay, "Wow! I Just Won the Lottery: Now What Do I Do?" *USA Today*, November 2000, 26–27.

previous sentence. These are the transitions that reveal cause or effect relationships between thoughts. The most common cause/effect transition words are listed below.

Cause/Effect Transitions

so	consequently
therefore	as a consequence
as a result	due to
thus	hence
because of	for this reason
in response	

The following pairs of sentences illustrate the use of cause/effect transitions:

High protein/low carbohydrate diets produce dramatic weight loss. *As a result*, many people are cutting bread, pasta, and cereal out of their meals.

Most head-on vehicle collisions occur when distracted drivers drift into oncoming traffic. *So* to reduce your risk of such an accident, drive more on divided highways with medians.

Many Americans choose to live in urban and suburban neighborhoods. *Consequently*, they separate themselves from a deep connection to the land and become indifferent to the environment.

Next, read a paragraph that uses cause/effect transition words (boldfaced and italicized). Notice how each transition indicates another effect.

Mother England made the mistake of withholding liberty too long from her "children" in the American colonies. They grew to be rebellious "teenagers" who demanded their freedom. *In response*, their "mother" refused to release them, and a war had to be fought. *As a consequence*, though, England did learn a valuable lesson from a painful experience, which is why she later granted a peaceful and orderly transfer of power to another tempestuous[1] offspring named India.*

1. **tempestuous:** stormy; agitated

---

* Adapted from Dr. James Dobson, "Focus on the Family," *News Herald* (Morganton, NC), July 22, 2001, 11C.

This paragraph is arranged according to the chain-reaction type of cause/effect paragraphs. Each transition indicates that the detail is the result of a previous occurrence.

Exercise 5.3

Fill in the blanks in the following sentences and paragraphs with appropriate cause/effect transitions. Choose words or phrases from the box on page 226. Try to vary your choices. Answers may vary.

1. Female elected officials are gaining more political power along with the public's trust. __As a result__, the United States will probably elect its first woman president during the twenty-first century.

2. There have been a few incidents involving children slipping under the water at the town pool this year. ____So____, the town representatives are making it mandatory[1] for children to wear safety vests at all times while at the pool.

3. __Because of__ teenagers' natural tendency to go to bed later and awake later, several school districts around the country have adjusted high school starting times.*

4. I have been eating more than I should, especially when it comes to dessert. __Therefore__, I have gained five pounds!

5. Many Americans are locked into a work-and-spend cycle. Their debts increase. __As a result__, they give up leisure time to make more money. The treadmill continues to roll, and some people become too tired to enjoy active leisure activities such as hiking, swimming, or playing a round of golf. __Consequently__, they engage in less satisfactory activities such as sitting passively in front of the television set. __Hence__, this work-and-spend cycle reduces quality of life.†

1. **mandatory:** required

* Adapted from Desda Moss, "Science Confirms What Parents Know," *USA Today*, March 12, 2004, 15A.
† Adapted from Barry L. Reece and Rhonda Brandt, *Effective Human Relations in Organizations*, 7th ed. (Boston: Houghton Mifflin Co., 1997), 462.

6. My grandfather's name was Charlie Bundrum, a tall, bone-thin man who worked with nails in his teeth and a roofing hatchet in his fist. He died in the spring of 1958, one year before I was born. _Consequently_, I knew almost nothing about him growing up because nobody in my mother's family talked about him. _____Thus_____, I made it my life's work to try to find out what kind of man Charlie Bundrum was.*

7. I was in high school when I realized my own possibilities. I had started a volunteer organization that matched students with senior citizens, and my teacher told me I was a good person. _As a result_, I felt very good about myself, and those few words literally changed how I saw myself. _Consequently_, I try to help young people understand the power they have to change the world. I cofounded the national organization Do Something based on the idea that life is most rewarding when we're helping others.†

Transition Words That Indicate Comparison/Contrast

Paragraphs include comparison transitions to help readers see similarities between two or more things. They include contrast transitions to point out differences.

First, let's examine the comparison transitions, which appear in the list below.

Comparison Transitions		
also	similarly	similar to
too	in like manner	in the same way
likewise	just like, just as	along the same line
		in both cases

---

* Adapted from Rick Bragg, "Charlie and the River Rat," from "Ava's Man," *Reader's Digest*, August 2001, 149.

† Adapted from Andrew Shue, "A Message from Andrew Shue," Special Advertising Section, *Reader's Digest*, August 2001, 160.

The following pairs of sentences illustrate the use of comparison transitions:

When you shop for a car, you look for the color, style, and features you want. ***Similarly***, new genetic[1] research may allow future parents to choose the characteristics they want in their children.

In the nineteenth century, large numbers of Irish, Italian, and Jewish immigrants struggled to blend into American society. ***Likewise***, today's Latinos and Asians are weaving themselves into this country's diverse[2] cultural mix.

Today's parents are objecting to the skimpy, skin-baring clothes their pre-teens are wearing. ***In the same way***, 1960s parents were horrified by their girls' hip-huggers and halter tops.

The following paragraph uses comparison transition words (boldfaced and italicized). Notice how each transition indicates another point of comparison.

The disputed[3] presidential elections of 1876 and 2000 shared some striking similarities. The 1876 election between Samuel Tilden and Rutherford B. Hayes was so close that the victory hinged upon just a few electoral votes. ***Likewise***, in 2000, the race between Al Gore and George W. Bush depended upon only a handful of electoral votes.[4] In 1876, the state of Florida played a major part in the election's outcome. ***Similarly***, Florida was cast into the national spotlight in 2000 when the election depended upon that state's poll results. The media of 1876 prematurely[5] assumed that Hayes had won. The media in 2000, ***too***, presumed George W. Bush the winner before they had all of the facts. ***In both cases***, the Supreme Court had to get involved to help settle the matter.*

5

1. **genetic:** related to genes, the units that determine the particular characteristics of an organism
2. **diverse:** different
3. **disputed:** argued about
4. **electoral votes:** votes from the body chosen to elect the president and vice president of the U.S.
5. **prematurely:** occurring before the right time

* Adapted from Jeremy F. Plant, "Déjà vu: Revisiting the 1876 Presidential Election," *USA Today*, May 2001, 16–18.

Exercise 5.4

Fill in the blanks in the following sentences and paragraphs with appropriate comparison transitions. Choose words or phrases from the box on page 228. Try to vary your choices. Answers may vary.

1. World War I changed the nature of war by introducing gas, trench warfare, tanks, submarines and aircraft. ___Likewise___, World War II changed fighting by adding rockets and atomic bombs.

2. Many antibiotics and drugs have been discovered in European rivers and tap water. _In like manner_, low levels of three antibiotics are present in West Virginia waters.

3. My biology textbook is colorful and breaks down information into small sections. _In the same way_, my economics textbook offers a chapter summary and beautiful illustrations to make the concepts easier to understand.

4. ___Just like___ you, I try to exercise at least a half an hour every day.

5. Many observers feared for the future of America's families at the ends of both the nineteenth and twentieth centuries. In the 1890s, the U.S. divorce rate was the highest in the world. ___Similarly___, the 1990s divorce rate was very high. In the 1890s, there was an epidemic[1] of sexually transmitted diseases. ___Along the same line___, such diseases were a problem in the late 1990s. Late nineteenth-century urban areas were plagued[2] by drug abuse. ___Likewise___, many late-twentieth-century Americans struggled with drug addiction and the crime it caused.*

6. Born in the Bronx and reared in a humble household on Long Island, Billy Joel[3] attended school by day and worked odd jobs at night to help support his single mother. ___Like___ half of the rest of the teenage world in the 1960s, he ___also___ played in a rock and roll band. Unlike most of the others, he stayed with it, developing a solo act and taking it to whatever places would hire him.†

1. **epidemic:** a disease affecting large numbers of people
2. **plagued:** afflicted; affected
3. **Billy Joel:** a popular singer/musician

---

* Adapted from Stephanie Coontz, "The American Family," *Life,* November 1999, 79.

† Adapted from Shanti Gold, "When the Ship Comes In: Downtown Man, Uptown Girl," *New York Daily News,* March 16, 2003, 39.

7. Although the positions they play couldn't be more different, pitchers and catchers share many of the same traits and characteristics. _Just as_ a pitcher can hold the fate of the whole ball game in his hands, a catcher can do the same by either tagging someone out at home and preventing a run from scoring or just the opposite—dropping the ball and letting the run score. _Likewise_, pitchers and catchers share the pain of sustaining major injuries, pitchers to their arms and shoulders, and catchers to any part of their body that can be hit by a bat or a ball. And _in the same way_ that pitchers are lifelong pitchers and never play another position, catchers are very loyal to the position, only moving if injury or the team manager makes them move.

Now, let's look at the contrast transitions.

Contrast Transitions

however	nevertheless	unfortunately
but	on the one hand	in contrast
yet	on the other hand	conversely
although	unlike	even though
instead	rather	still
in opposition	on the contrary	nonetheless
in spite of	actually	whereas
just the opposite	despite	in reality
though	while	as opposed to

The following pairs of sentences illustrate the use of contrast transitions:

Scientists agree that exercising the mind keeps it functioning well. *However*, they disagree about the best way to go about achieving mental fitness.

For a while, eggs fell out of favor because of their high cholesterol content. *But* the latest studies show they are both healthy and nutritious.

Photos of President John F. Kennedy's family at play only looked casual and spontaneous. *In reality,* they were professionally lit, and the people in them were styled and posed.

Next, read a paragraph that includes contrast transition words (boldfaced and italicized). Notice how each transition indicates another point of contrast.

Interactive and independent teaching styles differ in a number of various ways. The instructor whose style is *independent* is usually formal and businesslike with students and places more importance on individual effort than on group effort. **On the other hand,** the instructor whose style is *interactive* is usually informal with students and places more importance on group effort than on individual effort. The preferred teaching method of the independent instructor is lecturing, and he or she will often call on students rather than ask for volunteers. The interactive instructor, ***though,*** prefers small group activities and large group discussions. Rather than calling on students, he or she will usually ask for volunteers. Students usually feel competitive in the independent instructor's class. **Conversely,** they feel cooperative in the interactive instructor's class.*

Exercise 5.5

Fill in the blanks in the following sentences and paragraphs with the appropriate contrast transition. Choose words or phrases from the box on page 231. Try to vary your choices. Answers may vary.

1. Friendship ranks with marriage and kinship as one of the most important relationships in our lives. ____However____, it can be the most neglected.

2. ___Despite___ being one of the most beautiful and admired women in the world, Marilyn Monroe[1] suffered from depression.

3. You would think that a team with the high salary budget of the New York Rangers hockey team would have many championships in its history. _____But_____ the Rangers have only won two Stanley Cup championships in the last one hundred years.

4. Charles called to see if I was available to go to dinner. ____However____, I had another commitment.

1. **Marilyn Monroe:** a famous actress who committed suicide

---

* Adapted from Carol C. Kanar, *The Confident Student*, 5th ed. (Boston: Houghton Mifflin Co., 2004), 51.

5. Golf is really more of a game than a sport. Sports—such as basketball or tennis—require aerobic activity that increases the heart rate and makes players sweat. Golf, _on the other hand_, requires about the same physical conditioning necessary for stamp collecting. In sports like soccer and hockey, fans cheer, boo, and scream at the players. _In contrast_, in golf, the announcers whisper, and the spectators have to be quiet, clapping politely when a player hits a good shot. Sports—such as baseball and football—require uniforms, cheerleaders, and most importantly, real opponents. Golf, _though_, has none of these things.*

6. Some people say that reading the newspaper is a better way to get information than watching television. _However_, studies have shown that people who get their news exclusively from television news shows know almost as much about current affairs as people who read newspapers. _Nevertheless_, the debate rages on with some people favoring newspapers and some favoring television news shows.

7. Struggling students see themselves as victims, believing that what happens to them is determined mostly by external forces such as fate, luck, and powerful people. Successful students, _though_, accept personal responsibility, seeing *themselves* as the primary cause of their outcomes and experiences. Struggling students have difficulty sustaining motivation and often feel depressed, frustrated, or resentful about the lack of direction in their lives. _But_ successful students are self-motivated because they have discovered meaningful goals and dreams that give them purpose. Struggling students seldom identify specific actions needed to accomplish a desired outcome. Successful students, _however_, are good at self-management. They consistently plan and take purposeful actions in pursuit of their goals and dreams.†

Transition Words That Indicate Definition

One final set of transition words signals examples. Because the definition pattern or organization often includes one or more examples, this type of transition will often appear in definition paragraphs. However, transitions that

* Adapted from Bill Geist, "Planet Golf," *Reader's Digest*, August 2001, 121–122.
† Adapted from Skip Downing, *On Course*, 4th ed. (Boston: Houghton Mifflin Co., 2005), 1.

indicate example can appear in other types of paragraphs, too. Any time that authors want to illustrate an idea or make it clearer, they often identify the beginning of an example with one of the following transitions.

Definition (Example) Transitions

for example	as an illustration	in one case
for instance	in one instance	more precisely
to illustrate	such as	specifically

The following pairs of sentences illustrate the use of example transitions:

Volcanic explosions can be devastating. ***One illustration*** is Indonesia's Tambora Volcano, which killed 10,000 people when it exploded in 1815.

An autoimmune disease is one in which a person's immune system attacks the body's healthy tissue and organs. Lupus, ***for instance***, is one of about eighty such diseases.

Thousands of employers are attempting to reduce the cost of employee health insurance by regulating their employees' lifestyles. ***For example***, many companies require that employees don't smoke.

Now, read a paragraph that includes example transition words (boldfaced and italicized). Notice how the transition introduces the example.

When you reveal wrongdoing within an organization to the public or to those in positions of authority, you are a whistle blower. Whistle blowers are sounding alarms in industries from tobacco companies to airlines. ***For example***, Sylvia Robins reported that she knew about a procedural flaw at Unisys, a National Aeronautics and Space Administration subcontractor that produces software programs for the space shuttle program. Robins came forward to stop any further endangerment of space shuttle crews.*

This definition paragraph explains the meaning of the term *whistle blower*. After defining the term, it presents an illustration of one specific person who acted as a whistle blower.

* Adapted from Barry L. Reece and Rhonda Brandt, *Effective Human Relations in Organizations,* 7th ed. (Boston: Houghton Mifflin Co., 1999), 139–140.

Exercise 5.6

Fill in the blanks in the following sentences and paragraphs with appropriate example transitions. Choose words or phrases from the box on page 234. Try to vary your choices. Answers may vary.

1. One study of multivitamins found that one-third of brands don't contain what the label promises. <u>For example</u>, two brands of multivitamins for adults contained only 40 percent of the amount of vitamin A listed on the package.

2. There are many cars available today that are considered safe. <u>For instance</u>, the Volvo S70 scored extremely well in crash tests, making it one of the safest cars you can buy.

3. Dolphins have been shown to have superior thinking abilities and more than a little extrasensory perception, or ESP.[1] <u>In one case</u>, a dolphin swimming beside a young woman sensed that the woman was pregnant by nudging her abdomen, even though the woman herself did not know she was carrying a baby at the time!

4. Many American manufacturers of various products have facilities overseas. Dell, a Texas company that makes computers, <u>for instance</u>, owns a large plant in Ireland. Microsoft software runs computers all over the world. McDonald's franchises are operated in many foreign cities, including Moscow and Tokyo.*

5. I'm a nerd. While the Internet boom has lent some respectability to the term, narrow-minded stereotypes of nerds still linger. <u>For example</u>, nerds are supposed to be friendless bookworms who suck up to authority figures. <u>More precisely</u>, we're sissies.†

6. The categories of people to which you see yourself belonging and to which you always compare yourself are called *reference groups*. The performance of people in a reference group can influence your self-esteem.

1. **ESP:** knowing information that comes from outside of the normal range of senses

---

* Adapted from Carol C. Kanar, *The Confident Student*, 5th ed. (Boston: Houghton Mifflin Co., 2004), 357.

† Adapted from Tom Rogers, "My Kids Are Smarter Than Yours," *Reader's Digest*, August 2001, 69.

5

<u>For instance</u> , if being a good swimmer is very important to you, knowing that someone in your reference group swims much faster than you do can lower your self-esteem.*

7. Exporting is selling and shipping materials and products to other nations.

<u>To illustrate</u> , the Boeing Company exports its airplanes to a number of countries for use by their airlines. Importing is purchasing materials or products from other nations and bringing them into one's own country.

<u>For example</u> , American stores may purchase rugs in India or raincoats in England and have them shipped back to the United States for resale.†

Transition Words in Combinations of Patterns

Supporting details in paragraphs can be organized according to more than one pattern. For example, a paragraph may include *both* time order details and effect details. In such paragraphs, it will be particularly important for you to notice transition words and phrases, for they will provide clues about the various relationships among different kinds of details. For an example of a paragraph that includes more than one pattern and, therefore, different kinds of transitions, read the following.

Xenotransplantation is the use of animal organs as replacement for human organs. ***For example,*** surgeons have removed diseased livers from human patients and substituted livers taken from baboons. Such animal-to-human transplants began ***in the 1900s*** when doctors tried but failed to transplant kidneys from pigs, goats, apes, and lambs. ***In the 1960s,*** a number of primate[1]-to-human transplants were attempted, and several patients who received chimpanzee or baboon kidneys lived up to nine months following the operation. ***In 1983,*** a baby received a baboon heart, but her body rejected it twenty days later. ***During the early 1990s,*** doctors made three more attempts at

1. **primate:** mammals like apes and monkeys

* Adapted from Douglas A. Bernstein et al., *Psychology*, 5th ed. (Boston: Houghton Mifflin Co., 2000), 605. Copyright © 2000 by Houghton Mifflin Company. Reprinted with permission.

† Adapted from William Pride, Robert Hughes and Jack Kapoor, *Business*, 6th ed. (Boston: Houghton Mifflin Co., 1999), 60.

liver xenotransplantation. *Today,* researchers are still studying xeno-transplants and trying to make them a viable[1] option for people suffering from organ failure.*

This paragraph begins with the definition pattern, including an example. Then, it switches to the time order pattern as it explains the history of xenotransplant attempts. Therefore, it includes both example and time order transitions.

Exercise 5.7

Read each of the following paragraphs and then circle the transition words or phrases. Then, in the list below the paragraph, place a check mark next to each of the two patterns used to organize the details.

1. Although Columbus[2] was a great navigator and sailor, he was not a particularly good leader. Spanish officials and settlers were never loyal to him, and King Ferdinand and Queen Isabella of Spain eventually tired of him. (However,) unlike Columbus, Hernando Cortés[3] was a great leader and was able to help Ferdinand and Isabella realize their goals. (In 1519,) he and an army of six hundred Spanish soldiers landed in Mexico. (Within three years,) Cortés and his small force had defeated the mighty Aztec[4] empire. Establishing themselves in Mexico City, the Spanish took over the empire, bringing the Indian groups to the south under their rule.†

    _____ series

    ✔ time order

    _____ cause/effect

    ✔ comparison/contrast

    _____ definition

1. **viable:** capable of success; workable
2. **Columbus:** the first historically important European discoverer of the New World
3. **Hernando Cortés:** Spanish adventurer who conquered Mexico's Aztec empire
4. **Aztec:** an ancient civilization of Central Mexico

---

* Adapted from John J. Fung, "Transplanting Animal Organs into Humans Is Feasible," *USA Today*, November 1999, 54–55.

† Adapted from Carol Berkin et al., *Making America*, Brief 2nd ed. (Boston: Houghton Mifflin Co., 2001), 26.

2. If you feel like giving up when you encounter a very long or hard assignment, you probably have a low tolerance for unpleasant tasks. (However,) you can change your attitude toward unpleasant tasks so that you can concentrate and get them done. (First,) remind yourself that the sooner you start, the sooner you will finish. (Next,) remind yourself that your attitude toward studying may be causing you to lose concentration and may be keeping you from doing your work as well as you can. (Third,) make long or difficult assignments easier to handle by breaking them into smaller segments that you can complete in one sitting. (Then) reward yourself for doing the work.*

_____ series

__✔__ time order

_____ cause/effect

__✔__ comparison/contrast

_____ definition

3. A minority is a racial, religious, political, national, or other group that is regarded as different from the larger group of which it is a part and that is often singled out for unfavorable treatment. African Americans, (for example,) are considered a minority. (During the 1960s and 1970s,) the federal government passed a number of laws forbidding discrimination[1] in the workplace. (In 1965,) the first of these acts, entitled the Civil Rights Act, was passed. (Now) more than thirty-five years after passage of the Civil Rights Act, abuses still exist.†

_____ series

__✔__ time order

_____ cause/effect

_____ comparison/contrast

__✔__ definition

1. **discrimination:** showing prejudice or preference without considering individual merit

---

* Adapted from Carol C. Kanar, *The Confident Student*, 5th ed. (Boston: Houghton Mifflin Co., 2004), 258.

† Adapted from William Pride, Robert Hughes, and Jack Kapoor, *Business*, 6th ed. (Boston: Houghton Mifflin Co., 1999), 44.

4. (Because) so many children play at the Lexington Avenue Park every day, many children lose the toys they bring to play with, such as trucks, dolls, and balls. There are a few things you can do to avoid losing your children's toys at the park. (Before) you come to the park, label everything with your child's name and address. It is also a good idea to bring as few toys as you can and to make a list of the things that you bring with you. (While) you are at the park, keep your child's toys in a pile where he or she is playing, if possible. (Before) you leave, make a quick sweep of the park to see if your child has left anything behind. This will ensure that you leave with your child's toys.

_____ series

✔ time order

✔ cause/effect

_____ comparison/contrast

_____ definition

5. The Spanish Crown supported many exploratory ventures[1] to the "New World" by hiring *conquistadors*. A *conquistador* was the name given to a Spanish explorer who set out to overtake parts of the New World both in Mexico and what is now the United States. (For example,) Ponce de Leon, Hernando de Soto, and Francisco Pizarro were all conquistadors. (In 1513 and again in 1521,) Juan Ponce de Leon led expeditions to Florida. (In 1539,) the Spanish sent Hernando de Soto to claim the Mississippi River. (In 1533,) Francisco Pizarro conquered the Inca Empire, an advanced civilization that glittered with gold.*

_____ series

✔ time order

_____ cause/effect

_____ comparison/contrast

✔ definition

1. ventures: daring or dangerous undertakings

---

* Adapted from Carol Berkin et al., *Making America*, Brief 2nd Edition. (Boston: Houghton Mifflin Co., 2001), 26.

Exercise 5.8

The following groups of sentences have been scrambled. Number them in the order they should appear (1, 2, 3, and so on) so that they make sense. Use the transitions to help you figure out the right order. Then, in the list below each group, place a check mark next to the pattern or patterns used to organize the details.

1. __2__ First, write your positive statements—sentences like "I am intelligent," "I can handle my problems," and "I am creative"—on 3 × 5 index cards.

   __1__ One technique for improving self-esteem is designing positive self-talk statements.

   __4__ Then, each time you see one of these cards, review its message and believe the words.

   __3__ Next, attach your cards to your bathroom mirror, your refrigerator, your car dashboard, and your desk.*

   Pattern of organization:

   _____ series

   ✔ time order

   _____ cause/effect

   _____ comparison/contrast

   _____ definition

2. __4__ The catalog will also tell you whether a fee is involved in applying for a degree and under what conditions you can get your money back if you withdraw from a course.

   __2__ The calendar in your catalog, for example, is one of the items you will use most frequently.

   __1__ Your college catalog is a publication that contains a wealth of information about your college's programs, policies, requirements, and services.

* Adapted from Barry L. Reece and Rhonda Brandt, *Effective Human Relations in Organizations*, 7th ed. (Boston: Houghton Mifflin Co., 1997), 111.

___3___ It shows when classes begin and end, when holidays occur, when the drop-and-add period is over, when final exams are scheduled, and when you should apply for a degree.*

Pattern of organization:

___✔___ series

_____ time order

_____ cause/effect

_____ comparison/contrast

___✔___ definition

3. ___4___ Consequently, town residents who want to swim will have to join either the Silver Lake swim club or the Charles Cook Pool in Cortlandt Manor.

___2___ As a result, no swimming will be allowed during July and August.

___1___ Due to high levels of algae, the Duck Pond in the center of town has tested positive for a dangerous microbe.[1]

___3___ Because swimming won't be allowed, the Duck Pond in the center of town is being closed for the summer.

Pattern of organization:

_____ series

_____ time order

___✔___ cause/effect

_____ comparison/contrast

_____ definition

4. ___3___ In the early 1960s, Irving refined his storytelling skills at the University of Iowa, where he got a master's degree in creative writing.

1. **microbe:** a tiny life form

* Adapted from Carol C. Kanar, *The Confident Student*, 5th ed. (Boston: Houghton Mifflin Co., 2004), 20.

5

___1___ John Irving[1] grew up in Exeter, New Hampshire, where his step-father taught at exclusive Phillips Exeter Academy.

___2___ He took up wrestling at age fourteen to provide a much-needed outlet for his energy.

___4___ In 1964, he married photographer Shyla Leary, whom he met in college, and became a father at the age of 23.*

Pattern of organization:

_____ series

___✔___ time order

_____ cause/effect

_____ comparison/contrast

_____ definition

CHAPTER 5 REVIEW

Write the correct answer in each of the blanks in the following statements.

1. __Transitions__ are words and phrases whose function is to show the relationships between thoughts and ideas.

2. Some transitions are __synonyms__; in other words, they mean the same thing.

3. Some transitions can be used in more than one __pattern__ of organization.

4. Different transitions can create subtle but significant changes in the __meaning__ of sentences.

5. __Series__ transitions indicate the addition of another reason, example, type, or other point.

6. __Time order__ transitions signal another event, step, or stage within a chronological order of details.

1. **John Irving:** American writer whose novels include *The World According to Garp*

* Adapted from Kim Hubbard and Natasha Stoynoff, "Hands Full," *People* Magazine, July 30, 2001, 96–97.

7. _Cause/effect_ transitions indicate either a reason for or a result of an occurrence presented in a previous sentence.

8. _Comparison_ transitions point out similarities, and _contrast_ transitions point out differences.

9. _Definition_ transitions illustrate ideas in definition paragraphs as well as in other types of paragraphs.

10. _Paragraphs_ organized according to more than one pattern will often include different kinds of transitions.

Reading Selection

Practicing the Active Reading Strategy:
Before and As You Read

You can use active reading strategies before, as, and after you read a selection. The following are some suggestions for active reading strategies that you can employ before you read and as you are reading.

1. Skim the selection for any unfamiliar words. Circle or highlight any words you do not know.

2. As you read, underline, highlight, or circle important words or phrases.

3. Write down any questions about the selection if you are confused by the information presented.

4. Jot notes in the margin to help you understand the material.

Out of the Candlelight and Into the Spotlight
by Rochelle Jewel Shapiro

1 I dreamed I was in Barnes and Noble,[1] giving a reading of my very first novel, about a suburban psychic. The audience smiled expectantly, and as soon as I stopped reading, people rose from their seats. Whipping out my pen, I sat down at the table, ready to sign copies. But the crowd that rushed toward me held no books for me to sign. Instead, their hands were outstretched, grabbing for me. "We came to be read by you!" they shouted. I woke up in a cold sweat.

1. **Barnes and Noble:** a bookstore

2   In a few months, I'm supposed to go out and promote my novel. While I'm happy to talk to readers about plot and character, I dread being asked where I got my subject matter, how I did my research, and whether I really believe in psychics.

3   The fact is, I do. My Russian grandmother, who called herself a healer, was psychic. One look into a woman's eyes and she could tell if she was pregnant—and whether she was happy about it.

4   Bubbie suspected, even before I could talk, that I had her talent. When I was four, I told everyone that my mother's cousin Bertie was coming on a ship from London. The next day my mother got a call from the docks. "It's Bertie! Come pick me up!" No invitation, no warning. When Bubbie heard, she told me, "You have my gift."

5   But as I got older, being psychic began to seem too Old World to me. I wanted to do something modern, so after college I wrote for a magazine and then taught middle school. But wherever I worked, my psychic abilities came with me. I knew too much about other people, and that caused pain and embarrassment to me and them. I was gossiping with a coworker one day when I suddenly blurted out, "Congratulations! When is the baby due?" And then I saw a funny look on her face and knew she hadn't told anyone.

6   "How did you know?" she demanded.

7   "I don't remember," I lied.

8   A couple of days later, over lunch, I was moved to tell another coworker, "I'm sure your father is going to be OK."

9   "What are you talking about?" he said. "My father is perfectly fine." An hour later he got a call that his father had been in a car accident and was in intensive care.

10   As it happened more and more, I had to admit to my colleagues that I was clairvoyant.[1] Once I did, people no longer wanted friendship—they wanted the future. Finally, I stopped resisting my calling and became a professional psychic, though one who was in hiding. For more than twenty-five years, I've given readings over the phone and told all but my closest friends that I make my living as a writer.

11   Keeping my occupation under wraps hasn't been easy. I was once coaxed into attending the wedding of a client who believed my reading had led her to her husband-to-be. "Only if I can be incognito," I told her.

12   "Of course," she said.

13   At the ceremony, I joyfully wept at having had a hand in the young couple's destiny. But during the toasts, the bride stood up, lifted her glass, and said, "It was my psychic, Rochelle Shapiro, who brought Steve and me together." The photographer shone his lights on me. Guests rushed over as if I were the Viennese dessert table. "Will my son-in-law pass the bar exam this time?" one demanded. "Is my dead father around me?" another asked. "Can I take you to the track with me?" another said.

14   I was so unnerved that I would have left right away, but I had to stop at the ladies' room. "She's in here," I heard a woman say, seconds after I went in. "I recognize her shoes!"

15   "Where can I find a husband?" a woman called over the stall. "I'm next for the psychic," another woman argued. There was a

---

1. **clairvoyant:** able to see the future

crowd out there! "We should take numbers," I heard a man say. A man in the ladies' room! I had gone from being a phone psychic to a bathroom psychic.

16   I'm no longer surprised by how quickly people get carried away. Once, a woman I'll call Linda begged me to let her come to my house for a reading instead of doing it on the phone. "I need to be close to you when you contact my mother's spirit," she pleaded.

17   She sounded so distraught that I finally gave in, and after the reading, she looked so much happier that I considered working in person more often. She wanted to come back in two days, but I didn't have an appointment available for two weeks. "I'll just have to hold out," she sighed.

18   The next day, when I stepped out of my front door, Linda was standing there. "Mama!" she cried, and threw her arms around me as tight as a vise. After that, I couldn't help looking over my shoulder every time I left the house.

19   I don't want to use my ability to promote my writing career. I work by candlelight, not spotlight, and my gift might leave me if I abuse it. I want to use it to help people, not to sell books. I'll continue to give psychic readings, but I want to use my other gift, too, the one I practice in quiet when I'm alone—writing.*

VOCABULARY

Read the following questions about some of the vocabulary words that appear in the previous selection. Then circle the letter of each correct answer.

1. In paragraph 2, the author uses the word *psychic* for the first time. Using what you know about the author and what she does for a living, what does the word *psychic* mean?

   a. someone who knows a lot about different things
   b. someone who has a photographic memory
   c. someone who can see into the future
   d. someone who likes to work alone

2. If someone is your *colleague* (paragraph 10), who is the person?

   a. a coworker   c. a relative
   b. a neighbor   d. a close friend

3. "I was once *coaxed* into attending the wedding of a client who believed my reading had led her to her husband-to-be." (paragraph 11) What does *coaxed* mean?

   a. denied   c. allowed
   b. persuaded   d. permitted

* "Out of the Candlelight and Into the Spotlight" by Rochelle Jewel Shapiro from *Newsweek*, February 16, 2004. Copyright © 2004 Newsweek. All rights reserved. Reprinted by permission.

4. If you are *incognito* (paragraph 11), what are you?
   a. in disguise
   b. afraid
   c. speaking another language
   d. hiding behind a wall

5. If you are *unnerved* (paragraph 14), you are
   a. disgusted.
   b. secure.
   c. alone.
   d. anxious.

6. "She sounded so *distraught* that I finally gave in" (paragraph 17). What does *distraught* mean?
   a. happy
   b. upset
   c. content
   d. angry

MAIN IDEAS, IMPLIED MAIN IDEAS, AND TRANSITIONS

Respond to each of the following questions by circling the letter of the correct answer.

1. Which of the following paragraphs begins with a contrast transition?
   a. paragraph 3
   b. paragraph 5
   c. paragraph 10
   d. paragraph 17

2. What is the main idea of paragraph 5?
   a. The author couldn't deny her psychic abilities.
   b. The author liked to gossip.
   c. The author's coworkers didn't like her psychic abilities.
   d. The author lived in the Old World.

3. Which of the following sentences begins with a contrast transition?
   a. "Instead, their hands were outstretched, grabbing for me."
   b. "In a few months, I'm supposed to go out and promote my novel."
   c. "Finally, I stopped resisting my calling and became a professional psychic, though one who was in hiding."
   d. "The next day, when I stepped out of my front door, Linda was standing there."

4. Which of the following paragraphs DOES NOT include time order transitions?
   a. paragraph 3
   b. paragraph 4
   c. paragraph 5
   d. paragraph 10

5. What is the implied main idea of paragraph 13?
   a. The author's abilities were revealed by the bride, and she then became the center of attention.

b. The author enjoyed giving readings.

c. The author picked up some new clients that day.

d. The author angered the groom.

Practicing the Active Reading Strategy:

After You Read

Now that you have read the selection, answer the following questions, using the active reading strategies that you learned in Chapter 1.

1. Identify and write down the point and purpose of this reading selection.

2. Besides the vocabulary words included in the exercise on pages 245–246, are there any other vocabulary words that are unfamiliar to you? If so, write a list of them. When you have finished writing your list, look up each word in a dictionary and write the definition that best describes the word as it is used in the selection.

3. Predict any possible test questions that may be used on a test about the content of this selection.

4. How could you use the information contained in this selection? Does the information contained in the selection reinforce or contradict your ideas and experiences? Explain.

QUESTIONS FOR DISCUSSION AND WRITING

Answer the following questions based on your reading of the selection. Write your answers on the blanks provided.

1. How would you feel if you had the abilities that the author possesses? Would you be more open than the author is about what you can do and see? Why or why not? Answers will vary.

   _____

2. In your own words, describe how you think the author feels about having this special "gift." Do you think that she might see it as a curse?
   Answers will vary.

   _____

3. What does it mean when the author says that she works "by candlelight, not spotlight"? Why do you think that is? The author does not want her
   psychic abilities—and by extension, herself—to be the focus of attention. By

doing readings at home, without meeting her clients, she is able to stay out of the spotlight. She has had too many bad experiences in which people focused on her psychic ability rather than on her as a person, so she wants to remain "by candlelight."

▶ Vocabulary: The Explanation Context Clue

In Chapter 4, you learned about the definition/restatement context clue. A second type of context clue is **explanation.** In this type of clue, the words, phrases, or sentences near an unfamiliar word will explain enough about that word to allow you to figure out its meaning. For example, read this next sentence, which comes from one of the paragraphs in this chapter:

> Almost immediately, it began leaning because it was being erected on the soft *silt* of a buried riverbed.

What is *silt*? Well, you get several explanation clues in this sentence. First of all, it's soft, and secondly, it's found in buried riverbeds. It also caused the tower to lean. Therefore, you can conclude that it must be some type of wet, unstable sand.

Vocabulary Exercise

The following examples all come from paragraphs in Chapters 4 and 5. In each one, use the explanation context clue to help you determine the meaning of the boldfaced, italicized word and write a definition for this word on the blank provided.

1. From 1999 to 2001, engineers *excavated* soil from beneath the tower.
   Dug or scooped out

2. So to reduce your risk of such an accident, drive more on divided highways with *medians.* Dividing area between opposing lanes of traffic on highways

3. Mother England made the mistake of withholding liberty too long from her "children" in the American colonies. They grew to be rebellious "teenagers" who demanded their freedom. . . . As a consequence, though, England did learn a valuable lesson from a painful experience, which is

why she later granted a peaceful and orderly transfer of power to another *tempestuous* offspring named India. Stormy

4. The *disputed* presidential elections of 1876 and 2000 shared some striking similarities. The 1876 election between Samuel Tilden and Rutherford B. Hayes was so close that the victory hinged upon just a few electoral votes. Likewise, in 2000, the race between Al Gore and George W. Bush depended upon only a handful of electoral votes. Argued about

5. Sports—such as basketball or tennis—require *aerobic* activity that increases the heart rate and makes players sweat. Involving oxygen consumption by the body

6. The ancient Greeks would tuck rosemary twigs in their hair while studying to help them remember what they were learning. They also wore rosemary *garlands* to word off the "evil eye," a look or stare believed to harm others. Wreaths

7. He is also a master magician and makes friends and fights *mythic* battles against the forces of Darkness, which appeals to a wide variety of readers. Of or existing in myth; imaginary or fictional

8. And of course, Mike Tyson, formerly the best heavyweight boxer in the world, pleaded guilty in a Brooklyn court to *disorderly* conduct after a 5:30 AM fistfight with two men in a hotel lobby last June. disturbing, undisciplined, out of control

5

READING STRATEGY: Summarizing

When you **summarize** a reading selection, you briefly restate, in your own words, its most important ideas. A summary usually focuses on the most general points, which include the overall main idea and some of the major supporting details. As a result, summaries are much shorter than the original material. A paragraph can usually be summarized in a sentence or two, an article can be summarized in a paragraph, and a typical textbook chapter can be summarized in a page or two.

Continued

Summarizing is an important reading skill that you will use for three specific academic purposes: studying, completing assignments and tests, and incorporating source material into research projects.

Studying. Writing summaries is an effective way to gain a better understanding of what you read. If you need to remember the information in a textbook chapter, for instance, you will know it more thoroughly after you have summarized its main ideas. Also, the act of writing down these ideas will help reinforce them in your memory.

Completing assignments and tests. Summaries are one of the most common types of college writing assignments. Professors in a variety of disciplines often ask students to summarize readings such as journal articles. Also, "summarize" is a common direction in tests that require written responses.

Incorporating source material into research projects. You will use summaries of other sources to support your ideas in research projects such as term papers.

To write a summary, follow these three steps:

1. Using active reading techniques, read and reread the original material until you understand it.

2. Identify the main idea and major supporting points. In particular, underline all of the topic sentences. You might also want to create an outline or map that diagrams the general and specific relationships among sentences (in a paragraph) or paragraphs (in an article or chapter).

3. Using your own words, write sentences that state the author's main idea along with the most important major details. Your paraphrase should be accurate; it should not add anything that did not appear in the original or omit anything important from the original. It should also be objective. In other words, don't offer your own reactions or opinions; just restate the author's points without commenting on them. If you use a phrase from the original, enclose it in quotation marks to indicate that it is the author's words, not yours.

Follow the three steps described above to write a one-paragraph summary of the following newspaper article: Answers will vary.

"Getting Yourself Back on Track"

Five years after graduation, an economics major still temps[1] as a book-keeper. A legal secretary has dropped so many evening courses over twenty years that she still doesn't have her bachelor's degree. An audio-visual technician finds himself in one dead-end job after another.

These men and women share a common enemy: themselves. By pro-crastinating,[2] missing deadlines, and engaging in other self-defeating be-haviors, they routinely undermine their chances for success.

"Everybody ducks out of one challenge or another," says psychologist Kenneth W. Christian, author of *Your Own Worst Enemy: Breaking the Habit of Adult Underachievement*. "But if you're a chronic[3] underachiever, whenever you run into difficulty, you want to curl up and suck your thumb. You seek comfort rather than hard work. You make excuses to avoid facing your fears. And you end up with a life that's unfulfilling be-cause you miss out on the satisfaction that only comes from tackling something hard."

Underachievement—failure to live up to potential—exists in every age group at every job level and in every field, from sales to sports.

Christian estimates that one in four adults has the problem. But suf-ferers should take heart, notes psychologist Pamela Brill, author of *The Winner's Way*. "Underachievement isn't a permanent condition," she says, "but a mind-set—a behavior pattern that you can change."

The Roots of Self-Sabotage[4]

The key, psychological research reveals, is how much control you think you have over your life. "High achievers tend to assume responsibility, at-tributing[5] positive results to their own actions," says psychologist Susan Battley of Stony Brook, NY. "Underachievers may feel very little control over their lives, so they may not have the same motivation to work to make things happen. They like to believe things will turn out the same, whatever they do."

Continued

1. **temps:** works at a temporary job
2. **procrastinating:** putting things off
3. **chronic:** happening over and over
4. **self-sabotage:** harming oneself
5. **attributing:** crediting

Although underachievement can start in grade school, adults usually don't sense a problem until their late twenties. "The Bart Simpson, underachieving-and-proud-of-it thing isn't cute after a certain age," says Christian. "Often, young adults who don't want to leave behind the world of adolescence, where anything is possible, won't commit to any one job or career. They just drift along." Other underachievers hit a plateau[1] in their thirties and see younger colleagues advancing faster. As their self-defeating behavior continues, they sink deeper into disappointment.

"It doesn't take long before underachievers lose confidence that they could perform well even if they tried their best," Christian adds. "Instead of pursuing a path leading to a sense of meaning and delight, they lower their expectations and settle for less. Before they know it, they're forty and at the edge of depression, or fifty and having midlife crisis."

At any age, self-sabotage stems from fear—both of failure and of success. "If you're afraid of what success will bring, you'll find a way to fail," says Noah St. John, author of *Permission To Succeed*. "Success may bring higher standards, more work, more responsibilities. And the best way to stay in your comfort zone and not succeed is not to finish things. You can always find an excuse so it's not your fault, and people will expect less of you in the future."

How to Stop Shooting Yourself in the Foot

If you want to break the habit of underachievement, here are some ways to start.

- **Say goodbye to the way things were.** "Ask yourself what you would leave behind if you got a promotion," says Kenneth Sole, a consulting social psychologist in Lee, NH. "Would you miss the people you work with? Would you have to move? Only when people come to terms with the losses that any change brings can they see its benefits and move into the future."

- **Take a personal audit.** "Identify what you really want to achieve," says Kenneth Christian. "Get rid of everything that stands in the way. And keep working regardless of how frustrated or inadequate you may feel."

---

1. **plateau:** a stable, unchanging level

- **Put your goals in writing.** "High achievers have goals and plans," Susan Battley observes. "Underachievers live in wish mode."[1] Start with "stretch goals" that are both a reach and reachable so you can accumulate a confidence-building series of small wins. "And remember: Nothing becomes a goal until you write it down."

- **Use the language of change.** Tune in to the messages you send yourself. Eliminate "weasel words," such as "I'll try" or "I hope to," and declare what you will do positively. Switch from saying "I have to" and "I should"; instead, say "I will." Challenge automatic negative assumptions ("I couldn't do that") by asking yourself "Why not?" "Try to neutralize[2] irrational fear," says Battley.

- **Take baby steps.** "Think of *one* small thing you can do today that will make you feel better tomorrow," says Christian. "One daily change, especially if it helps you finish something you started, can change the trajectory[3] of your life."

- **Tackle self-defeating habits.** Identify three behaviors that have resulted in the most lost opportunities. For example, if you always procrastinate, open the mail as soon as it arrives and return e-mails the same day.

- **Get support.** Recruit a friend or colleague to encourage you to reach your goals. Surround yourself with positive people who don't make you feel inferior or defensive, and train yourself to tune out the negative words of others.

- **Be your own Monday-morning quarterback.** Top competitors analyze and learn from each performance. Like them, focus on what you did well and what you can correct—and aim to do better the next time.*

5

1. **mode:** state or condition   3. **trajectory:** path
2. **neutralize:** destroy

* "Getting Yourself Back on Track" by Dianne Hales from *Parade*, March 28, 2004. Reprinted with permission from *Parade* and Dianne Hales, copyright © 2004.

CHAPTER 5 TESTS

Name _____ Date _____

TEST 1

Choose the transition that would best complete the sentence. Circle the letter of the correct answer.

1. Phil spends a lot of time at the library. _____, his wife has never been there.

   a. Also

   b. Due to

   c.) On the other hand

   d. Finally

2. Recent court cases involving unethical[1] behavior have helped make business ethics a matter of public concern. _____, the Copley Company pled guilty to charges of faking drug reports to a government agency.

   a. Often

   b. Due to

   c. However

   d.) For instance

3. Infants have large heads in relation to their bodies, their faces are hairless and smooth-skinned, and they have a relatively large forehead and small chin so that the vertical placement of features is low in the infant's face. _____, infants' eyes are large, they have fine eyebrows, and their nose is small.

   a.) In addition

   b. Another

   c. As a result

   d. While

4. _____ the exceptionally cold weather this winter, many lakes have frozen over, making it possible for people to skate and play hockey.

   a. In contrast to

   b. Therefore

   c.) As a result of

   d. For example

1. unethical: morally wrong

_____

For additional tests, see the Test Bank.

5. _____ Wegman's grocery store now offers prepared foods for take-out, the Food Emporium has a wide selection of heat-and-eat dinners that busy people can buy and serve for dinner.

(a.) Just as   c. Due to

b. Yet   d. First

6. In the Middle Ages, the Black Death[1] wiped out over a third of Europe's population. Epidemics[2] of smallpox, measles, typhus, and other serious diseases took the lives of many Europeans, _____ .*

a. then   (c.) too

b. such as   d. in contrast

7. Yahoo![3] offers many great sites if you are interested in using the Internet for research. _____, Alta Vista[4] brings you good sites and interesting information that will help you do research.

a. Conversely   c. After

b. First   (d.) Similarly

8. _____ the concert ran late, the Tates were still able to make our dinner reservation.

(a.) Although   c. First

b. For example   d. Finally

9. Brainstorming[5] is a technique for finding solutions, creating plans, and discovering new ideas. _____, when you are stuck on a problem, brainstorming can help you clear your mind.†

a. Instead   c. Eventually

(b.) For example   d. In contrast

1. **Black Death:** a contagious disease caused by bacteria

2. **epidemics:** diseases affecting large numbers of people

3. **Yahoo!:** an Internet search engine company

4. **Alta Vista:** an Internet search engine company

5. **brainstorming:** generating ideas

---

* Adapted from Carol Berkin et al., *Making America*, 3rd ed. (Boston: Houghton Mifflin Co., 2002), 23.

† Adapted from Dave Ellis, *Becoming a Master Student*, 9th ed. (Boston: Houghton Mifflin Co., 2000), 228.

10. I locked my keys in the car. _____, we'll miss the beginning of the concert.

    a. Due to   c. Often

    (b.) As a consequence   d. Previously

11. My minivan is great because I can pack lots of groceries in the back when I go to the store. _____, there is plenty of room for my four children.

    a. First   c. Next

    (b.) In addition   d. Despite

12. Jack had used the local service station many times while he lived in Statesville. _____, he decided that its service was not very good and that its rates were high, so he changed service stations.

    a. Before   c. While

    (b.) Over time   d. Next

13. Polaner offers a low-fat strawberry jelly that has a lot of flavor. _____, Smucker's has a reduced-fat blueberry jam that can't be beat!

    a. Consequently   c. To illustrate

    (b.) Along the same line   d. While

14. There are many advantages to maintaining your car. _____, your car will last longer than a car that is not maintained.

    a. Also   (c.) First of all

    b. In spite of   d. Finally

15. Danielle read a book to two of her children before dinner. _____, her husband took the other child to the park.

    a. First   (c.) Meanwhile

    b. As   d. When

16. Children's movies seem to be more for adults. _____, *Shrek* has a lot of jokes that children wouldn't understand but that have adults howling with laughter.

    (a.) As an illustration   c. As a result

    b. In the beginning   d. On the contrary

17. Leanne Nakamura saw huge nets that had washed ashore from fishing boats digging into the sand on the island of Oahu. _____, damage was done to the beach and the coral reefs, and fish and sea turtles were dying.*

   a. While   c. Second
   b. Before   d. Consequently ⓓ

18. Jane's health club has a pool that members can use just by showing their membership card. _____, Frank's club has a pool that caters[1] exclusively to club members.

   a. In like manner ⓐ   c. Second
   b. First   d. Similar to

19. Many people use the Internet for a variety of activities including shopping, gathering information, and sending messages. _____, you will be able to send video messages to loved ones with just the click of a button!

   a. Eventually ⓐ   c. While
   b. Before   d. As a result

20. There are only a few parking spaces left on campus. _____, you should get over to the security office and get a parking pass as soon as possible.

   a. For this reason ⓐ   c. Meanwhile
   b. Now   d. During

21. Everyone at the dinner party praised Janet's attempt at baking a chocolate soufflé. _____, it was soggy and tasteless.

   a. In opposition   c. Nevertheless ⓒ
   b. Before   d. In addition

1. **caters:** attends to the desires and needs of

---

* Adapted from Maile Carpenter, "The Girl Who Helped Preserve Paradise," *Reader's Digest*, August 2001, 163–164.

22. There are a lot of new soft drinks on the market with extra vitamins for health. _____, any of the "Fresh Samantha" drinks are packed with vitamins.

    a. However

    b. After

    c. In spite of

    (d.) For example

23. How are you doing today? _____, have you recovered from your recent bout[1] of strep throat?

    a. In addition

    (b.) Specifically

    c. Third

    d. Though

24. I'm going to go swimming. _____ that I'm going to take a shower.

    a. While

    (b.) After

    c. Eventually

    d. Once

25. _____ he makes a lot of money, Donald never seems to have a dime to spare!

    a. However

    b. In opposition

    c. Before

    (d.) Even though

TEST 2

Read each of the following paragraphs and then respond to the questions by circling the letter of each correct answer.

A. (1) Here's a concept that everyone will applaud but few will put into practice: start a regular savings program at a very early age. (2) To begin, a child could put a certain percentage of his or her allowance into a savings account (or a piggy bank). (3) Later on, as the youngster receives payment for chores completed, this percentage would continue to be socked away. (4) When he or she gets a job, that same percentage can be put aside for the savings account. (5) Although the amount of money saved will vary from year to year, over time it will accumulate surprisingly quickly. (6) By the time the youngster has grown into a retiree, he or she will be astounded at how much money is now available!

1. **bout:** period or episode

1. Which of the following sentences begins with a contrast transition?
   a. sentence 1
   (c.) sentence 5
   b. sentence 3
   d. sentence 6

2. Which of the following sentences does NOT start with a time order transition?
   a. sentence 3
   (c.) sentence 5
   b. sentence 4
   d. sentence 6

B. (1) I have a word of advice for college students: consult a counselor. (2) When I went through college, I never spoke with a counselor to plan my future courses. (3) As a result, when graduation time came around, I was two credits short. (4) I had to take an extra semester just to obtain those two credits. (5) From then on, I was a semester behind all of the classmates with whom I'd gone through college. (6) For example, I couldn't apply for graduate school until a semester after they had applied.

3. Which of the following sentences begins with a cause/effect transition?
   a. sentence 2
   c. sentence 5
   (b.) sentence 3
   d. sentence 6

4. Which of the following sentences begins with a definition/example transition?
   a. sentence 2
   c. sentence 5
   b. sentence 3
   (d.) sentence 6

C. (1) Some people take the process of buying a new computer step by step. (2) They begin by educating themselves about computers and about which components would be right for them. (3) Next, they shop around by comparing computer sales ads and visiting the websites of computer companies. (4) Then they make a list of the features they need in a computer and try to match that list with the computers being offered in ads. (5) Finally, they call the computer company to order their computer. (6) On the other hand, there are also people who simply walk into the nearest computer store and buy the computer the salesperson recommends.

5. Which of the following sentences does NOT begin with a time order transition?
   a. sentence 3
   c. sentence 5
   b. sentence 4
   (d.) sentence 6

6. Which of the following sentences begins with a contrast transition?

   a. sentence 3   c. sentence 5

   b. sentence 4   (d.) sentence 6

D. (1) My first mistake was registering my e-mail address with a few websites that interest me. (2) After I did that, I started getting unwanted e-mails with advertisements all the time. (3) I then registered with a direct mail association to have my e-mail address put on a list of addresses not wanting advertising e-mail. (4) As a consequence, I seem to be getting more advertising e-mail than ever before. (5) Help!

7. Sentence 4 begins with a

   (a.) cause/effect transition.   c. time order transition.

   b. series transition.   d. comparison/contrast transition.

8. Sentence 2 begins with a

   a. definition/example transition.   c. series transition.

   b. cause/effect transition.   (d.) time order transition.

E. (1) Different people have different types of living styles. (2) You can look right on our block for perfect illustrations of this. (3) For example, the Hammonds' house down the block is a ramshackle[1] affair. (4) The paint is peeling, the driveway has ruts in it, and some windows are broken. (5) By contrast, just next door, the Rubellas' house is a model of upkeep. (6) It is freshly painted, all the fixtures look like new, and the greenery seems almost manicured.[2]

9. Sentence 3 begins with a

   a. series transition.   (c.) definition/example transition.

   b. cause/effect transition.   d. time order transition.

10. Sentence 5 begins with a

   a. cause/effect transition.   c. time order transition.

   (b.) comparison/contrast transition. d. series transition.

1. **ramshackle:** falling apart   2. **manicured:** groomed, trimmed, and clean

Patterns of Organization

GOALS FOR CHAPTER 6

▶ Define the term *pattern* as it relates to paragraphs.

▶ Name the five broad patterns for organizing supporting details in paragraphs.

▶ Recognize words in topic sentences that indicate certain patterns.

▶ Recognize supporting details within a series pattern.

▶ Recognize supporting details within a time order pattern.

▶ Recognize supporting details within a cause/effect pattern.

▶ Recognize supporting details within a comparison/contrast pattern.

▶ Recognize supporting details within a definition pattern.

▶ Take notes on a reading selection.

N ow that you've practiced examining supporting details and transitions, you're ready to look at some common patterns for arranging details. A **pattern** is a consistent form or method for arranging things. To find out what you already know about patterns of organization in paragraphs, take the test below.

TEST YOURSELF

Read each of the following paragraphs and decide which pattern of organization arranges the details. Write a check mark on the blank next to the correct pattern.

1. Smoking is the single most preventable risk factor for fatal illnesses in the United States. Indeed, cigarette smoking accounts for more deaths than all other drugs, car accidents, suicides, homicides, and fires combined. Further, nonsmokers who inhale smoke from other people's cigarettes face an elevated risk for lung cancer and other illnesses related to the lungs, a fact that has given rise to a nonsmokers' rights movement in the United States.*

* Adapted from Douglas Bernstein et al., *Psychology*, 5th ed. (Boston: Houghton Mifflin Co., 1999), 473.

_____ series

_____ time order

__✔__ cause/effect

_____ comparison/contrast

_____ definition

2. Therapists often teach clients desirable behaviors by demonstrating those behaviors. In modeling, the client watches other people perform desired behaviors to learn new skills without going through a lengthy process. In fear treatment, for example, modeling can teach the client how to respond fearlessly while getting rid of the fear responses the patient has.*

_____ series

_____ time order

_____ cause/effect

_____ comparison/contrast

__✔__ definition

3. The newly redesigned $20 bill, which was released in 2003, includes a number of enhanced security features that make it harder to counterfeit. For one thing, it includes an embedded plastic security thread that is visible from both sides. Also, it is printed with color-shifting ink. When the bill is tilted up and down, the color-shifting ink in the number *20* in the lower right corner changes from copper to green and back to copper. Finally, the bill includes a watermark.[1] When the bill is held up to the light, there appears to the right side of the portrait of Andrew Jackson a faint image that is similar to the portrait. It's part of the paper itself, and it can be seen from both sides.†

__✔__ series

_____ time order

1. **watermark:** a design impressed upon paper

---

* Adapted from Douglas Bernstein et al., *Psychology*, 5th ed. (Boston: Houghton Mifflin Co., 1999), 572.

† Adapted from U.S. Department of the Treasury Bureau of Engraving and Printing, "New $20 Bill: Security Features," 2003, http://www.moneyfactory.com/newmoney/main.cfm/learning/interactivebilltext.

_____ cause/effect

_____ comparison/contrast

_____ definition

4. Just before I went to college, I remember telling my father that I wanted to be an actress and to major in speech and drama. My father grew up poor in rural Mississippi, where being a teacher was the highest calling—the most honorable position a black person could hold, other than being a doctor, so he was not happy with my choice. Before I left, I got a scholarship so that my daddy wouldn't have to pay my tuition—and so that I would have control over my decision. Then, I attended college and majored in speech and drama. From there, I went on to become a newscaster and host of my own television show.*

_____ series

___✔___ time order

_____ cause/effect

_____ comparison/contrast

_____ definition

5. My two children are so different that it surprises me every day. For one thing, my older child is a girl, and my younger child is a boy. My daughter loves reading, going to the movies, and writing in her journal. My son, on the other hand, loves running, jumping, and swimming—anything that requires using energy. My daughter loves all different kinds of foods, but my son likes to eat only pizza. And while my son can't go a day without watching some kind of sporting event on television, my daughter will only watch a baseball game if nothing else is on.

_____ series

_____ time order

_____ cause/effect

___✔___ comparison/contrast

_____ definition

6

* Adapted from Oprah Winfrey, "Set Yourself Free," *O* Magazine, April 2001, 37.

To help readers find and comprehend supporting details more easily, paragraphs are usually organized according to at least one particular pattern. A **pattern** is a consistent, predictable form or method of putting something together. So if you learn the most common patterns found within paragraphs, you'll be able to:

1. Recognize supporting details more quickly and accurately.

2. Better understand the relationships among supporting details.

Both of these skills are essential to good reading comprehension.

This chapter presents five broad patterns of organization: **series, time order, cause/effect, comparison/contrast,** and **definition.** Each pattern type is illustrated by itself first, but it's important to realize that paragraphs often combine two or more of these patterns. The end of this chapter presents some examples of paragraphs that are organized according to two or more patterns.

Topic Sentences

As you read the example paragraphs and learn to recognize each pattern, note how the **topic sentence** often indicates the paragraph's pattern of organization. Alert readers know how to watch for clues within topic sentences, clues that indicate how the information is arranged. When you can see these clues, you'll be able to predict the paragraph's framework and see more easily how the details fit into it as you read.

Series

Many paragraphs organize supporting details as a series of items. A **series** is a number of things that come one after the other in succession. Series within paragraphs are often in the form of examples, reasons, types, or some other kind of point. Series of items all equally support the paragraph's topic sentence. For example, read the following paragraph:

> Many modern people are turning themselves into social victims. One example is a Tennessee woman who is suing McDonald's because she was badly burned on the chin by a hot pickle in her hamburger. A Canadian woman is another example. She wants to ban the *South Park* television show because her son Kenny is victimized by the show's Kenny character, who is killed in each episode. A third example is a group of European and Australian women who want to ban

urinals in men's restrooms because they require men to stand in a way that suggests violence toward women. Another victims' group called the American Association for Single People claims that single people are victimized because society ignores them.*

This paragraph offers a series of four equal examples to explain the topic sentence:

Example #1: Tennessee woman burned by a pickle

Example #2: Canadian woman who believes *South Park* damages her son

Example #3: Women who object to urinals

Example #4: Single people who feel ignored

Here's another paragraph that uses a series pattern:

I hit the beach with my new electronic book in hand, but e-books and the outdoors don't mix. They're impossible to read because bright sun reflects off the glass screen, turning it into a mirror. And they're fragile, too. I had to shield mine from sand and surf, but a computer just doesn't belong on the beach. Plus, I had to worry about my e-book being stolen while I took a dip in the ocean.†

The details in this paragraph are organized into a series of reasons. The main idea is "E-books and the outdoors don't mix," and the paragraph gives three reasons to support that idea.

Reason #1: They're difficult to read in a sunny setting.

Reason #2: They're too fragile.

Reason #3: They might be stolen.

If you were to map this paragraph, it might look like this:

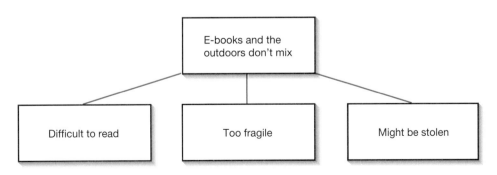

* Adapted from John Leo, "Victims of the Year," *U.S. News and World Report,* December 4, 2000, 24.
† Adapted from Jim Louderback, "E-books: Hot or Not?" *USA Weekend,* July 13–15, 2001, 4.

Series of supporting details all equally develop the topic sentence, so they can often be presented in any order. Authors, however, may choose to arrange them according to their order of importance so they can emphasize one of the points by either presenting it first or saving it for last.

A paragraph's topic sentence will often indicate that the details will appear as a series of items. For example:

We should eliminate pennies for a **number of reasons.**

There are **four major forms** of child abuse.

I began the New Year with **three major goals** in mind.

As you read, look for the following topic sentence words that indicate that a series will follow.

Words and Phrases That Indicate a Series Pattern

Quantity word	plus	Series word
several		examples
many		reasons
two, three, four, etc.		points
a number of		classes
numerous		types
		categories
		groups
		goals
		kinds
		characteristics
		methods
		advantages
		ways
		forms
		tips

Exercise 6.1

Read each of the paragraphs below and write the correct word in each of the blanks that follow. Then, insert abbreviated versions of the paragraph's sentences in the outline or map to indicate the series of *major* supporting details.

1. Isabelle Tihanyi, the founder and owner of the first and only for-women-only surfing schools, called Surf Diva, has a few goals for her surfers. First, she wants

them to have fun. Second, she wants them to learn to surf. And third, she wants them to enjoy the whole process of learning to surf, which means falling down, going under the water, and working hard to achieve something.*

Word(s) in the topic sentence that indicate a series: <u>A few goals</u>

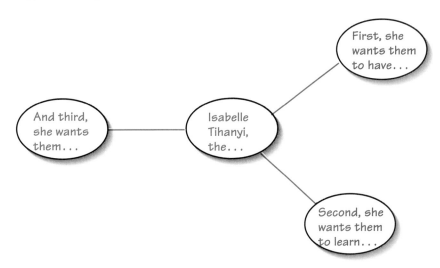

2. Several animated[1] programs on television today are designed to appeal specifically to adults. One example, *The Simpsons*, which started as short animated segments on *The Tracy Ullman Show*, is the oldest of the animated situation comedies for adults and deals with adult themes but in a lighthearted manner. Another example is *King of the Hill*, which focuses on a family and, again, deals with its problems and adult themes in a comedic way. Finally, *South Park*, although originally designed to appeal to and be viewed by adults, has found a following with the preteen and teen set, who memorize and recite lines from the program.

Word(s) in the topic sentence that indicate a series: <u>Several animated</u>

<u>programs</u>

	Several animated programs . . .	
One example is . . .	Another example is . . .	Finally, South Park . . .

1. **animated:** not live action; cartoons

---

* Adapted from David Leon Moore, "Surf Divas," *USA Today*, 1C.

3. For several reasons, *The Bold and the Beautiful*, a popular daytime drama, or soap opera, recently made the decision to add a Spanish-language simulcast[1] (the first in soap history) and a major story line featuring Latino characters. One reason is that the Hispanic population in the United States has surpassed[2] 35 million, and that vast audience, already a strong viewing base for Spanish-language soaps, or *telenovelas*, has American producers taking notice. Another reason is that the network that broadcasts the show is pressuring the producers to add Latino characters to make the show more ethnically diverse.[3] The network is also hoping that by adding some exciting Latino characters, it will expand its viewing base to include younger viewers whom advertisers seek when they buy time during a show.*

Word(s) in the topic sentence that indicate a series: For several reasons

I. Reasons for adding Spanish-language simulcast

A. Large Hispanic audience

B. Network pressure on producers to make shows more diverse

C. Network's hope of attracting younger viewers

4. There are four advantages to joining a weight loss program or group like Weight Watchers or Jenny Craig. First, if you choose a program suited to your personality and lifestyle, your chances of success are much higher. For instance, if you like to eat out a lot, a program that requires that you buy its food may not be for you, but one in which you can eat what you like, in moderation,[4] may be the answer. Second, some weight loss programs often offer different classes on portion control, exercise, and eating habits that may help you understand why you overeat at times. Third, weight loss programs are attended by a lot of different people, so you may find a built-in support group that can help you overcome the tough times when you are dieting. Finally, studies have shown that people who join weight loss programs often have greater success at losing weight and often keep the weight off longer than those who diet on their own.

Word(s) in the topic sentence that indicate a series: Four advantages

1. **simulcast:** simultaneous broadcast
2. **surpassed:** went beyond
3. **diverse:** different
4. **moderation:** medium or average amounts, not excessive amounts

* Adapted from Michael Logan, "Haute Tamale," *TV Guide,* July 21, 2001, 36.

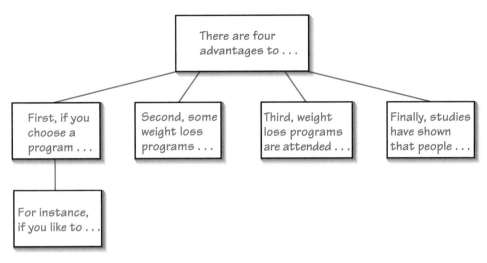

5. Family rules typically fall into five categories. The first category is safety rules such as "Stay in your car seat while riding in the vehicle." The second category is health, which includes hygiene and nutrition. For example, a common hygiene rule might be "Brush your teeth every morning." A third category of rules covers appropriate and inappropriate behaviors such as "Don't burp at the table." Next is the rights category, which includes rules like "Knock before you enter the bathroom." Finally, the fifth category concerns values. "We respect people's feelings" is an example of a values-type rule.*

Word(s) in the topic sentence that indicate a series: <u>Five categories</u>

6

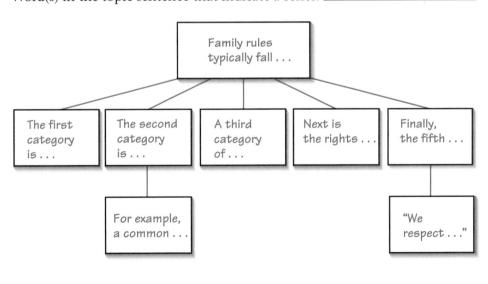

* Adapted from Nancy Seid, "How to Set Rules Your Kids Won't Break," *Parents*, August 2001, 109.

Time Order

The next common pattern for organizing details is time order. In **time order** paragraphs, the details are arranged according to their chronological relationships. In other words, time order paragraphs present details in the order in which they happened or should happen. Like the series pattern, the time order pattern includes items that follow each other in succession to support a main idea. However, these series are events, stages, or steps presented in the order in which they occurred or should occur. Unlike series paragraphs, these details cannot be rearranged because they would no longer make sense.

Two types of time order paragraphs are narrative and process. A **narrative** paragraph tells a story or recounts a sequence of events. Here is an example of a narrative paragraph that arranges details according to the time order pattern:

> The Lindbergh baby kidnapping was one of the biggest crime stories of the twentieth century. On March 1, 1932, Charles Lindbergh Jr., the beloved twenty-month-old son of the flying ace, was put to bed, as usual, at 7:30 PM. But when a nurse checked on the blond, curly-haired boy at 10 PM, his crib was empty, and the window to his second-floor bedroom was open. Police found a ransom note[1] on the sill. Whoever took the child wanted $50,000 to bring him back. Charles Lindbergh paid the money in marked bills. But on May 12, the baby's body was found in the woods near the Lindbergh house, and police believed he was killed the night he was kidnapped. In September 1934, detectives arrested Bruno Richard Hauptmann after finding thousands of dollars of the marked bills in his house. Hauptmann was convicted of the crime and executed in 1936 by electric chair.*

In this paragraph, the supporting details are all events presented in the order in which they occurred:

1. **ransom note:** note written by a kidnapper to demand money in exchange for the return of the kidnapped person

---

* Adapted from Angie Cannon and Kate V. Forsythe, "Crime Stories of the Century," *U.S. News and World Report,* December 6, 1999, 41ff.

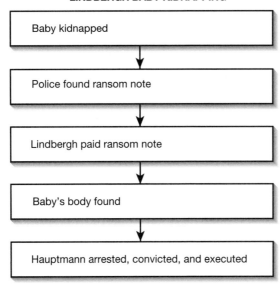

LINDBERGH BABY KIDNAPPING

Baby kidnapped

↓

Police found ransom note

↓

Lindbergh paid ransom note

↓

Baby's body found

↓

Hauptmann arrested, convicted, and executed

The second type of time order paragraph is **process.** A process paragraph explains how something is done or could be done. Its details are organized in the steps or stages, in the order in which they occur. Here is an example:

> The new gasoline-electric hybrid[1] cars work by transferring power back and forth between a gasoline engine and an electric motor. First, the car's batteries feed power to the electric motor to start the car. When the car accelerates to about 15 miles per hour, the gasoline engine takes over. It also sends backup power to a generator, which either feeds it back to the electric motor or sends it to recharge the batteries. As the car continues to accelerate, the batteries contribute power to the electric motor to help the gasoline engine. When the car slows down, the electric motor captures the energy from the spinning axles[2] and sends it to recharge the batteries.*

1. **hybrid:** something containing mixed parts

2. **axles:** shafts on which wheels revolve

---

* Adapted from William Holstein, "Green Cars and Red Ink," *U.S. News and World Report,* November 6, 2000, 42.

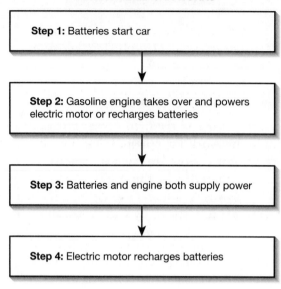

HOW A HYBRID CAR WORKS

Step 1: Batteries start car

Step 2: Gasoline engine takes over and powers electric motor or recharges batteries

Step 3: Batteries and engine both supply power

Step 4: Electric motor recharges batteries

Topic sentences in time order paragraphs will often indicate that a chronology will follow:

> To cope with stress more effectively, follow *six steps.*

> According to William Shakespeare,[1] a person's life moves through *seven stages.*

> Over the last one hundred years, women's swimwear has undergone *several developments.*

As you read, look for topic sentence words that indicate a time order pattern.

Words and Phrases That Indicate a Time Order Pattern

Quantity word	*plus*	*Time Order word*
several		events
two, three, four, etc.		steps
a number of		stages
over time		developments
in just one year		procedures
		processes

---

1. **William Shakespeare:** 17th century English writer of plays and poetry

Exercise 6.2

Read each of the paragraphs below and fill in the blanks that follow. Then, write abbreviated versions of the paragraph's sentences in the outline or map to indicate the *major* time order details.

1. Bozo the Clown, whose career spanned more than fifty years, was the longest-running children's TV star in the country. He was created in 1946 by Capitol Records and debuted on television in 1949. Though he never appeared on network TV, one local TV station after another began producing its own Bozo show with games, circus acts, and comedy. At the height of his popularity in the 1960s, Bozo appeared on 183 TV stations around the world, and fans put their names on waiting lists for years to get tickets to a show. By the 1990s, though, kids had access to cable TV and channels like the Cartoon Network and Nickelodeon, and stations began canceling their Bozo shows. The final Bozo show was taped in Chicago in June 2001, ending a long era of clowning around.*

Word(s) in the topic sentence that indicate time order: <u>Spanned more than fifty years</u>

   I. <u>Bozo the Clown's career</u>
     A. <u>Created in 1946 and debuted on TV in 1949</u>
     B. <u>Local TV stations began producing Bozo shows</u>
     C. <u>Height of popularity in 1960s</u>
     D. <u>Shows canceled in 1990s</u>
     E. <u>Final show in June 2001</u>

2. To maintain the sharpness of kitchen knives by using a steel rod, follow several easy steps. First, with one hand, hold the sharpening steel rod, point down, on a flat, stable surface like a cutting board. Second, with the other hand, angle the knife blade so that it is about 15 degrees from the rod. Third, pull the knife down the rod in a slight arc, pulling the knife handle toward you, stroking the entire blade edge from base to tip. Fourth, repeat this procedure on the other side of the blade. Repeat the entire process three to five times, alternating the right and left sides of the knife's cutting edge.†

* Adapted from Marc Peyser, "It's Bedtime for Bozo," *Newsweek,* June 25, 2001, 81.
† Adapted from "Sharpening Can Make Knives Safer," *Charlotte* (NC) *Observer,* February 11, 2004, 2A.

6

Word(s) in the topic sentence that indicate time order: <u>several steps</u>

SHARPENING A KNIFE

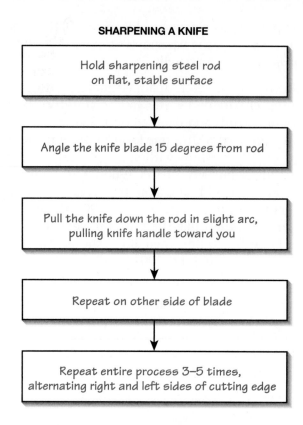

Hold sharpening steel rod
on flat, stable surface

↓

Angle the knife blade 15 degrees from rod

↓

Pull the knife down the rod in slight arc,
pulling knife handle toward you

↓

Repeat on other side of blade

↓

Repeat entire process 3–5 times,
alternating right and left sides of cutting edge

6

3. Many experienced cooks shy away from baking bread because it is a time-consuming task with many steps. The first step is to buy all of the necessary ingredients, including yeast and flour, the two main ingredients in any bread. The second step is to put your ingredients together. Then, the time-consuming part begins because the dough, or the combination of all of your ingredients, must sit for an extended period of time—anywhere from one hour to four hours—to allow the yeast in the dough to rise. After the dough-rising step has been completed, you must take the time to knead[1] the dough, which can also take a long time, depending on how much dough you have prepared. Finally, your risen, kneaded dough should be shaped and baked at the appropriate temperature for the period of time specified in your recipe.

1. **knead:** to work the dough with your
   hands and knuckles

Word(s) in the topic sentence that indicate time order: <u>Many steps</u>

    I. <u>Steps in baking bread</u>

       A. <u>Buy ingredients</u>

       B. <u>Mix ingredients</u>

       C. <u>Let dough rise for one to four hours</u>

       D. <u>Knead the dough</u>

       E. <u>Shape and bake dough</u>

4. Building on the disillusionment of the 1960s, Americans' distrust of the federal government has deepened over the last several decades. In the 1970s, the Watergate scandal and Richard Nixon's resignation from the presidency convinced many that politics was inherently[1] corrupt. In the 1980s, the administration of Ronald Reagan added the Iran-Contra scandal to the public's concerns about government corruption and cover-ups. And in the 1990s, Bill Clinton's White House was tainted[2] by a variety of special investigations and trials as well as allegations[3] about his character, like the one that he had extramarital affairs.*

Word(s) in the topic sentence that indicate time order: <u>Over the last several</u>

<u>decades</u>

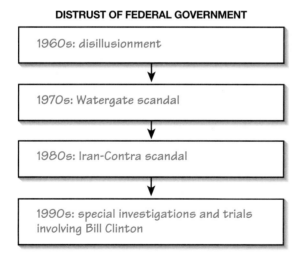

DISTRUST OF FEDERAL GOVERNMENT

1960s: disillusionment

↓

1970s: Watergate scandal

↓

1980s: Iran-Contra scandal

↓

1990s: special investigations and trials involving Bill Clinton

6

1. **inherently:** fundamentally   3. **allegations:** accusations
2. **tainted:** corrupted, spoiled

* Adapted from Mary Beth Norton et al., *A People and a Nation*, Vol. II, 5th ed. (Boston: Houghton Mifflin Co., 1998), 1002.

5. Christopher Columbus's[1] journey to the New World took just over two months. On August 3, 1492, in command of three ships—the *Pinta,* the *Niña,* and the *Santa Maria*—Columbus set sail from the southern Spanish port of Palos. The first part of the journey must have been very familiar, for the ships steered down the Northeast Trades to the Canary Islands. There Columbus refitted his square-rigged ships, adding triangular sails to make them more maneuverable.[2] On September 6, the ships weighed anchor and headed out into the unknown ocean. Just over a month later, pushed by the favorable trade winds, the vessels found land approximately where Columbus had predicted. On October 12, he and his men landed on an island in the Bahamas, which its inhabitants called Guanahani, but which he renamed San Salvador. Later he went on to explore the islands now known as Cuba and Hispaniola.*

Word(s) in the topic sentence that indicate time order: <u>Just over two months</u>

   I. <u>Christopher Columbus's journey</u>

      A. <u>August 3, 1492: set sail from Palos and traveled to Canary Islands</u>

      B. <u>September 6: headed out into unknown ocean</u>

      C. <u>October 12: landed on an island in the Bahamas</u>

      D. <u>Later: explored Cuba and Hispaniola</u>

Cause/Effect

When details are arranged in the **cause/effect** pattern, the paragraph intends to show how the details relate to or affect each other. Like a narrative paragraph, a cause/effect paragraph presents a series of occurrences. However, unlike a narrative, the cause/effect pattern reveals how one occurrence led to another. It might also demonstrate how a series of causes produced one particular effect, or result. The diagram on page 279 will help you visualize some common types of cause/effect patterns.

The first diagram shows a chain reaction of causes and effects while the second one indicates a separate series of effects that are not related. The third diagram shows a pattern in which several unrelated causes together produce one particular effect.

1. **Christopher Columbus:** the first historically important European discoverer of the New World

2. **maneuverable:** able to move

---

* Adapted from Mary Beth Norton et al., *A People and a Nation,* Vol. I, 5th ed. (Boston: Houghton Mifflin Co., 1998).

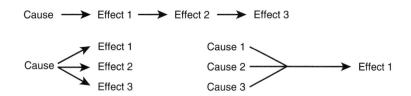

For an example of the cause/effect pattern, read the following paragraphs:

Several outcomes depend upon the results of the population census conducted in the United States every ten years. Political representation is affected by the census because population determines how many Congressional representatives each state can have. The census numbers are also given to local governments, which determine how many schools, hospitals, and firehouses to build to accommodate the number of people living in the area. The census results are given to businesses, too. They use the data to decide where to open businesses, where to close them, and even what kind and how many products to put on stores' shelves.*

In this paragraph, one cause produces three different effects:

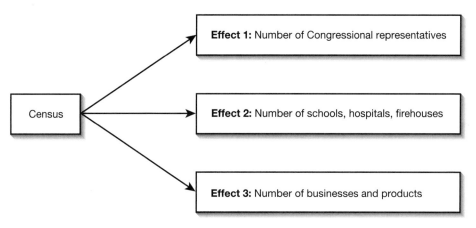

Here's a second example that is arranged according to a different cause/effect pattern:

The saga[1] of fiber and its protection against colon cancer reveals how uncertain science can lead to consumer confusion. In 1971, a British surgeon observed that Africans in rural areas had fewer bowel[2]

1. **saga:** long report or story

2. **bowel:** related to the intestines in the digestive system

* Adapted from Calvin Baker, "The Uncounted," *Life,* March 2000, 64.

disorders than Americans. He theorized[3] that the Africans' high-fiber diet made the difference. So scientists began experimenting with rats and mice, and the results seemed to indicate that fiber might help prevent colon cancer. Therefore, in 1984, the American Cancer Society recommended that people eat more fiber. That led to the Kellogg Company's printing a claim on All-Bran cereal boxes that suggested its product could reduce the risk of colon cancer. Other cereals followed suit even though it wasn't clear that *cereal* fiber was responsible. In the late 1980s and early 1990s, however, more clinical trials found that fiber's protection was much weaker than earlier studies had predicted.*

This paragraph explains a chain reaction. The British doctor's observation about Africans was the cause, and then a series of effects occurred as a result. You might map this paragraph as follows:

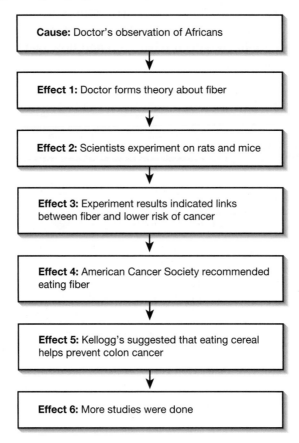

Cause: Doctor's observation of Africans

Effect 1: Doctor forms theory about fiber

Effect 2: Scientists experiment on rats and mice

Effect 3: Experiment results indicated links between fiber and lower risk of cancer

Effect 4: American Cancer Society recommended eating fiber

Effect 5: Kellogg's suggested that eating cereal helps prevent colon cancer

Effect 6: More studies were done

1. **theorized:** proposed as being true

* Adapted from Linda Kulman, "Food News Can Get You Dizzy, So Know What to Swallow," *U.S. News and World Report,* November 13, 2000, 70.

Topic sentences in cause/effect paragraphs will often indicate that an explanation of related occurrences will follow:

Stereotyping often **leads to** prejudice and discrimination.

The **results** of hypnosis can be fascinating.

A **chain reaction** of events **led to** the Great Depression of the 1930s.

As you read, look for the following topic sentence words that signal a cause/effect pattern.

Words and Phrases That Indicate a Cause/Effect Pattern

consequences	was caused by
effects	causes
results	chain reaction
outcomes	leads to
affect	factors
because	

Exercise 6.3

Read the paragraphs below and fill in the blanks that follow. Then, write abbreviated versions of the paragraph's sentences in the map to indicate the cause/effect relationships among the *major* supporting details.

1. Because of their negative effects, multiple births are frowned upon even by fertility doctors. One of the drawbacks to having four, five, or six babies at one time is poor health for the infants. Multiple births are often premature,[1] and premature babies usually require long periods of intensive care. Even if the babies are not born prematurely, they are more likely to suffer from afflictions,[2] such as heart problems or genetic[3] disorders, that can affect their lifelong health. These health problems lead to a second disadvantage: financial problems. Multiple birth babies can run up expensive medical bills. These bills, along with the daily demands of caring for several infants at one time, usually result in high levels of stress for the whole family.*

1. **premature:** occurring before the right time
2. **afflictions:** causes of suffering
3. **genetic:** related to genes, the units that determine the particular characteristics of an organism

---

* Adapted from Rita Rubin, "Little Safety in Numbers," *USA Today,* July 19, 2001, 8D.

Word(s) in the topic sentence that indicate cause/effect order: _Because, effects_

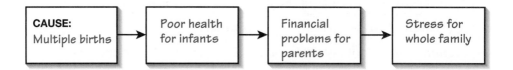

2. Negative beliefs lead to negative behaviors. For example, after a disappointing test score, a struggling student thinks, "I knew I couldn't do college math!" This belief will likely lead the student to miss classes and neglect assignments. These self-defeating behaviors lead to even lower test scores, reinforcing the negative beliefs. This student, caught in a cycle of failure, is now in grave[1] danger of failing math.*

Word(s) in the topic sentence that indicate cause/effect order: _lead to_

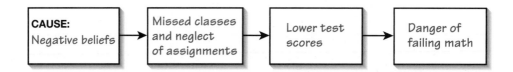

3. There are a number of factors that may be contributing to your getting sunburned every summer. If you wear sunscreen but still get sunburned, you may not be using a sunscreen with enough "SPF," the ingredient that shields your skin and indicates how long you can stay in the sun with protection. For instance, if you wear a sunscreen with SPF 30, you can stay in the sun thirty times longer than you could without protection. Second, you may not be reapplying sunscreen after every dip in the pool, ocean, or lake, and after intense physical activity. Third, in addition to sunscreen, you may not be wearing a hat and sunglasses to protect your face and eyes.

Word(s) in the topic sentence that indicate cause/effect order: _Factors,_

contributing

1. **grave:** serious

* Adapted from Skip Downing, *On Course*, 4th ed. (Boston: Houghton Mifflin Co., 2005), 5.

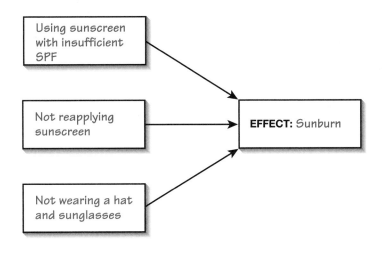

4. If companies shipped just 25 percent of their freight on trains instead of big trucks, traffic on America's overcrowded roads would decrease significantly. As a result, drivers' commuting time could decrease by 86 hours per year by 2020. So commuters would gain two full workweeks' worth of personal time. In addition, they would each save $1,127 in annual commuting costs. Plus, getting more big trucks off the roads would significantly reduce harmful emissions[1] that pollute our air.*

6

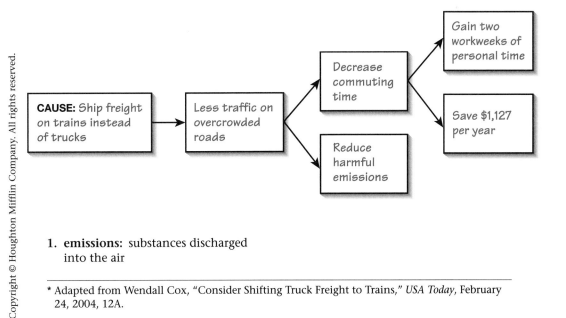

1. **emissions:** substances discharged into the air

_____

* Adapted from Wendall Cox, "Consider Shifting Truck Freight to Trains," *USA Today*, February 24, 2004, 12A.

5. Researchers have found that the average American is driving fifteen to twenty miles per hour faster than he or she did ten years ago, with serious consequences. As a result, the number of speeding tickets issued has risen by about 20 percent in the last ten years. More serious is the number of deaths associated with car accidents. Studies show that more people die as a result of speeding than any other driving-related factor such as bad weather, driver neglect, or driving under the influence of alcohol. Consequently, many states are considering lowering the speed limit by five or ten miles per hour.

Word(s) in the topic sentence that indicate cause/effect order: _Consequences_

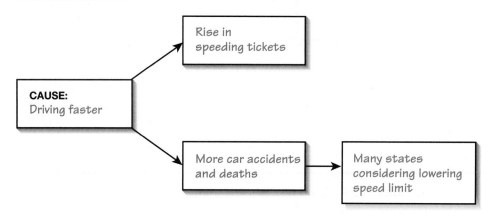

Comparison/Contrast

A third common pattern is comparison/contrast. **Comparison** means explaining the *similarities* between two or more things. **Contrast** means examining the *differences* between things. A paragraph can compare or contrast, or do both.

In comparison/contrast paragraphs, the supporting details are in the form of points of comparison. In other words, the paragraph concentrates on certain aspects or features of the subjects and explores their likenesses and/or differences in those areas. For example, a comparison of two different male singing groups might focus on the similarities in their style, the subjects of their songs, and the audiences they attract. Paragraphs arrange these details in one of two ways. One option is to focus on each subject in turn. The following paragraph, which deals only with similarities, provides an example of this pattern.

Abraham Lincoln was similar in many ways to Benjamin Franklin. Franklin received little schooling, dropping out at age ten to work. Yet he loved to read and write, and he wrote everything from articles to poetry. Franklin is famous for his inventions such as the Franklin stove and for his world-famous experiments with electricity. In addition, he was an able politician who helped to win America's independence and form its new government. Franklin was also an outspoken opponent of slavery. Like Franklin, Lincoln received little schooling, attending for only a year. However, he, too, loved to read and write, and he is famous for his eloquent[1] speeches such as The Gettysburg Address. Lincoln, like Franklin, was also an inventor; he is the only president to hold a patent.[2] And he is also known for his ability as a politician and his hatred of slavery.*

This paragraph groups the points of comparison by subject, discussing first Benjamin Franklin and then Abraham Lincoln. It would be outlined like this:

I. Similarities between Benjamin Franklin and Abraham Lincoln

   A. Benjamin Franklin
      1. Received little schooling
      2. Loved to read and write
      3. Inventor
      4. Able politician
      5. Opponent of slavery

   B. Abraham Lincoln
      1. Received little schooling
      2. Loved to read and write
      3. Inventor
      4. Able politician
      5. Opponent of slavery

6

A comparison/contrast paragraph can also be arranged so that it focuses on the points of comparison, alternating back and forth between the two subjects.

Even in preschool, boys and girls fall into very different play patterns. Boys tend to gather in larger groups while girls, early on, gather in small groups. Boys play games that have clear winners and losers and bluster[3] through them, boasting about their skills. Girls play theatrical games, such as playacting roles as members of a pretend family,

1. **eloquent:** vivid and expressive
2. **patent:** government grant giving sole rights to an invention to its creator
3. **bluster:** speak loudly and arrogantly

* Adapted from "Remarkable Similarities Between President Abraham Lincoln and Benjamin Franklin," http://www.theamericans.us/poparticle-Lincoln-Franklin.html.

that don't feature hierarchy[1] or winners. One study of children aged three to four found they were already resolving conflict in separate ways—boys resorting to threats, girls negotiating verbally and often reaching a compromise.*

This paragraph contrasts three aspects of preschool play groups: their size, type of games played, and ways conflict is resolved. You could outline the organization of these three points of comparison as follows:

I. Play patterns of boys and girls

   A. Size of play groups
      1. Boys
      2. Girls

   B. Types of games
      1. Boys
      2. Girls

   C. Conflict resolution
      1. Boys
      2. Girls

Topic sentences in comparison/contrast paragraphs often indicate that an explanation of similarities and/or differences is to follow:

Public schools and private schools *differ* in four significant aspects.

Although they share a few *similarities,* football and rugby are more *different* than *alike.*

In comparison to Japanese cars, American cars give you more for your money.

As you read, look for the following topic sentence words that indicate a comparison/contrast pattern.

Words That Indicate a Comparison/Contrast Pattern

similarities	differences
alike	different
likenesses	

---

1. hierarchy: groupings according to rank

* Adapted from Deborah Blum, "What's the Difference Between Boys and Girls?" *Life,* March 1999, 52.

Exercise 6.4

Read the following comparison/contrast paragraphs and answer the questions that follow by circling the letter of correct response or filling in the blanks.

> Though there are some differences between today's teenagers and those of previous generations, they are very much the same in many respects. It's true that modern teens must deal with problems—such as school shootings and AIDS—unknown to teens in other eras. Anorexia, bulimia,[1] and teen suicide are more prevalent,[2] too. But the teens of today still struggle with the same emotions and daily dramas as teens of yesterday. Teens still see adults as too critical. They still define themselves as different through their outward appearance. In previous generations, it was bell-bottoms and long hair. Today, it's green hair and body piercings. But what was true then and is today is that to be a teen is to be on the search for self. "Who am I?" and "How do others perceive me?" are two big questions for teenagers of any era.*

1. This paragraph (circle the letter of one answer):

   a. compares.
   b. contrasts.
   c. compares and contrasts.

2. What two subjects are being compared and/or contrasted?

   <u>Today's teenagers</u> and <u>teenagers of previous generations</u>

3. On what four similarities between the two subjects does the paragraph focus?

   1. <u>Struggles with emotions and daily dramas</u>
   2. <u>Opinion of adults as too critical</u>
   3. <u>Defining self through outward appearance</u>
   4. <u>Search for self</u>

> Although *USA Today* and the *New York Times* are both daily newspapers, they couldn't be more different. For one thing, *USA Today* caters[3] to the reader who wants lots of news about a lot of different subjects and who doesn't have a lot of time to devote to reading. The *New York Times*

1. **anorexia** and **bulimia:** two types of eating disorders
2. **prevalent:** widespread; common
3. **caters:** attends to the needs or desires

---

* Adapted from Kimberly Kirberger, "Are Today's Teens That Different?" *Life*, March 1999, 48.

features in-depth articles on fewer subjects and is known for its ground-breaking stories on news in the United States and abroad. *USA Today* is heavy on sports and entertainment reporting while the *New York Times* is noted for its number of articles on political issues. Finally *USA Today* is a daily paper that is only published Monday through Friday while the *New York Times* is published seven days a week, with an extensive weekend supplement most noted for its magazine section.

4. This paragraph (circle the letter of one answer):

   a. compares.
   b. contrasts.
   c. compares and contrasts.

5. What two subjects are being compared and/or contrasted?

   USA Today _____ and New York Times _____

6. On what three differences between the two subjects does the paragraph focus?

   1. Number of subjects covered _____
   2. Subject matter _____
   3. Number of days published _____

Mark and John—identical twins separated at birth—met for the first time at twenty-four years of age. They were physically alike; the same molars were giving them toothaches. There were also similarities in their behavior and mental processes. For example, they used the same aftershave, smoked the same brand of cigarettes, brushed with the same imported brand of tooth-paste, and liked the same sports. Both had served in the military, having joined within eight days of each other. Testing by a psychologist found they had nearly identical overall IQ scores.*

7. This paragraph (circle the letter of one answer):

   a. compares.
   b. contrasts.
   c. compares and contrasts.

8. What two subjects are being compared and/or contrasted?

   Mark _____ and John _____

* Adapted from Douglas Bernstein and Peggy Nash, *Essentials of Psychology*, 2nd ed. (Boston: Houghton Mifflin Co., 2002), 30.

9. On what four similarities between the two subjects does this paragraph focus?

1. _Physical similarities_

2. _Behavior and mental process similarities_

3. _Military service_

4. _Identical IQ scores_

George Clooney and Brad Pitt share many of the same characteristics but couldn't be more different. Both have been named to *People* Magazine's "50 Most Beautiful People" list, and both are adored by women in the United States and abroad. Both men have made a name for themselves acting as leading men in some highly publicized movies. However, Brad Pitt is a stay-at-home kind of guy, spending most, if not all, of his time by the side of his wife, Jennifer Aniston. George Clooney is known for being a bit of a playboy, having been seen around Hollywood with different women. One woman, who has known him for years, claims he will never settle down and get married whereas Pitt's friends say that he is doing exactly what he has always wanted to do by being married.

10. This paragraph (circle the letter of one answer):

    a. compares.
    b. contrasts.
    c. compares and contrasts.

11. What two subjects are being compared and/or contrasted?

    George Clooney and _Brad Pitt_

12. How are the two men compared? List three similarities:

    1. _Both named to People Magazine's "50 Most Beautiful People" list_

    2. _Both adored by women_

    3. _Both have been leading men in highly publicized movies_

13. How are they contrasted? _Clooney is a playboy, and Pitt likes being married._

Swimming in a lake and swimming in a pool are two different experiences. For one thing, swimming in a lake does not involve swimming in chemicals like chlorine, which you need in a pool to keep it clean. Another thing that makes the swimming experience different is that lake water is often very cold whereas pool water can get warm and stay warm due to the fact that it is in a closed container or area. Lake water is often very clear whereas pool water, if you don't maintain it properly, can get

6

cloudy and full of leaves and bugs. Finally, often you can see small fish and eels swimming with you in a lake, which is something you would never see in a pool!

14. This paragraph (circle the letter of one answer):

    a. compares.

    (b.) contrasts.

    c. compares and contrasts.

15. What two subjects are being compared and/or contrasted?

    Swimming in a lake _____ and swimming in a pool _____

16. On what four differences between the two subjects does the paragraph focus?

    1. Chemicals

    2. Water temperature

    3. Water clarity

    4. Water creatures

Definition

One last pattern you should learn to recognize is the definition pattern. **Definition** usually states the meaning of a particular word, term, or concept, and then goes on to illustrate it with one or more examples. Textbooks often use this pattern to explain a term being introduced for the first time. The following paragraph is organized according to the definition pattern.

> *Job sharing* (sometimes referred to as *work sharing*) is an arrangement whereby two people share one full-time position. One job sharer may work from 8 AM to noon and the other from 1 to 5 PM, or they may alternate workdays. For example, at a financial institution in Cleveland, two women share the position of manager of corporate communications. One works Tuesdays and Thursdays, and the other works Mondays, Wednesdays, and Fridays. They communicate daily through computers, voice mail, and fax machines to handle their challenging administrative position.*

* Adapted from William M. Pride et al., *Business,* 6th ed. (Boston: Houghton Mifflin Co., 1999), 237.

The example or examples within a definition paragraph may be arranged according to one of the other patterns. For example, the definition might be followed by an example that contains details organized with a *time order* pattern. Or the definition might be followed by *a series* of two or more examples. This next paragraph is a good example:

> Punishment involves the presentation of an unpleasant stimulus[1] or the removal of a pleasant stimulus in order to decrease the frequency of an undesirable behavior. One example is shouting "No!" and swatting your dog when it begins chewing on the rug. That illustrates a negative stimulus that follows a behavior you want to eliminate. Another example is taking away a child's TV privileges following a demonstration of rude behavior. This is a punishment, or penalty, that removes a positive stimulus.*

Topic sentences will often indicate that a definition will follow:

> Money *can be defined as* anything a society uses to purchase products, services, or resources.

> Personality *is* an individual's unique pattern of psychological and behavioral characteristics.

> To understand what a Republican believes, you must first know what the word *conservative* **means.**

As you read, look for the following topic sentence words that may indicate a definition pattern.

6

Words That Indicate a Definition Pattern

means	definition
meaning	is/are
define	

---

1. **stimulus:** something that causes a response

---

* Adapted from Douglas A. Bernstein, *Psychology,* 4th ed. (Boston: Houghton Mifflin Co., 1997), 209.

Exercise 6.5

Read each of the following definition paragraphs and then respond to the questions that follow by writing your answers on the blanks provided.

(1) People learn a lot from personal experience, but they can also learn by observing what others do and what happens to them when they do it. (2) Learning by watching others—a process called *observational learning*—is efficient and adaptive.[1] (3) We don't have to find out for ourselves that a door is locked or that an iron is hot if we have just seen someone else try to open the door or suffer a burn.*

1. What term is defined in this paragraph? <u>Observational learning</u>

2. Which sentence states the definition? <u>2</u>

3. How many examples are given as illustrations? <u>2</u>

(1) In a zoo, a "landscape immersion" exhibit is one that mimics[2] the natural habitats of animals. (2) This type of exhibit brings together different animals and vegetation from similar climate zones and allows the animals to interact as they do in the wild. (3) Also, zoos are extending the plants, rocks, and other natural features of the exhibits into areas where visitors walk, stand, and sit. (4) The jaguar habitat at Seattle's Woodland Park Zoo, for example, is designed so that the big cats can creep into tree branches and lurk over the heads of visitors. (5) The "Absolutely Apes" exhibit at the San Diego Zoo mocks an Asian rain forest, complete with fallen tree trunks. (6) And the National Aquarium in Baltimore includes a simulation of an Australian river canyon, complete with waterfall.†

4. What term is defined in this paragraph? <u>Landscape immersion exhibit</u>

5. Which sentence states the definition? <u>1</u>

6. How many examples are given as illustrations? <u>3</u>

7. Which pattern organizes the examples? <u>Series</u>

1. **adaptive:** capable of changing in response to new situations

2. **mimics:** copies

---

* Adapted from Douglas Bernstein and Peggy Nash, *Essentials of Psychology*, 2nd ed. (Boston: Houghton Mifflin Co., 2002), 167.

† From Tracey Harden, "Improving the Environment for Creatures of Two and Four Legs," *New York Times*, March 31, 2004, http://www.nytimes.com.

(1) A *nutraceutical* (a combination of the words *nutrition* and *pharmaceutical*) is either a pill or another pharmaceutical product that has nutritional value, or a food that has had its nutritional value enhanced by drugs. (2) One nutraceutical that has been in the news is beta-carotene, which is used as a dietary supplement[1] to prevent heart attacks. (3) The term also describes a number of vegetables that have been altered to contain elevated levels of naturally occurring substances believed to ward off cancer. (4) Many natural remedies that have been known for centuries—such as herbal teas—are also considered to be nutraceuticals.*

8. What word is defined in this paragraph? <u>Nutraceutical</u>

9. Which sentence states the definition? <u>1</u>

10. How many examples are given as illustrations? <u>3</u>

11. Which pattern organizes the examples? <u>Series</u>

(1) Many companies in the United States are adopting a "business casual policy" regarding how their employees dress. (2) What is *business casual*? (3) Business casual means that employees, who formerly wore suits and ties in the case of men, and suits and dresses in the case of women, are now permitted to wear more comfortable, less formal attire to the office. (4) An example of this would be khaki pants and a polo shirt for men. (5) For women, perhaps linen pants and a blouse would be appropriate.

12. What term is defined in this paragraph? <u>Business casual</u>

13. Which sentence states the definition? <u>3</u>

14. How many examples are given as illustrations? <u>2</u>

15. Which pattern organizes the examples? <u>Series</u>

(1) *Better* is a retail-fashion term that describes clothing lines that are not as expensive as designer collections—by implication,[2] those would be the "best"—and are affordable for most middle-class consumers. (2) Calvin Klein and Realities, for example, are two mid-priced lines at Lord and Taylor. (3) That store will also showcase the new Michael line from Michael Kors.

6

1. **supplement:** something added to complete something else

2. **implication:** suggestion

---

* Adapted from Michael Quinion, "Nutraceutical," *World Wide Words*, http://www.quinion.com/words/turnsofphrase/tp-nut1.htm.

(4) "Better is affordable luxury," says LaVelle Olexa, senior vice president of fashion merchandising at Lord and Taylor.*

16. What word is defined in this paragraph? _Better_

17. Which sentence states the definition? 1

18. How many examples are given as illustrations? 3

Combination of Patterns

Often, paragraphs include more than one pattern of organization. The major supporting details may be arranged according to one pattern, and minor details may be arranged according to another. For example, read the following paragraph:

> Quitting smoking is difficult because of the effects of nicotine in cigarettes. Nicotine produces pleasurable feelings and acts as a depressant.[1] As the nervous system adapts to nicotine, smokers tend to increase the number of cigarettes they smoke and, thus, the amount of nicotine in their blood. Therefore, when a smoker tries to quit, the absence of nicotine leads to two types of withdrawal. The first type of withdrawal is physical, which may include headaches, increased appetite, sleeping problems, and fatigue. The second type of withdrawal is psychological. Giving up a habit can result in depression, irritability, or feelings of restlessness.†

This paragraph begins with the *effects* of nicotine and ends with a *series* of two types of nicotine withdrawal.

Here is one more example:

> There are very different ways that men and women handle stress. Because women have a very different hormonal balance from men, researchers are finding that women are more prone to take on more stress in their daily living than men. The reasons are varied, but one reason is that women seem to have more stress in their lives. They "multitask," or do many things at once, to keep their family life

1. **depressant:** substance that lowers the rate of bodily activities

---

* Adapted from Isabel C. Gonzalez, "Turn for the Better," *Time*, March 22, 2004, 76.

† Adapted from American Cancer Society, http://www.cancer.org/tobacco/quitting.html.

coordinated and running smoothly. Men, on the other hand, focus on one task at a time. Another reason women have more stress than men is that women worry a lot more than men and about more things. While men may worry about one or two things in a day—their immediate family or money—women worry about their own families, their friends' families, their extended families, and other things.

Most of the details in this paragraph are arranged using the comparison/contrast pattern of organization. However, the paragraph also includes the causes of stress for both men and women, so the paragraph combines the comparison/contrast and cause/effect patterns.

Exercise 6.6

In the list following each paragraph, write a check mark in the blank before each pattern used to organize the supporting details.

1. *Retrograde amnesia* involves a loss of memory for events prior to some critical injury. Often, a person with this condition is unable to remember anything that took place in the months, or even years, before the injury. In most cases, the memories return gradually. For example, one man received a severe blow to the head after being thrown from his motorcycle. After regaining consciousness, he claimed that he was eleven years old. Over the next three months, he gradually recalled more and more of his life. He remembered when he was twelve, thirteen, and so on—right up until the time he was riding his motorcycle the day of the accident. But he was never able to remember what happened just before the accident.*

   _____ series

   __✔__ time order

   _____ cause/effect

   _____ comparison/contrast

   __✔__ definition

2. It was evident in the early 1970s that the United States was beginning to suffer economic decline. Recessions—which economists define as at least

* Adapted from Douglas Bernstein, *Psychology*, 4th ed. (Boston: Houghton Mifflin Co., 1997), 242.

two consecutive quarters of no growth in the gross national product[1]—began to occur more frequently. An eleven-month recession struck the country in 1969 and 1970, the first recession in almost a decade. Between 1973 and 1990, there were four more, and two were particularly long and harsh.*

_____ series

__✔__ time order

_____ cause/effect

_____ comparison/contrast

__✔__ definition

3. Three tools can help you better manage your time. The first one is a monthly calendar, which provides an overview of upcoming commitments, appointments, and assignments. The second self-management tool is a "next actions" list. On this list, record everything you want to do that day or as soon as possible, and as you complete each item on the list, cross it off. The third self-management tool is a tracking form, which allows you to schedule actions that need to be done repeatedly to reach a short-term goal. For example, if your short-term goal is to get an *A* in your sociology class, you could note on your tracking form to "Read the textbook one or more hours" and then check a box each time you complete that action. Researchers at the University of Georgia have found that engaging in these kinds of self-management activities positively affects college grades.†

__✔__ series

_____ time order

__✔__ cause/effect

_____ comparison/contrast

_____ definition

1. **gross national product:** the total market value of all of the goods and services produced in a nation

---

* Adapted from Mary Beth Norton et al., *A People and a Nation*, Vol. II, 5th ed. (Boston: Houghton Mifflin Co., 1998), 958.

† Adapted from Skip Downing, *On Course*, 4th ed. (Boston: Houghton Mifflin Co., 2005), 82–84.

4. Photographs sent back to Earth from the Mars rovers indicate that the Mars landscape is very similar to Earth's dry deserts. The Martian landscape, like deserts on Earth, is dry and has a mixture of rocks on the surface. Also, in both places there are channels that were formed by rain in the past. Scientists have concluded, therefore, that Mars may have been through the same kind of alternating wet and dry climate cycles that have affected our own planet's desert regions. And because scientists have discovered groundwater beneath deserts in Egypt, they wonder if there might be water beneath the Martian surface.*

_____ series

_____ time order

___✔___ cause/effect

___✔___ comparison/contrast

_____ definition

5. The police can search you under two circumstances—when they have a search warrant and when they have lawfully arrested you. A search warrant is an order from a judge authorizing the search of a place; the order must describe what is to be searched and seized, and the judge can issue it only if he or she is persuaded by the police that a good reason exists to believe that a crime has been committed and that the evidence bearing on that crime will be found at a certain location. In addition, you can be searched if the search occurs when you are being lawfully arrested.†

___✔___ series

_____ time order

_____ cause/effect

_____ comparison/contrast

___✔___ definition

---

* Adapted from "Scientist: Mars Rovers Show Deserts Similar to Earth," CNN.com, March 11, 2004, http://www.cnn.com/2004/TECH/space/03/11/mars.deserts.ap/.

† Adapted from James Q. Wilson, and John J. DiIulio Jr., *American Government: The Essentials*, 9th ed. (Boston: Houghton Mifflin Co., 2004), 452.

Exercise 6.7

In each of the following topic sentences, circle the clue word or words that suggest a particular pattern of organization. Then write a check mark next to the pattern indicated by the clue word(s).

1. Long-term overuse of aspirin can (cause) significant health risks.

   _____ series

   _____ time order

   _✔_ cause/effect

   _____ comparison/contrast

   _____ definition

2. For (three reasons) fly-fishing is a great hobby.

   _✔_ series

   _____ time order

   _____ cause/effect

   _____ comparison/contrast

   _____ definition

3. The personal computer's twenty-year history can be divided into (four major) (eras.)

   _____ series

   _✔_ time order

   _____ cause/effect

   _____ comparison/contrast

   _____ definition

4. Biometeorology (is) the new science of studying how the human body interacts with the weather.

   _____ series

   _____ time order

   _____ cause/effect

_____ comparison/contrast

✔ definition

5. Hearing and listening are very (different) actions.

_____ series

_____ time order

_____ cause/effect

✔ comparison/contrast

_____ definition

6. Shopping downtown and shopping in a mall (differ) significantly.

_____ series

_____ time order

_____ cause/effect

✔ comparison/contrast

_____ definition

7. A rude cell phone user exhibits (three inconsiderate behaviors.)

✔ series

_____ time order

_____ cause/effect

_____ comparison/contrast

_____ definition

8. A search engine (is defined) as a program that searches the Internet for documents that contain certain specified keywords.

_____ series

_____ time order

_____ cause/effect

_____ comparison/contrast

✔ definition

6

9. Canning your own vegetables requires following (six steps).

_____ series

✔ time order

_____ cause/effect

_____ comparison/contrast

_____ definition

10. MTV's (effects) on the music industry cannot be underestimated.

_____ series

_____ time order

✔ cause/effect

_____ comparison/contrast

_____ definition

CHAPTER 6 REVIEW

Write the correct word or words in the blanks in the following statements.

1. A ___pattern___ is a consistent, predictable form or method for putting something together.

2. Patterns help readers find _supporting details_ and understand their relationships.

3. Five broad patterns for organizing details include ___series___, ___time order___, ___cause/effect___, ___comparison/contrast___, and ___definition___.

4. _Topic sentences_ often include clues to a paragraph's pattern of arrangement.

5. A ___series___ is a number of things that follow each other in succession. Series in paragraphs may be examples, reasons, types, or other points.

6. _Time order_ paragraphs, which include narratives and processes, arrange details chronologically.

7. _Cause/effect_ paragraphs explain how supporting details are related to each other.

8. <u>Comparison/contrast</u> paragraphs examine two or more subjects' similarities, differences, or both.

9. The <u>definition</u> pattern includes a term's meaning plus one or more examples as illustration.

10. Paragraphs often use a combination of <u>patterns</u> to organize supporting details.

Reading Selection

Practicing the Active Reading Strategy:

Before and As You Read

You can use active reading strategies before, as, and after you read a selection. The following are some suggestions for active reading strategies that you can employ before you read and as you are reading.

1. Skim the selection for any unfamiliar words. Circle or highlight any words you do not know.

2. As you read, underline, highlight, or circle important words or phrases.

3. Write down any questions about the selection if you are confused by the information presented.

4. Jot notes in the margin to help you understand the material.

6

Jumping Jack's Still a Flash
by Rick Reilly

1 Here it comes, the festive day in this country, Sunday, February 1, when all Americans—men and women, young and old—gather together and give up on their New Year's resolutions. Your promise to eat right gets left. Your resolution to work out doesn't work out. Your solemn vow to lose weight dies somewhere between the Ding Dongs and the Domino's. And the last person you want to call to celebrate with is Jack LaLanne, the jerk who has ruined it for everybody by not missing a single daily workout in seventy-four years.

2 Remember *The Jack LaLanne Show*? Your mom doing jumping jacks in the family room? Jack in his short-sleeved jumpsuit? His German shepherd, Happy? Well, Happy's dead, but LaLanne is still at it. At 89, the 5'4" LaLanne has a 46-inch chest and a 31-inch waist and can still do 100 push-ups without

turning so much as light pink. His ninetieth birthday is coming up in September, and he wants to celebrate by swimming the 30 miles from Catalina Island to Long Beach, California, underwater, using air tanks. It'll take about 22 hours. (For my ninetieth, I also plan to use air tanks, at home in a hospital bed, gumming rice cakes.)

3   And when LaLanne looks out at this Cheez Doodle country of ours, most of us doing impressions of three-days-dead walruses, he wants to cry into his juicer. "We have no pride, no discipline in this country!" rants LaLanne. "We're serving junk food in schools! People think they can eat anything and just sit on their big, fat butts! Athletes are selling their souls to advertise crap that they know is no good for kids— milk and cheeseburgers and candy! Why can't people see that it's killing them! Any stupid ass can die! Living is hard! You've got to work at living!"

4   He's not a fan of the Atkins diet:[1] "It's a gimmick! All that meat! You need whole-grain bread and cereals!" Or dairy products: "Am I a suckling calf? No other creature uses milk after they wean." Or our eating habits: "Would you get your dog up in the morning and give him a cup of coffee, a cigarette, and a doughnut?"

5   Against all the unprincipled blowhards[2] and liars in this country, LaLanne stands out like a nun in a paddy wagon.[3] He works out every day from 5 AM to 7, pumping iron the first hour, swimming the next. His daily diet never sways: a protein soy drink for breakfast, five pieces of fruit and four egg whites for lunch, and a salad with ten raw vegetables, brown rice, and three ounces of grilled fish for dinner. And a glass of wine. Party!

6   He says he hasn't had a sweet since he was 15, and his wife and staff confirm it. "I tell him, 'A piece of carrot cake once in a while can be a very good thing,'" says his secretary, Liz, "but he'll never go for it."

7   Jack, are you nuts? "Yeah, I guess I am," he says. You don't know the half of it.

8   At 40, he swam from Alcatraz to Fisherman's Wharf handcuffed. At 60, he did it again, towing a rowboat with 1,000 pounds of sand. At 70, he jumped into Long Beach Harbor handcuffed and towed 70 people in 70 boats for a mile and a half. One birthday he did 1,000 chin-ups and 1,000 push-ups in 82 minutes.

9   Doesn't sound like a guy who once wanted to kill himself, does it?

10   A sugar addict at 15, he'd get splitting headaches and bang his head against the wall trying to get rid of them. He was so skinny the girls at his school beat him up. He set fire to his parents' house, tried to attack his older brother with an ax. "I considered suicide many times," LaLanne says. "I couldn't stand [my life] anymore."

11   And then his mom took him to a lecture by a nutritionist, who told him he was a human garbage can. That day, LaLanne resolved to eat right and start exercising— which is like saying, "That day, young Bill Shakespeare[4] resolved to try a little writing." LaLanne became captain of the high school football team and an all-conference wrestling

---

1. **Atkins diet:** a diet that consists mainly of proteins and vegetables
2. **blowhards:** braggarts; people who boast
3. **paddy wagon:** van used by police for taking suspects into custody
4. **Bill Shakespeare:** William Shakespeare, a great 17th century writer of plays and poetry

champion, and he was offered a pro baseball contract. He opened America's first health club, in 1936 in Oakland, and wound up with more than 100 clubs, which he eventually licensed to Bally. In 1951, he invented the television exercise program, *The Jack LaLanne Show*. People called him a crackpot[1] and said it would die in six weeks. It lasted 34 years.

12   Look around. Health clubs, health-food stores, jogging, Pilates, yoga, and personal trainers. It all started with Jack LaLanne.

13   To honor him, each one of us needs to wash-and-vac our bodies, give up sweets, get in shape, demand that our kids get gym class and healthy foods in schools, and rid this country of the plague of obesity.

14   First thing next year.*

VOCABULARY

Read the following questions about some of the vocabulary words that appear in the previous selection. Then circle the letter of each correct answer.

1. In paragraph 1, the author states: "Here it comes, the *festive* day in this country, Sunday, February 1, when all Americans—men and women, young and old—gather together and give up on their New Year's resolutions." What does *festive* mean?
   a. joyful
   b. unhappy
   c. distorted
   d. unwrapped

2. What is a *solemn vow*? "Your *solemn vow* to lose weight dies somewhere between the Ding Dongs and the Domino's." (paragraph 1)
   a. a sad song
   b. a serious promise
   c. a broken promise
   d. a depressed friend

3. What is a *gimmick*? "It's a *gimmick*," the author writes of LaLanne's opinion of the Atkins diet in paragraph 4.
   a. serious commitment
   b. publicity stunt
   c. serious illness
   d. deadly concept

4. What does it mean to *wean*? "No other creature uses milk after they *wean*." (paragraph 4)
   a. to give up breastfeeding from one's mother
   b. to start using a fork and knife
   c. to start eating red meat
   d. to stop eating red meat

1. **crackpot:** an odd or eccentric person

---

* Reprinted courtesy of *Sports Illustrated:* "Jumping Jack's Still a Flash" by Rick Reilly, January 26, 2004. Copyright © 2004 Time Inc. All rights reserved.

6

5. What is a *plague*? (paragraph 13) "and rid this country of the *plague* of obesity."

a. happy occurrence   c. cure

(b.) disease   d. misgiving

IMPLIED MAIN IDEAS, TRANSITIONS, AND PATTERNS OF ORGANIZATION

Respond to the following questions by circling the letter of the correct answer.

1. What pattern organizes the details in paragraph 8?

a. cause/effect   c. comparison

(b.) time order   d. definition

2. What is the implied main idea of paragraph 8?

a. Jack LaLanne is insane.

b. Jack LaLanne does everything for his wife.

(c.) Jack LaLanne is incredibly strong.

d. Jack LaLanne enjoys swimming.

3. What pattern organizes the details in paragraph 11?

a. series

b. definition

c. cause/effect

(d.) time order

4. Which of the following paragraphs begins with a series transition?

(a.) paragraph 3   c. paragraph 8

b. paragraph 5   d. paragraph 10

5. What is the implied main idea of paragraph 11?

(a.) LaLanne's visit to a nutritionist changed his life.

b. LaLanne's mother was worried about him.

c. LaLanne was a human garbage can.

d. LaLanne was too short to play professional sports.

Practicing the Active Reading Strategy:
After You Read

Now that you have read the selection, answer the following questions, using the active reading strategies that you learned in Chapter 1.

1. Identify and write down the point and purpose of this reading selection.

2. Besides the vocabulary words included in the exercise on pages 303–304, are there any other vocabulary words that are unfamiliar to you? If so, write a list of them. When you have finished writing your list, look up each word in a dictionary and write the definition that best describes the word as it is used in the selection.

3. Predict any possible test questions that may be used on a test about the content of this selection.

4. How could you use the information contained in this selection? Does the information contained in the selection reinforce or contradict your ideas and experiences? Explain.

QUESTIONS FOR DISCUSSION AND WRITING

Answer the following questions based on your reading of the selection. Write your answers on the blanks provided.

1. LaLanne's visit to a nutritionist changed his life. Have you ever had a life-changing experience? If so, what was it? *Answers will vary.*

_____

2. What kind of commitment do you think it takes to live a life like Jack LaLanne's? Why do you think he is so driven to live a healthy lifestyle? What motivates him, in your opinion? *Answers will vary.*

_____

3. Do you think that Americans are in better shape or worse shape than people in the rest of the world? Why? *Answers will vary.*

_____

▶ Vocabulary: The Example Context Clue

You've learned that a *context clue* is a word, phrase, or sentence that helps you understand the meaning of an unfamiliar word you encounter as you read. In Chapter 4, you practiced recognizing the definition/restatement context clue. In Chapter 5, you learned about the explanation context clue. The **example** is a third type of context clue that can give you a sense of a particular word's definition. In this type, an example somewhere near a word provides an

6

illustration that allows you to draw a conclusion about the word's meaning. For example, read the following sentence, which comes from one of the paragraphs in this chapter:

> Finally, the bill includes a *watermark*. When the [$20] bill is held up to the light, there appears to the right side of the portrait of Andrew Jackson a faint image that is similar to the portrait. It's part of the paper itself, and it can be seen from both sides.

What does the word *watermark* mean in this sentence? You get clues in the next two sentences, which give the example of a $20 bill. Phrases like "a faint image" and "it's part of the paper itself" help you conclude that a watermark is a design impressed upon paper.

Vocabulary Exercise

The following sentences all come from paragraphs in Chapters 3, 4, and 6. In each one, underline the example context clue that helps you understand the meaning of the boldfaced, italicized word. Then, on the blank provided, write a definition for the boldfaced, italicized word.

1. For example, a common *hygiene* rule might be "Brush your teeth every morning."

   Related to practices that preserve health

2. And in the 1990s, Bill Clinton's White House was tainted by a variety of special investigations and trials as well as *allegations* about his character, like the one that he had extramarital affairs.

   Unproven statements; accusations

3. Even if the babies are not born prematurely, they are more likely to suffer from *afflictions*, such as heart problems or genetic disorders, that can affect their lifelong health.

   Conditions of pain, suffering, or distress

4. Girls play *theatrical* games, such as playacting roles as members of a pretend family, that don't feature hierarchy or winners.

   Relating to dramatic performance

5. And the National Aquarium in Baltimore includes a *simulation* of an Australian river canyon, complete with waterfall.

   Imitation

6

6. A *nutraceutical* (a combination of the words *nutrition* and *pharmaceutical*) is either a pill or another ***pharmaceutical*** that has nutritional value, or a food that has had its nutritional value enhanced by drugs.

Related to drugs or medicine

7. Many Americans believe in the ***supernatural***. . . . A recent Gallup poll revealed that 69 percent of people believe in angels, half of them believe they have their own guardian angels, and 48 percent believe that there are aliens in outer space.

Things outside the natural, ordinary world

8. Another orangutan at a Seattle zoo came up with a ***ploy***, too, by pretending to drop or lose a piece of fruit and then asking for a replacement while actually hiding it.

A sneaky trick

9. The second rule for becoming rich is to avoid ***frivolous*** temptations. For example, don't drive expensive luxury cars; instead, buy medium-priced cars.

Silly or trivial

READING STRATEGY: Taking Notes

Learning how to take notes effectively is a vital skill for college students. You will often be tested on the information in reading selections such as textbook chapters, so you will need to make sure you're using all of the tools at your disposal to understand and retain this information. One of those tools is an active reading technique known as note taking. **Taking notes** means recording in writing the major information and ideas in a text. You might choose to take these notes in the margins of the book itself, or in a notebook, or on separate sheets of paper.

Regardless of where you write them, notes offer two important benefits. First of all, writing down information and ideas helps you to remember them better. For many people, taking the extra time to write the main points by hand helps implant those points in their memory more securely. As a result, retention and test performance tend to improve. Second, good notes are often easier to study because they provide you with a condensed version of the main points.

Continued

Good notes always begin with highlighting or underlining main ideas or key terms as you read, just as you learned to do in Chapter 1. When you write notes, they might take one or more of the following forms:

- **A list of the main ideas in all of the paragraphs.** Put them in your own words and condense them whenever possible. Don't try to include all of the details, just the most important points.

- **A summary of the chapter or article** (for an overview of this strategy, see Chapter 5).

- **An outline.** In previous chapters of this book, you've practiced filling out outlines that reveal the relationships among the details. You can use a Roman numeral outline, but the notes are usually for your eyes only, so you could also adopt or create a more informal system. No matter what kind of outline you use, though, make sure it clearly demonstrates the general and specific relationships among the ideas.

No matter what form they take, effective notes always possess three important characteristics. They should be

1. *Neat.* Skip lines between points and write legibly.

2. *Clearly organized.* Group related points together so they're easier to remember.

3. *Factual and objective.* Like summaries, notes should be free of your own opinions.

Actively read the following section from a textbook. Then, take notes by creating a list of the paragraphs' main ideas, by writing a summary, or by outlining the selection. Answers will vary.

Cooperative Learning: Studying with People

Education often looks like competition. We compete for entrance to school, for grades when we're in school, and for jobs when we leave school. In that climate, it's easy to overlook the power of cooperation.

Consider the idea that competition is not necessary for success in school. In some cases, competition actually works against your success. It is often stressful. It can strain relationships. According to staff members at the Institute for Cooperative Learning at the University of Minnesota, people can often get more done by sharing their skills and resources than by working alone.

We are social animals, and we draw strength from groups. Study groups feed you energy. Aside from offering camaraderie,[1] fellowship, and fun, study groups can elevate your spirit on days when you just don't want to work at your education. You might be more likely to keep an appointment to study with a group than to study by yourself. If you skip a solo study session, no one may know. If you declare your intention to study with others who are depending on you, your intention gains strength. In addition to drawing strength from the group when you're down, you can support others.

Almost every job is accomplished by the combined efforts of many people. For example, manufacturing a single car calls for the contribution of designers, welders, painters, electricians, marketing executives, computer programmers, and many others. Jobs in today's economy call for teamwork—the ability to function well in groups. That's a skill you can start developing by studying with others.

Study groups are especially important if going to school has thrown you into a new culture. Joining a study group with people you already know, as well as with people from other cultures, can ease the transition. Promote your success in school by refusing to go it alone.

In forming a study group, look for dedicated students. Find people you are comfortable with and who share some of your academic goals. You can include people who face academic or personal challenges similar to your own. For example, if you are divorced and have two toddlers at home, you might look for other single parents who have returned to school.

To get the benefit of other perspectives, also include people who face challenges different from yours. Studying with friends is fine, but if your common interests are beer and jokes, beware of getting together to work.

Look for people who pay attention, ask questions, and take notes during class. Ask them to join your group. Choose people with similar educational goals but different backgrounds and methods of learning. You can gain from seeing the material from a new perspective.

Ask two or three people to get together for a snack and talk about group goals, meeting times, and other logistics.[2] You don't have to make an immediate commitment. Limit groups to five or six people. Larger groups are unwieldy.[3] Test the group first by planning a one-time session. If that session works, plan another. After several successful sessions, you can schedule regular meetings.

Continued

1. **camaraderie:** companionship; friendship
2. **logistics:** details of an operation
3. **unwieldy:** difficult to manage because of size or shape

6

Another way to get into a group is to post a note on a bulletin board asking interested students to contact you. Or pass around a sign-up sheet before class. The advantage of these methods is that you don't have to face rejection. The disadvantages are that this method takes more time, and you don't get to choose who applies.*

6

* Adapted from Dave Ellis, *Becoming a Master Student*, 9th ed. (Boston: Houghton Mifflin Co., 2000), 190–191.

CHAPTER 6 TESTS

Name _____ Date _____

TEST 1

Read each par_____ and answer the question that follows. Circle the letter of the correct ans____

1. Experiment_____ __wn that relaxing before a learning session posi-tively affect____ When you take a few minutes to relax deeply, your brain v_____ 'own. When we experience alpha, or slower, waves, our mi_____ le to focus because it's less distracted by mus-cle tension or i_____ ights. Relaxation also appears to allow the two sides of our _____ ogical, linear left brain and the creative, holistic[1] right brain _____ ogether. All in all, alpha waves seem to tune up our brains fo_____ nental performance.*

   Which word in the top_____ indicates a cause/effect pattern?

   a. shown   __e
   (b.) affects   iments

2. Autism is a brain disorder t_____ in early childhood, affecting about two to five children per 1,0C_____ n. It is a disability marked by slow development of physical, soc_____ unication, and learning skills. For example, those who are affect_____ immature speech and use words without attaching the customa_____ igs to them. In addition, they are likely to display repetitive beha_____ h as rocking back and forth for long periods of time. They also h_____ irmal responses to sensations as well as abnormal ways of relating_____ e, objects, and events.

   Which word or phrase in the topic_____ indicates a definition pattern?

   (a.) is   c. begi
   b. disorder   d. affec

1. **holistic:** emphasizing the importance of the whole

* Adapted from Skip Downing, *On Course,* 4th ed. (B_____ ghton Mifflin Co., 2005), 6.

For additional tests on patterns o_____ iization, see the Test Bank.

3. There are numerous ways to begin the webbing[1] process. One is to brain-storm by listing anything you can think of related to the topic. A second technique is to identify questions and possible teaching techniques you could use to teach the topic. A third is to collect hands-on materials that are likely to pique[2] your interest and, eventually, that of your students.*

Which word or phrase in the topic sentence indicates a series?

a. numerous ways
b. are
c. begin
d. process

4. Although Vygotsky and Piaget are both considered to be major theorists[3] of children's cognitive development, their bodies of work are different. Piaget lived a long and productive life, published widely, and had time to modify and perfect his early ideas. His theory is thus whole and complete. Vygotsky, on the other hand, died young and published very little. He is known for only a few major ideas, but those ideas are among the most seminal[4] in all of developmental psychology.

Which word in the topic sentence indicates a comparison/contrast pattern?

a. considered
b. major
c. theorists
d. different

5. Dutch elm disease (actually, the disease came from Asia by way of the Netherlands) occurs in a number of stages. First, tiny beetles burrow into the bark of a tree, carrying the spores[5] of the disease-causing fungus. The fungus spreads through the tree's system of tubes, blocking the dispersal of fluids and nutrients. The fungus eventually plugs the tubes, resulting in, at first, a few yellowed leaves but, eventually, death of the tree.†

Which word or phrase in the topic sentence indicates time order?

a. disease
b. occurs
c. actually
d. a number of stages

1. **webbing:** creating a web or diagram
2. **pique:** provoke
3. **theorists:** people who formulate the-ories (explanations)
4. **seminal:** highly influential
5. **spores:** single-celled bodies capable of growing into new organisms

* Adapted from David Welton and John Mallan, *Children and Their World: Strategies for Teaching Social Studies*, 7th ed. (Boston: Houghton Mifflin Co., 2002), 231.

† Adapted from Bernd Heinrich, *The Trees in My Forest* (New York: Harper Perennial, 1998), 52.

6. For a juicy and delicious roast chicken, follow these simple steps. First, coat the entire chicken before roasting with a fat such as olive oil. Cover the chicken breast with cheesecloth,[1] dipped in olive oil, before roasting and place the chicken, on its back, on a rack in a roasting pan. Preheat the oven to 500 degrees, but turn the oven down to 350 degrees as soon as you put the chicken in. Baste[2] the chicken every 15 or 20 minutes, and roast for no more than 15 minutes per pound.

Which word or phrase in the topic sentence indicates time order?

a. roast
b. chicken
c. these
d. simple steps

7. There are several steps in matching your topic to your audience's interests. First, list your personal interests and make a similar listing of the presumed[3] interests of your classmates. Do this by considering what topics spark class discussions. Study the two lists together, looking for shared interests. Then use those shared interests to generate possible speech topics.*

Which word or phrase in the topic sentence indicates time order?

a. there
b. several steps
c. topic
d. interests

8. What happened to America's banks illustrates the widespread consequences of bank failure. Banks tied to the stock market or foreign investment were badly weakend by the decline in stock prices. When nervous people withdrew money from banks, panic set in. In 1929, 659 banks folded; in 1930, the total was 1,350. The Federal Reserve Board drastically raised interest rates, tightening the money markets just when loosening was needed. In 1931 and 1932, more than 3,600 banks shut their doors.†

Which word in the topic sentence indicates a cause/effect pattern?

a. happened
b. illustrates
c. consequences
d. failure

1. **cheesecloth:** loosely woven cotton cloth
2. **baste:** moisten with liquid or juices
3. **presumed:** believed, thought to be true

* Adapted from Michael and Suzanne Osborn, *Public Speaking*, 5th ed. (Boston: Houghton Mifflin Co., 2000), 129–130.

† Adapted from Mary Beth Norton et al., *A People and a Nation*, Vol. II, 5th ed. (Boston: Houghton Mifflin Co., 1999), 722.

9. "Soft" skills are defined as abilities that are essential to success in any job or career. They are the portable skills that you can take with you even if you change from one career to a completely different one. The soft skills identified by a U.S. government panel in the 1990s include taking responsibility, making effective decisions, setting goals, managing time, prioritizing tasks, and persevering.[1] Other soft skills are giving strong efforts, working well in teams, communicating effectively, and having empathy.[2] Knowing how to learn, exhibiting self-control, and believing in one's own self-worth are soft skills, too.*

Which phrase in the topic sentence indicates a definition pattern of organization?

a. skills   c. abilities
(b.) are defined as   d. job or career

10. The German states were locked in a political stalemate[3] as a result of certain factors. After Austria and Russia had blocked Frederick William's attempt to unify Germany "from above," tension grew between Austria and Prussia as each power sought to block the other within the German Confederation. Stalemate and reaction also prevailed[4] in the domestic politics of the individual German states in the 1850s.†

Which word or words in the topic sentence indicate a cause/effect pattern?

(a.) result, factors   c. locked
b. were   d. stalemate

11. Tree buds can take a number of different forms. Some are clusters of bare miniature leaves (as in hickory and butternut). Others hold only tiny unfurled[5] flowers (as in alder and hazelnut). A third kind includes both tiny new leaves and flowers, encased together in a protective package (as in apple, cherry, and shadbush). Some are sticky, some smooth, but all are packed with nutrients and are eagerly sought out as food by deer, birds, and other wildlife during the lean winter months.‡

1. **persevering:** not giving up   4. **prevailed:** won out; triumphed
2. **empathy:** understanding of others'   5. **unfurled:** not open
   feelings
3. **stalemate:** a situation in which further action is blocked

---

* Adapted from Skip Downing, *On Course*, 4th ed. (Boston: Houghton Mifflin Co., 2005), 15–16.

† Adapted from John McKay et al., *A History of World Societies*, Vol. II, 4th ed. (Boston: Houghton Mifflin, 1998), 833.

‡ Adapted from Bernd Heinrich, "Grand Opening," *Natural History*, February 2002, 26.

Which word or phrase in the topic sentence indicates a series?

a. tree buds   c. a number of different forms
b. can take   d. different

12. All teachers believe in the importance of authentic[1] activities, but their definitions of those activities differ greatly. Is an activity authentic just because it involves building something rather than filling out a classroom worksheet? In that case, the infamous[2] building-an-igloo-out-of-sugar-cubes activity would classify as authentic, and we believe it is not. No, authentic activities are those that incorporate the ordinary practices of a culture. These might include setting up a play store or any of the imaginary play activities that children engage in spontaneously.

Which word in the topic sentence indicates a comparison/contrast pattern?

a. all   c. differ
b. definitions d. greatly

13. Some schools have had success with a particular process of teaching students to drive. Students begin by taking a driver's education course in school. During the course, they begin taking driving lessons with a qualified instructor in the passenger seat. Then, they take the state's written driving test. Once they pass the written test, they receive a six-month learner's permit, which allows them to drive only with an adult licensed driver in the car. After six months, they may take a driving test at a state driving examination center. If they pass the driving test, they receive a full driver's license. But even then, they are not allowed to drive with other teens in the car for six months.

Which word in the topic sentence indicates a time order pattern?

a. particular   c. drive
b. teaching   d. process

14. Modern scientists see many similarities between early modern humans and Neanderthals.[3] Certainly, the bodies of the two are very similar, and Neanderthals had, if anything, the advantage in brain size. Both used fire, made tools, and lived in social groups. Even more significant, the fossil record shows that both buried their dead and cared for the elderly and sick among them.

1. **authentic:** worthy of trust, reliance, or belief
2. **infamous:** having a bad reputation
3. **Neanderthals:** extinct race of early human beings

Which word in the topic sentence indicates a comparison/contrast pattern?

a. scientists   (c.) similarities

b. many   d. between

15. A *prediction* is defined as a decision made beforehand about the outcome of an event. Predictions are based on assumptions. Because you believe that certain things are true, you expect or believe that certain things will happen. If you believe, for example, that you are good at math, then you can predict that you will do well in a math course. If you have a favorite author who has just published a new book, you can predict that you will probably like it. Your prediction is based on the assumption that the new book will be similar to others by this author that you have read and enjoyed.*

Which word in the topic sentence indicates a definition/example pattern?

a. prediction   (c.) defined

b. decision   d. event

16. The Navigation Acts, passed between 1651 and 1673, established three main principles. First, only English or colonial merchants could trade in the American colonies. Second, certain particularly valuable products, such as wool, sugar, and tobacco, could be sold only in the mother country or in other British colonies. Third, all foreign goods to be sold in the colonies had to be shipped by way of English ports. Later, a fourth principle was added: that the colonies could not export items that competed with English goods.†

Which word or phrase in the topic sentence indicates a series?

a. passed   (c.) three main principles

b. between   d. established

17. Although the phrase *oral literature* seems like a contradiction[1] in terms, it actually has a distinct meaning to scholars. Many societies in Africa, the Middle East, and early Europe relied on an oral tradition to transmit their most important works of literature. An oral tradition relies, first and

1. **contradiction:** inconsistency

---

* Adapted from Carol C. Kanar, *The Confident Student*, 5th ed. (Boston: Houghton Mifflin Co., 2004), 63.

† Adapted from Mary Beth Norton et al., *A People and a Nation*, Vol. I, 5th ed. (Boston: Houghton Mifflin Co., 1999), 83.

foremost, on the memory of those who transmit the works to each new generation. This memory is aided by repetition of key words and phrases and by other poetic formulas that make the work pleasing to the ear. When such a work is written down and read, most likely in translation, much of its unique flavor is lost.

Which word in the topic sentence indicates a definition pattern of organization?

a. phrase
b. contradiction
c. terms
d. meaning

18. Katherine Sherwood's career as an artist has proceeded through a number of surprising stages. Fearful of bad reviews, Sherwood did not originally intend to become a painter. However, she created a unique body of work that incorporated found objects into painted canvases. In 1997, a stroke paralyzed Sherwood's right side and made her unable to paint with her right hand. Gradually, Sherwood learned to walk and talk again and finally forced herself to begin painting again with her left hand. In the process, her creativity was freed, and her work became richer, deeper, and more eagerly sought after by collectors.*

Which phrase in the topic sentence indicates time order?

a. Katherine Sherwood's career
b. as an artist
c. has proceeded
d. a number of surprising stages

19. The use of appropriate reinforcers[1] often leads to surprising improvements in children's behavior. A child who does not routinely raise her hand to answer questions will often begin to do so if she knows the result will be a star or happy face sticker. Other appropriate reinforcers include praise (verbal or in writing), sending a note home to parents, and allowing the child to tutor other children or to run errands.

Which phrase in the topic sentence indicates a cause/effect pattern?

a. use of
b. appropriate reinforcers
c. leads to
d. improvements in

1. reinforcers: rewards

* Adapted from Thomas Fields-Meyer and Lyndon Stambler, "A Near Brush," *People* Magazine, December 3, 2001, 111–114.

20. One important difference between physical development of girls and boys is timing. Girls tend to reach puberty[1] around age twelve while the average age of puberty for boys is approximately fourteen. Children of both sexes undergo a growth spurt during the one and two years that precede sexual maturity. The growth spurt of boys is more extreme, resulting in taller adult stature.[2]

Which word in the topic sentence indicates a comparison/contrast pattern?

a. important   c. physical
(b.) difference   d. development

TEST 2

Read each of the following topic sentences and then circle the letter of the clue word or words that suggest a particular pattern of organization. Then circle the letter of the correct pattern indicated by those clue words.

Research shows that there are similarities between babies learning to talk and birds learning to sing.

1. What clue word indicates a pattern?

a. research   (c.) similarities
b. shows   d. learning

2. What pattern is indicated by this topic sentence?

(a.) comparison/contrast   c. cause/effect
b. definition   d. time order

Categorizing is defined as the grouping together of ideas that have common features.*

3. What clue word(s) indicate(s) a pattern?

a. categorizing   c. group together
(b.) is defined as   d. features

1. **puberty:** stage of adolescence in which an individual becomes capable of sexual reproduction

2. **stature:** height

---

* From Paul Burns, Betty Roe, and Elinor Ross, *Teaching Reading in Today's Elementary Schools*, 7th ed. (Boston: Houghton Mifflin Co., 1999), 436.

6

4. What pattern is indicated by this topic sentence?

   a. comparison/contrast   c. series
   b. cause/effect   (d.) definition

The protection of people with severe psychological disorders, when they are accused of crimes, takes two forms.*

5. What clue word(s) indicate(s) a pattern?

   a. the protection   (c.) two forms
   b. with severe   d. when they are accused

6. What pattern is indicated by this topic sentence?

   a. cause/effect   c. time order
   b. definition   (d.) series

Certain illnesses can lead to severe damage to the placenta[1] and embryo[2] if a woman contracts an illness while pregnant.†

7. What clue word(s) indicate(s) a pattern?

   a. certain illnesses   c. if a woman
   b. severe damage   (d.) can lead to

8. What pattern is indicated by this topic sentence?

   a. comparison/contrast   c. time order
   (b.) cause/effect   d. series

There were several developments in the area of cancer research in the 1990s.

9. What clue word(s) indicate(s) a pattern?

   a. there were   c. in the area
   (b.) several developments d. in the 1990s

10. What pattern is indicated by this topic sentence?

    a. comparison/contrast   (c.) time order
    b. definition   d. series

1. **placenta:** lining of the uterus (womb) during pregnancy

2. **embryo:** an organism in its early stages of development

---

* Adapted from Douglas Bernstein/Peggy Nash, *Essentials of Psychology,* 2nd ed. (Boston: Houghton Mifflin Co., 2002), 444.

† Adapted from Douglas Bernstein/Peggy Nash, *Essentials of Psychology,* 2nd ed. (Boston: Houghton Mifflin Co., 2002), 303.

6

TEST 3

In the list following each paragraph, write a check mark on the appropriate blank(s) to indicate the pattern(s) used to organize the supporting details.

1. A search engine is a program that collects and indexes information from webpages, allowing you to search the indexes by topic. Using a search engine, you can generate a list of resources on a topic of your choice, survey the list, and select possible sites to visit. To use a search engine, first choose an engine such as AltaVista or Yahoo! and go to its website. Next, select a few keywords that describe or relate to your topic. Then, type your keywords in the appropriate area on the engine's webpage. Finally, click on Search or Enter.*

   _____ series

   __✔__ time order

   _____ cause/effect

   _____ comparison/contrast

   __✔__ definition

2. Frogs and toads are different in some ways, but they are similar in a few ways, too. Toads have dry, wart-covered skin while frogs have wet, smooth skin. Frogs have tiny teeth, but toads have none. Frogs have longer back legs than toads, so frogs jump while toads hop. However, both are amphibians,[1] and both are similar in appearance. Both have voices and can make sounds. Both must reproduce in a body of water. Usually in the spring or early summer, toads and frogs find water. Then, the males begin broadcasting their mating calls. The females enter the water and lay their eggs, and the males fertilize them. In about ten days, the eggs hatch into tadpoles. Both the young froglets and toadlets share many of the same enemies, including fish, turtles, snakes, and birds.†

   _____ series

   __✔__ time order

1. amphibians: animals capable of living both on land and in water

---

* Adapted from Carol C. Kanar, *The Confident Student*, 5th ed. (Boston: Houghton Mifflin Co., 2004), 210.

† Adapted from Renie Burghardt, "What Is the Difference Between Frogs and Toads?" 2002, http://www.ak.essortment.com/whatisdiffererkwt.htm.

_____ cause/effect

___✔___ comparison/contrast

_____ definition

3. Several factors contributed to the fact that many people in many parts of Europe lived on the edge of disaster in 1300. Growing numbers of people competed for land to farm and for jobs. Also, farm sizes declined throughout Europe as parents tended to divide their land among their children. Rents for farmland increased as landlords found they could play one land-hungry farmer against another. Competition for jobs kept wages low, and when taxes were added to high rents and low wages, many peasants and artisans found it difficult to marry and raise families.*

_____ series

_____ time order

___✔___ cause/effect

_____ comparison/contrast

_____ definition

4. There are many contrasts between middle-and working-class membership in the United States. The middle class often earns income sufficient to permit savings and has both advanced education and marketable skills. Its members have what is called a *conceptual* orientation, using their mental capacities to solve problems, and their jobs often involve the manipulation of symbols rather than objects. Their working life focus is on occupational advancement and competent performance, and their jobs are often quite specialized and responsible. Members of the working class, on the other hand, typically have more serious financial concerns and not enough salary to permit savings. They are more likely to have on-the-job training than a formal education. Their orientation toward life is considered to be *motoric*, in that they manipulate objects rather than symbols.†

_____ series

_____ time order

_____ cause/effect

* Adapted from Thomas Noble et al., *Western Civilization* (Boston: Houghton Mifflin Co., 2002), 370.

† Adapted from Seymour Fishbach et al., *Personality*, 4th ed. (Boston: Houghton Mifflin Co., 1996), 50.

   ✔   comparison/contrast

   ✔   definition

5. How can you as a regular education teacher be effective in teaching children with disabilities in your classroom? There are a number of ways. First, be open to the idea of including students with disabilities in your classroom. Learn about each child's limitations and potential, and about available curriculum[1] methodologies[2] and technologies to help the child learn. Insist that any needed services be provided. Pair students with disabilities with children who can help them. Use a variety of teaching strategies, including hands-on activities, peer tutoring, and cooperative learning strategies. The outcome will be a rich, diverse[3] classroom filled with learning.*

   ✔   series

        time order

   ✔   cause/effect

        comparison/contrast

        definition

1. **curriculum:** related to courses of study

2. **methodologies:** a set of practices, procedures, and rules

3. **diverse:** different

---

* Adapted from Kevin Ryan and James Cooper, *Those Who Can, Teach,* 9th ed. (Boston: Houghton Mifflin Co., 2000), 127.

CHAPTER **7**

Reading Visual Aids

GOALS FOR CHAPTER 7

▶ Define the term *visual aid*.

▶ Summarize the reasons authors incorporate visual aids into texts.

▶ Describe three general steps to follow to interpret a visual aid.

▶ Define the term *table* and identify its purpose and parts.

▶ Define the term *organizational chart* and identify its purpose and parts.

▶ Define the term *flow chart* and identify its purpose and parts.

▶ Define the term *pie chart* and identify its purpose and parts.

▶ Define the term *line graph* and identify its purpose and parts.

▶ Define the term *bar graph* and identify its purpose and parts.

▶ Define the term *diagram* and identify its purpose and parts.

▶ Define the term *map* and identify its purpose and parts.

▶ Write a reading journal entry.

As you read, you will often encounter visual aids such as graphs, tables, and diagrams. Learning how to read and interpret these visuals will improve your overall comprehension of a text. To discover what you already know about visuals, complete the following test.

TEST YOURSELF

A. Look at the following visual from *USA Today* and then answer the questions that follow by writing your responses on the blanks provided.

Favorite Life Saver Flavors

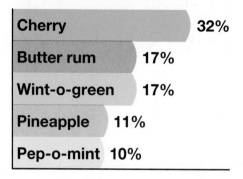

Source: *USA Today,* July 30, 2001, 1D. Copyright © 2001 by *USA Today*. Reprinted with permission.

1. What does this visual describe? <u>Percentages of people who like specific flavors</u>
   <u>of Life Savers</u>

2. What percentage of people enjoy pineapple Life Savers? <u>11%</u>

3. Are butter rum or pep-o-mint Life Savers more popular? How can you tell?
   <u>Butter rum is more popular; 17% of people like butter rum, while 10% like pep-o-mint.</u>

4. What flavor Life Saver is the least favorite among the people surveyed?
   <u>Pep-o-mint</u>

5. What flavor Life Saver is the most popular? <u>Cherry</u>

B. Study the pie chart on the next page entitled "Where We Buy Books" and answer the questions that follow by writing your responses on the blanks provided.

6. How many places where you can buy books are included in the pie chart?
   <u>10</u>

7. What percentage of the book-selling market do book clubs have?
   <u>19%</u>

8. From what year is this market share data based? <u>2002</u>

9. What is the source of this information? <u>American Booksellers Association</u>

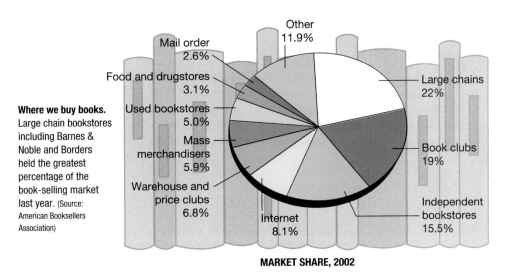

Mail order 2.6%

Other 11.9%

Food and drugstores 3.1%

Large chains 22%

Used bookstores 5.0%

Where we buy books. Large chain bookstores including Barnes & Noble and Borders held the greatest percentage of the book-selling market last year. (Source: American Booksellers Association)

Mass merchandisers 5.9%

Book clubs 19%

Warehouse and price clubs 6.8%

Internet 8.1%

Independent bookstores 15.5%

MARKET SHARE, 2002

Source: *The News Herald* (Morganton, NC), November 23, 2003, 9C. Reprinted by permission of Associated Press.

10. What type of bookseller holds the largest percentage of the business?

   large chains

Visual aids, which are also known as *graphics*, are types of illustrations that represent data or information in a visual form. Visual aids include tables, charts, different types of graphs, diagrams, and maps. You will often encounter all of these kinds of visuals when you read, especially when the purpose of a reading selection is to inform or explain. Publications such as textbooks, magazines, journals, and instruction manuals will often include visuals to aid, or help, the reader in understanding the information. Many job-related documents will also contain visual aids.

   Texts include visual aids for many reasons. For one thing, they can summarize a lot of information or complex information in a relatively small space. Think about a flow chart, for instance. A flow chart provides a visual summary of the steps in a process. It allows you to see a condensed version of even a complicated procedure.

   Another reason for visual aids is their ability to clarify and reinforce textual explanations. In most publications, visual aids do not substitute for written presentation of information. Instead, they provide another way of "seeing" what the words are saying. A diagram in an instruction manual is one example. When you are assembling something like a grill or a child's swing set, it's helpful to check your understanding of the directions by

7

looking at a diagram that labels the parts and shows how they fit together. You use both the written explanation and the visual aid to figure out what you need to do.

Visual aids also allow readers to see quickly the important data or facts. For instance, a graph reveals, at a glance, trends over time. An organizational chart allows readers to quickly grasp the chain of command within a company.

Finally, visual aids provide a way for readers to find a particular detail quickly and easily. A table, for example, that organizes facts into columns and rows allows a reader to easily locate one specific piece of information he or she needs.

General Tips for Reading Visual Aids

The following tips will help you improve your comprehension of reading selections that include visuals:

- **Don't skip a visual aid.** Passive readers ignore visual aids because they don't want to take the time to read them. Skipping visual aids, however, robs you of chances to improve and/or reinforce your understanding of the information in the text. When authors invest the time and effort necessary to create a visual, they do so because they believe a visual representation is particularly important. Therefore, get in the habit of reading over each visual as well as the text.

- **Look at a visual aid when the text directs you to do so.** As you read, you'll come across references to visual aids. Resist the urge to "save them for later." Instead, when a sentence mentions a visual, as in "See Figure 2," or "Table 1 presents the results . . ." and tells you where to find it (below, to the left, on page 163, etc.), find the visual and read it before going any further. Remember, most visuals reinforce information in a text. The writer's explanation will often state the conclusion you should draw from the visual, and the visual provides more insight into the textual explanation. Therefore, you'll get more out of both of them when you read a passage and its corresponding visual together.

- **Follow a three-step procedure for interpreting the information in a visual aid:**

1. First, read the title, the caption, and the source line. The title and caption, or brief description, will usually identify the visual aid's subject and main point. They will help you understand what you're seeing. The source line, which identifies where the information comes from, will help you decide whether the information is accurate and trustworthy.

2. Next, study the information represented in the visual and try to state the relationships you see in your own words. For example, you might say, "This graph shows that sales of sport utility vehicles have been growing since 1985," or "This table shows that teachers in the Midwest earn higher salaries than teachers in the rest of the country."

3. Finally, check your understanding of the relationship against its corresponding explanation in the text. Locate where the visual is mentioned and verify that the conclusion you drew is accurate.

The remainder of this chapter will cover the most common types of visual aids and provide you with more specific tips for improving your understanding of each kind.

Common Types of Visuals

As you read, you'll most often encounter tables, charts, graphs, diagrams, and maps.

Tables

A *table* is a visual aid that organizes information or data in rows and columns. A table might list types, categories, figures, statistics, steps in a process, or other kinds of information. Its purpose is to summarize many related details in a concise format so that readers can read them easily and find specific facts quickly.

Tables contain the following parts:

- **Title.** The title states the visual aid's subject.

- **Column headings.** These labels identify the type of information you'll find in the vertical lists.

- **Row headings.** These labels identify the type of information you'll find in each horizontal list.

- **Source line.** The source line identifies who collected or compiled the information in the table.

These parts are labeled in the table on the next page.*

* Excerpted from Sharon S. Brehm et al., *Social Psychology,* 5th ed. (Boston: Houghton Mifflin Co., 2002), 159.

Title

TABLE 7.1   Gender Differences in Specific Occupations in the United States

Recent labor statistics reveal that men and women occupy very different positions in the U.S. work force.

Column headings

Occupation	% Women	% Men
Architect	16	84
Athlete	28	72
Bartender	48	52
Child-care worker	97	3
Computer systems analyst	29	71
Construction worker	3	97
Cook	44	56
Dental hygienist	99	1
Dentist	16	84
Dietician	84	16
Financial manager	51	49
Firefighter	2	98
Lawyer, judge	29	71
Licensed nurse	95	5
Mechanical engineer	7	93
Medicine and health manager	77	23
Physician	24	76
Physician's assistant	53	47
Police, detective	14	86
Psychologist	65	35
Sales (apparel)	78	22
Sales (motorized vehicles and boats)	11	89
Secretary	98	2
Speech therapist	93	7
Teacher (college)	42	58
Teacher (elementary school)	84	16
Truck driver	5	95
Waitress/waiter	77	23

Row headings

Source line

(Data from U.S. Bureau of Labor Statistics, 2000.)

To understand the information in a table, first read the title, which will identify the kind of information the table includes. Next, familiarize yourself with the column and row headings. They will identify the kind of details included. Then, form an understanding of the relationships first by moving your eyes down each column to see how details compare and then across each row to see how those details are related. Finally, try to state in your own words the overall point revealed by the table's lists.

In the table on page 328, the title states that this visual aid will focus on gender differences in specific occupations in the United States. The occupations are listed in the first column. The second and third columns include corresponding numerical data for each of the two genders (women and men). The headings of the second and third columns indicate with a percent (%) sign that the numbers are percentages. To find information, locate the occupation that interests you and follow the row across to find the corresponding numbers. For example, you can see that architects are 16 percent women and 84 percent men. You also might want to find the occupations that attract the most numbers of men (construction workers, firefighters, and truck drivers) and the occupations that attract the most numbers of women (child-care workers, dental hygienists, licensed nurses, and secretaries).

Exercise 7.1

Study the table* below and then answer the questions that follow by writing your responses on the blanks provided.

Table 7.2   Growth of World Population

Year	Population
1825	1.0 billion
1925	2.0 billion
1976	4.0 billion
1990	5.3 billion
2025 (projected)	8.5 billion

Source: Paul Kennedy, *Preparing for the Twenty-first Century* (New York: Random House, 1993), 22–23.

7

1. How many years are listed in the table for comparison? <u>5</u>

2. In what year did the world's population reach 2 billion? <u>1925</u>

3. What is the projected world population for the year 2025? <u>8.5 billion</u>

4. In what year was the world's population at 1 billion? <u>1825</u>

5. What was the world's population in 1990? <u>5.3 billion</u>

* From Richard Bulliet et al., *The Earth and Its Peoples,* Brief Edition. (Boston: Houghton Mifflin Co., 2000), 596.

Charts

There are different types of charts. Three of the more common are organizational charts, flow charts, and pie charts. Each kind presents a different kind of relationship.

An **organizational chart** is one that shows the chain of command in a company or organization. It uses rectangles and lines to show the managerial relationships among the individuals within a group. Its purpose is to represent the lines of authority and responsibility in the organization.

An organizational chart contains the following parts:

- **Title.** The title usually identifies the organization or the part of an organization being described.

- **Boxes.** Each box, or rectangle, represents one entity within the organization. That entity might be an individual or a group of individuals, such as a department. Each box will be labeled with a name, a job title, or a department name. These boxes are arranged in a hierarchy, or ranking: the person or group with the most authority and responsibility is at the top of the chart. Each subsequent row of boxes represents the next layer of authority, a group of people or groups who are equal in rank and who all report to the individual(s) in the layer above.

- **Lines.** The lines connect boxes to show managerial relationships. They indicate who reports to whom. The source line, if applicable, identifies who collected or compiled the information in the chart.

These parts are labeled in the following organizational chart:

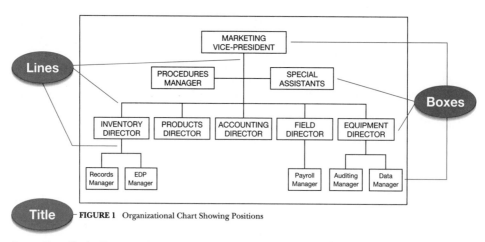

FIGURE 1 Organizational Chart Showing Positions

Source: From Charles Brusaw et al., *The Business Writer's Handbook*, 5th ed. (New York: St. Martin's Press, 1997), 422. Copyright © 1997 by Bedford/St. Martin's. Reprinted with permission of Bedford/St. Martin's.

To understand an organizational chart, begin at the top. Read the label in the box at the top and then follow the lines to see which individuals and groups are related to each other.

The portion of the organizational chart on page 330 shows a company structure that places the marketing vice-president at the top of the hierarchy. That individual has the most authority and responsibility. The staff positions listed beneath the vice-president advise him and report to him, but they do not supervise the different directors who make up the next layer of authority. Those directors report to the vice-president. The branching lines that descend from each box in the chart indicate the number and titles of individuals who are managed by that person.

Exercise 7.2

Study the organizational chart and then answer the questions that follow by writing your responses on the blanks provided.

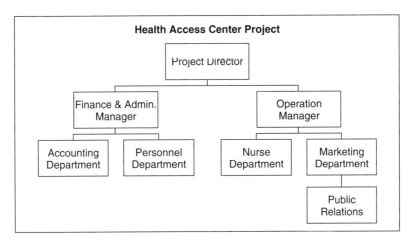

Source: William Murdick, *The Portable Business Writer.* (Boston: Houghton Mifflin Co., 1999), 129. Copyright © 1999 by Houghton Mifflin Company. Reprinted with permission.

1. What is the title of the person in charge of the Health Access Center Project? _Project Director_

2. List the two departments that report to the Finance and Administration Manager. _Accounting and Personnel_

3. List the two departments that report to the Operation Manager. _Nurse and Marketing_

4. To what department does the Public Relations department report?

Marketing

5. Who reports directly to the Project Director? Finance and Administration

Manager and Operation Manager

A **flow chart** is a visual aid composed of boxes, circles, or other shapes along with lines or arrows. The purpose of a flow chart is to represent the sequence of steps or stages in a process.

The parts of a flow chart are:

• **Title.** The title identifies the process or procedure summarized in the chart.

• **Boxes or other shapes.** Each box contains one step in the process. The boxes are arranged either top to bottom or left to right.

• **Lines or arrows.** Lines or arrows show the sequence of steps.

• **Source line.** The source line, if applicable, identifies who collected or compiled the information in the chart.

These parts are labeled in the following flow chart:

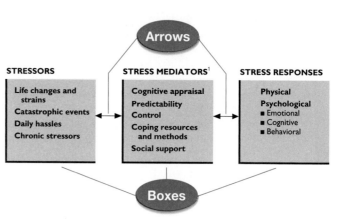

Source: Douglas Bernstein et al., *Psychology,* 6th ed. (Boston: Houghton Mifflin Co., 2003), 488.

1. **mediators:** intermediate (middle) agents

To interpret a flow chart, first read the chart's title so you'll know what process is being summarized. Next, begin with the box at the top, if the chart is organized vertically, or the box at the far left, if the chart is organized horizontally. Read each step in order, following the lines and arrows to understand their sequence.

As the title indicates, the simple flow chart on page 332 summarizes the process of stress. The process begins with stressors, which are listed in the box at the far left. The arrow indicates that the next step is the addition of stress mediators, or factors that lower the stress response. The third step lists the types of reactions that can occur as the result of the stressors and/or mediators. As the caption explains and the arrows in the chart indicate, the process moves backward as well as forward. In other words, certain reactions can improve or strengthen the mediators, which, in turn, actually lessen the stressors.

Exercise 7.3

Study the flow chart below and then write your answers to the questions that follow by writing your responses on the blanks provided.

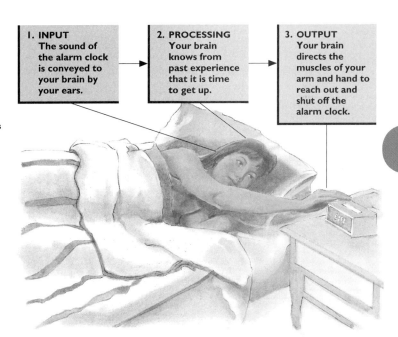

Three Functions of the Nervous System

The nervous system's three main functions are to receive information (input), integrate that information with past experiences (processing), and guide actions (output). **When the alarm clock goes off, this person's nervous system, like yours, gets the message, recognizes what it means, decides what to do, and then takes action, by getting out of bed or perhaps hitting the snooze button.**

1. INPUT The sound of the alarm clock is conveyed to your brain by your ears.

2. PROCESSING Your brain knows from past experience that it is time to get up.

3. OUTPUT Your brain directs the muscles of your arm and hand to reach out and shut off the alarm clock.

Source: Douglas Bernstein et al., *Psychology*, 6th ed. (Boston: Houghton Mifflin Co., 2003), 56.

1. What are the three major functions of the nervous system? <u>Input, processing, output</u>

2. What example is used to illustrate the three functions of the nervous system on the flow chart? <u>Someone responding to an alarm clock</u>

3. As illustrated on the flow chart, what happens during the "input" stage? <u>The sound of the alarm clock is conveyed to your brain by your ears.</u>

4. According to the chart, what happens during step 2, or during the "processing" part illustrated on the flow chart? <u>Your brain knows from past experience that it is time to get up.</u>

5. During what stage illustrated on the flow chart does your "brain direct the muscles of your arm and hand to reach out and shut off the alarm clock"? <u>Output</u>

A third kind of chart is called a **pie chart.** This visual aid is a circle that is divided into wedges or slices, like the pieces of a pie. The purpose of a pie chart is to show the composition of something; it indicates the amounts of each part that make up the whole. Each part is identified with a percentage or other quantity that indicates its size in relation to all of the other parts. One common use of pie charts is to represent financial information such as budgets or expenditures.

Pie charts contain the following parts:

- **Title.** The title identifies the whole entity that is being divided into parts.

- **Lines.** The lines radiate from the center of the circle, dividing the pie in pieces that represent the amount of each part. These pieces are different sizes because they are designed to be proportional to the whole.

- **Labels for names of parts.** Each piece is labeled to identify one part and its quantity in relation to the whole.

- **Source line.** The source line identifies who collected or compiled the information.

These parts are labeled in the following pie chart:*

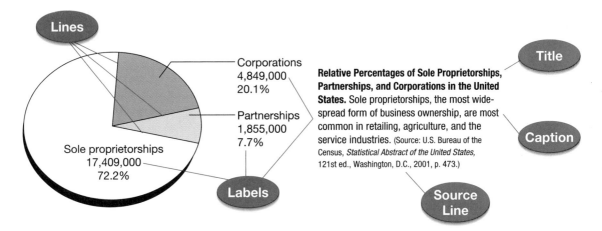

To read a pie chart, first look at its title so you'll know the whole entity that is being divided. Then, read each label and amount. Try to summarize in your own words the relationships you see and notice the biggest part, the smallest part, and parts that are about equal.

The pie chart above shows the numbers and percentages of three forms of business ownership. The largest piece of the pie represents sole proprietorships, which account for about 72 percent of all businesses. Corporations are the next biggest group, and partnerships are the smallest. The percentages all add up to 100 percent to represent the whole. The caption provides more information by naming some examples of specific sole proprietorship businesses.

Exercise 7.4

Study the pie chart on page 336 and then write your answers to the following questions by writing your responses on the blanks provided.

1. What percentage of people spend between 16 and 30 minutes with their doctor during an office visit? _32.7%_____

2. What percentage of people spend the least amount of time with their doctor during an office visit? _3.6%_____

3. What percentage of people spend the most amount of time with their doctor during an office visit? _8.4%_____

* From William Pride et al., *Business,* 8th ed. (Boston: Houghton Mifflin Co., 2005), 137.

4. What percentage of people spend between 6 and 10 minutes with their doctor during an office visit? _21.8%_____

5. According to the caption that accompanies the pie chart, how many office visits did Americans have with a physician in 1999? _724 million visits_

 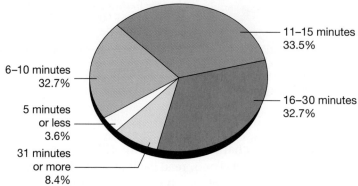

Time we spend with the doctor. Americans had 724 million office visits with a physician in 1999. A breakdown of how much time actually was spent with the doctor during those visits:

6–10 minutes
32.7%

5 minutes
or less
3.6%

31 minutes
or more
8.4%

11–15 minutes
33.5%

16–30 minutes
32.7%

Source: *USA Today*, July 24, 2001, 1A. Copyright © 2001, *USA Today*. Reprinted with permission.

Graphs

A **graph** is a visual aid composed of lines or bars that correspond to numbers or facts arranged along a vertical axis, or side, and a horizontal axis. The purpose of a graph is to show changes or differences in amounts, quantities, or characteristics. Two types of graphs are the line graph and the bar graph. Each one presents information differently.

A **line graph** is composed of points plotted within a vertical axis and a horizontal axis and then connected with lines. Line graphs typically reveal changes or trends in numerical data over time. They demonstrate how two factors interact with each other. The horizontal axis is labeled with increments of time, such as years or minutes. The vertical axis is labeled with quantities. For each point in time, a dot on the graph indicates the corresponding quantity. Then, these dots are all connected to show upward and downward movement.

Line graphs contain the following parts:

- **Title.** The title points out the type of numbers being examined. It corresponds to the label of the vertical axis.

7

- **Vertical axis.** This line, which runs up and down, is divided into regular increments of numbers that correspond to the type of data being tracked. This axis is labeled to identify the type of data.

- **Horizontal axis.** This line, which runs from left to right, is divided into segments of time. It, too, is labeled to identify the kind of time factor being used.

- **Points.** Numerical data are plotted at the points where numbers and time factors intersect on the grid. These points may be labeled with specific amounts.

- **Lines.** Points are connected with lines to show trends.

- **Source line.** The source line identifies who collected or compiled the information in the graph.

These parts are labeled on the following line graph:*

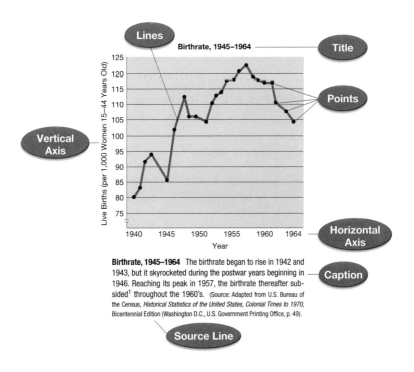

Birthrate, 1945–1964   The birthrate began to rise in 1942 and 1943, but it skyrocketed during the postwar years beginning in 1946. Reaching its peak in 1957, the birthrate thereafter subsided[1] throughout the 1960's. (Source: Adapted from U.S. Bureau of the Census, *Historical Statistics of the United States, Colonial Times to 1970,* Bicentennial Edition (Washington D.C., U.S. Government Printing Office, p. 49).

1. subsided: sank or fell to a normal level

* From Mary Beth Norton et al., *A People and a Nation,* 7th ed., Vol. II. (Boston: Houghton Mifflin Co., 2005), 801.

To read a line graph, begin with the title. Read it carefully to understand the numerical value on which the graph focuses. Then, read the labels on the vertical and horizontal axes to understand what two factors are interacting. Finally, examine the line that connects the points and try to state in your own words the trends being revealed by the numbers. Do the numbers increase, decrease, or both? When? How much overall change has occurred during the time span indicated on the horizontal axis?

As the title indicates, the line graph on page 337 illustrates the birthrate in America between 1945 and 1964. The vertical axis is divided into numbers of live births. The horizontal axis is divided into years. The points plotted on this grid are connected, which clearly reveals, among other things, that the birthrate climbed steadily between 1950 and 1957, the year it reached its peak, and then began a steady decline.

Exercise 7.5

Study the line graph below and then answer the questions that follow by writing your responses on the blanks provided.

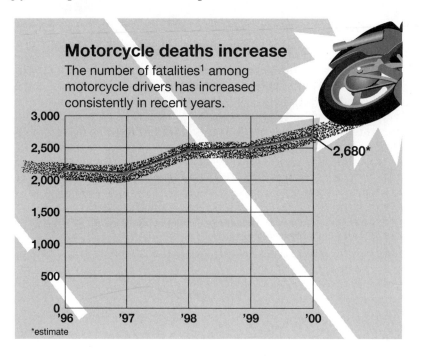

Motorcycle deaths increase

The number of fatalities[1] among motorcycle drivers has increased consistently in recent years.

*estimate

Source: *USA Today,* July 30, 2001, 1A. Copyright © 2001 by *USA Today.* Reprinted with permission.

1. fatalities: deaths

1. In 1997, did motorcycle deaths increase or decrease? _decrease_

2. In 1998, did motorcycle deaths increase or decrease? _increase_

3. How many people died as a result of a motorcycle accident in the year 2000? _2,680_

4. In what year were the number of motorcycle deaths the highest? _2000_

5. In what year were the number of motorcycle deaths the lowest? _1997_

A second kind of graph is a **bar graph.** Bar graphs indicate quantities of something with bars, or rectangles. These bars can run upward from the horizontal axis or sideways from the vertical axis of the graph. Each bar is labeled to show what is being measured. While the line graph includes a time factor, the bar graph may not; it focuses on varying quantities of some factor or factors, although it may include several sets of bars that correspond to different time periods.

A bar graph includes the following parts:

- **Title.** The title reveals the entity that's being measured. Depending on how the graph is arranged, this subject may correspond to either the vertical or the horizontal axis.

- **Vertical axis.** This line, which runs up and down, is labeled with either a kind of quantity or the entities being measured.

- **Horizontal axis.** This line, which runs from left to right, is labeled to identify either a kind of quantity or the entities being measured.

- **Bars.** Each bar rises to the line on the grid that matches the quantity it represents. Each bar may be labeled with a specific number.

- **Key.** If entities are broken down into subgroups, the graph may include bars of different colors to represent each group. In that case, a key, or explanation of what each color signifies, may accompany the graph.

- **Source line.** The source line identifies who collected or compiled the information in the bar graph.

These parts are labeled on the bar graph on page 340.

To interpret the information in a bar graph, read the title first to find out what is being measured. Next, read the labels of the vertical and horizontal axes to understand how the graph is arranged and what type of quantity is being used. Finally, examine each bar and try to state, in your own words, the

7

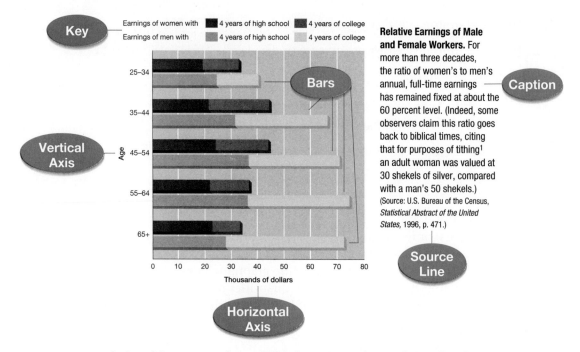

relationship among them. Which entity is largest? Smallest? Are there large discrepancies between two or more of the entities?

The bar graph* above shows how much money men and women with different levels of education earn at different ages. Among the notable relationships indicated by the bars are the following:

• College-educated men and women always earn more than high school graduates.

• At any age or education level, men always earn more than women earn.

• Men between the ages of 55 and 64 with only a high school education earn almost as much as women of the same age who have a college education.

• Men earn their highest salaries—up to $75,000—when they are between 55 and 64 years of age.

• Women earn their highest salaries—up to $45,000—when they are between 35 and 44, although the 45–54-year-old age group is a close second.

Notice how the four different shades are identified in a key at the top to help you understand all of the different groups represented in this one graph.

1. **tithing:** contributing a percentage of one's income

* From William Pride et al., *Business,* 6th ed. (Boston: Houghton Mifflin Co., 1999), 45.

Exercise 7.6

Study the bar graph below and then answer the questions that follow by writing your responses on the blanks provided.

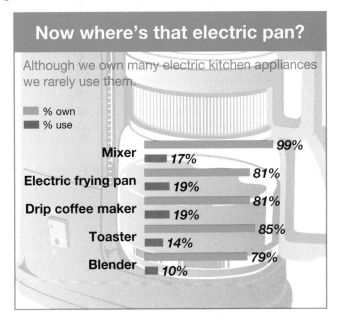

Now where's that electric pan?

Although we own many electric kitchen appliances we rarely use them.

- % own
- % use

	% own	% use
Mixer	99%	17%
Electric frying pan	81%	19%
Drip coffee maker	81%	19%
Toaster	85%	14%
Blender	79%	10%

Source: *USA Today*, July 24, 2001, 1D. Copyright © 2001, *USA Today*.
Reprinted with permission.

1. What percentage of Americans own an electric frying pan? _81%_____

2. What percentage of Americans use a toaster? _14%_____

3. Of all of the appliances listed, which one is owned by the largest percentage of Americans? _Mixer_____

4. Of all the appliances listed, which two appliances are used by the largest percentage of Americans? _Electric frying pan and drip coffee maker__

5. How many Americans actually use their blenders? _10%_____

Diagrams

A **diagram** is a visual aid that includes a pictorial illustration, usually in the form of a drawing created by hand or by computer. The purpose of diagrams

7

is to clarify and condense written information through images, so they are very common in instruction manuals and textbooks. They often illustrate processes or sequences of information.

A diagram typically contains these parts:

- **Title.** The title identifies the subject of the drawing.

- **A picture or series of pictures.** Diagrams communicate information through images.

- **Labels.** Parts or areas of the images will often be labeled to identify what they are.

- **Key.** A diagram that contains special symbols, colors, or shading will usually include a key to explain what these features represent.

These parts are labeled on the following diagram:

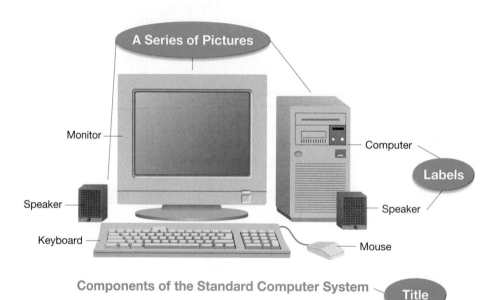

Source: From William Murdick and Jonathan C. Bloemker, *The Portable Technical Writer* (Boston: Houghton Mifflin Co., 2001), 170.

Reading a diagram begins with understanding the subject and main point identified in the title. Then, you can examine the labeled parts of the diagram to understand how they illustrate that point. Also, make sure you review the key, if applicable, to help you draw accurate conclusions.

The diagram illustrates the components of a standard computer. It includes line drawings of the various parts along with labels to identify each part.

Exercise 7.7

Study the diagram below and then write your answers to the questions that follow by writing your responses on the blanks provided.

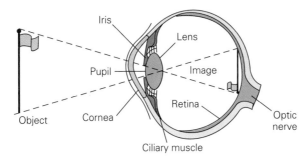

The Human Eye

The lens of the human eye forms an image on the retina, which contains rod and cone cells. The rods are more sensitive than the cones and are responsible for light and dark "twilight" vision; the cones are responsible for color vision.

Source: James Shipman et al., *An Introduction to Physical Science*, 10th ed. (Boston: Houghton Mifflin Co., 2003), 160. Copyright © 2003 by Houghton Mifflin Company. Reprinted with permission.

1. What is the topic of this diagram? <u>The human eye</u>

2. What is the object that the eye sees in this diagram? <u>A flag pole with a</u>
   <u>waving flag on top</u>

3. According to the text accompanying the diagram, which are more sensitive, rods or cones? <u>Rods</u>

4. Which parts of the eye are responsible for color vision? <u>Cones</u>

5. What part of the eye, according to the graph, is at the back of the eye?
   <u>Optic nerve</u>

Maps

A **map** is a visual depiction of an area and its physical characteristics. Maps illustrate spatial relationships; for example, they show sizes and borders and distances from one place to another. They can also be used to make comparisons. For instance, a map of the United States may color in the states that apply the death penalty in red and color those that don't blue.

Here are the parts of a map:

- **Title.** The title identifies either the area itself or the relationships among different areas.

- **A diagram of the area.** A map includes a proportionate drawing that represents the geographical features and spatial relationships.

- **Key.** Many maps incorporate symbols, so the key explains what these symbols mean.

- **Labels.** Maps will usually label parts or features that help the reader understand the overall point stated in the title.

- **Source line.** The source line identifies who collected or compiled the information shown in the map.

The map below labels all of these parts:

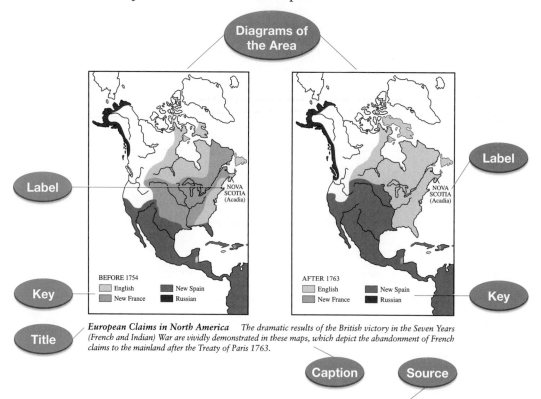

European Claims in North America   *The dramatic results of the British victory in the Seven Years (French and Indian) War are vividly demonstrated in these maps, which depict the abandonment of French claims to the mainland after the Treaty of Paris 1763.*

Source: Mary Beth Norton et al., *A People and a Nation,* 7th ed., Vol. I. (Boston: Houghton Mifflin Co., 2005), 122.

To interpret a map, read the title first to understand the idea or information on which you should focus. Then, familiarize yourself with symbols in the key (including the scale that indicates distance, if applicable) and read the labels that name different areas. If the map is illustrating some comparison, try to state in your own words a conclusion based on that comparison.

The visual aid on page 344 is composed of two maps that illustrate several different sets of relationships. In the first map, as the key indicates, the English claims in North America before 1754 were roughly equal to those of the French and Spanish. Notice how the continent is shaded with different shadings that correspond to the four different nations. These shadings show the relationship of the areas to each other. The second map, which represents these same countries' claims after 1763, reveals a much different distribution. France (represented by a light shading) has been virtually eliminated, and the English and Spanish have overtaken France's former areas. Taken together, the two different maps show the significant changes that occurred in less than ten years in North America.

Exercise 7.8

Study the map on page 346 and then write your answers to the questions that follow by writing your responses on the blanks provided.

1. Name three cities that qualify as Federal Reserve branch cities. Seattle, Portland, Los Angeles, Salt Lake City, Helena, Denver, El Paso, San Antonio, Houston, Omaha, Little Rock, Oklahoma City, New Orleans, Miami, Jacksonville, Birmingham, Memphis, Nashville, Louisville, Pittsburgh, Baltimore, Buffalo, Charlotte, Cincinnati, Detroit (Answers will vary.)

2. Name three cities that qualify as Federal Reserve Bank cities. Kansas City, Dallas, San Francisco, Minneapolis, Chicago, Richmond, Philadelphia, New York, Boston, St. Louis, Atlanta, Cleveland (Answers will vary.)

3. What city is home to the Board of Governors of the Federal Reserve System? Washington, DC

4. How would you classify Boston: as a Federal Reserve Bank city or a Federal Reserve branch city? Federal Reserve Bank city

5. How would you classify El Paso: as a Federal Reserve Bank city or a Federal Reserve branch city? Federal Reserve branch city

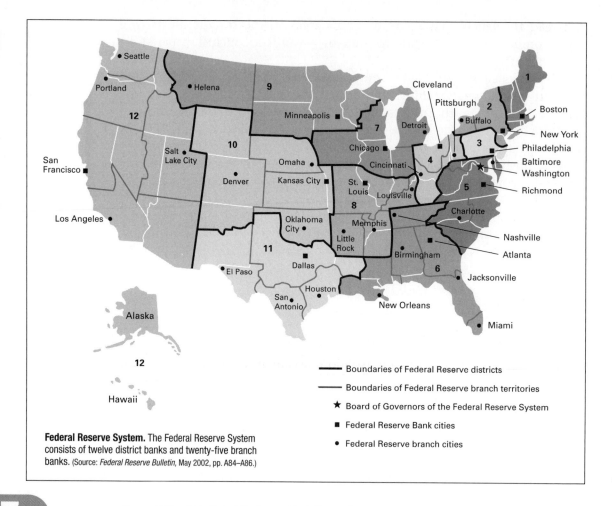

Federal Reserve System. The Federal Reserve System consists of twelve district banks and twenty-five branch banks. (Source: *Federal Reserve Bulletin*, May 2002, pp. A84–A86.)

— Boundaries of Federal Reserve districts

— Boundaries of Federal Reserve branch territories

★ Board of Governors of the Federal Reserve System

■ Federal Reserve Bank cities

• Federal Reserve branch cities

Source: William Pride, Robert Hughes, and Jack Kapoor, *Business*, 8th ed. (Boston: Houghton Mifflin Co., 2003), 574.

7

CHAPTER 7 REVIEW

Write the correct answer in each of the blanks in the following statements.

1. ___Visual aids___ are types of illustrations that represent data or information in a visual form.

2. Visual aids ___summarize___ information in a small space, clarify and reinforce ___textual explanations___, allow readers to see important ___relationships___ easily, and provide a way for readers to find a particular ___detail___ quickly.

3. To interpret the information in a visual aid, first read the ___title___, caption, and ___source line___. Next, try to state in your own words the relationships you see. Finally, check your understanding of those relationships by reviewing the corresponding explanation in the ___text___.

4. A ___table___ is a visual aid that organizes information or data in rows and columns. It summarizes related details so readers can find them quickly and easily.

5. An ___organizational chart___ is a hierarchy of boxes and lines that are connected to show lines of authority and responsibility in an organization.

6. A ___flow chart___ represents the sequence of steps in a process.

7. A ___pie chart___ is a circle divided into wedges that indicate the amounts of each part that make up a whole.

8. A ___line graph___ plots points on a grid and then connects them to show changes or trends in numerical data over time.

9. A ___bar graph___ identifies quantities of something.

10. A ___diagram___ is a pictorial illustration, usually in the form of a drawing created by hand or by computer.

11. A ___map___ is a visual depiction of an area and its physical characteristics. It illustrates spatial relationships and/or makes comparisons.

Reading Selection

Practicing the Active Reading Strategy:
Before and As You Read

You can use active reading strategies before, as, and after you read a selection. The following are some suggestions for active reading strategies that you can employ before you read and as you are reading.

1. Skim the selection for any unfamiliar words. Circle or highlight any words you do not know.

2. As you read, underline, highlight, or circle important words or phrases.

3. Write down any questions about the selection if you are confused by the information presented.

4. Jot notes in the margin to help you understand the material.

The Path to Cloud 9
by Bob Holmes

1 It is the subject of countless writings and self-help books. In the United States, the quest for it is stated right in the Declaration of Independence. Now, investigating happiness has become an academic discipline. You can find "professors of happiness" at leading universities. Happiness even has its own journal, the *Journal of Happiness Studies.* Here are science's latest findings.

1. Stop Comparing Your Looks With [Those of] Others . . .

2 First the bad news. Good-looking people really are happier. Ed Diener, a psychologist at the University of Illinois at Urbana–Champaign, got people to rate their own looks, both with and without makeup. He found a "small but positive effect of physical attractiveness on well-being."

3 The good news is that you can cash in on beauty's emotional high, even if you are no oil painting. The secret is to believe you look great. Unfortunately, this is harder than it sounds. Only one in twenty people accurately judge their own attractiveness. Most have a distorted self-image that tends toward hating rather than loving, according to Alan Feingold at Yale University. Women tend to think they are too fat. Men worry about being small and weak.

2. Desire Less . . .

4 According to wise men throughout the years, decreasing your desires is a surer route to happiness than a fat bank balance. And they may be right.

5 In the 1980s, political scientist Alex Michalos, now at the University of Northern British Columbia in Prince George, asked 18,000 college students in thirty-nine countries to rate their happiness on a numbered scale. Then he asked them how close they were to having all they wanted in life.

6 He found that the people who are less happy are those with desires (not just for money, but for friends, family, job, health, money, the works) that far exceeded what they already had. The size of the gap predicted happiness about five times as well as income alone.

7 This "aspiration gap" might explain why most people fail to get much happier as their salaries rise. Instead of satisfying our desires, most of us merely want more.

3. Earn More Money (Up to a Point) . . .

8 Can money buy happiness? The short answer is "yes." But it doesn't buy you very much. And once you can afford to feed, clothe, and house yourself, each extra dollar makes less and less difference.

9 Whenever and wherever they look, researchers find that, on average, wealthier people are happier. "There are rich people who are miserable. There are poor people who are happy all the time. But if you're an unhappy rich person, you're going to be happier than if you were poor," says Robert Frank, an economist at Cornell University in Ithaca, New York.

4. Don't Worry If You Aren't a Genius . . .

10 Few surveys have examined whether smart people are happier. But they have usually found that intelligence has no effect. At first glance, that seems surprising because brighter

people tend to earn more money, and richer people tend to be happier. Still, "I think if you were entering the world today with a choice 15 between being born smart and not smart, it wouldn't be a hard choice," says Frank.

5. Make the Most of Your Genes . . .

11 Are some people born happy or unhappy? Personality and happiness do seem to be linked. Many studies have shown that outgoing people tend to be happier than most 16 people and a lot happier than people who are not outgoing. This could be because outgoing people are more likely to do the things 17 that bring happiness. For example, they have friends, climb the job ladder, join a hang-gliding club, and get married. Or it could just mean that being happy makes you outgoing.

12 But being outgoing doesn't always bring happiness. It depends on your environment, 18 too. Gerhard Kette at Johannes Kepler University in Linz, Austria, found that in prison, people who are not outgoing are happier than outgoing people are. They are more used to being distant from others.

6. Get Married . . .

13 In an analysis of reports from forty-two countries, a team in the United States found that married people are consistently happier than singles. The effect is small, accounting for between about 1 percent and 2 percent in the difference in well-being.

14 But that still begs the question. Does marriage make you happy, or are happy peo- 20 ple simply more likely to get married? Both may be true. In a study that followed more than 30,000 Germans for fifteen years, Diener found that happy people are more likely to get married and stay married. And 21 it seems there's something special about signing that piece of paper. The research

shows that you can't get as much benefit from simply living with someone.

"My hunch is that couples [who live together] lack the deeper security that comes with the formal band of gold, and that is why they are not quite so happy," says Oswald. "Insecurity, we know from all data, is bad for human beings."

7. Find God (or a Belief System) . . .

16 Of the dozens of studies that have looked at religion and happiness, the vast majority have found a positive link.

17 Harold Koenig at Duke University Medical Center in Durham, North Carolina, found 100 papers on the subject. Seventy-nine of them showed that people who get involved in a religion are happier or more satisfied with their lives than others.

18 But why? Believing in God or an afterlife can give people meaning and purpose. Also, says Koenig, it reduces the feeling of being alone in the world, especially as people get older. "You really see the effect in times of stress. Religious belief can be a very powerful way of coping with [hard times]."

19 And it seems you're better off sticking to some belief system than none at all. Gary Reker at Trent University in Peterborough, Ontario, says this is most apparent when it comes to fear of death. Those who are deeply religious and those who are deeply nonreligious have described themselves as less fearful of death than others, he says.

20 "The most fearful are those who are uncertain, or uncommitted, to any specific belief system."

8. Do Someone a Good Turn . . .

21 Several studies have found a link between happiness and altruistic behavior. But it is not always clear whether doing good makes

you feel good, or whether happy people are more likely to help others.

22   Again, both could be true. In a study of 3,617 people who were interviewed once and then three years later, Peggy Thoits and Lyndi Hewitt of Vanderbilt University in Nashville found that happy people were more likely to sign up for volunteer work. But they also found that the more volunteer work they did, the happier they got.

9. Grow Old Gracefully . . .

23 Elderly people are on average just as happy as the young. They actually rate themselves more satisfied with their lives overall. In one study, old people reported positive emotions as often as young people did. But older people reported negative emotions much less frequently.

24   Why are old people so happy? Some researchers suggest they may expect life to be harder and learn to live with it. Or they're more realistic about their goals, setting only ones that they know they can achieve. Or perhaps older people have learned to regulate their own emotions. They focus on things that make them happy and let go of those that don't.

25   "People realize not only what they have but also that what they have cannot last forever," says Laura Carstensen, a psychology professor at Stanford University in California. "A goodbye kiss to a spouse at the age of eighty-five, for example, may elicit far more complex emotional responses than a similar kiss to a spouse at the age of twenty."*

Table 7.3 Happiness and Life Satisfaction: Averages for Different Periods

The proportions of people giving different happiness answers in the United States 1972–1998

	1972–1976	1977–1982	1983–1987	1988–1993	1994–1998
All–not too happy	14%	12%	12%	10%	12%
All–pretty happy	52	54	56	58	58
All–very happy	34	34	32	33	30
Male–not too happy	14	12	13	9	11
Male–pretty happy	54	56	57	58	58
Male–very happy	32	32	30	34	31
Female–not too happy	13	12	12	11	13
Female–pretty happy	51	53	56	57	59
Female–very happy	36	35	33	32	29

Source: David C. Blanchflower and Andrew J. Oswald, "Well-Being Over Time in Britain and the USA," June 2002, www2.warwick.ac.uk/fac/soc/economics/staff/faculty/oswald/finaljpubecwellbeingjune2002.pdf.

* "Reasons to be Cheerful" by Bob Holmes from *New Scientist*, October 4, 2003. Reprinted by permission.

VOCABULARY

Read the following questions about some of the vocabulary words that appear in the previous selection. Then circle the letter of each correct answer.

1. An academic *discipline* (paragraph 1) is
   - (a) an area of study.
   - b. a classroom.
   - c. a section in the library.
   - d. a type of professor.

2. What is an *aspiration*? (paragraph 7)
   - a. an improvement
   - (b) a goal
   - c. a daydream
   - d. a nightmare

3. If you are *altruistic* (paragraph 21), you are
   - (a) unselfish.
   - b. stupid.
   - c. ill.
   - d. depressed.

4. "A goodbye kiss to a spouse at the age of 85, for example, may *elicit* far more complex emotional responses than a similar kiss to a spouse at the age of 20." (paragraph 25) What does *elicit* mean?
   - a. reduce
   - b. increase
   - (c) bring forth
   - d delay

TOPICS, TRANSITIONS, AND VISUAL AIDS

Respond to the following questions by circling the letter of the correct answer.

1. What is the topic of paragraph 11?
   - a. happiness
   - b. genetic research
   - (c) personality's effect on happiness
   - d. extroverted people

2. Which of the following paragraphs begins with a time order transition?
   - (a) paragraph 5
   - b. paragraph 10
   - c. paragraph 14
   - d. paragraph 19

3. Study Table 7.3 on page 350. Between the years 1977 and 1982, what percentage of people were pretty happy?
   - a. 52 percent
   - (b) 54 percent
   - c. 34 percent
   - d. 12 percent

4. Most recently, according to the table, what percentage of people were very happy?
   - (a) 30 percent
   - b. 50 percent
   - c. 60 percent
   - d. The table doesn't say.

7

5. Between 1994 and 1998, what percentage of men reported that they were pretty happy?

a. 11 percent   c. 31 percent
b. 58 percent   d. 13 percent

Practicing the Active Reading Strategy:
After You Read

Now that you have read the selection, answer the following questions, using the active reading strategies that you learned in Chapter 1.

1. Identify and write down the point and purpose of this reading selection.

2. Besides the vocabulary words included in the exercise on page 351, are there any other vocabulary words that are unfamiliar to you? If so, write a list of them. When you have finished writing your list, look up each word in a dictionary and write the definition that best describes the word as it is used in the selection.

3. Predict any possible test questions that may be used on a test about the content of this selection.

4. How could you use the information contained in this selection? Does the information contained in the selection reinforce or contradict your ideas and experiences? Explain.

QUESTIONS FOR DISCUSSION AND WRITING

Answer the following questions based on your reading of the selection.

1. Can money buy happiness? Discuss your opinion of this question or write a response to it. Answers will vary.

2. Do you think that volunteering will bring happiness to the volunteer? Why or why not? Write your answer on the lines provided.
Answers will vary.

3. Who are the happiest people and why? What are the components of their lives? Write your answer on the lines provided. Answers will vary.

◗ Vocabulary: The Contrast Context Clue

In Chapters 4, 5, and 6, you learned about the three different types of context clues: definition/restatement, explanation, and example. One last type of context clue is **contrast**. In this type of clue, nearby words, phrases, or sentences may give the *opposite* meaning of the unfamiliar word, allowing you to conclude what it means by noticing this contrast. For example, read this next passage, which comes from one of the paragraphs in Chapter 4.

> When Sir Edmund Hillary and Tenzing Norgay planted the first flag atop Mount Everest on May 29, 1953, they surveyed an utterly *pristine* place. Nearly fifty years later, dozens of teams line up to take their crack at the sacred Nepalese monolith. Scores of guides jockey to get high-paying clients to the top. Trash on the roof of the world has become so bad that climbers mount expeditions specifically to clean up after past expeditions.

If you're wondering what *pristine* means, you can look at the next three sentences, which include a contrast clue. The word is contrasted with "dozens of teams," "scores of guides," and "trash." Therefore, it must mean the opposite: "pure and unspoiled by civilization."

Vocabulary Exercise

The following examples all come from paragraphs in Chapters 2, 3, and 4. In each one, use the explanation context clue to help you determine the meaning of the boldfaced, italicized word and then write a definition for this word on the blank provided.

1. People used to stop their lives to pay close attention when astronauts went into space, but now, the Space Shuttle goes up and comes back with little ***fanfare.*** Showy reception; hubbub

2. Different people have different types of living styles. You can look right on our block for perfect illustrations of this. For example, the Hammonds' house down the block is a ***ramshackle*** affair. . . . By contrast, just next door, the Rubellas' house is a model of upkeep. falling apart

3. Authoritarian parents tend to be strict, ***punitive,*** and unsympathetic. They value obedience from children and try to shape their children's behavior to meet a set standard and to curb the children's wills. They do not encourage independence. They are detached and seldom praise their youngsters. In contrast, permissive parents give their children complete freedom and lax discipline. Punishing

7

4. Authoritarian parents tend to be strict, punitive, and unsympathetic. They value obedience from children and try to shape their children's behavior to meet a set standard and to curb the children's wills. They do not encourage independence. They are detached and seldom praise their youngsters. In contrast, permissive parents give their children complete freedom and *lax* discipline. <u>Easygoing, loose, relaxed</u>

5. As I looked back and evaluated my own college training, I saw that the training and experience I had had in public speaking had been of more practical value to me in business—and in life—than everything else I had studied in college all put together. Why? Because it had wiped out my *timidity* and lack of self-confidence and given me the courage and assurance to deal with people. <u>shyness; fear</u>

READING STRATEGY: Keeping a Reading Journal

In Chapter 1 of this book, you learned that active readers are those who interact with the text by thinking about what they read. Active researchers also consciously try to connect the text's information to their own experiences and beliefs. One useful strategy for understanding and absorbing new information you read is to keep a reading journal, a notebook in which you record your thoughts about the things you read. These thoughts could include a brief summary of the selection, a list of new ideas or new information you learned, or your reactions to or opinions about the text.

Keeping a reading journal offers two important benefits. First of all, the act of writing helps your thoughts become clearer. You may have some vague ideas or reactions after finishing a text. When you write them down, however, you'll find that trying to find the right words to express what you think will actually result in a better understanding of those thoughts. Therefore, the act of writing your response becomes a tool for learning about what that response is. A second benefit comes from creating a written record of your ideas. An entry for each article, chapter, or essay you read for a class, for example, can provide you with a handy reference for study. Later, when you're preparing for a test or completing an assignment, you can simply reread your entries to refresh your memory about the content of each text.

To keep a reading journal, obtain a notebook with blank pages inside. Immediately after you read a text, first write down its title, the author's name, and the date you read it or finished reading it. Then, let your purpose for reading the text determine the type of response you compose. If you'll be expected to discuss the content of the selection in class or to write about its topic for an assignment, you may want to record several or all of the following:

- A brief summary of the text

- Your reaction (your feelings or your own opinions about the subject)

- Your judgment of the selection's merit or accuracy

- A comparison of this work with other works you've read

- Your experiences or observations that either support or refute the text's ideas and conclusions

- Your questions about the text

If you are reading for your own pleasure or to expand your general knowledge about a particular topic, you might want to focus on just one or two of the items in the list above. No matter what your purpose, though, plan to put forth the little bit of extra effort it takes to better understand what you've read.

Read the following article and then write a reading journal entry that includes at least three of the items in the bulleted list above. Answers will vary.

Love Your Problems (and Experience Your Barriers)*

We all have problems and barriers that block our progress or prevent us from moving into new areas. Often, the way we respond to our problems puts boundaries on our experiences. We limit what we allow ourselves to be, do, and have.

Our problems might include fear of speaking in front of a group, anxiety about math problems, or reluctance to sound silly trying to speak a foreign language. We might have a barrier about trying a new thing and looking silly. Some of us even have anxiety about being successful.

Problems often work like barriers. When we bump up against one of our problems, we usually turn around and start walking along a different path. And all of a sudden—bump!—we've struck another barrier. And we turn away again.

Continued

7

* Adapted from Dave Ellis, *Becoming a Master Student*, 9th ed. (Boston: Houghton Mifflin Co., 2000), 98–100.

As we continue to bump into problems and turn away from them, our lives stay inside the same old boundaries. Inside these boundaries, we are unlikely to have new adventures. We are unlikely to improve or make much progress.

The word *problem* is a wonderful word coming from the ancient Greek word *proballein,* which means "to throw forward." In other words, problems are there to provide an opportunity for us to gain new skills. If we respond to problems by loving them instead of resisting them, we can expand the boundaries in which we live our lives. When approached with acceptance and even love, problems can "throw" us forward.

Three Ways to Handle a Barrier

It's natural to have barriers, but sometimes they limit our experience so much that we get bored, angry, or frustrated with life. When this happens, consider the following three ways of dealing with a barrier. One way is to pretend it doesn't exist. Avoid it, deny it, lie about it. It's like turning your head the other way, putting on a fake grin, and saying, "See, there's really no problem at all. Everything is fine. Oh, that problem. That's not a problem; it's not really there."

In addition to looking foolish, this approach leaves the barrier intact, and we keep bumping into it. We deny the barrier and might not even be aware that we're bumping into it. For example, a student who has a barrier about math might subconsciously avoid enriching experiences that include math.

A second approach is to fight the barrier, to struggle against it. This usually makes the barrier grow. It increases the barrier's magnitude.[1] A person who is obsessed with weight might constantly worry about being fat. He might struggle with it every day, trying diet after diet. And the more he struggles, the bigger the problem gets.

The third alternative is to love the barrier. Accept it. Totally experience it. Tell the truth about it. Describe it in detail. When you do this, the barrier loses its power. You can literally love it to death.

The word *love* might sound like an overstatement. Here, the word means to accept your problems, to allow and permit them. When we fight a problem it grows bigger. The more we fight against it, the stronger it seems to become. When we accept the fact that we have a problem, we are more likely to find effective ways to deal with it.

1. **magnitude:** greatness in size or significance

Suppose one of your barriers is being afraid of speaking in front of a group. You can use any of these three approaches.

First, you can get up in front of the group and pretend you're not afraid. You can fake a smile, not admitting to yourself or the group that you have any concerns about speaking—even though your legs have turned to rubber bands and your mind is jelly. The problem is, everyone in the room will know you're scared, including you, when your hands start shaking and your voice cracks and you forget what you were going to say.

The second way to approach this barrier is to fight it. You could tell yourself, "I'm not going to be scared," and then try to keep your knees from knocking. Generally, this doesn't work. In fact, your knee-knocking might get worse.

The third approach is to go to the front of the room, look out into the audience, and say to yourself, "I am scared. I notice that my knees are shaking, my mouth feels dry, and I'm having a rush of thoughts about what might happen if I say the wrong thing. Yup, I'm scared and that's OK. As a matter of fact, it's just part of me, so I accept it and I'm not going to try to fight it. I'm going to give this speech even though I'm scared."

You might not actually eliminate the fear; however, your barrier about the fear—which is what stops you—might disappear. And you might discover that if you examine the fear, love it, accept it, and totally experience it, the fear itself also disappears.

Applying This Process

Applying this process is easier if you remember two ideas. First, loving a problem is not necessarily the same as enjoying it. Love in this sense means total and unconditional acceptance.

Second, unconditional acceptance is not the same as unconditional surrender. Accepting a problem is different from giving up or escaping from it. Rather, this process involves escaping from the grip of the problem by diving *into* the problem head first and getting to know it in detail.

Loving a problem does not need to keep us stuck in the problem. When people first hear about this process, they often think it means to be resigned to the problem. Actually, loving a problem does not stop us from acting. Loving a problem does not keep us mired in it. In fact, fully accepting and admitting the problem usually assists us in taking effective action—and perhaps in freeing ourselves of the problem once and for all.

7

CHAPTER 7 TESTS

Name _____ Date _____

TEST 1

Study the table below and then answer the questions that follow. Circle the letter of each correct answer.

Periods of Egyptian History

Period	Dates	Significant Events
Archaic	3100–2660 BC	Unification of Egypt
Old Kingdom	2660–2180 BC	Construction of the pyramids
First Intermediate	2180–2080 BC	Political chaos
Middle Kingdom	2080–1640 BC	Recovery and political stability
Second Intermediate	1640–1570 BC	Hyksos "invasion"
New Kingdom	1570–1075 BC	Creation of an Egyptian empire Akhenaten's religious policy

Source: John McKay et al., *A History of World Societies*, Vol. I. (Boston: Houghton Mifflin Co., 2001), 21. Copyright © 2001 by Houghton Mifflin Company. Reprinted with permission.

1. What was the period of the Middle Kingdom?
   a. 3100–2660 BC
   b. 2080–1640 BC
   c. 1570–1075 BC
   d. 2180–2080 BC

2. Which significant event occurred during the Archaic period?
   a. Unification of Egypt
   b. Hyksos "invasion"
   c. Recovery and political stability
   d. Political chaos

3. Which of the following periods came first, according to the table?
   a. Second Intermediate
   b. New Kingdom
   c. Middle Kingdom
   d. Old Kingdom

4. The period of 1570–1075 BC is called the
   a. Archaic period.
   b. First Intermediate period.
   c. New Kingdom.
   d. Old Kingdom.

5. Political chaos occurred during the
   a. First Intermediate period.
   b. New Kingdom.
   c. Archaic period.
   d. Middle Kingdom.

TEST 2

Study the organizational chart below and then answer the questions that follow. Circle the letter of each correct answer.

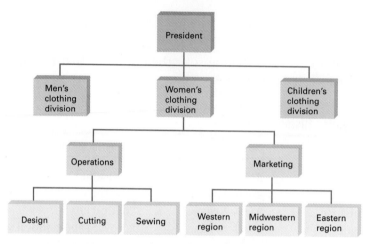

Multibase Departmentalization for New-Wave Fashions, Inc.   Most firms use more than one basis for departmentalization to improve efficiency and to avoid overlapping positions.

Source: William Pride et al., *Business*, 8th ed. (Boston: Houghton Mifflin Co., 2005), 229.

1. To what division does Marketing directly report?
   a. Children's clothing division   (c.) Women's clothing division
   b. President   d. Midwestern region

2. The Sewing department is on the same organizational level as
   a. Operations.   c. the President.
   b. Marketing.   (d.) Cutting.

3. What are two of the three departments that report to Marketing?
   (a.) Eastern region and Midwestern region
   b. Children's clothing division and Women's clothing division
   c. Midwestern region and Operations
   d. Cutting and Sewing

4. The Men's clothing division reports directly to
   a. Women's clothing division.   c. Operations.
   (b.) the President.   d. Children's clothing division.

5. Design, Cutting, and Sewing report directly to
   a. the President.   c. Marketing.
   b. the Men's clothing division.   (d.) Operations.

TEST 3

Study the flow chart below and then answer the questions that follow. Circle the letter of each correct answer.

▼ **Flow Chart for a Writing Plan**

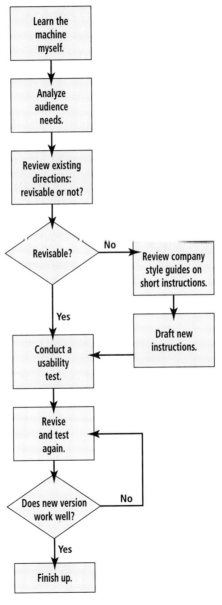

Source: William Murdick and Jonathan C. Bloemker, *The Portable Technical Writer* (Boston: Houghton Mifflin Co., 2001), 72.

1. The third step in the writing plan is

   a. review company style guidelines on short instructions.
   b. learn the machine myself.
   c. analyze audience needs.
   d. review existing directions: revisable or not?

2. The final stage in the writing plan is

   a. revise.   c. finish up.
   b. edit.   d. draft new instructions.

3. If the existing directions are not revisable, what is the first thing you should do?

   a. Draft new instructions.
   b. Review company style guides on short instructions.
   c. Conduct a usability test.
   d. Revise and test again.

4. The first thing you should do before you begin writing is

   a. examine the guidelines.   c. look at the instructions.
   b. learn the machine.   d. analyze audience needs.

5. If the new version does not work well, you should

   a. revise and test again.   c. conduct a usability test.
   b. finish up.   d. draft new instructions.

TEST 4

Study the pie chart* on page 363 and then answer the questions below. Circle the letter of each correct answer.

1. What percentage of businesses are wholesale businesses?

   a. 22.7%   c. 1.7%
   b. 37.6%   d. 8.0%

2. 22.7% of small businesses are

   a. construction businesses.   c. service businesses.
   b. retailing businesses.   d. transportation businesses.

* From Ricky Griffin, *Management*, 7th ed. (Boston: Houghton Mifflin Co., 2000), 294.

Small Businesses (Businesses with Less Than Twenty Employees) by Industry

Small businesses are especially strong in certain industries such as retailing and services. On the other hand, there are relatively fewer small businesses in industries such as transportation and manufacturing. The differences are affected primarily by factors such as the investment costs necessary to enter markets in these industries. For example, starting a new airline would require the purchase of large passenger aircraft and airport gates and hiring an expensive set of employees.

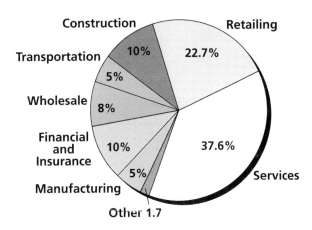

Source: U.S. Census Bureau, *Statistical Abstract of the United States: 1999*, 119th edition, Washington, DC, 1999.

3. According to the chart, besides the "Other" category, small businesses have the smallest percentage in which two industries?
   a. transportation and manufacturing
   b. financial and insurance
   c. retailing and services
   d. wholesale and manufacturing

4. The "Other" category of small businesses accounts for what percentage on the pie chart?
   a. 22.7%
   b. 5%
   c. 1.7%
   d. 37.6%

5. After retailing, the largest percentage of small businesses are
   a. construction.
   b. wholesale.
   c. wholesale and construction.
   d. construction and financial and insurance.

TEST 5

Study the line graph* below and then answer the questions that follow. Circle the letter of each correct answer.

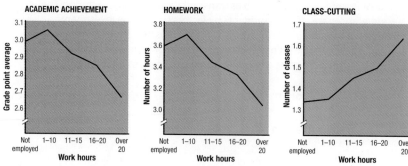

Adolescent Employment and School Achievement

This figure shows the relationship between hours of work per week and grade point average, time spent on homework, and class cutting. As adolescents spend more hours at work, their grade point averages decline, they spend less time on homework, and they cut more classes.

Source: Steinberg and Dornbusch, 1992, 308.

1. This chart represents
   a. adolescent employment and school achievement.
   b. work hours of adolescents in America.
   c. how many students cut class to go to a job.
   d. how many students are employed.

2. The grade point average of students who worked over twenty hours a week was approximately
   a. 3.1 percent.
   b. 3.0 percent.
   c. 2.7 percent.
   d. 2.0 percent.

3. "Not employed" students spent approximately how many hours a week on homework, according to the chart?
   a. 3.6
   b. 3.4
   c. 3.2
   d. 3.0

4. Students who worked between 1 and 10 hours per week cut approximately how many classes per week?
   a. between 1.2 and 1.3
   b. between 1.3 and 1.4
   c. between 1.5 and 1.6
   d. almost 2

5. Who spends the most time on homework per week, according to the chart?
   a. students who work over twenty hours a week
   b. students who work between 1 and 10 hours per week

* From Paul S. Kaplan, *Adolescence* (Boston: Houghton Mifflin Co., 2004), 421.

c. students who work between 16 and 20 hours per week

d. students who are not employed

TEST 6

Study the bar graph* below and then respond to the questions that follow by circling the letter of each correct answer.

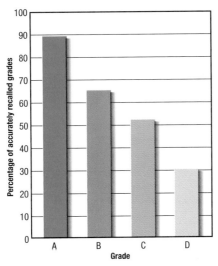

Distortions in Memory of High School Grades
College students were asked to recall their high school grades, which were then checked against their actual transcripts. These comparisons revealed that most errors in memory were grade inflations. Lower grades were recalled with the least accuracy (and the most inflation). It appears that people sometimes revise their own past to suit their current self-image. (Source: Bahrick et al.,1996.)

1. This graph represents

a. distortions in memories of college students.

(b.) distortions in memory of high school grades.

c. percentage of grade inflations.

d. current self-image of college students.

2. Approximately what percentage of students accurately recalled getting Ds as grades?

a. 10 percent

b. 20 percent

(c.) 30 percent

d. 40 percent

3. Approximately what percentage of students accurately recalled getting As as grades?

(a.) 90 percent

b. 80 percent

c. 70 percent

d. 60 percent

4. On the graph, what grade was most accurately remembered (got the highest percentage)?

(a.) A

b. B

c. C

d. D

* From Sharon S. Brehm, *Social Psychology,* 5th ed. (Boston: Houghton Mifflin Co., 2002), 64. Reprinted by permission of Houghton Mifflin Company.

5. Which grade did approximately 50 percent of students accurately recall?

    a. A   (c.) C

    b. B   d. D

TEST 7

Study the diagram below and then answer the questions that follow. Circle the letter of each correct answer.

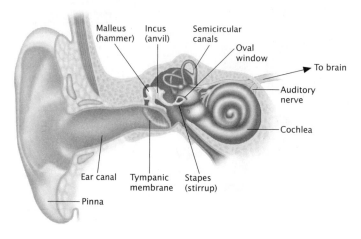

Source: Douglas Bernstein et al., *Psychology,* 6th ed. (Boston: Houghton Mifflin Co., 2003), 107.

1. What is the topic of this diagram?

    a. how we use our ears to hear   c. the eardrum

    (b) the structures of the ear   d. the ear canal

2. Which component of the ear is nearest the stirrup?

    a. hammer   c. brain

    b. auditory nerve   (d.) oval window

3. The only part of the ear that we normally see is the

    a. cochlea.   c. anvil.

    (b.) pinna.   d. semicircular canals.

4. The part of the ear that leads directly to the brain is the

    (a.) auditory nerve.   c. stirrup.

    b. semicircular canals.   d. ear canal.

5. The ear canal joins the pinna to the

    a. oval window.   (c.) eardrum.

    b. hammer.   d. brain.

7

TEST 8

Study the map below and then respond to the questions that follow by circling the letter of each correct answer.

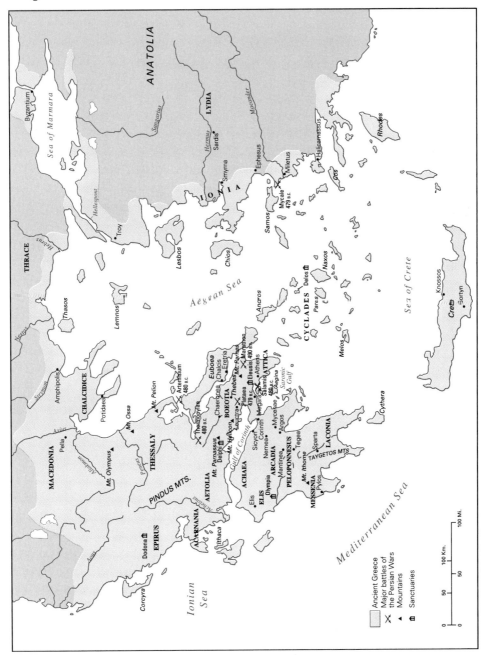

Source: Thomas Noble et al., *Western Civilization,* 4th ed. (Boston: Houghton Mifflin Co., 2005), 72. Copyright © 2005 by Houghton Mifflin Company. Reprinted with permission.

1. According to the map, Marathon would be considered which of the following?

    a. a sanctuary
    b. part of the mountains
    c. Anatolia
    (d.) a major battle site of the Persian Wars

2. Which area is located closest to the Sea of Marmara?

    a. Macedonia   c. Thrace
    (b.) Byzantium   d. Chalcidice

3. What do Dodona and Delos have in common?

    (a.) They were both sanctuaries.
    b. They were both sites of major battles of the Persian Wars.
    c. They are both located in Thessaly.
    d. They are both in the Sea of Crete.

4. Which of the following is not a sea on this map?

    a. The Mediterranean Sea   (c.) The Black Sea
    b. The Ionian Sea   d. The Aegean Sea

5. In what year did the war of Salamis take place?

    a. 580 BC   c. 490 BC
    b. 479 BC   (d.) 480 BC

7

Inferences

GOALS FOR CHAPTER 8

▶ Define the term *inference.*

▶ Explain how inferences are made.

▶ State three reasons for asking readers to make inferences.

▶ Use guidelines to make accurate inferences from reading selections.

▶ Explain and apply the steps of the REAP strategy.

Reading selections don't always state everything you should know about a subject. Instead, you're expected to figure out information that's not actually in the text by drawing inferences, or conclusions. To see how well you already do this, take the test below.

TEST YOURSELF

Read the following sentences and then respond to each question that follows by circling the correct answer.

1. I threw the stick, and he fetched it.

   What can you infer about the "he" in the sentence?

   a. He is my son.   c. He is a tree.
   b. He is a dog.   d. He is a squirrel.

2. Frank pulled the car over and asked the driver for his license.

   What can you infer about Frank from this sentence?

   a. Frank is a car thief.   c. Frank is a police officer.
   b. Frank needs a ride home.   d. Frank's car has broken down.

3. The "flawed masterpiece" *Apocalypse Now* was one of the most talked-about screen undertakings—even before anyone had seen it—since *Gone with the Wind.*

What can you infer about *Apocalypse Now*?

a. It is a book.

b. It is a television show.

(c.) It is a movie.

d. Francis Ford Coppola directed it.

4. John was a bright fellow who had been in college for seven years without graduating. During a class discussion, he related an experience that he said was typical of him: He had been studying for a midterm test in history when a friend called and asked for help with a test in biology, a course John had already passed. John set aside his own studies and spent the evening tutoring his friend. The next day John failed his history exam.*

What can you infer about John from this passage?

(a.) John cares about his friends more than he cares about his grades.

b. John knows a lot about history.

c. John is a *C* student.

d. John finds studying boring.

5. In Phoenix, about two-thirds of the incoming ninth graders read at least a year below grade level. And the statistics from other cities are similar. That reading lag, experts say, is largely why almost every big-city school district has at least twice as many ninth graders as twelfth graders.†

What can you infer from this passage?

a. Small-town school districts are better than big-city districts at teaching kids how to read.

b. Overcrowded schools are to blame for kids' problems with learning how to read.

(c.) Many teenagers with reading problems drop out of school and don't graduate.

d. Twelfth grade is much more difficult than ninth grade.

Inferences

Writers do not write down everything they want you to understand about a topic, but they expect you to figure out this information anyway. How? They

---

* From Skip Downing, *On Course*, 4th ed. (Boston: Houghton Mifflin Co., 2005), 112.

† Adapted from Tamar Lewin, "In Cities, a Battle to Improve Teenage Literacy," *New York Times*, April 14, 2004, http://www.nytimes.com/2004/04/14/education/14read.html.

know you make inferences while you read. An **inference** is a conclusion you draw that's based upon the stated information. You made one type of inference when you learned how to determine implied main ideas in Chapter 4. When you consider a group of related supporting details and draw a conclusion about the point they suggest, you're inferring that main idea. But you make many more kinds of smaller inferences, too, as you read. For example, read the following sentences.

> A mother thought her three-year-old child was playing too quietly, so she went into the living room to check on the youngster. The child was not in the room, and the front door was wide open. Their dog was gone, too. She panicked and called the police. When they arrived, they began searching the neighborhood. One of the searchers saw a dog barking and running into and out of a wooded area beside the road. He followed the excited dog and found the three-year-old, crying and trembling, hiding behind a tree.

Did you conclude that the child left home and got lost but was rescued when the family dog revealed his or her whereabouts? If you did, you made quite a few inferences to reach that conclusion. For instance, the passage never says that the child was at home, so how do you know that? You figure that out because the child, the child's mother, and the dog are all there, and the child is in the living room. Therefore, you conclude that they're all in the house where they live. How did you—and the mother—know the child had wandered off? You get three clues: the child is gone, the door is open, and the mother panics. You add these three pieces of information together to make your conclusion. How do you know that the dog helps rescuers find the child? The animal tries to attract their attention by barking and running back and forth, and the child is found where the dog is exhibiting these behaviors. You put those clues together to figure out that the dog was "telling" rescuers where they could find the child. Therefore, even though the passage does not tell you exactly what happened, you still understand because of your ability to make inferences. *To infer* means "to read between the lines." You see more than what is actually there because you bring your own knowledge, experiences, and observations to your reading, allowing you to fill in the gaps. For instance, you've noticed before that a burning building sends black smoke into the sky, and you know that fire trucks rush to a fire with their sirens on. Therefore, when you see smoke and hear sirens, you conclude that something is on fire. You apply these same experiences and observations as you read.

Here is another example that illustrates how you use your previous knowledge to make inferences:

> Some people ask me if I worry about my girlfriend's getting off work late at night. I don't, though, because she has her black belt in karate.

8

These two sentences ask you to make a couple of inferences. The first sentence assumes that you know why people would worry; it asks you to access your memory of news stories, observations, or your own personal experiences that have taught you that a woman alone at night can be vulnerable to an attack. Then, the second sentence assumes you know that someone who possesses a black belt in karate is a practiced fighter who can defend herself against attackers. Even though these two pieces of information are never stated, you easily infer the meaning of these sentences because you use your previous knowledge to understand.

As you read this next group of sentences, think about what knowledge you must possess in order to make the right conclusions:

> In New York, former Mafia[1] boss John Gotti had his hair trimmed daily by a barber as he sat in a professional barber's chair installed in his Queens headquarters. In prison, he got a haircut once a month from an inmate barber paid 40 cents an hour by the Bureau of Prisons.*

First of all, the passage asks you to interpret what having your hair trimmed daily means. Do you have your hair trimmed that often? Probably not. You might conclude, therefore, that John Gotti was very concerned about his looks and that he had plenty of money to pay for a service that most people can afford only occasionally. This passage also expects you to know that 40 cents an hour is far less than most people make for the work they do. Finally, then, you are expected to conclude that Gotti fell from the heights of luxury and pampering to the no-frills lows of prison life.

Exercise 8.1

Read the following comic strips and look at the following photographs and then write a check mark next to each statement that expresses an accurate inference.

1. Mafia: a criminal organization

---

* Adapted from Rick Hampson, "Curtains Descend on Gotti Family," *USA Today*, July 25, 2001, 3A.

Calvin and Hobbes
by Bill Watterson

Calvin and Hobbes © 1988 Watterson. Reprinted with permission of Universal Press Syndicate.
All rights reserved.

1. __✔__ Calvin doesn't like to take baths.

   _____ Calvin spends a lot of time on the roof.

   _____ Calvin's mother is having a good time.

   _____ Calvin lives in a very expensive house.

MOTHER GOOSE & GRIMM
BY MIKE PETERS

Mother Goose and Grimm © Grimmy, Inc. Reprinted with special permission of King Features
Syndicate.

2. _____ The restaurant's chef does not know how to cook steaks.

   __✔__ The buzzard likes its meat bad or rotting.

   _____ The waitress hears many complaints about the food.

   _____ The prices at this restaurant are very high.

© Will Hart / PhotoEdit

3. _____ These two boys live in Atlanta.

_____ These two boys fight a lot.

__✔__ The boys are brothers.

_____ The younger boy attends a private school.

© Elizabeth Crews

4. _____ These three people are students.

__✔__ The woman in the middle is the teacher, and the other people are her students.

_____ The students have just taken a test.

_____ The woman in the middle is angry at the other two people.

© Hans Pennink, *The Daily Gazette*

5. _____ The truck is going too fast.

   _✔_ The "Daddy" mentioned in the sign's message is a road construction worker.

   _____ A child made the sign.

   _____ It is rush hour on this highway.

Exercise 8.2

Read the following paragraphs and then respond to the questions that follow by circling the letter of each correct answer.

1. Barney-haters may have fresh ammo. According to researchers at Seattle's Children's Hospital and Regional Medical Center, toddlers who watch television are more likely to have attention problems later on.*

---

* Adapted from Nancy Shute, "Programmed for Trouble?" *U.S. News & World Report*, April 19, 2004, 76.

The author assumes you know that Barney is a

   (a.) children's television character.   c. television brand name.
   b. famous researcher.   d. name of a child.

2. Thirty years after the first Ali-Frazier fight, Laila Ali, daughter of Muhammad Ali, and Jacqui Frazier-Lyde, daughter of Smokin' Joe Frazier, reignited the family feud with a bout in upstate New York in June of 2001.*

The author assumes that you know that the women mentioned in the sentence are daughters of

   a. famous scientists.   (c.) famous heavyweight boxers.
   b. famous fireworks specialists.   d. famous civil rights activists.

3. *American Idol* fans are not happy. And *24* devotees are upset. On chat sites, viewers voiced their opposition to Fox's scheduling changes, made so that the network could air President Bush's news conference Tuesday night.†

The author assumes that you know that *American Idol* and *24* are

   a. titles of books.
   (b.) names of TV shows.
   c. websites.
   d. titles of CDs.

4. There are guys in my neighborhood who still sport their college's name on their car window. And they're in their 60s.‡

The author wants you to infer that

   (a.) the men to whom he or she is referring are too old to be displaying their college's name on their car windows.
   b. the men to whom he or she is referring own cars.
   c. the men to whom he or she is referring have gray hair.
   d. the men to whom he or she is referring went to his college.

5. Sundee Hughes, 23, who has been working since she was 15, was laid off from a local hosiery plant and has been looking in vain for full-time work for four months. She has applied at factories, convenience stores, and

---

* Adapted from Alisha Davis, "Newsmakers," *Newsweek*, June 11, 2001, 53.
† Adapted from Ann Oldenburg, "'Idol' and '24' Fans Annoyed at White House," *USA Today*, April 14, 2004, 3D.
‡ From Craig Wilson, "Picking a Future Alma Mater Is Anything but Academic," *USA Today*, July 25, 2001, 1D.

restaurants and has employment services helping her look. So far, all she's managed are some temporary stints[1] at a furniture plant.*

The author wants you to infer that Sundee Hughes

a. wants to return to work at the hosiery plant.
(b.) wants and needs to find a full-time job.
c. is named after a day of the week.
d. is homeless.

Writers rely on readers' ability to make inferences for three reasons. First of all, passages that spelled out every detail would be boring and tedious to read. Second, they would be unnecessarily long. And finally, they would deprive readers of the pleasure they experience in figuring out some things for themselves.

Guidelines for Making Accurate Inferences

How can you make sure you're drawing the right conclusions from information in a text? Follow these guidelines:

- **Focus only on the details and information provided, and don't "read in" anything that's not there.** It's surprisingly easy to take just a little bit of information and jump to unfounded conclusions. For example, think back to the earlier example about the three-year-old who wandered away from home. Would you say that the child's mother was careless in allowing the child to get away? Many people would; they would say that she should have been watching her child more carefully. Can you really make that assumption, though? Could there have been someone else in the house who may have been responsible for looking after the child? The passage did not say that anyone else was in the house, but it also didn't say that the mother and child were the only ones home. We read that into the story. Because we know that the mother is often the primary caretaker in a household, we also assume that it's her fault when something happens to the child. Now, without looking back at the passage, answer this question: Who rescued the child? Did you answer "a police officer"? Why? Because the mother called the police, who came and searched the neighborhood. But the person who found the child was actually referred to simply as a

8

1. **stints:** fixed amounts of time

* Adapted from George Hager, "Portrait of a Town in Trouble," *USA Today*, July 30, 2001, 3B.

"searcher." That person could have been a neighbor rather than a police officer. We don't get enough information to be able to answer that question, so we should not leap to inaccurate conclusions.

Next, read another passage:

Michele Fricheteau was waiting inside the hotel she and her husband owned for 170 British musicians who had booked rooms for the night. She heard the roar of the supersonic Concorde jet plane lifting off, as it did every afternoon. But then came the deafening bang and the anguished screams, as flames ripped through the building, searing[1] her face.*

Would it be accurate to infer from the last two sentences that the Concorde hit the hotel Michele Fricheteau owned? Yes, that's correct. Why? Because she was inside the hotel, and the flames from the crash burned her face. Could you infer that the 170 British musicians she was waiting for were on the Concorde when it crashed? No, nothing in the passage says they were, and besides, the Concorde was taking off when it crashed. The musicians would not have been flying away from the hotel if they were scheduled to stay there that night. Was Michele killed by the crash? No, the passage says only that she was burned. Could you infer that the plane was on fire when it hit the hotel? No, the passage says that flames were present, but it does not say if the plane was burning when it crashed, so we should not make that particular conclusion.

- **Don't ignore any details.** The details provide the important clues. For instance, in the earlier example, was the missing three-year-old child enjoying his or her time out of the house? Of course not. The paragraph says the child was "crying and trembling," two details that indicate the child's fear.

Here's another paragraph in which you must notice the details to make the right inferences:

When students were asked to warm up with ten minutes of simple writing exercises while soothing classical music played, hundreds of them made fewer mistakes on their homework. And Hungarian researchers found that students who warmed up this way could concentrate harder for longer periods of time. The reason? Handwriting activates the logical mind, and the music calms the emotional mind,

1. **searing:** burning

---

* Adapted from Vivienne Walt, "In Gonesse, Concorde Crash Is 'Always a Presence,'" *USA Today*, July 25, 2001, 11A.

so the logical mind can take over. Kids become instantly more attentive to new information and better able to retain it. The result is higher grades.*

Now, try to recall the details as you consider whether or not the following inferences are correct.

> Any kind of music provides the necessary calming effect for the emotional mind.

> The act of handwriting seems to activate the whole brain.

> To improve concentration, you should write as long as possible.

Think about how the details affect the inferences you make. The first statement is incorrect because the paragraph states that *classical* music is the kind researchers played during their experiment. You should not infer, then, that other kinds of music have the same effect. The second statement is also incorrect. The passage says that writing activates the logical mind only; it is the *music* that calms the emotional mind. Finally, the third statement is incorrect, too. The passage clearly states that the experiment lasted only ten minutes, and it makes no indication that longer periods of handwriting produce other results.

- **Make sure nothing contradicts your conclusion.** Try not to overlook one or more details that may conflict with any preliminary conclusion you make about a passage. For example, read the following:

> Years ago a professor overheard me talking with other engineers about the engineering dropouts who then go into business. "Don't laugh," he said. "In five years, one of them will be your boss."†

In this passage, you can infer that the writer is an engineer because he's talking with "other engineers." Next, you're supposed to infer how these engineers feel about engineering dropouts. Are they sympathetic? Are they sad for the people who can't make it through the engineering program? If you answer yes to either of those questions, you are overlooking one important detail: the professor tells them not to "laugh." If you miss that detail, you won't accurately conclude that the engineers are making fun of those who failed.

- **Don't let stereotypes and/or prejudices color your interpretation.** When you think back to that story about the missing three-year-old and try to picture the child in your mind, do you picture a boy or a girl? The

8

---

* Adapted from Barbara Hustedt Crook, "Your Child Can Write Her Way to Better Grades," *Woman's World*, January 9, 2001, 44.

† Adapted from Steven Parish, "'Show and Style' vs. Experience," *USA Today*, July 30, 2001, 11A.

passage never identifies the child's gender, but many readers think of the child as male. Why? Because we rely upon the stereotype that little boys are, in general, more adventurous and more disobedient. Therefore, a boy would be more likely to wander off and get lost. However, we should resist making that inference if there is no information in the passage that supports it, and we recognize that some of our assumptions are based on generalizations that may be incorrect.

For example, read the following passage:

> Keiko, the killer whale made famous by the *Free Willy* movies, has died in Norwegian coastal waters, where he remained after millions of dollars and a decade of work failed to coax him back to the open sea, his caretakers said early Saturday. The whale, who was 27, died Friday afternoon after the sudden onset of pneumonia . . . . He was old for an orca in captivity, though wild orcas live an average of 35 years.*

Would you say that the people who kept Keiko in captivity were to blame for his inability to return to the wild? Do you believe that these people were ultimately responsible for his premature death? If you answered yes to either question, you're letting your opinions about holding sea creatures captive color your interpretation of the information. Actually, the passage never suggests that Keiko's captivity caused his refusal to be set free. And the passage indicates that Keiko died of pneumonia. Thus, readers who conclude that Keiko would still be free and happy today if he hadn't been in captivity get no information in this passage to support that conclusion.

Exercise 8.3

Read the following passages and then circle the letter of the correct answer for each of the questions that follow.

Twenty-four-hour service is catching on all across America. In Milwaukee, for example, Joe Valenti operates Valenti's Hair Studio, a 24-hour hair salon. He lives upstairs from the shop near downtown. He'll give you a new 'do at 3 AM. But it'll cost you. He doubles his prices after 10 PM, when a $16 haircut becomes a $32 job. The night work adds 15 percent to his earnings. He started it on a whim only to discover that people wanted it.†

* Adapted from "'Free Willy' Whale, Keiko, Dies," CNN.com, December 13, 2003, http://www.cnn.com/2003/SHOWBIZ/Movies/12/12/obit.keiko.ap/.
† Adapted from Bruce Horovitz, "24/7 Almost a Way of Life," *USA Today,* August 1, 2001, 2A.

1. What can you infer from the information that Joe Valenti "lives upstairs from the shop near downtown"?

   a. Because Joe Valenti lives in the downtown area, he is obviously a hip and trendy person.

   (b.) Because Joe lives so close to his salon, he can get to work easily at any hour of the day or night.

   c. Because Joe lives so close to his salon, he obviously can't afford a house.

   d. Because Joe lives so close to his salon, he must not have anything else to do besides work.

2. Based on the details in this paragraph, which of the following inferences is most accurate?

   a. Joe wasn't making enough money, so he had to open for business 24 hours a day.

   (b.) Many people find it convenient to get their hair done in the middle of the night.

   c. Joe has more customers at night than he does in the daytime.

   d. People who pay double for a haircut are wasting their money.

3. The reader can infer that Joe doubles his prices after 10 PM because

   a. he's greedy.

   b. only rich customers want their hair done after 10 PM.

   c. he's better at his job during nighttime hours.

   (d.) he works all day, too, so he has to charge extra to make the additional service worth his time.

On the bank of the Ottawa River, at 6 AM, Colorado Avalanche hockey coach Bob Hartley removed the championship Stanley Cup trophy from its case like a father cradling a baby out of a crib, joking that he thought it was still sleeping. If the 108-year-old Stanley Cup did start its day well rested, it was unlike most of Hartley's friends. About 60 showed up at the docks starting at 5:30 AM to fish with Hartley and the Cup, or at least to help launch his official day with what is arguably professional sports' most storied[1] trophy and the Holy Grail of hockey. While Hartley fished, the crowd started to build at the PPG Industries plant, a windshield manufacturing facility where Hartley worked in the 1980s. By 11 AM, about 1,200 employees and their family members had gathered to have a photo snapped with Hartley and the Cup.*

1. **storied:** celebrated or famous

* Adapted from Kevin Allen, "At Home with the Cup," *USA Today*, August 2, 2001, 1C.

4. What can you infer from the fact that Bob Hartley had the Stanley Cup in his possession?

   (a.) The Colorado Avalanche won the Stanley Cup.
   b. Bob Hartley had stolen the Stanley Cup.
   c. Bob Hartley is a hockey fan.
   d. The Colorado Avalanche had borrowed the Cup.

5. What can you infer from the fact that Bob Hartley once worked at a windshield manufacturing plant but now is in possession of the Stanley Cup?

   a. He loved his job at the plant.
   b. He didn't want to move to Colorado.
   (c.) He has had great success as a hockey coach since leaving the plant.
   d. He was always a fan of the Colorado Avalanche.

6. The reader can infer that Bob Hartley's "official day" is a result of his

   (a.) coaching a Stanley Cup–winning team.
   b. retirement from the windshield manufacturing plant.
   c. having grown up in Canada.
   d. being a great fisherman.

Six months after taking office, the president will begin a month-long vacation Saturday that is significantly longer than the average American's annual getaway. If the president returns as scheduled on Labor Day, he'll tie the modern record for presidential absence from the White House. That was held by Richard Nixon at 30 days. Ronald Reagan took trips as long as 28 days.*

7. What can you infer from the term *president* as used in the paragraph?

   a. The author is referring to Jack Welch, president of General Electric.
   b. The author is referring to Bill Gates, president of Microsoft.
   (c.) The author is referring to the president of the United States.
   d. The author is referring to Martin Sheen, who plays the president on a popular television show.

8. What can you infer about the length of time the president is taking for vacation?

   (a.) The president is using his position to justify taking a vacation longer than one that the average American would take.
   b. The president is not really going to be away that long.

* Adapted from Laurence McQuillan, "White House to Move to Texas for a While; President Takes Month Off for Working Vacation at His Ranch," *USA Today,* August 3, 2001, 10A.

    c. The president is going to be traveling extensively while on vacation, and that's why he needs a month.

    d. The president might not return on Labor Day, as promised.

9. What can you infer about other presidents not mentioned in the paragraph and the length of time that they took for vacation?

    a. You can infer that they took vacations, too.

    (b.) You can infer that they took less time than the presidents mentioned in the paragraph.

    c. You can infer that they didn't take vacations.

    d. You can infer that their vacations were longer than the ones taken by presidents mentioned in the paragraph.

They got up with the birds, fought traffic on the Pennsylvania Turnpike, crowded four into a hotel room, and spent hours dressing up to look like their idol, singer Madonna. They paid $336 apiece for a package that included concert tickets, hotel, preconcert party, and transportation to the show. For good luck, they brought a shrine: a framed picture of Madonna and a little altar with candles. They decorated their hotel rooms with Madonna banners, posters, and even a Madonna throw rug.*

10. What can you infer about the people referred to in the paragraph?

    (a.) They are fans of Madonna.

    b. They became fans of Madonna when they were children.

    c. They own birds.

    d. They like driving on the Pennsylvania Turnpike.

11. What is one other thing that you can infer about the people referred to in the paragraph?

    a. They like to wear costumes.

    b. They dress up like Madonna on Halloween.

    (c.) They would have done just about anything to see Madonna in concert.

    d. They have seen the movie *Desperately Seeking Susan* a hundred times.

12. What can you infer from the statement "They got up with the birds"?

    a. The people going to the Madonna concert slept late.

    b. The people going to the Madonna concert overslept.

    (c.) The people going to the Madonna concert got up very early.

    d. The people going to the Madonna concert stayed up late the night before.

8

* Adapted from Maria Puente, "Mad About Madonna," *USA Today,* July 25, 2001, 1D.

Last month, nine women wearing black caps and gowns walked onto a podium[1] here and received their college diplomas as their friends and family members wept and cheered. It was an unusual ceremony because all the graduates were convicted felons, and it took place in a gym embraced by locked metal gates and razor wire at the Bedford Hills Correctional Facility, a maximum security women's prison.*

13. What can we infer about the graduates from the paragraph?
   a. They had committed serious crimes.
   b. They were going to be in jail for life.
   c. They all had children.
   d. They didn't care about the graduation ceremony.

14. What can we infer from the statement "It was an unusual ceremony"?
   a. There was no music at the ceremony.
   b. Graduation ceremonies usually don't take place at prisons.
   c. It was unusual because the graduates were wearing caps and gowns.
   d. It was unusual because all of the graduates were women.

15. What can we infer about the friends and families of the graduates and the fact that they "wept and cheered"?
   a. They were very saddened by the event.
   b. They had come long distances to see the graduation.
   c. They were very proud of the graduates.
   d. They were not proud of the graduates.

Exercise 8.4

Read the following passages and then write a check mark next to each statement that expresses an accurate inference.

1. Upset that your husband forgot to call? Think telling him off will make you feel better? Not so, says psychologist Brad Bushman, PhD, whose research shows that venting anger actually ends up making people unhappy. Why? We often say things we later regret, studies show. A better idea, according to Bushman, is reading a good book, watching a funny TV show, or listening to a favorite CD. You'll soon calm down enough to deal

---

1. **podium:** elevated platform

---

* Adapted from Robert Worth, "Bringing College Back to Bedford Hills," *New York Times,* June 24, 2001, Sec. 14,1.

more productively with the situation by having a calm discussion with whoever made you angry.*

_____ 1. Women vent their anger more than men do.

✔ 2. Venting anger often involves hurtful verbal criticism.

✔ 3. Venting anger can damage the relationship between two people, leading to more unhappiness.

_____ 4. Women have a right to feel angry when their husbands forget them.

_____ 5. A primary goal of the media is to help people better manage their anger.

2. Medical experts have warned for years that anorexia and bulimia can be deadly, but a growing number of teens are celebrating their eating disorders on the Web and sharing their tips and strategies for losing weight and exercising. It's a trend that worries and disturbs eating-disorder experts. "I love the feeling I get when I can feel my bones sticking out. I love feeling empty, like a hollow gourd.[1] I love knowing I went the whole day without eating." So says a posting on one website promoting eating disorders as a lifestyle.†

✔ 1. Teens don't take eating disorders as seriously as medical experts do.

_____ 2. Medical experts think that teens are stupid.

✔ 3. Medical experts are disturbed by how teens are dealing with eating disorders.

_____ 4. Teens think that medical experts don't know what they are talking about.

_____ 5. Teens with eating disorders don't care about other people.

3. It's 6:35 in the morning, and Cheryl Nevins, thirty-four, is dressed for work in a silky black maternity blouse and skirt. Ryan, two and a half, and Brendan, eleven months, are sobbing because Reilly, the beefy family dog, knocked Ryan over. In a blur of calm, purposeful activity, Nevins, who is

8

1. **gourd:** hollowed-out shell of certain fruits

---

* Adapted from Barbara Hustedt Crook, "Feel Happier Just by Doing These Six Simple Things," *Woman's World,* July 10, 2001, 21.

† Adapted from Nanci Hellmich, "Super-thin, Super-troubling," *USA Today,* July 25, 2001, 7D.

eight months pregnant, shoves the dog out into the backyard, changes Ryan's diaper on the family-room rug, heats farina[1] in the microwave, and feeds Brendan cereal and sliced bananas while crooning "Open, Shut Them" to encourage the baby to chew. Her husband, Joe, normally out the door by 5:30 AM for his job as a finance manager at Kraft Foods, makes a rare appearance in the morning muddle. "I do want to go outside with you," he tells Ryan, who is clinging to his leg, "but Daddy has to work every day except Saturdays and Sundays. That stinks."*

_____ 1. Cheryl Nevins has nice maternity clothing.

__✔__ 2. Cheryl Nevins has very busy mornings before she leaves for work.

__✔__ 3. Cheryl Nevins's husband is not around to help much in the morning.

_____ 4. Cheryl Nevins is regretting having another child.

_____ 5. Cheryl Nevins serves her children convenience foods when she can.

4. She walks down the sidewalk of one of Cincinnati's meanest streets. Young toughs, pants low on their hips, slouch on the corner. As she approaches, they straighten up. "Good afternoon, Miz Mattie," they say to the seventy-four-year-old woman. She cuts them the briefest of nods. She disapproves of idleness, but she's kind and charitable, too. She's head of "Grandma's Hands," a place where volunteers teach girls from the meaner streets of Cincinnati to cook and sew.†

__✔__ 1. Mattie wants to help the girls of her community.

__✔__ 2. Mattie lives in a dangerous neighborhood.

_____ 3. Mattie is a nun.

_____ 4. Mattie doesn't really care about young men in her community.

_____ 5. Mattie goes to church every day.

5. Resisting slavery seemed second nature to Harriet Tubman. Born a slave on a Maryland plantation in 1820, she quickly developed a fiery spirit

1. **farina:** cooked cereal

---

* Adapted from "The Case for Staying Home," by Claudia Wallis, *Time*, March 22, 2004, 51.
† Adapted from Laura Pulfer, "Mattie's Mission," *Rosie*, August 2, 2001, 55.

and was not shy about protesting bad treatment. One such incident so angered the plantation overseer that he hit her over the head with a lead weight, inflicting a permanent brain injury that would cause her to suddenly lose consciousness several times a day for the rest of her life. To overcome this disability, she worked on building herself up physically, becoming an uncommonly strong woman. It was said that she could single-handedly haul a boat fully loaded with stones, a feat[1] deemed impossible for all but the strongest men.*

___✔___ 1. Harriet Tubman was an African American.

___✔___ 2. Harriet Tubman is now dead.

___✔___ 3. Harriet Tubman stood up for herself.

_____ 4. Men were frightened of Harriet Tubman.

_____ 5. Harriet Tubman freed herself from slavery.

Exercise 8.5

Read the following Aesop fable. This fable is written in the style of a parable, or story, written to make a point. Respond to each of the questions that follow by circling the letter of the correct answer.

The tortoise and the hare argued over which was the swifter. So, as a result, they agreed on a fixed period of time and a place and parted company. Now the hare, trusting in his natural speed, didn't hurry to set out. He lay down at the side of the road and fell asleep. But the tortoise, well aware of his slowness, didn't stop running, and, overtaking the sleeping hare, he arrived first and won the contest.†

1. What can you infer about the hare from this selection?
   a. He assumed that he could beat the tortoise.
   b. He was very tired.
   c. He had won many speed contests.
   d. He did not like the tortoise.

8

1. feat: an act of strength or courage

---

* From Carol Berkin et al., *Making America* (Boston: Houghton Mifflin Co., 2001), 276.

† Aesop fable from *The Complete Fables,* translated by Olivia and Robert Temple (New York: Penguin, 1998). Copyright © 1998 by Olivia and Robert Temple. Reprinted by permission of the authors.

2. What can you infer about the tortoise from this selection?

   a. The tortoise assumed that he could beat the hare without too much effort.

   (b.) The tortoise was aware of his slowness and worked hard to win the race.

   c. The tortoise wasn't as tired as the hare.

   d. There is nothing to infer about the tortoise from this selection.

3. What inference can you make about what the author is trying to convey in this selection?

   a. The author is warning against thinking too much of oneself.

   b. The author is saying that speed wins over intellect any day.

   (c.) The author is saying that hard work often triumphs over talent if the talents are not used effectively.

   d. The author isn't really saying anything worth mentioning.

CHAPTER 8 REVIEW

Fill in each of the blanks in the following statements by writing the correct answer.

1. An ____inference____ is a conclusion you draw that's based upon the stated information.

2. ____Readers____ use their knowledge, experiences, and observations to help them make inferences.

3. Writers ask readers to make inferences to keep their writing ____brief____, ____interesting____, and fun for the reader.

4. To make accurate inferences, readers should avoid ____"reading in"____ information that's not in a text. On the other hand, they should not ignore any details provided.

5. To make accurate inferences, readers should make sure nothing ____contra-dicts____ a conclusion, and they should avoid letting stereotypes or ____prejudices____ affect their conclusions.

8

Reading Selection

> ## Practicing the Active Reading Strategy:
> ### Before and As You Read
>
> You can use active reading strategies before, as, and after you read a selection. The following are some suggestions for active reading strategies that you can employ before you read and as you are reading.
>
> 1. Skim the selection for any unfamiliar words. Circle or highlight any words you do not know.
>
> 2. As you read, underline, highlight, or circle important words or phrases.
>
> 3. Write down any questions about the selection if you are confused by the information presented.
>
> 4. Jot notes in the margin to help you understand the material.

What a Way to Live, What a Way to Die!
by Al Neuharth

1 He reminded people of all ages how to live with life's little disappointments. And to laugh about them. For fifty years.

2 Now he has shown us how to die. Charles Schulz died in his sleep just when his farewell comic strip of *Peanuts* was being inserted and distributed in the Sunday papers.

3 Schulz was much more than a cartoonist. He was a philosopher. His teachings were more useful than those of such noted philosophers as Aristotle or Confucius or Plato or Socrates. Here's why: He knew life is not always fair, but it can still be fun.

4 He and his *Peanuts* gang took life very seriously, but never took themselves too seriously. So Charlie Brown always missed the football and always got his kite stuck in a tree. So Linus always sucked his thumb and carried his comfort blanket. So Snoopy was a sleepy-eyed beagle who dozed at the typewriter. So Lucy's curbside psychiatric clinic didn't offer a nickel's worth of good advice. So what? That's life. It made kids of all ages laugh because they could relate.

5 Some Schulz critics suggested he should create winners, not just losers. His response: "You can't create humor out of happiness." Yet the few times I was in his presence, I sensed a serene sort of happiness about him.

6 My feeling of kinship goes back to our Midwestern upbringing. His father was a barber in Minnesota; mine, a farmer in South Dakota. We both entered the army at Fort Snelling, in St. Paul, in 1943 for World War II. He served as a sergeant in the 20th Armored Division in Europe. I was

a sergeant in the 86th Infantry Division in Europe and the Pacific.

7   After the war, we returned home, both hoping to find fame and fortune in newspapering. He began by drawing comics for the *St. Paul Pioneer Press.* I wrote news stories

for the *Rapid City* (South Dakota) *Journal.* The rest, as they say, is history.

8   Charles Schulz showed me and the 355 million of you around the world who read him regularly how to live. Now he has shown us how to die. What a way to be and to go!*

Peanuts reprinted by permission of United Feature Syndicate, Inc.

VOCABULARY

Read the following questions about some of the vocabulary words that appear in the previous selection and then circle the letter of each correct answer.

1. As used in paragraph 2, what does the word *distributed* mean?
   a. taken away
   (b) given out
   c. cleaned up
   d. put together

2. "Schulz was much more than a cartoonist. He was a *philosopher*" (paragraph 3). What does *philosopher* mean?
   a. professor
   b. artist
   (c) wise person
   d. painter

3. "I sensed a *serene* sort of happiness about him" (paragraph 5). What does *serene* mean?
   a. disturbed
   b. happy
   (c) calm
   d. sad

4. When someone has a "feeling of *kinship*," what does that mean (paragraph 6)?
   (a) a feeling of being connected or friends with someone
   b. a feeling of being unhappy with someone
   c. a feeling of being like a child
   d. a feeling of being out of place

* Adapted from Al Neuharth, "What a Way to Live, What a Way to Die!" *USA Today,* March 21, 2000. Reprinted by permission of the author.

TOPICS, TOPIC SENTENCES, AND INFERENCES

Respond to the following questions by circling the letter of each correct answer.

1. The topic of paragraph 3 is
   a. cartoonists.
   b. philosophers.
   c. Charles Schulz.
   d. cartoons.

2. What is the topic sentence of paragraph 4?
   a. sentence 1
   b. sentence 2
   c. sentence 3
   d. sentence 4

3. Based on the information presented in the selection, which of the following statements best expresses an inference that you can make from reading the selection?
   a. *Peanuts* was not a popular cartoon.
   b. Charles Schulz had a hard life.
   c. Schulz had a lot of critics.
   d. The author of this selection has a great deal of respect for Charles Schulz and his work.

4. What is another inference you can make about Al Neuharth and Charles Schulz as people, based on the last few paragraphs of the selection?
   a. Neuharth and Schulz had nothing in common, but Neuharth still respected Schulz as an artist.
   b. Neuharth and Schulz had a lot in common, from their upbringing to different events that took place in their lives.
   c. Neuharth and Schulz were very patriotic.
   d. Neuharth enjoyed serving in World War II, but Schulz did not.

5. Look at the cartoon that accompanies the reading selection. What can you infer from the cartoon?
   a. People shouldn't try to tame wild birds.
   b. All children like birds.
   c. The birds get a lot of satisfaction from being patted on their heads by Linus.
   d. The birds leave because they do not like being patted on their heads.

Practicing the Active Reading Strategy:
After You Read

Now that you have read the selection, answer the following questions, using the active reading strategies that you learned in Chapter 1.

8

1. Identify and write down the point and purpose of this reading selection.

2. Besides the vocabulary words included in the exercise on page 390, are there any other vocabulary words that are unfamiliar to you? If so, write a list of them. When you have finished writing your list, look up each word in a dictionary and write the definition that best describes the word as it is used in the selection.

3. Predict any possible test questions that may be used on a test about the content of this selection.

4. How could you use the information contained in this selection? Does the information contained in the selection reinforce or contradict your ideas and experiences? Explain.

QUESTIONS FOR DISCUSSION AND WRITING

Write your answers to the following questions on the blanks provided based on your reading of the selection.

1. Why do you think the selection is called "What a Way to Live, What a Way to Die"? What does the author want to say about Charles Schulz? The author wants to express his gratitude to Schulz for his cartoons and for the way he lived his life.

2. Do you agree or disagree with this statement in paragraph 5: "You can't create humor out of happiness"? Why? Answers will vary.

3. Based on the information in paragraph 4, why do you think that the comic strip "made kids . . . laugh because they could relate"? Answers will vary.

▶ Vocabulary: Formal vs. Informal Language

When you read, you should be able to distinguish between formal and informal language. **Formal language** is usually serious, businesslike, and often sophisticated. This is the type of language that is most prevalent in scholarly, academic, and business writing. Most textbooks, college assignments, and business reports, for example, are written using formal language. **Informal language** is closer to that of conversation. It is more casual, often including colloquial (everyday) words, slang terms, idioms (expressions like "She's trying to butter me up"), abbreviations, and even humor.

The level of formality in a reading selection helps the reader know how the author feels about his or her subject. A passage or document written in a formal style communicates the author's belief that the subject is important and significant. A more informal style can suggest that the author is more lighthearted about the topic.

To understand the difference between formal and informal language, first take a look at an informal statement from one of the examples in this chapter:

> There are *guys* in my neighborhood who still *sport* their college's name on their *car* window.

The boldfaced, italicized words are colloquial and casual. Notice, though, how the substitution of different words increases the sentence's formality:

> There are *gentlemen* in my neighborhood who still *affix* their college's name to their *vehicle* window.

Vocabulary Exercise

Use the boldfaced, italicized words in each of the following sentences to decide whether the language is formal or informal, then on the blank after each sentence, write *FORMAL* or *INFORMAL*.

1. He'll give you a new *'do* at 3 AM. INFORMAL

2. One such *incident* so *angered* the plantation overseer that he hit her over the head with a lead weight, *inflicting* a permanent brain injury that would cause her to suddenly *lose consciousness* several times a day for the rest of her life. FORMAL

3. *Mess up* one word and *you're history.* INFORMAL

4. [The middle class] have what is called a *conceptual orientation*, using their *mental capacities* to solve problems, and their jobs often involve the *manipulation of symbols* rather than objects. FORMAL

5. *Barney-haters* may have fresh *ammo.* INFORMAL

6. *Nerds* are supposed to be friendless *bookworms* who *suck up* to authority figures. Furthermore, we're *sissies.* INFORMAL

8

READING STRATEGY: REAP

REAP (Read-Encode-Annotate-Ponder) is a strategy that guides you to respond to a text to improve your reading and thinking skills. This method provides you with a system of four steps. When you follow these steps, you'll be training yourself to look deeper into the texts you read so you can more fully understand and evaluate them. As a result, your comprehension and critical thinking skills will improve.

STEP 1: Read. The first step involves carefully reading the text to understand the author's ideas and information.

STEP 2: Encode. Next, you translate the text's message into your own words. This step asks you to paraphrase the ideas or information to put it in language you understand.

STEP 3: Annotate. To *annotate* means to write notes or comments about a text. You can record these in the margins of the text, or in a notebook, or on separate sheets of paper. These notes can take the form of objective summaries or more subjective reactions to the ideas and information. For example, you could jot down your own feelings, opinions, or judgments.

STEP 4: Ponder. Finally, you continue to reflect on what you have read and the notes you have written. In this stage, you also read or discuss other people's responses to the same text in order to more fully explore its content. This sharing can take place formally in classroom settings or informally outside of the classroom.

Here is a sample passage annotated according to the REAP method:

Street Art

It's been called trash, scratching (by the ancient Greeks) and a crime (in today's society). Although many people see graffiti as a sign of gang activity or plain old defacement,[1] this very American grassroots[2] art form blossomed in New York in the late 1960s, when inner-city

> Most people are critical of graffiti. It seems like property destruction to me, but a new book claims that graffiti was more than just spray paint on walls.

1. **defacement:** spoiling the surface or appearance of something

2. **grassroots:** related to the people or society at a local level rather than at the political center

kids just wanted to get noticed. Now a new book shows there's more to crafting graffiti than just spraying your name on a wall in black Rust-Oleum.

The work of one such artist is chronicled in *Dondi White Style Master General: The Life of Graffiti Artist Dondi White* (Regan Books). Dondi, aka Donald White—who died of AIDS in 1998 at age 37—was one of the first "taggers," who used spray paint to transform subway cars and tunnels into irreverent[1] art galleries. What easier audience to capture than thousands of commuting strap-hangers?[2]

New book celebrates art of Dondi White. "Taggers" spray-painted subway cars and tunnels.

"His work looked like it had been taped off or die-cut.[3] Dondi made it look easy when, in fact, his planning was meticulous[4] and exhaustive,"[5] says Andrew "Zephyr" Witten, a friend who cowrote the book with the artist's brother, Michael.

Dondi's friends and family believe he was very talented.

Yesterday's trash has become today's treasure. While billions of dollars are spent each year to remove graffiti from public property, the works of White and other early taggers sell for thousands in galleries. And "bombing"—creating graffiti in one spurt—is sporadic[6] now, Witten says.*

Graffiti is expensive art now. Question: what form does the graffiti take? How can you buy paintings that were on subway walls?

Now, practice the REAP method yourself by reading and annotating the following passage. Then, discuss your reactions with a partner or a group of your classmates.   Answers will vary.

Continued

8

1. **irreverent:** disrespectful
2. **strap-hangers:** subway riders who stand and hang on to straps
3. **die-cut:** cut out by a machine
4. **meticulous:** extremely careful and precise
5. **exhaustive:** thorough
6. **sporadic:** occurring irregularly

---

* Reading strategy adapted from "Street Art" by Robin Reid, as first appeared in *USA Weekend*, November 23–25, 2001, 17. Reprinted with permission of the author.

Choose Your Conversations

We can choose our conversations. Certain conversations create real value for us. They give us fuel for reaching our goals. Others distract us from what we want. They might even create lasting unhappiness and frustration.

We can choose more of the conversations that exhilarate[1] and sustain us. Sometimes we can't control the outward circumstances of our lives. Yet no matter what happens, we retain the right to choose our conversations.

Before choosing whether to participate in a particular conversation, we can pay attention to several characteristics of that conversation: *time frame, topic,* and *attitude.* When we choose conversations that are more balanced within each of these areas, our lives will be more balanced as well.

First, we can notice the *time frame* of the conversation—whether it is about the past, the present, or the future. Most people spend most of their conversation time talking about the past. Often, they are blaming ("If he wasn't such a jerk, I wouldn't be in this mess"), justifying ("I would have been on time, but between my crazy kids and the crazy traffic, I had a terrible morning"), or regretting ("If only I had bought that land before they started to develop it").

Conversations about the past can be fun and valuable. These conversations can help us learn from our mistakes, celebrate our successes, grieve over our losses, and enjoy fond memories. The problem arises when our conversations are out of balance. When the majority of our conversations are about the past, then both our thoughts and our actions become predominantly[2] influenced

1. **exhilarate:** cause to feel happily energetic

2. **predominantly:** mostly

by the past. With so much focus and attention on the past, our future could be little more than a repetitive variation of the past.

An alternative is to balance our conversations. We can limit our conversations about the past to approximately one-third of our time. Then we can devote a third of our conversation space to the present, and another third to the future. Shifting conversation to the present offers many benefits. Much of our pleasure comes from paying attention to what we're doing in the present moment—enjoying great food, performing well in sports, or becoming lost in captivating[1] music. As we engage in conversations about the present, we enhance the richness and quality of our lives.

Benefits also come from conversations about the future. These conversations help us create the most wonderful life possible. Instead of worrying about the future, we can create ways to live the life of our dreams. We can enjoy our creativity and use our planning skills.

In looking for ways to balance our conversations, we can select among the *topics* of things, others, self, or "us." Most conversations fall into one of these four categories. Like the time frame of conversations, the topics of most conversations are unbalanced. Most people talk about things (cars, houses, trips, football games, weather) and others (politicians, actors, neighbors, kids, coworkers) far more than they talk about themselves or about their relationships.

Of course, there is no problem in having conversations about things and others. But when we talk mostly about things and others, we neglect the rich intimacy[2] that comes from revealing ourselves to another person. When we

Continued

8

1. **captivating:** interesting

2. **intimacy:** close association or familiarity

choose our conversations thoughtfully, we can share our heartfelt desires, fears, joys, and celebrations. We can also choose to talk about the quality of our relationships and how they can be improved.

Depending on our *attitude,* we might choose to dwell in conversations about problems, or we might prefer to engage mostly in conversations about solutions. Most people's conversations are out of balance in this area. They spend about 90 percent of their time complaining and talking about what is not working. And they spend only about 10 percent looking for solutions and celebrating what *is* working.

We can reverse these percentages. We can spend about 10 percent of our conversation space looking at and defining problems. Then we can invest the rest of our time discussing solutions, exploring new possibilities, discovering exciting new passions and potentials, and achieving amazing results.*

8

* Adapted from Dave Ellis, *Becoming a Master Student,* 9th ed. (Boston: Houghton Mifflin Co., 2000), 217–218.

Name _____ Date _____

TEST 1

Read the following sentences and then respond to the questions that follow by circling the letter of each correct answer.

1. It took me a long time to clean the house today.

   What can you infer about the state of the house from this statement?

   a. The house was very neat and tidy before it was cleaned.
   b. The house was very dirty and needed to be cleaned.
   c. The house is old.
   d. The house is very small.

2. Patrick likes to have his mother read books to him before he goes to bed.

   What can you infer about Patrick's age from this statement?

   a. Patrick is very young.
   b. Patrick is a teenager.
   c. Patrick is an old man.
   d. Patrick is a second grader.

3. With all the new rules at airports these days, you'd think that Americans would have figured out a way to travel lighter.*

   What can you assume about the number of bags Americans bring onto airplanes these days?

   a. They bring on fewer bags.
   b. They bring on heavier bags.
   c. They bring on lighter bags.
   d. They bring on as many bags as they did before, if not more.

4. I've seen an eighty-year-old lady in a wheelchair have her tennis shoes removed and checked for explosives at the airport. A five-year-old girl's doll

* From Gene Sloan, "Americans Carry a Lot of Baggage," *USA Today*, March 8, 2002, 1D.

For additional tests on inferences, see the Test Bank.

carrier was hand-searched. A flight attendant's bag was emptied and her clean and neatly folded clothes scrambled.*

What can you infer about airline security from this passage?

a. It is not strict.
(b.) It is very strict with nobody above being searched.
c. It is for the very old.
d. It is only for the very young.

5. Six months after Pearl Harbor, June 7, 1942,[1] Americans did not have the luxury of wallowing[2] in self-obsessed thoughts on the meaning of it all. The pivotal[3] Battle of Midway had ended just the day before.†

What can you infer about America in 1942 from this passage?

a. The country was in a recession.
b. The country was in the midst of good economic times.
(c.) The country was at war.
d. The country was in the midst of a presidential election.

6. When John Burrows arrived at the Hilton New York last month and found himself stalled in the long check-in line, his eye wandered to a bank of polished, electronic kiosks.[4] A hotel employee asked Burrows if he wanted to take the new machine for a test spin. "About a minute later I was on my way to my room, while everyone else was still waiting," Burrows remembers.‡

The author assumes you know that the kiosks may contain

a. very fast elevators.
(b.) computers that allow guests to check themselves in.
c. access to the Internet.
d. bellmen driving high-tech golf carts.

7. Sandra Levison of Atherton, California, remembers listening to six-year-old daughter Alexa sleep: "She sounded horrible. . . . It wasn't a real snore,

8

1. **Pearl Harbor:** A military base in Hawaii that was attacked by the Japanese; the attack caused the United States to enter World War II.

2. **wallowing:** indulging

3. **pivotal:** vitally important

4. **kiosks:** small structures, such as booths

---

* Adapted from Al Neuharth, "Hassle, Not Fear, Is Crippling Air Travel," *USA Today*, March 8, 2002, 11A.

† Adapted from Walter Shapiro, "Americans Strangely Fixated on Tragic Anniversary," *USA Today*, March 8, 2002, 6A.

‡ Adapted from Christopher Elliott, "Invasion of the Kiosks," *U.S. News & World Report*, March 15, 2004, 82.

but breathing was very loud and labored. And she'd flip and flop and move all over." During the day, Levison says, Alexa, a first grader, had no apparent problems with attention or schoolwork, but she was grumpy and cried easily. Levison took up the problem with Alexa's pediatrician and then with Dr. Messner, who took out Alexa's tonsils and adenoids. "For the first time, her breathing was actually silent" when she slept, Levison says. And Alexa's daytime mood has improved.*

What does the author expect you to infer from this passage?

(a.) Alexa's tonsils were causing her sleep problems and making her irritable.
b. Alexa was extremely overweight.
c. Alexa had had problems sleeping during her infancy.
d. Alexa's pediatrician was not a very good doctor.

8. Believe it or not, filmmakers try to avoid having their work slapped with an R rating. By banning unchaperoned[1] teens, the R automatically stunts a movie's box office potential. But Robert Altman is different. When he heard that *Gosford Park,* his 1930s comedy of British manners and murder, had earned an R for its curse words, his reaction could be summed up with a four-letter word: Cool.†

What can you infer about Robert Altman from this passage?

a. He is a producer.
(b.) He is a director and filmmaker.
c. He is British.
d. He is a poet.

9. On a cold afternoon about a week before Valentine's Day, Meichelle Jackson, 41, sits with 18 other students in a classroom in rural Caddo County, Oklahoma, and listens to a lecturer discuss communication and conflict resolution in marriage. The course is part of Oklahoma's Marriage Initiative, a controversial $10 million program that uses welfare money to lower the state's sky-high divorce rate. Many of the students doodle[2] and giggle, but Jackson listens courteously.‡

1. **unchaperoned:** in attendance at an event without adult supervision   2. **doodle:** draw on paper

* Adapted from Kim Painter, "Take Out the Tonsils, Solve a Sleep Problem," *USA Today,* April 14, 2004, 4D.
† Adapted from Jim Jerome, "Inside Outsider," *People,* March 18, 2002, 109.
‡ From Peg Tyre, "Giving Lessons in Love," *Newsweek,* February 18, 2002, 64.

What can you infer about Meichelle Jackson from this passage?

a. She is interested in making friends with her 18 classmates.

b. She is married.

(c.) She is interested in learning new skills in the program.

d. She doesn't want to become friends with anyone in her class.

10. Two students from Professor Hallengren's English composition class sat in the cafeteria discussing the approaching deadline for their fourth essay.

"There's no way I can get this essay done on time," Tracy said. "I've turned in every essay late, and I still owe him a rewrite on the second one. Professor Hallengren is going to be furious!"

"You think you're in trouble!" Ricardo said. "I haven't even turned in the last essay. Now I'm going to be two essays behind."

"How come?" Tracy asked. "I would have thought a young guy right out of high school would have all the time in the world."

"Don't ask me where my time goes," Ricardo answered, shrugging. "Deadlines keep sneaking up on me, and before I know it, I'm weeks behind. I live on campus, and I don't even have to commute. But something always comes up. Last weekend I was going to write that other essay and study for my sociology test, but I had to go to a wedding out of state on Saturday. I was having such a good time, I didn't drive back until Monday morning. Now I'm even further behind."*

What can you infer about Ricardo from this passage?

a. He is Tracy's son.

(b.) His schoolwork is not always his top priority.

c. He is a better student than Tracy.

d. He has to work to pay for school.

TEST 2

8

Read the following passages and then respond to the questions that follow by circling the letter of each correct answer.

A. Earthwatch recruits volunteers to help scientists conduct field research in locations throughout the world. Most of the trips are for two weeks and cover

---

* From Skip Downing, *On Course,* 4th ed. (Boston: Houghton Mifflin Co., 2005), 93.

everything from excavating[1] a Roman fort in England to studying manatees[2] in Florida. The cost of these expeditions averages $1,600 to $1,800, without airfare. Participants stay in dorms or guesthouses and generally cook meals together.

Earthwatch has fared well considering the downturn in travel, with just over two dozen cancellations out of an expected 4,000 volunteers this year, according to Earthwatch spokesperson Blue Magruder. "They know that the scientists need them badly," she says.

Two-thirds of Earthwatch participants are from the United States, and the other third come from 46 other countries. Magruder emphasizes that this diversity plays an important role in building much-needed global camaraderie.[3]*

1. Based on the passage, the people who spend their vacations with Earthwatch prefer

   a. relief from a stressful life.
   b. to do something meaningful.
   c. to get away from other people.
   d. to relax in luxury.

2. According to spokesperson Magruder, diversity in Earthwatch participants

   a. creates many problems due to language barriers.
   b. gives Earthwatch scientists a large talent pool to use.
   c. is one of the reasons for the downturn in Earthwatch involvement.
   d. helps build worldwide support for Earthwatch efforts.

3. What would you most expect to experience on an Earthwatch vacation?

   a. golf, tennis, and swimming
   b. plenty of hard work
   c. music and dancing
   d. two weeks of complete leisure

B. We came in 1970. No minister visited to encourage us to worship on Sunday; no neighbor dropped in with a plate of brownies. Several times I stopped at neighboring farms to say hello and announce our presence and

8

1. **excavating:** removing by digging
2. **manatees:** aquatic mammals found in warm coastal waters
3. **camaraderie:** goodwill among friends

* Adapted from Kathy McCabe, "Volunteer Vacations Benefit Many," usatoday.com Travel Guide, November 30, 2001.

was met in the yard by the farmer, and we spent an uncomfortable few minutes standing beside my car, making small talk about the weather, studying the ground, me waiting to be invited into the house, him waiting for me to go away, until finally I went away. In town the shopkeepers and the man at the garage were cordial,[1] of course, but if I said hello to someone on the street, he glanced down at the sidewalk and passed in silence. I lived south of Freeport for three years and never managed to have a conversation with anyone in the town. I didn't have long hair or a beard, didn't dress oddly or do wild things, and it troubled me. I felt like a criminal.*

4. Which of the following inferences is accurately based on the information given?

    a. People in this town are cruel to strangers.
    b. Shopkeepers don't like conversation.
    ⓒ People in this town do not welcome strangers.
    d. New people are welcomed here.

5. Which of the following inferences is accurately based on the information given?

    a. The writer was a criminal.
    ⓑ The writer was friendly and looked similar to the people who lived in the town.
    c. The writer is a churchgoing person.
    d. The writer did favors for the townspeople.

6. Which of the following inferences is accurately based on the information given?

    ⓐ The writer tried to make friends in the town.
    b. The townspeople sensed something unusual about the writer.
    c. The writer did not like making small talk.
    d. The writer came to hate the townspeople.

C. "Help!"

It came from the lips of a young woman in pajamas perched on the front-porch roof of a house set supernaturally aglow by the fresh fire consuming the place her family called home. In her arms she held her daughter, also in pajamas and just three.

1. **cordial:** friendly

---

* From Garrison Keillor, "In Search of Lake Wobegon," *National Geographic*, December 2000, 102.

"Help! Help!"

Suddenly, a stranger emerged from the Brooklyn Avenue freeze-frame. He called up: "Throw the baby! I will catch her! Hurry! Throw the baby."

The woman, Nicole Walkes, hesitated. She was nineteen years old and new to adulthood. Behind her, a fire that would kill her own mother; before her, a stranger urging her to part with her baby, her Tiara. She kept hesitating, and he kept calling up.

"I promise! I will catch the baby!"

On the words of a stranger, the young mother tossed her toddler into the cold night air.

The stranger's name is Alberto Wickehem, and he says that he has "excellent" hands. He played a lot of football in his day, first at Midwood High School and then for a couple of semiprofessional teams. "I had my game on," the former halfback says.*

7. What can you infer about Nicole Walkes's hesitation to throw the baby?

   a. She didn't know Alberto Wickehem and thought he might steal her baby.
   (b.) She didn't trust Wickehem to catch the baby.
   c. She thought that she and Tiara could get out on their own.
   d. She was confident that the firefighters would arrive soon.

8. What can you infer about what time of day the fire started?

   a. The fire began in the middle of the day.
   b. The fire began at dinner time.
   c. The fire begin around 9 AM.
   (d.) The fire began while everyone was sleeping, probably during the night.

9. What can you infer about Wickehem from this selection?

   (a.) He caught the baby.
   b. He dropped the baby.
   c. He enjoys seeing fires.
   d. He is married and has his own children.

D. "The Delaware people have lost so much," says Lucy Parks Blalock of Quapaw, Oklahoma. "Our language is almost gone and our culture forgotten. When I was a girl, the white kids teased us so much that some were ashamed to be Indian. . . . It is hard now for many Delawares to imagine how to do things the traditional way. They no longer remember."

* From Dan Barry, "Mother Hesitated in Making Her Choice," *Charlotte* (NC) *Observer*, February 8, 2004, 14A.

Mrs. Blalock, also known as *Oxeapanexkwe,* or "Early Dawn Woman," does remember. Born on June 14, 1906, in Indian Territory shortly before it became the state of Oklahoma, she is one of a handful who can still speak her native tongue (the Unami dialect[1] of the Delaware language) and who attended important ceremonies that died out during the 1920s and 1930s.*

10. What can you infer about how Mrs. Blalock feels when she says, "It is hard now for many Delawares to imagine how to do things the traditional way"?

    a. She has no feeling one way or the other about it.
    b. She thinks it's a good thing that the traditional ways are being forgotten.
    c. She does not like observing the traditions.
    d. She is sorry that the traditional ways are being forgotten.

11. From the information provided, do you think Mrs. Blalock is "ashamed to be Indian"?

    a. Yes; it is because she was teased as a child.
    b. On the contrary; she is proud of her heritage.
    c. She doesn't have any opinion about it.
    d. She has forgotten her heritage.

12. From the information provided, what can you infer that Mrs. Blalock would like to do?

    a. enjoy living in the present
    b. change all the bad memories of the past into happy ones
    c. forget the present day and relive the past so she can improve on it
    d. help remember the traditions and native language of her heritage

8

1. **dialect:** a regional version of a language

---

* From David M. Oestreicher, "Lucy Blalock: Rescuing a Language from Oblivion," *Natural History,* October 1996, 20.

Critical Reading: Fact, Opinion, Purpose, and Tone

GOALS FOR CHAPTER 9

▶ Define the term *critical reading*.

▶ Explain the difference between a fact and an opinion.

▶ Label statements as either facts or opinions.

▶ List the three purposes for writing.

▶ Define the term *bias*.

▶ Explain why readers should learn to detect bias in texts.

▶ Identify examples of positive and negative bias.

▶ Define the term *tone*.

▶ Recognize different types of tone in reading selections.

▶ List the characteristics of a sound main idea.

▶ Define the term *evidence*.

▶ List the two essential qualities of sound evidence and distinguish between informed and uninformed opinions.

▶ Explain the three purposes for skimming and describe the steps involved in skimming a text.

College students are expected to read critically. Professors assign textbook chapters, journal articles, and other readings not just to have you memorize facts. They also want you to think about the texts so you can expand and refine your ideas. To discover how well you already can read critically, complete the test that follows.

9

TEST YOURSELF

A. Are the following statements facts or opinions? On the blank provided, write an **F** for fact and an **O** for opinion after each statement.

1. Mars is a planet. _____F_____

2. Some people call Mars the red planet. _____F_____

3. The *Washington Post* is a newspaper that is published every day. _____F_____

4. The *Washington Post* is the best newspaper published today. _____O_____

5. Some professional baseball teams now have Japanese players. _____F_____

6. Some players on the Little League World Series team from New York are so big that they're probably older than the twelve-year-old age limit. _____O_____

7. The Jersey Shore beaches are the most beautiful in the world. _____O_____

8. The Empire State Building was once the tallest building in the world. _____F_____

9. The Statue of Liberty was given to America by the French. _____F_____

10. Jackie Robinson was the first African American to play professional baseball. _____F_____

B. What is the tone of each of the following paragraphs? Circle the letter of each correct answer.

11. No one with an e-mail account needs to be told that unwanted commercial messages, better known as *spam,* are a bad problem that is getting worse. America Online reports that 70 percent of the e-mail its users receive is now junk and that the quantity has doubled just since the beginning of this year. Much of the increase is being fueled by Internet marketing companies, which charge as little as $500 to send out a million e-mail messages. Internet service providers have taken steps to clamp down on spam, but the tools at their disposal are limited. Congress needs to help.*

   a. amused   c. neutral
   b. sad   (d.) critical

* Adapted from "Crack Down on Spam," *New York Times,* April 29, 2003, www.nytimes.com.

9

12. It's wedding season again. You can tell because the average bridal magazine currently weighs more than the average bride.

      Bridal magazines are massive because they carry enormous amounts
of advertising designed to convince the bride-to-be that her wedding will
be a hideous disaster if it costs less than a nuclear aircraft carrier.

      There are no magazines for grooms, of course. The groom's sole wed-
ding responsibility is to arrive at the ceremony wearing pants and not actively throwing up. Everything else is up to the bride, who must make
thousands of critical wedding decisions, such as: Should she invite all her
relatives, or just the attractive ones? Where should the guests sit? Should
they shoot firearms into the air?

      On that last question, my advice is: No.*

  (a.) amused   c. neutral
  b. sad   d. critical

C. Read the following letter to the editor from *USA Today* and then respond to
the questions that follow by circling the letter of each correct answer.

I am truly sick of people discrediting[1] MTV because they have outgrown it.

      MTV has maintained the same target audience for the past twenty years
by continuing to reinvent itself and remain in touch with its viewer base of
teenagers and twentysomethings.

      If commentary writer Mark Goldblatt doesn't like MTV's programming,
then most probably it's because he's too old. I don't hear anyone providing
the same commentary on how childish or immature the programming is on
Nickelodeon.[2]

      Additionally, the social strides that MTV has made have been remarkable.
Yes, maybe there is sophomoric[3] programming, but MTV has provided role
models for people of color and homosexuals time and again.

      MTV also has made countless strides to get today's youth thinking "out-
side the box," and the network's recent year-long initiative to stop hate crime
in America is one example of what I consider to be very brave and powerful
programming.

      If Goldblatt isn't concerned about what is on kids' minds, maybe he
shouldn't watch MTV.†

1. discrediting: damaging the reputation   **3. sophomoric:** juvenile or immature
2. Nickelodeon: a TV channel for chil-
   dren's programs

9

* Dave Barry, "Firearms May Put a Damper on Wedding," *Miami Herald*, April 4, 2004,
  www.miami.com.
† From Jimmy Szczepanek, "Letter to the Editor," *USA Today*, August 3, 2001, 12A. Reprinted by
  permission of the author.

13. The main point of this letter can be paraphrased:

   (a.) MTV has had some beneficial influence and does not deserve criticism.
   b. Today's teenagers have no taste when it comes to music.
   c. MTV is just not for older people.
   d. Music is an important cultural influence.

14. The purpose of this passage is

   a. to entertain.   (c.) to persuade.
   b. to inform.

15. The author's tone is

   a. amused.   c. neutral.
   (b.) critical.   d. admiring.

16. In your opinion, does the author support his main point with sufficient

   and appropriate evidence? Why or why not? <u>Answers will vary.</u>

   _____

Critical reading does not mean reading to criticize or find fault with a text. Instead, **critical reading** involves noticing certain techniques that the writer is using to try to convince you of the validity and worth of his or her ideas or information. Once you learn to recognize these techniques, you will be better able to evaluate a reading selection and decide what it means to you.

The ultimate goal of critical reading is critical thinking, an important skill in all areas of life, not just in your academic courses. Critical thinkers don't just believe everything they hear or read. Instead, they approach new ideas and information with a healthy skepticism. They have learned how to analyze texts and ideas not only to understand them better but also to decide whether they should accept those ideas, reject them, or think about them further.

This chapter will help you develop your own critical reading skills by showing you how to examine important features of a text as you evaluate it. First, you'll learn to distinguish facts from opinions. Then, you'll get some practice with asking two key questions to further guide your analysis.

Distinguishing Fact from Opinion

The first essential skill in critical reading is the ability to distinguish between facts and opinions. **Facts** are information that is verifiably true.

They are based upon direct experience and observation, so they often include specific data such as numbers, dates, times, or other statistics. They also include information like names of people, places, or events. Therefore, facts can be proven. The following statements are all examples of facts.

> In 2000, 17.6 percent of the American population spoke a language other than English while at home.

> The last major eruption of Mount Etna, Europe's largest volcano, occurred in 2001.

> NASCAR[1] champion Dale Earnhardt was killed on February 18, 2001, during the final lap of the Daytona 500.

You should be aware as you read that a statement presented as a fact can be incorrect. Writers are not always right, and sometimes they include inaccurate information by accident or even on purpose. If that's the case, how does a reader know what to believe? That question will be answered more fully in a later section of this chapter.

Opinions are statements that express beliefs, feelings, judgments, attitudes, and preferences. They cannot be verified because they are based on an individual's perceptions of the world. Thus, they are subject to change as a person modifies his or her views. They can also be argued or disputed. Here are some examples of each kind of opinion.

> BELIEF: Human cloning is morally wrong.

> FEELING: The lack of patriotism among young people is sad and disturbing.

> JUDGMENT: People who drive a sport utility vehicle obviously don't care about the environment.

> ATTITUDE: The majority of television shows are boring.

> PREFERENCE: Coffee is better than hot tea.

When you are trying to decide whether a statement is a fact or an opinion, you can look for some clue words that often appear in statements of opinion. One kind of clue is words that indicate the relative nature of something, words like *bigger, most important, strangest,* and *silliest.* These words

9

----

1. **NASCAR:** National Association for
   Stock Car Auto Racing

relate and compare the subject with something else. For example, notice the boldfaced, italicized words in the following opinions.

Alaska is one of the ***most beautiful*** states in America.

Teenagers today are much ***lazier*** than they used to be.

Tiger Woods is a ***better*** golfer than anyone else who's ever played the game.

Another kind of clue is words that either qualify or limit statements or turn them into absolutes. Qualifying words and phrases include *some, several, many, quite a few, a lot, most, a majority, large numbers, usually, often, sometimes, frequently, seldom,* and *rarely*. Absolute words and phrases include *all, every, never, each, always, none,* and *no*. For example, notice the boldfaced, italicized words in the following opinions.

Allowing children to ride in the front seat of a vehicle will ***usually*** put them at higher risk in an accident.

All voters should be required to produce identification when they arrive at the polls to vote.

Space travel is ***always*** a waste of taxpayers' money.

One last type of clue is words or phrases that admit there are other possibilities. These terms include *may be, could be, seems, appears, probably, possibly, apparently,* and *seemingly*. This type of clue is boldfaced and italicized in the following examples.

There is a real ***possibility*** that life exists on another moon or planet.

Passing a law that outlaws a parent from leaving a child in the back seat of the car is ***probably*** a waste of time.

Apparently, fans are turned off by the commercialism of sports.

Exercise 9.1

Read the following statements carefully and then label each of them by writing **F** on the blank provided if it is a fact and **O** if it is an opinion.

   F   1. Some day care centers are open twenty-four hours a day.

   O   2. Phil Jackson, coach of the Los Angeles Lakers, is the greatest basketball coach of all time.

   F   3. Phil Jackson has won many NBA championships as the coach of the Chicago Bulls and the Los Angeles Lakers.

_F_   4. The temperature is 90 degrees today.

_O_   5. Paris is the most beautiful city on the planet.

_O_   6. The Grand Canyon is one of the wonders of the world.

_O_   7. Writing a first draft is a lot harder than revising and editing that draft.

_O_   8. Raising children is the most difficult job on earth.

_F_   9. Some newspapers publish editions only during the week and not on weekends.

_O_   10. Space travel is very exciting.

Exercise 9.2

Read the passages and then label each of the sentences in the list by writing **F** on the blank provided if it offers a fact and **O** if it offers an opinion.

1. (1) Despite the widespread emphasis on raising academic standards, the performance of high school seniors on a nationwide science test has declined since 1996, with 18 percent of those tested in 2000 proving proficient[1] in the subject. (2) The scores of eighth graders who took the test, the National Assessment of Educational Progress, improved so slightly as to be statistically insignificant. (3) The scores of fourth graders remained flat. (4) These results underscore[2] the urgent need for highly skilled science and mathematics teachers, as well as other improvements at the high school level.*

   _F_ Sentence 1

   _F_ Sentence 2

   _F_ Sentence 3

   _O_ Sentence 4

2. (1) The most overrated chief executive is John Adams, the second president of the United States. (2) He is justly honored as a patriot and a diplomat. (3) John's biographers overplay their hand, however, when

1. **proficient:** showing knowledge, ability, or skill

2. **underscore:** emphasize

9

---

* Adapted from Abby Goodnough, "National Science Scores for 12th Graders Slip," *New York Times*, November 21, 2001.

they defend his presidency. (4) Confronted by a menacing France, he lurched[1] from war hawk[2] to peacenik[3] with an abruptness that finished his career and the Federalist party.[4]*

____O____ Sentence 1

____O____ Sentence 2

____O____ Sentence 3

____O____ Sentence 4

3. (1) Today, several credit cards are designed specifically for high school and even middle school students: the Cobaltcard from American Express, Capital One's High School Student Card, and the Visa Buxx card. (2) With these programs, children as young as twelve or thirteen can have their very own accounts, with lines of credit up to $1,000. (3) According to many adults, this trend will create a generation of overspenders with no concept that just because you charge it doesn't mean it's free. (4) In my view, however, kids having credit cards is a good thing. (5) These young people will learn how to spend their money more wisely now and in the future. (6) They need more practice with managing their money, and credit cards can help teach them important financial lessons.†

____F____ Sentence 1

____F____ Sentence 2

____O____ Sentence 3

____O____ Sentence 4

____O____ Sentence 5

____O____ Sentence 6

4. (1) Nearly half of all grades at Harvard University last year were A or A-minus, says a university study that follows reports of grade inflation at the Ivy League school. (2) The report found that As and A-minuses grew from

1. **lurched:** moved suddenly
2. **war hawk:** someone who supports war
3. **peacenik:** someone who is against war
4. **Federalist party:** early American political party

---

* Adapted from Richard Brookhiser, "Overrated, Underrated," *American Heritage,* September 2001, 26.

† Adapted from Robin Marantz Henig, "Teen Credit Cards Actually Teach Responsibility," *USA Today,* July 31, 2001, 15A.

33.2 percent of all grades in 1985 to 48.5 percent last year. (3) Failing grades, Ds, and Cs accounted for fewer than 6 percent. (4) The higher grades may be deserved, as students work harder and are better prepared. (5) But it's hard to believe that so many students are performing at that level.*

___F___ Sentence 1

___F___ Sentence 2

___F___ Sentence 3

___O___ Sentence 4

___O___ Sentence 5

5. (1) Clinton's presidency got off to a slow and shaky start. (2) One of his first actions was to attempt to fulfill a campaign pledge to change the national health insurance system. (3) Chaired by his wife, the Task Force on National Health Care Reform in 1993 proposed providing universal insurance primarily by mandating[1] that employers offer health insurance to their employees. (4) Much criticism greeted the task force's report. (5) Businesses objected to providing mandated health insurance. (6) The American Medical Association complained that adopting the recommendations would mean that government would decide how much health care an individual could receive and deny an individual's choice of doctors. (7) Such complaints found their mark in a public suspicious of big changes in medical care. (8) By mid-1994, it was apparent that health care reform was a dead issue.†

___O___ Sentence 1

___F___ Sentence 2

___F___ Sentence 3

___F___ Sentence 4

___F___ Sentence 5

___F___ Sentence 6

___F___ Sentence 7

___F___ Sentence 8

9

1. **mandating:** requiring

* Adapted from "Study Shows Harvard Has Boosted Its A's," *USA Today,* November 26, 2001, 9D.
† Adapted from Carol Berkin et al., *Making America,* 2nd ed. (Boston: Houghton Mifflin Co., 2001), 724.

Why do you need to recognize the difference between a fact and opinion? The distinction matters because you are going to see both used to explain and support ideas in reading selections. If you need to evaluate whether a text is valid, you'll have to sort out what is definitely true from what the writer *believes* to be true. Understanding the difference allows you, the reader, to make more sound interpretations. If a writer offers little more than a string of opinions and few facts to back them up, then his or her point may not hold as much weight. Learning how to distinguish facts from opinions allows you to make more reliable judgments about the worth of information and ideas.

Exercise 9.3

Read each passage and then decide whether it contains mostly facts or mostly opinions. Then circle the letter of the correct answer of the question that follows.

1. Despite all of the media's warnings, plastic surgery is relatively safe. In the United States, only one in every 250,000 people who goes under the knife actually dies, usually due to complications from anesthesia. Clearly, our doctors are all competent professionals who know what they're doing. They are the smartest people in all of America, and they are very well-trained. Our hospitals, too, are the best in the world, with the best equipment and the most advanced technologies. Therefore, people should not let a very tiny amount of risk prevent them from improving their personal appearance. Everyone should get that facelift or nose job or liposuction[1] that he or she has always wanted because when you look your best, you feel your best.

   This passage contains mostly

   a. facts.
   b. opinions.

2. You've probably heard that Americans are drowning in debt. However, statistics show that this just isn't true. In reality, 55 percent of Americans owe nothing at all to credit card companies. Almost 24 percent of American households have no credit cards at all, and another 31 percent of households that do have credit cards paid off their most recent balances. According to the Federal Reserve's 2001 Survey of Consumer

---

1. **liposuction:** surgical procedure involving the removal of fatty tissue

Finances, only about one in twenty American households owes $8,000 or more on credit cards. Most households that carry balances owe about $2,000 or less.*

This passage contains mostly

(a.) facts.
b. opinions.

3. Everyone should get married and stay married. Having a long-term companion is absolutely necessary to human beings' happiness. Having someone else to care for gives your own life meaning and purpose. Only when you're married will you have the comfort of knowing for sure that someone will be there to help you, encourage you, and support you during difficult times. Marriage will also give you a sense of belonging and structure that you need in order to be mentally healthy.

This passage contains mostly

a. facts.
(b.) opinions.

4. Cultures may breed war, but war may have helped to nourish some of our most cherished—and peaceful—cultural innovations.[1] California State University–Fresno classicist[2] Victor Davis Hanson points out that the classical Greeks invented not just democracy but also infantry[3] battles. In the *Western Way of War: Infantry Battle in Classic Greece,* he argues that the equality and interdependence in Greek military units helped set the stage for consensual[4] government. And in the Valley of Oaxaca in Mexico, notes University of Michigan archaeologist Joyce Marcus, writing seems to have been first used—and perhaps invented—in order to record the names of deposed[5] enemy rulers.†

This passage contains mostly

(a.) facts.
b. opinions.

1. **innovations:** things newly introduced
2. **classicist:** scholar who studies ancient Greece or Rome
3. **infantry:** combat troops on foot
4. **consensual:** involving the willing participation of all parties
5. **deposed:** removed from power

9

* Adapted from Liz Pulliam Weston, "The Truth About Credit Card Debt," *MSN Money,* http://www.moneycentral.msn.com/content/SavingandDebt/P74808.asp.

† Excerpted from Thomas Hayden, "So What's War Good For Anyway?" *U.S. News & World Report,* April 26, 2004, 50.

5. Because today's "performers" have no talent, they have to rely on their sex appeal and shocking antics to get attention. Britney Spears is the perfect example. She can't carry a tune, and she really has no business charging people money to attend her concerts. She really should be concentrating on getting voice lessons, but instead she wears overly sexy, revealing clothes and pulls publicity stunts like getting married in Las Vegas and then having the marriage annulled[1] just two days later. People should let her know that they're on to her by refusing to buy her records.

This passage contains mostly

a. facts.
b. opinions.

Just as they know that some "facts" may be inaccurate, critical readers are also aware that some opinions are more valid than others. Everyone has opinions, but they may not always be sound. First of all, some opinions can be unreasonable. For example, many opinions that include the absolute words mentioned earlier can be too all-inclusive to be valid. An author who claims, for example, that *everyone* feels a certain way or that *all* things of a certain type share some characteristic is probably not allowing for reasonable exceptions. Secondly, some opinions are based on shaky or inadequate evidence. Some people believe, for example, that the moon landings of the 1960s and 1970s never happened, and they manage to ignore all of the proof that they *did* happen. A later section in this chapter will further discuss how to evaluate the evidence offered in support of an opinion.

Exercise 9.4

Is each of the following opinions reasonable or unreasonable? Circle the letter of each correct answer, and then write your explanations on the blanks provided.

1. All of today's teenagers lack common sense.

a. reasonable
b. unreasonable

Explanation: The word all makes the statement too all-inclusive to be valid.

1. **annulled:** declared void or invalid

2. The Holocaust, German leader Adolph Hitler's supposed imprisonment and execution of Jewish citizens, never actually happened.

   a. reasonable

   (b.) unreasonable

   Explanation: _There is plenty of proof—including survivors' eyewitness accounts—_
   that it did happen.

3. Aliens from outer space have not only visited Earth, but they are also living among us right now.

   a. reasonable

   (b.) unreasonable

   Explanation: _The evidence to support this statement is shaky or inadequate._

4. Oprah Winfrey is the only person in this entire country who would make a good president.

   a. reasonable

   (b.) unreasonable

   Explanation: _This statement unreasonably rejects the idea that there might be_
   more than one person qualified for the job.

5. The United States should send astronauts to explore Mars.

   (a.) reasonable

   b. unreasonable

   Explanation: _Many people would agree, and based on the United States' past_
   successes with its space program, the idea seems possible.

6. People who live in California are much odder than residents of the rest of America.

   a. reasonable

   (b.) unreasonable

   Explanation: _This is a sweeping generalization about millions of people, so_
   it cannot be valid.

7. Everyone should take a cruise for his or her next vacation.

   a. reasonable

   (b.) unreasonable

   Explanation: _The word everyone makes this statement too all-inclusive to be valid._

9

8. Wild animals like tigers should not be caged and forced to perform for humans' amusement.

   (a.) reasonable

   b. unreasonable

   Explanation: Many people would agree, and the idea can be supported with valid evidence.

9. Because vehicles are causing so much traffic and pollution, Americans must give up their cars, vans, and trucks and begin using horses to get around.

   a. reasonable

   (b.) unreasonable

   Explanation: The suggestion that Americans should do away with modern forms of transportation is, of course, ridiculous.

10. Many of today's antipollution laws are inadequate and too weak.

    (a.) reasonable

    b. unreasonable

    Explanation: Many people would agree, and there is evidence to support this claim.

Three Critical Reading Questions

Now that you've practiced distinguishing between facts and opinions, you're ready to probe a text more deeply to understand *what* it says and *how* it says it. To do that, you can use three questions to guide your critical reading:

What is the author's purpose?

Does the author reveal bias or a certain tone?

What is the main point, and what evidence is offered to support that claim?

When you actively search for the answers to these questions, you are examining the features of a text that will indicate its validity.

Question #1: What Is the Author's Purpose?

Every book, article, or any other document you read has a purpose behind it. The writer recorded his or her thoughts for one or more of three main purposes:

1. **Entertain:** to entertain or amuse you

2. **Inform:** to give you more information about a topic

3. **Persuade:** to convince you to change an attitude, belief, or behavior

Everything you read has been written for at least one of these purposes. It's important to realize, too, that a particular reading selection can have more than one purpose. For example, a persuasive essay can also be informative. An entertaining novel might also teach you something new. Good reading comprehension includes the ability to recognize these different purposes so that you'll know what the author wants you to do with the information.

Purpose: To Entertain.   Some works are written either to entertain or to amuse you. Much creative writing, such as novels, stories, poems, and plays, is created solely for the reader's enjoyment. For example, read the following excerpt from a newspaper column.

I live in Florida, where we have BIG cockroaches.

Q. How big are they?

A. They are so big that when they back up, they are required by federal law to emit warning beeps.

These cockroaches could harm Florida's image. But we Floridians solved that problem by giving them a new name, *palmetto bugs,* which makes them sound cute and harmless. So when a guest walks into a Florida kitchen and screams at the sight of an insect the size of Charles Barkley,[1] we say: "Don't worry! It's just a palmetto bug!" And then we and our guest have a hearty laugh because we know there's nothing to worry about, as long as we do not make any sudden moves toward the palmetto bug's sandwich.*

The sole purpose of this story is to entertain you and make you laugh. How do you know? It's a personal story, for one thing. In addition, it includes humor such as exaggeration and amusing descriptions. It makes no attempt to teach you anything or convince you of something.

1. **Charles Barkley:** a professional basketball player

9

---

* Excerpted from Dave Barry, "North Dakota Wants Its Place in the Sun," *Miami Herald,* August 12, 2001.

Purpose: To Inform.   Much writing is intended to increase your knowledge or understanding about a subject. A work with an informative purpose is designed to teach you something. Textbooks, most sections of the newspaper, and reference works such as encyclopedias are created with an informative purpose in mind. For example, read the following passage from an American government textbook.

> America is a nation of immigrants. Some have arrived legally, others illegally. An illegal, or undocumented, alien is subject to being deported. With the passage in 1986 of the Immigration Reform and Control Act, illegal aliens who have resided in this country continuously since before January 1, 1982, are entitled to amnesty[1]—that is, they can become legal residents. However, the same legislation stipulated[2] that employers (who once could hire undocumented aliens without fear of penalty) must now verify the legal status of all newly hired employees; if they knowingly hire an illegal alien, they face civil and criminal penalties.*

The topic of this paragraph is illegal aliens, a topic about which people have different opinions. However, the writers of this selection present neutral and factual information about the subject. They are not attempting to persuade you to think one way or another, so the purpose here is simply to inform.

Purpose: To Persuade.   Works with a persuasive purpose attempt to convince you to change or to adopt a belief, an attitude, or a behavior. These readings are said to be arguments, for they argue a point in hopes of getting the reader to agree. An editorial in a newspaper, for example, may argue that you should support a particular cause. A self-help book may urge you to think and act differently to improve a personal problem. An essay in a magazine might attempt to convince you to interpret a current event in a certain way. For example, look at the following excerpt from a newspaper editorial.

> American schoolchildren should not be required to recite the Pledge of Allegiance. The law is clear: It is impermissible[3] to hold religious ceremonies in public schools. Asking students to affirm a belief in God is an inherently[4] religious act. The place for religious declarations, including a belief in God, is in our hearts, our homes, and our

1. **amnesty:** general pardon granted by a government
2. **stipulated:** required or specified
3. **impermissible:** not allowed
4. **inherently:** essentially

---

* Excerpted from James Q. Wilson and John J. DiIulio Jr., *American Government: The Essentials,* 9th ed. (Boston: Houghton Mifflin Co., 2004), 484.

place of worship—but not in official public school activities. It's dangerous when we start injecting God into political debates, and there's something wrong about asking schoolchildren to declare their belief in God at the same time that we ask them to pledge their loyalty to their country.*

In this passage, the authors hope to persuade the reader to agree with their opinion that children should not have to recite the Pledge of Allegiance while at school. The authors take a clear stand on a debatable point, and they provide reasons why readers should agree. Thus, their purpose is to persuade.

Determining the Purpose.   When you read a passage, how can you determine the author's purpose? The passage itself will usually provide a number of clues that will help you decide on the author's intentions.

- **The Main Point.** An entertaining passage may not have a main point at all, or the main point may focus on something that the writer learned from some experience. The main point of an informative passage will usually state a fact or describe some state of affairs without offering any judgment about it. The main point of a persuasive passage, however, will be to present an opinion. Its persuasive purpose is often indicated with words like *should, must,* and *have to* because the author wants to convince the reader to change or to adopt a belief or a behavior.

- **The Supporting Details.** In entertaining passages, supporting details are often stories or descriptions, both of which might be humorous. In an informative passage, the details take the form of facts that can be verified, and they do not offer the writer's opinions about those facts. A persuasive passage, too, can include facts; however, also watch for more opinions that are used to justify the main point.

- **The Sources of the Information.** In an entertaining passage, there are usually no sources provided. An informative passage will often cite sources, and those sources will usually be informative in nature themselves. Persuasive passages may also cite sources, but those sources may very well be ones that favor the author's point of view.

- **The Author.** Pay attention to any information you get about the writer's background, qualifications, experience, and interests, for these characteristics will help you evaluate what he or she intended by writing the passage. Sometimes, authors will directly state their purpose by announcing it or by summarizing their credentials. They may offer you some details about their

* Adapted from Erwin Chemerinsky and Sheryl McCarthy, qtd. in "Pledge Debate Divides Nation," *USA Today,* October 17, 2003, 15A.

9

background that led them to write about the topic. However, even if a text reveals little or nothing about the writer, you will still be able to gain a sense of who the writer is and what he or she hopes to achieve. The words authors choose and even the way that they put their sentences together can reveal a great deal about their feelings, their attitudes, and their goals. Specifically, you can learn to recognize bias and to determine the tone of a text, topics that are discussed in the next section.

You should get in the habit of examining all these aspects of a reading selection so that you can begin to think more critically about the ideas and information it includes.

Exercise 9.5

Read each of the following passages and then respond to the questions that follow by circling the letter of the correct answer.

1. Studies of cheerleaders in junior high school demonstrate the difference between having a high social status and being well liked. At the beginning of seventh grade, newly chosen cheerleaders were not only popular but also well liked. Many girls sought them out as friends to gain the prestige[1] that comes with friendship with individuals who have a high social position. As time went by, the cheerleaders became more choosy about whom they associated with and narrowed their associations. Other students considered them to be "stuck-up," and they became more disliked. At this point, few girls sought out these cheerleaders for new friendships, and though still considered popular by other students, they were in fact disliked by many.*

The author's primary purpose is to

a. entertain.
b. inform.
c. persuade.

2. I'm a pretty good housekeeper. Ask anybody. No, wait: Don't ask my wife. She and I disagree on certain housekeeping issues, such as whether it's OK for a house to contain dirt. Also smells. If NASA[2] scientists really want to know about life on Mars, instead of sending up robots that keep finding

1. **prestige:** respect or high standing

2. **NASA:** National Aeronautics and Space Administration

* Adapted from Paul S. Kaplan, *Adolescence* (Boston: Houghton Mifflin Co., 2004), 193.

rocks, they need to send my wife and have her take a whiff of the Martian atmosphere. If there's a single one-celled organism anywhere on the planet, she'll smell it. And if the other astronauts don't stop her, she'll kill it with Lysol. This is why her approach to leftovers baffles me. I am opposed to leftovers. I believe the only food that should be kept around is takeout Chinese, which contains a powerful preservative chemical called "kung pao" that enables it to remain edible for several football seasons. All other leftover foods should be thrown away immediately.*

The author's primary purpose is to

(a.) entertain.
b. inform.
c. persuade.

3. President George Bush seems to want to minimize the suffering of our military family to help his election chances in the fall. And his Democratic opponents seem eager to exploit every dead and wounded soldier to defeat him. Neither side seems genuinely interested in the human cost and sacrifice. Maybe this is because some of the people who run for national office these days, or who manage their campaigns, do not have a child deployed[1] in harm's way. I find that the whole debate about how to treat the subject of our war dead is mostly being carried on by people with no skin in the game. This is hypocritical.[2] Each side wants to use the war on terrorism and the fighting in Iraq and Afghanistan for political ends. They should earn the right in lost sleep over a child sent to war before they speak to the issue. And they should stop trying to find military parents or personnel to quote to support their political agendas.†

The author's primary purpose is to

a. entertain.
b. inform.
(c.) persuade.

1. **deployed:** sent into combat or action

2. **hypocritical:** professing to have feelings or virtues that one does not actually possess

9

* Adapted from Dave Barry, "Forget Mars, Just Open the Refrigerator," *Miami Herald*, March 14, 2004.

† Adapted from Frank Schaeffer, "For War Families, It's Not Political," *USA Today*, May 6, 2004, 13A.

4. Most people use the terms *Web* and *Internet* interchangeably, but technically the Internet and the Web are two different beasts. The Internet is a global network of millions of computers that began in the late 1960s as a tool for university research and national defense. Information that travels over the Internet does so in a variety of languages (known as *protocols*). Think of the many languages that are spoken over the telephone wires. In order to have true communication with the person on the other end, you both need to speak the same language. Technically, the Web (and its HTTP protocol) is just one of the languages spoken on the Internet. Others include e-mail, FTP (file transfer protocol), and Usenet news groups. So the Web is just a portion (albeit[1] a large one) of the Internet. It consists of multimedia (pictures, sounds, movies, and words) viewed through a browser such as Netscape Navigator or Internet Explorer.*

The author's primary purpose is to

a. entertain.
b. inform. *(circled)*
c. persuade.

5. No doubt you've heard something recently about carbohydrates and their role in diet and weight loss. With a long history of providing science-based weight-loss programs that are safe, healthy, and focused on the long term, you can count on Weight Watchers to give you sound information. No- and low-carb diets may be the latest "craze" in weight loss, but they've taken the sound idea of cutting back on empty calories and hijacked it into extreme, flawed thinking. If you need to cut calories to lose weight, should you cut out all carbs? No! Many carbs—including fruits, vegetables, whole grains, and nonfat dairy—provide essential nutrients and are vital to your health and well-being. On the other hand, excess consumption of saturated fat and trans fat has been repeatedly shown to hurt your long-term health. So, although weight loss is an important health goal, finding a smart, healthy way to lose the weight and keep it off is what counts.†

The author's primary purpose is to

a. entertain.
b. inform.
c. persuade. *(circled)*

9

1. **albeit:** although

---

* Adapted from Barbara J. Feldman, "What's the Difference Between the Web and the Internet?" iVillage.com.

† Adapted from Weight Watchers, "The Truth About Carbs," WeightWatchers.com, October 21, 2003.

Question #2: Does the Author Reveal Bias or a Certain Tone?

One of the main reasons to determine an author's purpose is so that you can detect any bias the author might have about his or her subject. **Bias** is an inclination toward a particular opinion or viewpoint. The term describes our tendency to feel strongly that something is right or wrong, positive or negative. Even authors who try to present information neutrally, without revealing any of their own feelings about the topic, will often allow their own prejudices to creep into their writing. Conversely, authors can also make their bias perfectly clear. They often do so in hopes that they will influence the reader to agree with them.

Authors communicate their bias by using words that urge the reader to feel a certain way about a topic. Many of these words are emotional, and they provoke strong reactions in readers, encouraging them to feel either positive or negative. For example, the word *psychiatrist* is a respectful term, but the word *shrink* is negative and disrespectful. In the following pairs of sentences, the first sentence includes words that are relatively neutral. Notice how the substitution of a few more emotional words injects bias into the statement.

Neutral: Our desire to own private property is the motivation that drives humans to want to achieve.

Emotional: Our materialistic natures are the only thing preventing us all from becoming fat and lazy couch potatoes.

Neutral: The recording industry should not sell records that contain objectionable lyrics to children.

Emotional: The money-hungry recording industry is guilty of destroying children's morals with lewd and violent song lyrics.

Neutral: The Egyptian pyramids are interesting for many reasons.

Emotional: The awe-inspiring Egyptian pyramids will no doubt fascinate and astonish modern visitors.

In the second sentence of each pair, you can see that the choice of words makes the author's opinion more emotionally forceful.

Exercise 9.6

In each of the following statements, underline the words or phrases that reveal the author's bias. Then, on the blank provided, write *POSITIVE* if the words encourage you to feel positive about the subject or *NEGATIVE* if they urge you to feel negative.

1. Like a <u>fox</u> in a hen house, <u>ruthless</u> collectors are <u>plundering</u>[1] Africa's cultural heritage by encouraging <u>poor</u> Africans to sell stolen treasures. __NEGATIVE__

2. Ken Burns's <u>spectacular</u> outline of jazz history will surprise no one; in *Jazz*, his <u>beautiful</u> miniseries on the subject, Burns <u>delights</u> in the details. __POSITIVE__

3. Tyler Chicken turns your dinners into something to talk about—where ordinary meals become <u>masterpieces</u>. __POSITIVE__

4. Critics say that the McMahon family—the founders and gatekeepers of the World Wrestling Federation—are a <u>menace to society</u>. __NEGATIVE__

5. The artificial heart may just be the most <u>momentous</u>[2] invention of the late twentieth century because of its ability to prolong the lives of those who suffer from heart ailments. __POSITIVE__

6. Many people who engage in skydiving describe the event as <u>exhilarating, heart pounding, and just plain fun</u>. __POSITIVE__

7. A <u>ferocious and vicious</u> pit bull was responsible for the <u>damage</u> to my front tire. __NEGATIVE__

8. <u>Lovely bright</u> purple and white flowers <u>blanketed</u> the <u>peaceful</u> landscape. __POSITIVE__

9. There's no <u>better</u> place to watch TV sports than leaning back in a <u>nice, comfy</u> recliner. __POSITIVE__

10. Many recliners are <u>ugly—bulky and overstuffed</u>—sort of like football linemen. __NEGATIVE__

1. **plundering**: robbing   2. **momentous**: important